—

THE FEUDAL NOBILITY AND THE KINGDOM OF JERUSALEM,

1174–1277

THE FEUDAL NOBILITY AND THE KINGDOM OF JERUSALEM, 1174–1277

JONATHAN RILEY-SMITH

'Clad like women in soft robes . . . they have learned so to qualify what they say with well-ordered words, like barren willow-trees covered and bedecked with beautiful leaves but with no fruit, that those who do not by experience fully know them can scarcely see through the dissimulation in their hearts and in their speech and avoid being deceived by them.'

JAMES OF VITRY,
BISHOP OF ACRE, 1216–1228

ARCHON BOOKS 1973

Library of Congress Cataloging in Publication Data

Riley-Smith, Jonathan Simon Christopher, 1938–
   The feudal nobility and the kingdom of Jerusalem,
1174–1277.

    Bibliography: p.
     1. Jerusalem—History—Latin Kingdom, 1099–1244.
  2. Feudalism—Jerusalem (Latin Kingdom, 1099–1244).
  3. Feudal law—Jerusalem (Latin Kingdom, 1099–1244).
  I. Title.
D183.R55   1973   956.94′4   73–526
ISBN 0–208–01348–2

© Jonathan Riley-Smith 1973

Published 1973 by The Macmillan Press Ltd., London and Basingstoke,
and in the United States of America as an Archon Book by
The Shoe String Press, Inc., Hamden, Connecticut

Printed in Great Britain

For My Wife

CONTENTS

LIST OF ILLUSTRATIONS
AND MAPS

PREFACE

THIS book is far from being a comprehensive history of the Latin Kingdom of Jerusalem. I wrote it because I wanted to investigate the constitutional ideas of certain learned and politically active Palestinian lords in the thirteenth century and to find out how they tried to put their theories into practice. But by limiting myself in one way I have been able to extend myself in another, because in order to understand my subject I have had to look closely at the feudatories themselves and the way they ran their estates and so I have been led step by step into a study of aspects of government and society in Latin Palestine.

There is little direct evidence for the legislation of the Kings of Jerusalem before 1187, but there survive seven law-books written in Palestine and Cyprus in the course of the thirteenth century.[1] Five of these, composed by members of the knightly class after 1250, described with remarkable consistency a feudal system that seemed to have ossified since its introduction in the late eleventh century at the time of the First Crusade. The milieu responsible for such a prolific output of legal treatises has its own interest, but the work of scholars in the last fifty years has given the law-books an even greater importance than was first supposed. The historians who took them at their face-value imagined the Kingdom of Jerusalem to have been an extraordinary example of pure feudalism in action, a state which throughout the two centuries of its existence continued to be run on archaic principles,[2] but in the 1920s a revolution in attitudes was made possible by the work of M. Grandclaude, who identified those laws referred to in the treatises that could definitely be attributed to the period between 1099 and 1187.[3] Since the Second World War a group of historians led by Professors Jean Richard and Joshua Prawer have worked on the foundations laid by Grandclaude and have shown that, far from being the *fainéant* rulers of a static feudal state, the Kings of Jerusalem before 1187 were vigorous and aggressive, governing a kingdom the institutions of which were developing and changing like any other.[4] It is possible to wonder whether the pendulum has now swung too far in another direction and suggest that the twelfth-century monarchy was never as strong as it is sometimes said to have been, but one must also recognise that the picture drawn of it in the thirteenth-century law-books was a caricature.

It is in the nature of historical discoveries that they pose new problems. If before 1187 the crown was comparatively strong, how was it possible for it to be described seventy years later as being weak? And if part of the answer is that the jurists were theorists as much as observers, what were the political ideas that conditioned their approach to the constitution? It is obvious that answers to these questions can only be found in a study of the vassals in the kingdom, for the jurists were themselves lords or the dependants of lords. One of the leading historians of Latin Syria has seen the weakening of the monarchy, already apparent before 1187, as in some way linked to the growing power of the nobility: in the early years, he has argued, chronic warfare and continual waves of migration resulted in lordships quickly changing hands; stability and with it the growth of privilege came only after 1130 – with this, it will be seen, I disagree – and at the same time royal lands, always more extensive than those of the vassals, were reduced by the creation of new lordships.[5] But neither he nor his colleagues have studied in depth the crucial period between 1170 and 1260: they have only turned to the thirteenth century to examine particular problems[6] or in the large-scale narrative histories to describe the general course of events.[7]

It was the absence of any satisfactory description of the political ideas of the jurists or the constitutional crises in which they were involved that led me to this work. I could never claim that I have here dealt with all the facets of my subject, but I have tried to consider it in the context of economics and government in Latin Palestine, having some regard for the institutions which gave Palestinian society its own particular features. In many cases the mechanics of administration can be described and the legal status of individuals defined; and this approach is necessary not only because it is impossible to discuss a matter like the wealth of the lords without some knowledge of the means by which they raised revenues, but also, I believe, because it helps one to comprehend their motives and ideals. When making any decision, I myself will take into account certain assumptions that are based on my knowledge of my environment: that trains run on time, that I am unlikely to be robbed in the streets, that I can rely on the telephone or electricity or stable government at a national and local level, that food will arrive in the shops or, conversely, that there is no guarantee that a letter posted today will reach its destination tomorrow. These assumptions will play a significant part in the conclusions I reach, although I may not even be conscious of them, and behind them is the machinery that makes it possible to live in an organised society. The institutional structure of a thirteenth-century state was simpler than is ours, but it was still complex and by studying it we draw nearer to those who lived in it.

I have tried to give this book a form suitable for an examination in depth of a small but by no means insignificant subject. I have studied the development of a school of jurists within the ranks of the Palestinian nobility and I have described their political ideas. I have tried to show how between 1174 and 1277 they developed in political action two themes, one the form they believed resistance should take to what in their eyes were unconstitutional acts by their rulers and the other their theories on the appointment and powers of regents. It is this, the second part of the book, that has determined its terminal dates: a coherent baronial movement only emerged in the 1170s, reached its apogee in two peaks, one political in 1229 and the other literary in about 1260, and had to accept a humiliating reversal in 1277. But the ideas and activities of the vassals can only be understood against the background provided in the first part of the book where I have tried to explain the system of feudal relationships in the Latin kingdom and to describe the structure of the greater fiefs which provided the nobles with the foundations of their power. I felt that here I could not be bound by the terminal dates of the constitutional narrative and I have used evidence provided by the material surviving from the two centuries of the western occupation of Palestine and also, where relevant, of the near-by Latin states of Antioch, Tripoli and Cyprus.

I am very conscious of the dangers inherent in the historical method I have used, for it has entailed the comparison of phrases and even words in documents often distantly separated from each other in space and time.[8] I have noticed, for instance, that perhaps because of their position and past history there were important differences in the ways in which the ports of Acre, Tyre and Antioch were organised, but on other matters I may well have missed local variations and my conclusions may thus have become distorted. Some of the evidence moreover is so fragmentary that two phrases, occurring in documents that date from a century apart, may have been laid under contribution to support a finding which ignores developments that must have taken place. I have had of course to cope with documentary evidence that is very unsatisfactory. The archives of the crown and the secular lords are now lost: only that relating to the fief of Joscelin of Courtenay remains in a more or less complete state. The surviving documents of Latin Palestine come in the main from the archives of churches, monasteries and religious orders or from those of merchant communities: from the institutions, in other words, with centres in the West to which they could retire after the Holy Land had fallen to the Muslims. Although their cartularies contain many charters issued to them by lay lords it will be understood that my study has been deprived of what would have been its foundations and for it I have had to use material relating primarily to others.

If the absence of solid documentary evidence is the Scylla past which I must navigate, my Charybdis is provided by the narrative sources, the chronicles, annals and law-books, for with them I am faced by other kinds of difficulty. The standard edition of the law-books could hardly be worse[9] and the variant manuscripts present many problems which will not be resolved until they are subjected to a critical textual examination by a future editor. In the course of this some of my conclusions may become suspect. Most of these treatises moreover were written by members of the baronial movement; and one could scarcely avoid being struck by the chief defect of the main narrative sources, the Latin Chronicle of William of Tyre and a group of Old-French Continuations of it,[10] the 'Annales de Terre Sainte' and a curious compilation called 'Les Gestes des Chiprois', containing an account by one of the leading jurists of his part in the civil wars in the 1230s and a chronicle of the later years of the thirteenth century written by a man who had been a page of a Lord of Tyre and was associated with the Order of the Knights Templar. William of Tyre was a fierce partisan of that group of men who can be considered as the founding fathers of the baronial party and his successors seem to have had the same political views.[11] The picture presented by the authors of the narrative sources is very one-sided and while they provide important evidence for the ideas and aims of the lords, they cannot be treated as trustworthy witnesses. I have tried to look beneath their platitudes and apologetics, searching for inconsistencies that might lead me to the truth, and I have been careful not to take them on trust unless I have been able to find some supporting evidence for what they have said.

Three years hence I would still have been grappling with the intricacies of feudal law in the Latin East had it not been for the generosity of the Trustees of The Leverhulme Trust Fund, who granted me a Fellowship and therefore the time I needed to finish off this work. The head of the Department of Medieval History in St Andrews, Professor L. H. Butler, who has always encouraged my researches, generously supported my application for leave. I gladly acknowledge again my very great debt to Dr R. C. Smail, whose pupil I once was. He has always given me encouragement and advice and his criticisms of the typescript, which he read in the difficult final stages, were of the greatest value to me. So were the comments of Dr David Chambers on the typescript, part of which was also read by Miss Ann Kettle. I benefited a good deal from correspondence with Professor H. E. Mayer and Professor Joshua Prawer and from discussions over a long period with Dr M. C. Lyons of Cambridge, who sent me some valuable evidence from oriental sources, and Mr Meron Benvenisti of Jerusalem. My theories were first tried out on those students in St Andrews who attended my seminar on the Kingdom of Jerusalem and I alone know how much I learnt from their enthusiasm and the arguments that raged round my table; I owe the same debt to the challenging ideas on allied subjects of my research students, Dr Bruce Beebe, Miss Joyce McLellan and Mr Peter Edbury.

I had much help from the staffs of the libraries of the Universities of St Andrews and Cambridge, the Reading Room of the British Museum and the London Library; and I would like especially to thank Miss Cecily Baird of St Andrews who acquired books on loan and xerox-copies of printed documents which would not otherwise have been available to me. The manuscript was typed by Mrs Dunn, Mrs Davies, Mrs O'Connor and Mrs Starnes of that most valuable institution, the University Aunts of Cambridge – long may it flourish! Mr T. M. Farmiloe of Macmillan was again always ready to assist me and was prepared to accept a very different sort of book from that which he originally expected.

My father, as ever, gave me moral support. And I owe most to my wife. Those who are married to authors will know of the demands which have been made of her; and other authors will understand how much I have relied on her. Her self-sacrifice and support greatly eased the task of producing this book and it is therefore with very real gratitude as well as love that I dedicate it to her.

St Andrews   J. S. C. R.-S.
July 1972

I

LORDS
AND LORDSHIPS

I

FEUDALISM IN PALESTINE

In one sense feudalism can be described as being a system in which, for the class of men to whom it applied, government, the possession of property and social status were based on personal ties. The king's relations with the more important of his subjects were circumscribed by the terms of private contracts made with each of them individually; and a landowner's relations with many of his own tenants were governed by similar compacts. The parties to a feudal contract, like those entering on any formal agreement, were bound by rights and duties and a feudal king or lord claimed certain services from his vassal, who enjoyed in return his protection and a grant of maintenance which, taking the form of land, rents or property, enabled him to live and fulfil his obligations. Since in all feudal societies the rights of both parties were widely interpreted, misdemeanours that in another kind of state might have been seen as offences against public order were regarded as breaches of the contract and as acts of personal disloyalty. And so jurisdiction came to mean for the most powerful section of the community decisions on alleged violations of contracts.

Just such a system of contractual relationships is described in the thirteenth-century law-books of Jerusalem, but it is an example of the way in which minds can be conditioned and sensibilities dulled that this no longer greatly surprises us. Feudal society had developed in the West because of the needs of rulers and subjects in the seventh, eighth and ninth centuries when the old instruments of administration had rotted away; society had disintegrated to the point at which men had to rely on their private loyalties and rulers had a desperate need for services for which lands or upkeep in their households had become the only worthwhile rewards. The decline of feudalism in Europe naturally coincided with economic recovery: with the re-emergence of a monetary economy, the growth of the towns and the reappearance of a class of citizens who held property under conditions that had nothing to do with the feudal contract. These changes were only just beginning to have an effect at the time of the First Crusade, but Palestine, on which the crusaders superimposed a society organised on the lines they had known in the West, was an area with an already developed administration, flourishing cities and a monetary economy. Palestinian feudalism was in fact inappropriate, corrupt and characterised by a loose definition of terms, which may help to explain why the jurists re-created in the law-books an archaic, rarified system of contractual obligations: in a world so unlike their model they were self-consciously acting out parts based on cardboard exemplars of chivalry imported from Europe.

In Palestine as elsewhere the homage paid by a vassal to his lord was the visible sign of the making of the contract between them. From this in theory all else followed, including the services enjoyed by the lord and the fief held by the vassal, and it remained one of the foundations upon which were built the political theories of the feudatories. But by the thirteenth century the fief had in practice become the centre-piece, for which contracts were entered into and services performed. According to one of the greatest of the jurists,

> the promise of faith is contained . . . in homage and homage is made for the fief, so that if one can renounce a fief [he was speaking of those circumstances in which this could be done] one can indeed renounce the faith that is given in exchange for the fief.[1]

We shall see that only knights could hold those fiefs for which was owed *service de chevalerie*, but there may have been many sergeantries – in 1261 21 out of 27 fiefs in the lordship of Arsur[2] – although it is not possible to make any estimates for the kingdom as a whole. The existence of these sergeantries, often held by native-born tenants,[3] highlights the curiously impractical way in which the feudal system had been imposed on Palestine. In the West they date from the time when money was scarce and it was easier to pay in land for the many different services required by a lord.[4] These conditions never existed in the East and it seems that sergeantries were created simply out of convention, although the fact that they were hereditary may have led to pressure for them from the vassals themselves. Those of Arsur, which not unexpectedly were held as minor offices – by the lord's carpenter,

dragoman, viscount, *scribanus* and scribes, butler, cooks, chaplain
and marshal – were mixed fiefs in money, land and kind for which
payment could easily have been substituted and the same is true of
the *scribanages* and dragomanates in the lordships of Caesarea and
Jaffa and in the minor seigneuries in the royal domain near Acre.[5]
There seem to have been few principles behind their creation :
they were the same 'hotch-potch of tenures that did not, for one
reason or another, conveniently fit into the general scheme of
social grouping', as one historian has described them with reference to England,[6] and no rules governed their size or the kind of
person who was granted them. The great offices of the crown were
sergeantries and among them it is noteworthy that the marshal
held his fief not immediately of the king but of the constable.[7]
Some sergeants performed military services and they perhaps included those who owed the services of turcopoles.[8] Sergeantries
could of course be held by knights and they were subject to the
same laws on sale and partition among heirs as other fiefs[9] and to
the jurisdiction of seigneurial courts,[10] although the jurists never
regarded the simple sergeant as the equal of a knight.[11]

There were many kinds of fief.[12] A vassal might be given lands
and villages, making up what was called a *fié en terre* or *fié en
casau* :[13] at its greatest it was a barony or lordship and at the other
end of the scale was an estate of only one or two villages.[14] But
prevalent in the thirteenth century – indeed it has been suggested
that it was the norm[15] – was the fief in money or kind. This, the
fief-rente, had in the West gradually become quite common in the
eleventh and twelfth centuries, reaching the height of its popularity in the thirteenth and fourteenth. It could be confiscated on
breach of contract more easily than a territorial fief and it could be
given to a man who lived a long way from the domain of the
grantor. To flourish it needed a society in which a strong feudal
system was in balance with a monetary economy[16] and just such
conditions existed in the East. There it took several forms. It
could be paid in what were known as *livreisons* or *estoveirs*: victuals
and rations for men and horses that although granted both to
knights and sergeants seem to have been given more commonly to
the latter.[17] Alternatively a man might enjoy a rent in kind, collecting corn, vegetables or oil from certain villages after the
harvests or from his lord's storehouses at specified times in the
year;[18] those fiefs known as *fiés en villains* may have been similar,

for villagers provided returns in kind, as we shall see.[19] The money-fiefs proper, the *fiés en besans*, fell into three categories. First, a lord might commit himself simply to pay a vassal a fixed sum each year: it is possible that in 1198 many of the knights in Acre were enjoying this sort of maintenance, for King Aimery made them choose two of their number to help supervise the collection of revenues and the payment of the fiefs.[20] Secondly, an annual payment might be assigned on the revenues of a village or a group of them;[21] a man might also be given a rent from a monopoly within a village like the communal cistern or the tax-farm over a country district or even over encampments of Bedouins.[22] The most usual kind of money-fief, however, was assigned on the revenues collected in a town by one of the lord's offices: one finds references to fiefs granted on the revenues from the markets for meat, fish, fruit, cloth, wine, oil and musical instruments; from mills, mints, tanneries, soap-works and dyeworks; from the exchanges where were the tables of the money-changers, the gates where entry and exit dues were levied, and the 'loge', presumably some sort of bazaar; but above all from the *fondes*, the groups of markets on some of which were centred the international spice trade, and the *chaines* or custom houses.[23] The departments involved were under the supervision of each lord's central financial office, known in the royal domain as the *secrete*. It is not surprising to find that proof of possession of a money-fief held of the king was made by consulting the records of the *secrete*, in which notes of payment were entered.[24]

Many vassals held mixed fiefs, consisting partly of land and partly of rents in money or kind. Only one of the fiefs in the lordship of Arsur in 1261 was held entirely in land and only one other entirely in cash; the rest were held in various combinations in which were involved sums of money, produce, rations, land and the profits and perquisites of offices.[25] To find an example of what a greater man might possess we have only to look at the properties accumulated by Joscelin of Courtenay in 1182 and 1183: rents of 500 besants in Acre and Tyre, a castle in northern Galilee with the villages around and three other fiefs, one of which he exchanged for a village and a rent of 1,000 besants, while another itself consisted of villages and a rent of 800 besants.[26] It is probable that in the thirteenth century most of the great lords held in addition to their territories money-fiefs in the cities of the royal domain.

Fiefs-rentes could be used flexibly: they could be granted in all sorts of combinations and we will see that, like lands, rear-fiefs could be created or eleemosynary grants made out of them. Their popularity must have been one of the reasons why so many of the knights lived in the towns, near their sources of income. And the opportunities for creating money-fiefs grew with the prosperity of the cities in the first half of the thirteenth century, compensating in terms of military service for the lands alienated to the Military Orders[27] and conquered by the Muslims: it is clear that the feudal host was not reduced in proportion to the territories and therefore fiefs that were irretrievably lost to Saladin in 1187.[28]

One of the jurists defined a fief as being 'anything which owes service'.[29] And although another argued that the king could grant maintenance without the obligation of service in return if he so wished, it must be suspected that here he was putting forward a view of his own rather than accurately commenting upon custom, for he went on to write that the king could freely alienate land to the Church, a practice which certainly had not been given an unqualified *imprimatur* in the earliest of the law-books.[30] There certainly existed lay *fiés francs*, some being the result of special grants and others being perhaps established in the period of uncertainty that immediately followed the conquest,[31] but it was not in the interest of the lords to lose service, as they themselves knew well: we will see that its commutation for money payments was extremely rare; religious houses like the Military Orders, whose grants, when eleemosynary, exempted them from the usual services, were at times specifically made liable for them;[32] in one case the service due from lands given to an order was guaranteed by the donor;[33] and sometimes seigneurs gave notice that they would only confirm gifts to the Church provided that they lost no service.[34]

On rendering homage a vassal was above all bound to his lord by faith. I shall return to this ideal in a later chapter. Here it suffices to say that the authors of the earliest of the law-books, the 'Livre au roi', expressed a solemn principle when they stated that

> the king is held by faith to his liegeman and liegewoman as that liegeman is held to him; and also the king must guarantee and save and defend his liegemen against all those who would do them wrong, as the liegemen are held to guarantee and save him against all men.[35]

A vassal was committed to protect the body and honour of his lord not merely in the negative sense, for he should take active steps to oppose any plans to harm him of which he heard and was bound to make extraordinary efforts in times of need, such as when his lord was a prisoner of the enemy, contributing to the ransom by taxing his property at 1% or even selling his fief if it was of the kind that was not heritable.[36] Upon correct summons[37] and provided he was aged between 15 and 60 years[38] he gave his lord services that are usually grouped under the headings of *auxilium* and *consilium*. Those performed in person were commonly referred to as *services de cors* and were differentiated from the rest : when the Hospitallers took over the fief of Arsur in 1261 they promised to perform the services due, except for *service de cors*, which presumably their Master could not or would not fulfil.[39] *Service de cors* was normally carried out only inside the kingdom – perhaps defined in the thirteenth century as being west of the river Jordan[40] – and the king could only ask for it beyond the frontiers in three matters: negotiations for his marriage or that of his children; the guarding of his faith and honour; and the apparent needs of his lordship or the common profit of the land. Around 1200 a man could only be called upon to serve as a messenger abroad for the last of these reasons, but no vassal need perform military service outside the kingdom unless the king himself was present and while in the army he would be provided with rations.[41]

'There are great advantages,' wrote one of the jurists, 'in the different kinds of service that the vavasour can pay.'[42] The first of the *auxilia* was military service. A vassal answered the summons for it by going to the place of assembly with his arms and a given number of horses. Within the borders of the kingdom he remained with the feudal host for as long as had been specified in the summons up to one year, whether his king or lord was present or not.[43] He might also have to perform castle guard, garrison duties at his lord's fortress: although there is no good evidence for its performance generally, it was owed by the knights of the fief of Margat in the Principality of Antioch and in the mid-thirteenth century one can find vassal-castellans of Arsur and Beirut.[44] Great and lesser sergeants carried out the duties of their offices as *auxilia*. And a liege-woman, who could not of course render personal military aid, owed *service de mariage* which was treated in the same way as an *auxilium*: upon summons she was bound to marry one of three candidates for her hand presented to her by her lord, provided they were her equals, so that her consort could perform the personal services due from her fief.[45] Of more importance to this study were those services that can be collected under the second heading of *consilium*. This meant more than the giving of advice : it involved the vassal in judgements on the behaviour of his lord as well as his peers, since it bound him to take part in the seigneurial court in which were considered breaches of the feudal contract. Procedure in the courts will be discussed in a later chapter. Here it need only be said that when called upon a vassal had to participate in the decisions of the court, serve on inquiries into murders, homicides and the boundaries of fiefs, deliver summonses to service, act as a messenger for his lord and as counsel to pleaders and defendants before the court.[46] We will see that this last duty, the *service de conseil*, was one of the main reasons for the appearance of a school of practising vassal-lawyers.

The tenants of many fiefs had to bring to the feudal host additional knights, sergeants-at-arms or even esquires.[47] Many of these were of course rear-vassals, but another quite common form of *auxilium*, *service des compaignons*, was one by which a fief-holder raised mercenaries and guaranteed their wages, thus being absolved from the need to alienate his holding into a commensurate number of rear-fiefs.[48] There survives an incomplete list of the knights' service owed by fiefs, probably compiled in the decade before 1187,[49] but there is some evidence that the figures for *servitia debita* were subject to reassessment and so did not remain constant. The fief of St George maintained a return of 10 knights over two decades,[50] but Maron's *servitia* seem to have increased from 3 to 4 knights in the 1180s[51] and, although the services of the lordship of Arsur before 1187 are not known, the 6 knights and 21 sergeants owed in 1261 look like a very small burden in comparison with what similar fiefs had owed in the twelfth century.[52] In the first half of the thirteenth century the service of two knights was due for two villages near Tripoli. In 1254 the lord, the Order of St John, took one of the villages into its own hands in exchange for a remission of it, but laid down that on the death of the present tenant the service of both knights would be demanded in exchange for possession of only one of the villages. Although this was not put into effect,[53] it suggests that rising land-values led lords to

demand additional services from territorial fiefs. At the same time
there was inflation and one would expect to see money-fiefs increasing in size as the value of money declined. In the century
1165–1265 we can say that the service of one knight was never
owed for less than 300 besants a year and never for more than
1,000 besants and that the smallest sergeantry known was one in
which was combined a rent of 100 besants and 4 carrucates of
land.[54] Around 1200 the writers of the 'Livre au roi' assumed that
a rent of 300 besants a year was enough to provide for a knight,
but by the 1260s the value of such a fee could in the eyes of the
jurists stand at between 900 and 1,000 besants.[55] We would perhaps not be far wrong in suggesting that the rising value of land
meant that lords continually demanded more services from it,
while inflation led the vassals to ask for larger *fiefs-rentes* to support
their *auxilia*. Inflation of course must be set against the rising
revenues of the cities when we consider how far in the first half of
the thirteenth century they compensated for the territorial losses
of the twelfth. And after 1250, with a decline of commerce and the
loss to the Muslims of many of the smaller ports, the numbers of
knights serving in the feudal host must have fallen rapidly.

Most of the knights were Europeans, although there is quite good
evidence for a number of the native-born among them. The best
known of these was a knightly family, known as the Arrabi and
clearly of native origins, who made their appearance in 1122 when
Muisse Arrabi was in the entourage of Prince Hugh of Jaffa.
Muisse had a brother called Baldwin and a son called George who
in his turn had four children, Henry, Peter, John and Maria. Had
the members of this family not chosen to use their distinctive
cognomen, their Christian names would for us have merged all
but Muisse himself into the mass of the Latin settlers.[56] In the
twelfth century non-European knights were also to be found in
the royal domain round Jerusalem, Nablus and Acre and in the
lordships of Oultrejourdain and Haifa;[57] in 1253 a man called
Walter Qelbe Arab was a liegeman of Jerusalem; in 1282 a knight
called Paul Elteffaha was a vassal of the Templars; and in Maronite
sources were preserved grants to indigenous persons in 1255 and
1280 by Julian of Sidon and Humphrey of Beirut, the second of
which seems to have been the gift of a fief.[58] Whatever his origins,
however, a knight had to be a Latin Christian: otherwise he could

not give *consilium*, for only Latins could sit in a seigneurial court. By the thirteenth century the liege-knights had become a caste, their privileged position confirmed by law 'on account of the honour and highness that knights and chivalry have and ought to have over all other manner of men'.[59] They could not be arrested for debt[60] and could not be appealed in court by anyone save a peer for any crime except that of murder.[61] Only they were permitted to buy those fiefs owing knights' service that were put up for sale;[62] and although in Palestine there were many knights who were landless mercenaries,[63] by *chevaliers* the writers of the lawbooks usually meant fief-holders. The development of an *ordo* of chivalry was common in the feudal West, where it found expression in the elaboration of initiation ceremonies into knighthood. In thirteenth-century Palestine a knight had to be dubbed before enfeoffment, for otherwise he could not wear the armour proper to his station and essential to his *auxilium*.[64] While any knight could dub another – the young Balian of Arsur was made a knight by St Louis in 1254[65] – it seems to have been regarded as usual for lords to perform the ceremony for their own men: in 1187 Balian of Nablus, who had taken charge of the defence of the city of Jerusalem against Saladin, dubbed many knights in order to increase the number of defenders, but he only did this after he had been received by the city as its lord and homage had been paid him.[66] While it was by no means impossible for burgesses to be made knights – Balian of Nablus elevated some sons of burgesses in 1187 and at least one branch of the Antiaume family reached the ranks of knighthood early in the thirteenth century[67] – only those legitimately descended from knightly families could normally expect the honour.[68]

The position of the knights so far described was not markedly different from that of their cousins in the West, but it was affected by the working of certain special laws and customs. Some of these tended to weaken their standing. An early *assise* – the usual word for a law – had laid down that no knight already holding a fief could enter into possession of another coming to him by common rights of inheritance, but must renounce it in favour of a relative who was not already enfeoffed. The jurist Philip of Novara believed that this *assise* was a consequence of the purist feudal *dictum* that no one could perform service in person for two different fiefs, but doubtless it was made to prevent the accumulation of

properties in the hands of a small number of vassals and to en-
large the class of knights.[69] It was however modified later in the
twelfth century by another *assise* which allowed a man to succeed
to a second fief on condition that he provided for it the service of
a salaried companion in place of his *service de cors*. No longer was
a man to be hindered from acquiring several fiefs, so long as he
guaranteed the services required from each of them.[70]

The effects of this change in the law were moderated by the
growth of a custom that upon the death of a man who held two
or more fiefs these would have to be shared out among his
descendants so that service in person could be performed for each
of them.[71] In one court case relating to this a knight called Anjou
of Malembec, who had inherited two fiefs from his father, was
sued for one of them by his sister. Anjou at first defended the plea
but at length agreed to grant her a money-fief of 400 saracen
besants a year. On her death and that of her husband Thomas of
St Bertin this fief escheated back to Anjou, but it was claimed by
her son Walter, who brought an action for it in the High Court in
Acre. The result of his plea is not known, but it and other cases
gave rise to arguments among the feudal lawyers over whether
daughters, who certainly had rights when there were no male
heirs, were to be treated in these circumstances as co-inheritors
with sons. One view, held by the prestigious John of Beirut and
Philip of Novara, was that the existence of a male heir cancelled
the rights to inheritance of daughters, so that all the fiefs would
pass even to an only son. Another opinion was expressed by the
equally prestigious Balian of Sidon, who argued that, since
daughters could inherit in those cases in which a male heir could
not perform *service de cors* because of physical and mental dis-
abilities, a plurality of fiefs should be shared out among sisters as
well as brothers, for they were, he reminded his listeners, discussing fiefs for which a male heir could certainly not perform service
in person.[72] John of Beirut's view seems to have prevailed – it was
one that suited the feudatories – but even the modified custom
must have helped to prevent the concentration of properties in the
hands of a small group of vassals and must have led to a scattering
of fiefs among the cadets of the knightly families.

Another early *assise* forbade the tenant of a fief for which the
service of several knights or sergeants was owed to sub-infeudate
a greater proportion of it than he himself retained. By the middle

of the thirteenth century the interpretation of this law had become the subject of an argument that was never resolved. Must the value of all the rear-fiefs combined amount to less than half the value of the whole fief, or should the lord merely keep in his own hands more than was held by each of his vassals? The second interpretation would have permitted far more sub-infeudation, but it is clear that either way the law was still being observed and it must have prevented the development of large private armies, although it would also have ensured that seigneurial domains could never be reduced by massive alienations.[73]

On the other hand the feudal class was strengthened by the far-reaching consequences of other laws. The *Assise sur la ligece* of *c.* 1166 will be considered in detail below, but one result of it was that all the feudatories, whether they held fiefs immediately of the crown or were rear-vassals, were in theory bound to make liege-homage to the king and so became peers, entitled, from the greatest baron to the smallest vavasour, to sit in the High Court at the apex of feudal jurisdiction. The concept of peerage, the idea that liege-homage to the crown bound the vassals not only to the king as their common lord but also to one another by reason of the ties they all shared, increased each man's consciousness of belonging to a class. The words of the jurist Geoffrey Le Tor, if rather extreme, give us some idea of the thinking of a knight on the subject in the thirteenth century.

> Because I have spoken of peers, [he wrote] so I wish to explain what peerage is. All liege-knights of the king in the High Court are peers, whoever they are, high or low, poor or rich, in so far as they protect one another in their rights and maintain one another in law and also as they are called upon to act as counsel, to give judgements and issue *recorts*. And the speech of one carries as much force as that of any of the others.[74]

The knightly class was given further cohesion by particularly rigid laws of inheritance. The rights of heirs to a fief were affected by the means by which it had come into the hands of its last tenant – whether by inheritance or by acquisition – and by the terms laid down for inheritance in the original grant. Most fiefs were known as *fiés d'escheete*, for they had escheated through inheritance to their holders who could not dispossess their descendants by disposing of them, except in very special cases: perhaps an eleemosynary grant to a religious house – only possible with the permission of

the lord, who would lose service, and of the heirs, if the property
made returns they would never enjoy[75] – and certainly a sale to
pay off debts. The jurists argued that such a sale, governed by a
law known as the *Assise des ventes*, did not damage the position of
heirs, because they would otherwise have inherited the debts; in
Cyprus, at least, these heirs had the first chance to buy back the
fief themselves.[76] But the law relating to a *fié de conquest*, a fief that
had first been granted to its present possessor, was carefully
differentiated from that concerning the *fié d'escheete*. A *fié de conquest*
could be renounced and the heirs thus dispossessed by the vassal
who had acquired it; and a case in which the most famous of all
the jurists had given up a fief he had held from the Count of
Tripoli had aroused great interest early in the thirteenth century.[77]
The acquirer of a *fié de conquest* moreover need not transmit it to
the nearest of his heirs, but could bestow it as he wished, provided
that the man chosen was among those permitted to inherit by the
terms of the original grant: the jurists were insistent that if heirs
could be disinherited by renunciation, it followed that the
acquirer of a fief had a freedom of action with regard to his
descendants that was denied to other vassals. But this was a very
rare occurrence and of course once a *fié de conquest* had passed to an
heir by the common laws of inheritance it became a normal *fié
d'escheete*, subject to the usual entails. The charters granting *fiés de
conquest* always seem to have specified as heirs the children of the
beneficiary's espoused wife and by the thirteenth century this was
the normal way of defining the rights of succession to new fiefs. It
was known, however, that the terms of older grants had given
rights of inheritance to all relatives and this was regarded as being
a characteristic of escheats in Palestine.[78]

Inheritance followed the doctrine of *plus dreit heir aparant*, so
prevalent that it is to be found applying to all heirs from those to
the monarchy down to those to a native sergeantry.[79] A *plus dreit
heir aparant* was the nearest relative to the last in possession of a
fief, being in such a relationship to him that he could legally inherit; he must be capable of performing the services due and he
had to be resident in the East. The rules of primogeniture were
usually followed in establishing relationship, but these could be
overturned where there were no direct heirs, because the closeness
of a claimant's relationship to the last possessor of a fief was more
important than the branch of the family to which he belonged.

According to John of Jaffa and Geoffrey Le Tor the elder of two men who were not sons of but were in the same degree of relationship to the last tenant would inherit, irrespective of whether he belonged to an elder or younger branch of the family, but we will see that this may have been a new custom established in the 1260s: it was not known to the authors of the 'Livre au roi'.[80] An heir also had to be capable of performing the services required, which meant that a male had precedence over a female who was otherwise as closely related to the last possessor as he was,[81] and he had to be resident in the East.[82] Fiefs could not legally be partitioned among male heirs, but if a fief owed the service of more than one knight or sergeant it was possible to share it among the descendants, provided that the most rightful heir held the tenancy-in-chief and presumably the bulk of the property and the others became his rear-vassals: on his deathbed in 1236 John of Beirut granted some rear-fiefs to his younger sons.[83] This practice was always followed when a tenant of a large fief was survived only by daughters. In the early years of the settlement the eldest of them had inherited and the thirteenth-century jurists ascribed the change in the law to the initiative of Stephen of Champagne, Count of Sancerre, who had paid a short and rather ill-tempered visit to Palestine in 1171 and had suggested that the fief of the recently dead Henry Le Buffle should be divided in this way among his three daughters, the eldest of whom was to owe homage and *service de cors* to the crown.[84]

The doctrine of *plus dreit heir aparant*, with its emphasis on rights based on relationship to the last man physically in possession of an estate, could have curious results, especially to be seen in the application of a custom known as *Fors de Turs tolt saisin*. It was believed that when the continuous occupation of a fief was broken by Muslim conquest the man who would succeed to it once it came back into Christian hands must be that person closest in degrees of relationship to the last actually in possession. His rights overruled all claims by those who would normally have inherited by primogeniture. The great jurist John of Jaffa gave as an example of this custom at work what happened to Ibelin in southern Palestine, the fief from which his family took its name. Ibelin had been held by Balian of Nablus when it was lost in 1187 and it was not reoccupied by the Christians until 1241, by which time he and all his children save one daughter, Margaret of

Caesarea, were dead. The fief, therefore, was inherited not by his heir by primogeniture, Balian of Beirut who was the eldest son of his eldest son, but by Margaret and it passed into the possession of the house of Caesarea.[85]

Among the feudatories of Jerusalem there was a group called high men, rich men or barons. In the West the word *baro* first appeared in eighth-century dog-latin when it simply meant man as opposed to woman – in thirteenth-century Palestine an echo of this primitive meaning was to be found in its use also to denote a husband[86] – but, although it was never adequately defined, in the course of time it came to describe a vassal and then a king's vassal and in France could be used of a tenant-in-chief of the crown who exercised jurisdiction with High Justice, the ability to condemn a man to mutilation or death, as against a vavasour or simple knight who enjoyed no such right.[87] It is in this general sense that the word will be used throughout this book and it might be as well to state here that regarded as baronies will be the Principality of Galilee, the County of Jaffa and Ascalon and the Lordships of Beirut, Sidon, Tyre after 1246, Toron, Scandelion, Chastiau-dou-rei, Nazareth, Haifa, Caesarea, Bethsan, Arsur, Lydda, Blanchegarde and Oultrejourdain.

In the middle of the thirteenth century the greatest of the Palestinian jurists, John of Ibelin Count of Jaffa, gave the title a far narrower definition. He ranked as barons only the Count of Jaffa, the Prince of Galilee, the Lord of Sidon and the Count of Tripoli, although he admitted that there was doubt about the last of them, his position being challenged in the opinion of some by the Lord of Oultrejourdain. What for John distinguished these four from the rest of the lords were that each had the duty of rendering the king the service of 100 knights and the right of employing among his seigneurial officers both a constable and a marshal. And while the four could join with the other liegemen in the High Court in judgement on any knight,

> the highness and the franchise that the four barons enjoy above all other vassals . . . is . . . that none (of them) can by the *assise* or custom of this kingdom be judged on matters concerning his body, honour or fief – that is those things that appertain to his barony – save by his peers . . . the other barons, if he wishes to defend himself.

In what was clearly a reference to contemporary French law John was reluctant to give the high officers of the crown, the seneschal and the constable, parity with his barons,[88] to whom he gave the right to carry the crown and orb at a coronation.[89] In one of the very rare instances where he was sure there had existed an *assise* – certainly it was similar to practice in western Europe – he argued that each of the four baronies was indivisible and so could not be partitioned by inheritance or dower.[90]

This treatment of the baronage, giving a privileged position in law to a small group within the nobility, ran counter to that spirit of equality among the feudatories upon which, we will see, their methods of resisting the crown were based. One of the finest contemporary historians has concluded that it had little correspondence with reality, but was a proud fantasy of the higher nobles, perhaps under the influence of French law.[91] One cannot disagree with this, but it should be pointed out that John of Jaffa's approach to the subject was remarkably consistent: it permeated his long legal treatise in which, over and over again, baronies were carefully differentiated from lordships, barons from other 'rich men' and both barons and 'rich men' from the mass of the liegemen.[92] It is clear from the words he used that there had taken place much discussion on the four baronies[93] and some echoes of this can be found elsewhere. John's contemporary Philip of Novara usually referred in his own law-book to the great fiefholders as rich men, but on at least one occasion he distinguished barons from them.[94] And although to the jurist James of Ibelin and to the compiler of the laws of the burgess court of Acre a baron was simply a great tenant-in-chief, while Geoffrey Le Tor seems to have been strongly opposed to the concept of the peerage of the four barons, a writer of one of the continuations of the chronicle of William of Tyre reported that to royal procurators before the Roman curia in the 1270s the judgement of cases concerning the crown of Jerusalem belonged to 'the barons and peers of the kingdom'.[95]

It is worth investigating the use of *baro* before John of Jaffa defined it. Before 1188 one finds the title given not only to all those lords who enjoyed rights of High Justice, but also to humbler tenants of the crown;[96] as late as the 1160s lords were using it of their own vassals;[97] and in 1187 among the 'barons' advising Conrad of Montferrat in Tyre there were the Viscounts

of Nazareth and Legio, who were not even officers in the
royal domain.[98] In one sense therefore a baron may have
been any vassal called upon to give counsel to the crown or, before 1170, to his own lord. This definition may sometimes have
been used in the thirteenth century: in 1231 the lieutenant of the
regent, certifying the sale of a fief, announced that it had been
carried out 'in our presence and that of the other barons of the
court'.[99]

It is, however, clear that the word also had a stricter meaning,
perhaps already in use in the first half of the twelfth century in the
County of Tripoli, where certain charters appear to differentiate
barons from other knights.[100] In the Kingdom of Jerusalem itself
the first sign of this is to be found in a charter of 1155, in which
Hugh and Baldwin of Ibelin, later Lord of Ramle, Philip of
Nablus, Guy Francigena, Henry Le Buffle, Humphrey of Toron,
Hugh of Caesarea and John Gottman were ranked as barons, the
last three being separated in the list of witnesses from the 'men of
the king'. What entitled these men to be called barons now escapes
us, for Guy Francigena, Henry Le Buffle and John Gottman, although substantial fief-holders, had, as far as we know, none of
the rights to jurisdiction enjoyed by the others.[101] But clearly some
differentiation was now being made between them and the other
vassals, and this is confirmed elsewhere: the witness lists to a
group of charters of 1160 were headed: 'Of the barons and the
men of the king';[102] William of Tyre at one of the very rare points
in his chronicle when he wrote the word *baro* – interestingly in his
treatment of the constitutional crisis in 1174 in which the baronial
movement can first be discerned – used it of Humphrey of Toron,
Reynald of Sidon, Baldwin of Ramle and his brother Balian, who
was later to enjoy the royal apanage of Nablus;[103] a royal proc-
lamation of 1183, imposing a general tax on the kingdom, made
reference both to barons and vavasours;[104] a continuator of the
chronicle of William of Tyre, relating the tragic annihilation of
the Christian army at Hattin in 1187, wrote that one privilege of a
baron was that he commanded the first squadron in battle, the
vanguard in advance and the rear-guard in retreat, when the army
of the kingdom was marching through his barony – this right was
claimed by Raymond of Tripoli while the Christian forces were in
the Principality of Galilee;[105] between 1198 and 1205 the authors
of the first of the law-books knew that barons, landholders and

vassals all had different rights, although they nowhere defined them;[106] in 1205 'the barons and knights' were present at the appointment of John of Beirut as lieutenant and in 1207 it was 'the barons and knights' who swore to abide by the terms of the marriage pact between King Hugh of Cyprus and Alice, the elder daughter of Henry of Champagne.[107] There survives no explanation of the differences that were obviously known to exist, but if before 1225 men felt no need to make definitions, we may assume that the issue was not to them one of much practical importance. Certainly visitors to the kingdom seem to have felt no difficulties : on the eve of Saladin's conquests in 1187 the anonymous writer of a tract on the Holy Land appears to have believed that all the greater lords ranked as barons and so some forty years later did James of Vitry, Bishop of Acre.[108]

What is certain is that there was in the early thirteenth century no concept of the four baronies proposed by John of Jaffa. The very vagueness that surrounded the term would have been reason enough for the jurists to look for some definition of it and a sign that it had become a subject for discussion may be the sudden appearance or reappearance of constables and marshals among the officers of the fiefs John of Jaffa ranked as baronies: it will be remembered that he argued that the right to have both of these officers was a distinguishing mark of baron. The Principality of Galilee had constables from 1121 to 1179[109] and marshals from 1121 to 1170;[110] after a long interval they reappeared in 1253[111] and 1234[112] respectively. A constable of Jaffa, in fact the founder of the house of Ibelin, held office from before 1115 to 1126;[113] the post is never to be found again in the surviving documents, but a marshal of Jaffa was in existence in 1256.[114] There was a constable of Sidon in 1158,[115] and this officer only reappeared in 1253;[116] while a marshal of Sidon is first to be found in 1228.[117] It looks as though the lords of the great fiefs after 1228 were trying to reestablish what they believed to be their rights, and it may be no coincidence that in a charter issued by the Hospitallers in 1256 both John of Jaffa and Philip of Montfort, who as Lord of Toron was heir to the lost fief of Oultrejourdain, were referred to as barons; this title was again used of Philip in a treaty he made in 1264 with the Genoese,[118] although it is possible that this reflected a belief, almost certainly erroneous, that Philip had been made one of the twelve peers of France.[119] The concept of the four baronies,

although unhistorical and never, it seems, entirely accepted, is one
of many examples in this book of the thought of a remarkable
group of men in a dominant position in the kingdom and it is to
them that we must now turn.

2

LORDS, LORDSHIPS AND VAVASOURS

IN September 1268 Pope Clement IV gave the Patriarch of Jerusalem permission to dispense Margaret, the sister of the King of Cyprus, from impediments to marriage

> because in the Kingdoms of Jerusalem and Cyprus one cannot easily find any noble, worthy by reason of his estate and origins to be her husband, who is not related to her within the degrees of consanguinity or affinity prohibited for the contracting of marriage.[1]

By this time the nobility of Jerusalem was made up of a small group of families, closely related to one another. Foremost were the Ibelins, who rose to prominence in the twelfth century, shone with brilliance in the thirteenth and faded into obscurity in the fourteenth. Once they had achieved fame they liked to think of themselves as the descendants of the French Viscounts of Chartres, but in fact their origins were undistinguished and Barisanus, who founded their fortunes when he became Constable of Jaffa before 1115, was probably a Norman knight from southern Italy.[2] In 1144 his son Balian was granted the castle of Ibelin from which the family took its name and he began the family tradition of making good marriages by wedding the heiress to the important fief of Ramle; of his sons Hugh and Baldwin of Ramle and Balian of Nablus it was the last who made the best match of all, one that linked the Ibelins to the royal house and helped to give them an international reputation, for he married Maria Comnena, the grand-niece of the Byzantine Emperor Manuel and widow of King Amalric. Early in the thirteenth century at least four of Balian and Maria's children survived. John, the eldest and known to later generations as the 'Old Lord of Beirut' was born in 1177 or 1178. By 1194 he was Constable of Jerusalem and thereafter he played a prominent part in the kingdom's affairs, not least because he was the half-brother of Queen Isabella who gave him the

important fief of Beirut.[3] He married first a daughter of the house
of Nephin in Tripoli and then in 1207 Melisende, Lady of Arsur.
From him descended two lines of lords, for his eldest son Balian
inherited Beirut, while Arsur passed to the younger John, who
himself married Alice, a daughter of Lord Rohard of Haifa, thus
bringing another noble house into the family orbit. Close to John
of Beirut was his younger brother Philip, Bailli of Cyprus, whose
career belongs more to the history of the island than the mainland.
By his marriage to Alice of Montbéliard, however, he fathered the
greatest figure of the next generation, the jurist John of Jaffa and
was probably the grandfather of another jurist, James.

Both of John of Beirut's sisters married into branches of
another great family, the Greniers, the descendants of Eustace, a
knight from Flanders who had travelled out to Syria some time
between 1099 and August 1105. He had soon become one of the
king's most trusted advisers: he may have been viscount of the
city of Jerusalem, was constable of the kingdom between 1120 and
1123 and in the latter year was elected regent after King Baldwin II
had been captured by the Muslims. By September 1110 he had
been granted the fief of Caesarea and in December of that year he
was also given the newly conquered Lordship of Sidon. When he
died in June 1123 his fiefs, in an act foreshadowing the custom
that governed pluralism, were separately inherited by his twin
sons, who were to be the progenitors of the two lines of Grenier
lords: Eustace II became Lord of Sidon and Walter Lord of
Caesarea.[4] It is possible – it was so reported by John of Jaffa in his
law-book[5] – that Caesarea was held by the cadet branch from their
cousins as a rear-fief. Evidence from the twelfth century, however,
especially the fact that long before the issuing of the *Assise sur la
ligece* a Lord of Caesarea can be seen participating at a meeting of
the High Court as a tenant-in-chief of the crown, makes this unlikely.[6] Before 1210 Margaret, the elder of John of Beirut's sisters,
married Walter III of Caesarea, who became a loyal supporter of
her family.[7] We shall encounter their son John, 'the young Lord
of Caesarea', as one of the most violent partisans of the baronial
movement. The younger of the Ibelin sisters, Helvis, married
Reynald of Sidon, by whom she had a son and two daughters.
The son, Balian of Sidon, became one of the most distinguished of
the jurists and the daughters Euphemia and Agnes married Otto
and Ralph of Tiberias, of the house of the Princes of Galilee. The

genealogy of this family is very complicated: by the late 1160s the principality had passed to Otto and Ralph's parents, Walter of Falconberg and Eschiva of Bures, both descendants of Hugh of Falconberg, the son of a Provost of St Omer, who had been given Galilee in 1101.[8] Of the four Falconberg sons, unquestionably the most important was Ralph, who himself may have had an Ibelin grandmother and is a key figure in the story that will follow. It was he who inherited the principality.

But if the Palestinian aristocracy was inter-married, a feature of it was the way in which new blood was infused by migrant members of the European nobility. The diversion of the Fourth Crusade to Constantinople bitterly disappointed the Franks in Syria, but it brought to the East three important new families. In 1204 Guy of Montfort, brother of the great Simon who was to be leader of the French forces on the Albigensian Crusade, married Helvis of Ibelin, now Reynald of Sidon's widow. Their son Philip was brought up in the West, but he came to Palestine in 1239 with the crusade of Thibaut of Champagne and in the following year married Maria of Armenia, the heiress to the Lordships of Toron and Oultrejourdain;[9] the fief of Toron later passed to their son John together with the Lordship of Tyre, one of the richest slices of the royal domain. The fortunes of the family of Montbéliard in the East were laid by Walter, a younger son of Count Amadeus of Montbéliard, who travelled out to Cyprus and married Burgundia, the daughter of King Aimery and Eschiva of Ibelin. Walter, whose sister married Philip of Ibelin, became Regent of Cyprus on Aimery's death in 1205. He had two children: Eschiva, who was to become the second wife of Balian of Beirut; and Odo who, as Constable of Jerusalem and lieutenant for the Emperor Frederick II, was to play a leading part in the stirring events of the 1230s. Odo himself married another Eschiva, the elder daughter of Ralph of Tiberias and Agnes of Sidon, and their daughter married James of Ibelin.[10] Lastly, coming East at the same time as Guy of Montfort and Walter of Montbéliard was William of La Mandelée, a knight from Calabria. Like them he made a good match, wedding Agnes, one of the daughters of Joscelin of Courtenay, the titular Count of Edessa who had acquired an important group of fiefs in northern Palestine. Their son James married Alice of Caesarea, the 'young lord's' sister and herself half an Ibelin; and James and Alice's son William married Agnes,

the heiress of Scandelion, bringing another of the small fiefs into
the network of blood relationships.[11]

It is important to remember how closely related to one another
were the dominant figures in the thirteenth-century baronial
movement. Of the leaders between 1174 and 1192 Balian of
Nablus and Baldwin of Ramle were brothers, but Raymond of
Tripoli and Reynald of Sidon were not related to them and were
only very distantly related to each other.[12] Of their successors
however Ralph of Tiberias was the brother-in-law of Balian of
Sidon, who was himself a nephew of John the 'Old Lord of
Beirut', while Odo of Montbéliard was John's cousin and Ralph's
son-in-law; of the next generation, Balian of Beirut and John of
Arsur were brothers and Philip of Montfort, John of Jaffa and
John of Caesarea were their first cousins; and the leaders in the
1270s, Balian of Arsur and James of Jaffa, were second cousins.
The web of family ties spread even further: the Kings of Jerusalem
were related to the Ibelins through their common ancestress,
Maria Comnena, and the royal house of Cyprus was descended
from John of Beirut's cousin, Eschiva of Ibelin; that relationship
was cemented by the marriages of Kings Hugh II and Hugh III to
Ibelins and of Hugh III's sister Margaret to John of Montfort. By
the middle of the thirteenth century the house of Ibelin was at the
centre of a network of alliances by blood that encompassed all the
important fiefs in Palestine and the two royal lines of Jerusalem
and Cyprus. No wonder members of the family had an intense
pride in their lineage which was reflected in the writings of their
vassal Philip of Novara but was most vividly expressed in a speech
made by James of Jaffa in 1271:

> Further we can certainly show by the testimony of men still living
> that the vassals of the Kingdom of Cyprus have served the house of
> Ibelin outside the said kingdom more often than they have my lord
> the king or his ancestors; and if the custom of their service binds
> them, then the house of Ibelin can call upon their services in the
> same way as can my lord the king.[13]

John of Jaffa wrote that Godfrey of Bouillon

> and the other lords and kings of the kingdom who came after him
> gave to certain high men of the kingdom baronies, lordships, courts
> and rights to seals and justice, for which they owed them service of
> their bodies and a number of knights.[14]

ARSUR. The castle-mound and the port below it can be seen near the top of the photograph. The town lay to the east and south of the castle.

By the middle of the thirteenth century all the greater lordships were of the same pattern. The centre of a seigneurie's administration would be the town in which stood the lord's chief castle; it was a market for the surrounding area and if on the coast might be a minor port; in many cases it was also the seat of a bishop. Around it lay the territories of the lordship, but the lord himself would hold properties beyond its borders, usually including a house in Acre,[15] and *fiefs-rentes* which must have been accumulated over many years. A brief description of two Palestinian fiefs will show the similarities. The southern borders of the Lordship of Sidon and the annexed fief of Beaufort followed the course of the river Litani and to the east the frontier ran along the line of the Lebanon mountains; in the north it perhaps approached to within 6 km of the city of Beirut.[16] The town of Sidon, a prosperous though comparatively small port and the centre of a diocese, was dominated by two citadels, both in the hands of the lord, who also had possession of other castles in the countryside: Beaufort, only reoccupied in 1240 and one of the finest in the kingdom, standing on a hilltop to the south-east of Sidon; the grotto-fortress of the Cave de Tyron on the lordship's eastern frontier;[17] and perhaps the little castle of Belhacem a few miles to the east of Sidon itself. The lord also owned villages in the territories of Tyre and Galilee and a palace in Acre.[18] By comparison the fief of Arsur was small, extending over the coastal plain of southern Palestine from the al-'Auja' river in the south to the Wadi Faliq in the north and reaching inland to the foothills of Samaria. Like so many towns on the Levantine coast Arsur was rectangular in shape, enclosed by the sea on the west and by walls to north, east and south. In the north-western angle of walls and sea was its citadel, immediately beneath which lay a small harbour. The lord had properties in and near Acre, including a house, and probably drew money-fiefs from the revenues of Acre and the lost royal domain round Nablus.[19]

The territorial lordships, established soon after the arrival of the crusaders, often followed administrative boundaries which had existed long before: that part of the Principality of Galilee which was in Palestine proper was nearly co-terminous with Byzantine Palaestina Secunda; the lordship of Caesarea had the same borders as had the city territory of Caesarea in the seventh century; the lordship of Arsur covered the same area as had the

Muslim *kura* administered from it.[20] It will be seen below that the
lords seem to have taken over not only the lands that lay within
the ancient boundaries, but also the bureaucracies that had run
them, so that for the exploitation of their fiefs they had at their
disposal already developed instruments of government with their
own local traditions which could be used with little reference to
central authority. But they also had jurisdictional independence,
perhaps based on generous terms in the original charters which
created the lordships, although we cannot be certain because none
survive. The early royal grants to the Italian merchants were
liberal in order to encourage them to come and trade,[21] and it may
be that in the same way the need to attract settlers led the crown
to give away a good deal of its authority to prospective lords.
Perhaps it was only after a period ending in 1120 with the Council
of Nablus, at which the king tried unsuccessfully to reserve certain
kinds of case to his own jurisdiction,[22] that the rulers began to try
to reverse the process of decentralisation: certainly their attitude
towards the Italians had changed by the middle of the twelfth
century.

Authority in a medieval state was normally exercised through
the administration of justice and the rights of jurisdiction enjoyed
by the crown and local interests are a guide to their relative
powers. The privileges of the lords in their own fiefs were defined
by the authors of the 'Livre au roi', who believed they had been
confirmed by *assise*: they could grant fiefs and lands to vassals and
could seal the charters of gift with their own lead seals, validating
them in the same way as did the king when he made grants out of
the royal estates; they could exercise jurisdiction over all those
living in their lordships, their vassals being judged in seigneurial
courts and other freemen in burgess courts; from these they could
take the profits of justice in the forms of amends, fines and confiscations; and they could punish malefactors with death – in
other words they could administer High Justice or Justice of
Blood, which in a centralised state would have been reserved to
the crown.[23] These rights, known as those of *court, coins et justise*,[24]
made the lordships palatinates in which jurisdiction was concen-
trated in their lords' hands rather than under royal officers. The
independence of the greater lords was later reinforced by the
exercise of two other privileges which had been originally royal
prerogatives: in the middle of the twelfth century King Amalric

gave the lords of maritime fiefs the right to shipwreck, a proportion of the cargoes jettisoned in times of storm and washed on to
Palestinian shores and timbers from the ships wrecked on the
coast;[25] and within a few years another regalian right, the minting
of coins, was usurped by the barons, for money is known to have
been struck in the Lordships of Jaffa, Sidon, Beirut, Toron and
Tyre after its acquisition by Philip of Montfort.[26] By 1200 it was
believed that, except when a man alienated lands to a religious
house in such a way that services to the crown would be reduced,
the king had no right to interfere in the granting of fiefs within a
lordship. Gifts made by him within a vassal's tenement had no
validity unless his charter was countersealed by the vassal himself,
although one of the jurists advised a rear-vassal whose immediate
lord had no court to get his tenure confirmed in the High Court
where at least he was a peer through the liege-homage he had paid
the king. And no men who were not tenants in a particular lordship could sit in its seigneurial court, not even the great men of the
High Court, unless they had been given special licence at the request of the lord involved.[27]

The great lords also conducted their own foreign policies,
making peace treaties or war with the neighbouring Islamic states
with little or no reference to the central government, although
this practice is only apparent in periods like the 1180s and the
years after 1250 when the kingdom was under pressure from the
Infidel. Raymond of Tripoli in his wife's lordship of Galilee had
a highly individual relationship with Saladin in the years immediately preceding the Battle of Hattin.[28] At the same time
Reynald of Châtillon, the Lord of Oultrejourdain, was claiming
not to be bound by a peace treaty made by the king with Saladin,
'because he too was lord in his land, just as (the king) was in
his'.[29] In 1192 the Lords of Haifa, Caesarea, Arsur and Sidon seem
to have regained their old fiefs or parts of them directly from
Saladin, who also granted Caymont to Balian of Nablus; it is possible that they entered into a feudal relationship with the sultan.[30]
In the 1260s the Mamluk Sultan Baibars commented on the independence in this respect of the Christian lords[31] and their
activities at the time bear him out. In the previous decade John of
Jaffa had been conducting on his own a very aggressive policy towards the Egyptians, but he and his relative John of Beirut made
treaties with Baibars in 1261.[32] In 1263 Philip of Montfort at Tyre

had even entered into an alliance with the sultan aimed against the government of the regent in Acre, with whom he was on very bad terms,[33] and ten years later Haymo l'Estrange, the Lord of Beirut, put his wife the Lady Isabella and her fief under the protection of Egypt on his deathbed, a move aimed at thwarting the rights of the king who was prevented from receiving Isabella's *service de mariage* :[34] it is interesting to note that the king's treaty with Baibars in 1272 made no reference to the Lordships of Tyre or Beirut.[35] Although we have no evidence that the lords followed their own foreign policies before the 1180s – the strength of character of the kings in the middle years of the twelfth century would have made any course of this kind a dangerous one for a lord to take – it was precisely this privilege that was being granted to the Military Orders in the northern Christian states of Tripoli and Antioch from the 1140s onwards[36] and it may be that the counts and princes were only following precedents already established soon after the conquest of the Levant by the crusaders and to be found in privileges in the foundation charters of the lordships.

'There is not a prince of this world,' wrote the Master of the Templars in 1261, 'who on one and the same day could hold seven great castles without much inconvenience and keep them in a defensible state and fortified against this multitude' – by which he meant the Mongols.[37] At the time he was writing many of the great fortresses in the kingdom – Beirut, Tyre, Toron, Haifa, Caesarea, Arsur and Jaffa – were not in the hands of the government or the Military Orders, but were held by feudatories; and the guard of two others, Sidon and Beaufort, had only just been renounced by their lord. The enormous amounts spent by the Military Orders in the defence of the Holy Land are well known: the rebuilding of Saphet by the Templars, begun in 1240, cost them over two and a half years 1,100,000 saracen besants, over and above what the castle's domain returned in rents, and thereafter their building expenses were running at 40,000 saracen besants a year; it was estimated that Saphet's garrison, 1,700 strong in peacetime and 2,200 in time of war, consumed annually 12,000 muleloads of grain.[38] But historians have ignored the fact that much the same burdens were shouldered by feudatories, who had not behind them great international organisations geared to providing them with finances. Heavy and recurring expenses must have been involved in the repairing and improvement of fortifications, the building and storing of machines of war and the hiring and provisioning of mercenaries: we have seen that the law of the kingdom not only permitted the service of salaried companions in place of rear-vassals, but also forbade fief-holders to sub-infeudate more of their assets than they themselves held, so that to defend his lands a lord could never rely only on the service that he would receive from them.

When their expenses are taken into account the lords' achievement in the defence of the Holy Land is scarcely less remarkable than their writings on the law. For the first half of the thirteenth century, the years in which the baronial movement was most active, the frontiers with the infidel were generally quiet. But once the Christian settlements came again under pressure after 1244 and particularly in the 1250s and the 1260s, after the coming to power in Egypt of the Mamluks and the arrival in the Near East of the Mongols, the burdens associated with defence greatly increased. The Mamluks and Mongols between them moreover seem to have been responsible for a decline in the trade that passed through the Palestinian ports, because the area became troubled at the same time as Mongol rule in central Asia permitted the reopening of more northerly trade routes that by-passed Palestine and Syria. The dependence of the Latins on trade will be shown in a later chapter; here it need only be said that increased military expenses coincided with a reduction in the profits from commerce. It is not surprising that the 1260s should have been marked by the alienation of some fiefs to the Military Orders and the loss of large tracts of territory to the Muslims. For a long time the brothers of the Military Orders had been contributing to the defence of the Holy Land not only by garrisoning their great castles, but also by taking over the custody of stretches of city-walls;[39] and in the twelfth century they were already helping to defend some lordships: Kerak in 1152,[40] Baniyas in 1157,[41] Sidon in 1162[42] and Ascalon in 1177.[43] In 1186 the Hospitallers were granted the whole of the fief of Margat in the Principality of Antioch because its lord could no longer afford to hold it.[44] But apart from Margat and Baniyas, the grants from fief-holders to the Orders had consisted only of small stretches of fortifications and when in 1206 the Lady of Caesarea gave the Teutonic Knights some towers on the

walls of her city, she specified that in time of war these were to be
returned to her.[45] It was in the late 1250s that Julian of Sidon
began to give away parts of his fief to the Teutonic Knights[46] and
in 1260 he leased the rest of it to the Templars, after negotiating
with the Hospitallers on the same matter.[47] A heavy gambler and
in many ways rather a stupid man, Julian was at the same time a
brave and shrewd military commander.[48] His lordship had
suffered greatly from the Muslims,[49] but the final straw for him
seems to have been a raid by the Mongols in which they pene-
trated his city and knocked down its walls: he simply could not
afford to have them rebuilt.[50] In the following year Balian of
Arsur leased to the Hospitallers his fief, the castle of which had
been re-fortified by his father in 1241.[51]

It must be emphasised that the Lords of Sidon and Arsur were
exceptions. What remained of Galilee was protected by the
Templars at Saphet and the Hospitallers on Mt Thabor, but
Caesarea and Jaffa were in lay hands when they fell to Baibars in
1265 and 1268 and so until the end in 1291 remained Haifa,
Scandelion, Tyre and Beirut, although a heavy ransom charged by
his Muslim captors on John of Beirut in 1260 forced him to
alienate some of his lands to the Teutonic Knights.[52] The most
heroic of the lords was John of Jaffa, who acquired his county
shortly before June 1247. The town of Ascalon, which had once
been part of it, had been re-fortified by Richard of Cornwall and
had been granted by Frederick II to the Hospitallers, but it fell to
the Egyptians in the following October. The Hospitallers claimed
repayment of the expenses incurred in its defence and by 1256
John, obviously to reinforce his right to the county, had taken
upon himself the responsibility for compensating them, which he
did in the following year by promising them land near Ascalon
once it had been reoccupied by the Christians.[53] Jaffa was re-
fortified by Louis of France in 1252,[54] but John also concerned
himself with improvements to it: in 1253 Pope Innocent IV was
offering an indulgence to those who helped him repair the port.[55]
In 1255 the county was excluded from a ten-year truce made with
Damascus and negotiated for the kingdom by John himself.[56]
This may have been engineered by John, for in the following year
there was a successful Christian raid into the interior, although
John had to resign the regency of the kingdom to defend his fief
against an Egyptian counterstroke; a treaty with Egypt followed

from which Jaffa was again excluded.[57] John was conducting an aggressive policy at a time when he was short of money: in 1256 Pope Alexander IV, having heard that in the custody of his castle he had spent all his movable goods and much of his patrimony and was now gravely in debt, ordered the Templars to give the Patriarch of Jerusalem for expenditure on Jaffa up to 1,000 silver marks of money deposited with them by a past patriarch; and in the following year he ordered the brothers to hand the sum directly to John himself.[58] In 1261 John and his cousin John of Beirut made treaties with Baibars, and John of Jaffa and the sultan seem to have entered into a new peace treaty covering Jaffa and Arsur in 1263.[59] In spite of a raid from Jaffa into the territory of Ascalon in 1264 to force the Muslims to release his castellan,[60] John's relations with Baibars were good in the early 1260s; he seems to have been prepared to enter into some sort of feudal relationship with him and even to allow his port to be used as a supply point for the Egyptian field-army.[61] It may be that in spite of all his efforts Jaffa was still not in a defensible state: in 1264 Pope Urban IV was directing part of the quinquennial hundredth collected in France to be spent at once on the fortification of the castle, which, it was noted, was especially in need of attention, although the pope insisted that John should not be allowed to spend the money himself.[62] In the end all these efforts were to no avail: the truce was invalidated by John's death in 1266 and Jaffa fell to the Muslims in 1268. But one must admire John's stubborn fight for his fief and when it is considered that at this time he was composing his great law-book and was playing an important part in the government of the kingdom one can only wonder at his industry.

The Count of Jaffa was not alone in receiving papal moneys to help him defend his fief: early in the century 'the Old Lord' had spent 'Christian alms' on the re-fortification of Beirut.[63] But even allowing for occasional subsidies from the Church the role of the barons as defenders of the Holy Land is a tribute to their wealth: John of Beirut was reputedly very rich when he entered the Order of the Templars just before his death in 1236.[64] Without money the lords could not have played the part they did in constitutional struggles and their financial circumstances will be given much attention in this book. It seems that in the middle of the twelfth century a landlord could expect a return of about 10% on an investment in property,[65] but we have very little knowledge of the capital value of the great lordships or even of their annual revenues. There is evidence that early in the 1240s the inland Seigneurie of Toron was valued at 60,000 saracen besants.[66] Arsur was leased to the Hospitallers in 1261 for 4,000 besants a year, but only when its lord could no longer afford to hold it. We might expect that district's total revenues to have been more than twice the amount of the rent by adding to it an equal sum to cover the value of the rear-fiefs: we know that the lord handed out each year to his own vassals 2,349 besants, a very large quantity of rations for men and horses, 137 *modii* of wheat, 245 of barley, 23 of vegetables and 127 litres of oil. But we must assume that the returns of Arsur averaged much more than 8,000 besants, for without some profit it is unlikely that the Hospitallers would have taken over the burdens of its defence, and we know that excluded from the lease of Arsur were the lord's possessions elsewhere in the kingdom, including properties in Acre that may have been considerable.[67] It is clear moreover that most of the Palestinian lords had lands in Cyprus that provided them with additional revenues.[68] But although we have a very inadequate knowledge of the income of the greater lords it is possible to describe in detail the sources from which they drew most of their revenues. This is valuable because many of their reactions to political events were conditioned by their desire to preserve rich assets from what they believed to be threats to them.

Every lordship can be divided into two parts. We have seen that more than half of it had to be retained by the lord for his own exploitation and this, known as the domain,[69] will be considered in the next two chapters. The rest could be granted out in rear-fiefs, although at least one Lord of Arsur in the middle of the thirteenth century preferred to exploit nearly all his territory himself, handing out a proportion of its revenues in money and kind to his men.[70] The vassals of Arsur, already described, were all small men, most being sergeants holding tiny fiefs; slightly more prosperous were two knights in the territory of Tyre who were vassals of the Venetians in 1243. William Jordan had three villages in the countryside, a third of the revenues of another, two gardens, a piece of land and a *gastina*[71] in the well-watered environs of Tyre, and in the city a house, an oven and a rent of 60 besants a year. The fief of Roland Contarini had been somewhat reduced when an ancestor, perhaps his grandmother, had left her dower to the crown, but he held two villages in the interior and had a third share in two others, together with two pieces of land near Tyre and a house in the town. The villages of William Jordan and Roland Contarini were scattered throughout the district and this must have been characteristic of many lesser fiefs,[72] although the greater rear-fiefs like Ramle were compact territorial units and smaller blocks of land held in fief were to be found in the royal domain near Acre in the twelfth century [73] and in the Lordship of Sidon in the middle of the thirteenth. Not very much is known about the lordship of Adelon in the south-western corner of that seigneurie, but details have survived of two estates in the central march of its eastern borders. Here an area called Shuf was divided between the lords and a family whose administration was centred on the village of Niha and had another fief around Gezin. The estates round Niha and Gezin consisted of some 26 villages with their dependent *gastinae*, most of which ran in a solid block for over 20 km up the frontier, although there were one or two in other parts of the lordship and the family had three *gastinae* near Sidon and houses in the town itself. The fiefs of Gezin and Niha may have been coterminous with the old Muslim *iklim* or administrative district of Jazzin, but it is noteworthy that the Cave de Tyron, the castle at the centre of this territory, seems to have remained in the Lord of Sidon's possession.[74]

The richer rear-vassals would naturally have vassals of their own and this could lead to very extended lines of dependence. Until 1176, for instance, the knight John Arrabi held a village north-east of Ascalon from Balian of Nablus, who was vassal for it of his brother Baldwin, Lord of Ramle; in his turn Baldwin held it from the king.[75] Rear-fiefs which were held in plurality by one tenant would be subdivided by partition among heirs, the younger children holding their lands from the eldest: such seems to have been the state of affairs on the eastern borders of Sidon in 1257, for there Andrew of Shuf held the fief of Gezin from his brother John who had made homage to the Lord of Sidon for the whole march.[76] But except in the case of a very large rear-fief like Ramle the lesser tenants did not have courts of their own other than for their villagers: indeed the unlawful exercise of jurisdiction, when it had not been expressly granted by a lord competent to give such a privilege, was regarded as a serious breach of the feudal contract[77] and it was the custom for a rear-vassal to make his own gifts in the court of his immediate lord, asking him to seal his charters.[78]

It must be emphasised that while rear-vassals owed their lord the same services as he owed the king, they also claimed from him the same rights as he demanded from the crown. When a writer like John of Jaffa defined the duties of the monarch towards himself he was at the same time describing the limitations on his own conduct towards his tenants, for he believed that the laws and customs of Jerusalem were applicable throughout the kingdom, not just within the royal domain. He argued that not only the king, but also 'all the vassals and the vassals of vassals' ought to swear to keep the laws; all lords should know them, as should the tenants who sat in their seigneurial courts;[79] these rear-vassals were peers, bound to their lord and to one another just as were the liegemen of the crown.[80] To the jurists the same criteria for validity were applied to the grants both of kings and lords, none of whose gifts had any worth unless witnessed by their men;[81] a lord, like the king, was bound by his contractual obligations and could not lay hands on the body or fief of a vassal without the formal judgement of that man's peers in a court in which he or his representative[82] acted only as president; and rear-vassals had the same means of resisting their lords as had the vassals of the king.[83]

In theory, the rights of rear-vassals were buttressed by a famous law, the *Assise sur la ligece*, which, according to the jurists of the mid-thirteenth century, had been issued after a King of Jerusalem, probably Baldwin III,[84] had taken up arms against Lord Gerard of Sidon, who had dispossessed one of his vassals without the judgement of his seigneurial court. Gerard had been forced to submit, return the fief to his man and compensate him for the damage he had done. Then, at a full meeting of the High Court, the *Assise* had been established by Amalric, Baldwin's successor. Although its actual wording does not seem to have been known in the thirteenth century, it was accepted that it had laid down that in future all rear-vassals were to make liege-homage to the king for their fiefs – homage which had precedence over but did not supersede that paid to their immediate lords – and that it had formalised the way in which this *ligece* should be made. All – king, tenants-in-

chief and rear-vassals who had made *ligece* – were now bound together by the bonds of homage and held to one another by their
reciprocal oaths, and it seems that some statement to this effect
had been included in the original law. The king could also demand
fealty from other freemen in a fief held in-chief, although this does
not seem to have been obligatory on him.[85]

Many of the consequences of this *Assise* will be considered
later, but an immediate effect of it was to give those rear-vassals
who made liege-homage peerage with their own lords in the High
Court, where they could sit and decide even cases concerning their
own superiors.[86] And while there could be no appeal to the High
Court from a judgement of a seigneurial court,[87] the procedure for
complaining before the king if there had been a failure on the part
of a lord to accord a man a hearing in his own court was strengthened, although this was never explicitly stated by the jurists, for
the voice of the lowliest knight could be raised in the highest
court in the land. The law provided the machinery for bringing
seigneurial injustices to the notice of the king and justification for
royal intervention, because as liege-lord the king had the duty and
right to see that their immediate lords did not oppress his liegemen
either by arbitrary acts or by the failure to give them justice. If a
tenant-in-chief acted wrongly towards one of his men he could be
summoned to the High Court; and if he refused to make amends
the king could restore a confiscated fief to the rear-vassal, presumably by the use of physical force, or by his court's judgement
deprive the lord of the right to exercise jurisdiction for the rest of
his life.[88]

Those rear-vassals who were now bound directly to the king by
liege-homage owed him duties that sometimes took precedence
over their services to their immediate lords. If warfare broke out
between the king and one of his tenants-in-chief, or if that tenant-
in-chief refused to stand trial in the High Court, or if the rear-
vassals knew that he had committed or was contemplating some
act against the rights of the crown, they had to try to persuade
him to submit to a trial at which they, as his vassals, would support him. But if after forty days he was still obdurate, they were
bound to go over to the side of the king and serve him, on condition that they were guaranteed the restoration within a further
forty days of the fiefs they would naturally lose and were compensated for any damage done to them; if the king was not able to

fulfil these conditions, they were free to return to their own lord.[89] Seen from the point of view of the king the descending lines of feudal dependence were now by-passed and he had established a direct relationship with all fief-holders whether or not they were his own immediate vassals; seen from the point of view of the feudatories, the rights of the rear-vassals were strengthened and the obligations towards them of the tenants-in-chief made more binding.

That was the theory; but one is here faced by a problem. The *Assise* should have resulted in all rear-vassals being liegemen of the crown. But the authors of the 'Livre au roi', compiled between 1198 and 1205, referred at one point to them as *liegemen of their lords*;[90] and some vassals were so described in charters issued concerning the lordships of Haifa in 1234,[91] Nazareth in 1255,[92] Sidon in 1254 and 1257,[93] Scandelion in 1263,[94] and Tyre in 1261 and 1277.[95] A knight of Arsur called John of Arsur, who in the 1260s held a *fief-rente* in the lordship, was in one charter specifically excluded from the ranks of the liegemen of the crown.[96] When in 1249 Louis IX of France granted a charter to the archbishop of the newly-conquered Damietta in Egypt, a land over which he himself was planning to retain overlordship, he gave him 'the fiefs of 10 knights *who will make liege-homage to the archbishop* and are held to serve him for their fiefs *according to the custom of the Kingdom of Jerusalem*'.[97] What are we to make of this evidence, which conflicts with the unanimous opinion of the great jurists of the mid-thirteenth century, although there are references in their law-books which suggest that they knew that theory and practice did not always coincide?[98] It should be remembered that there are inconsistencies in some of these documents: in most of Julian of Sidon's charters his tenants were simply called vassals and there are only two surviving references to them as his 'liegemen'; and there were vavasours who do not seem to have held fiefs in the royal domain but participated in meetings of the High Court, which suggests that they had made *ligece*.[99] There may be no easy way out of our difficulties and it is possible that we are faced sometimes with bad terminology, but also sometimes with a consequence of the absence in the middle years of the thirteenth century of a resident king to whom the vassals could unreservedly make liege-homage. At the very least we must not take too literally the picture painted by the jurists of a host of feudatories all bound together by the peerage that resulted from the making of *ligece*.

It is worth while examining a little more closely through seigneurial charters issued between 1241 and 1271 the persons who held rear-fiefs in the lordships.[100] They seem to have made up a close society, sharing among themselves the seigneurial offices, many of them as sergeantries. Among them are to be found relatives of the lords,[101] as well as members of other well-known families in the East.[102] The most interesting detail brought to light however is that several rear-vassals enjoyed fiefs in more than one lordship. Peter of Avelon, Lord of Adelon in the territory of Sidon, was also Constable of Tiberias;[103] John Harneis seems to have been at the same time a vassal of Nazareth and Marshal of Sidon;[104] Amalric of St Bertin, presumably related to the family with a fief in the royal domain, was a vassal of Caesarea in the 1250s and of Tyre around 1270.[105] Two important political figures were members of this group. Stephen of Sauvegny, active in the High Court and its representative in negotiations with Ancona in 1257, held fiefs of the Count of Jaffa and the Lord of Sidon.[106] James Vidal, a French knight who was a fief-holder in Palestine by April 1249,[107] appeared regularly among the witnesses from the High Court to charters until 1271.[108] By the 1260s he was an important man, attending with other leaders of the kingdom a meeting called by the papal legate to restore order after the War of St Sabas and acting as the spokesman of the High Court in 1268 and 1269 when it accepted Hugh of Antioch-Lusignan as regent and then as king;[109] in 1273 he was a member of the delegation sent to the Council of Lyons to argue Hugh's case for the crown against the claims of Maria of Antioch, but while in France he seems to have turned coat, only returning to Syria in 1277 with Odo Poilechien, one of the Angevin officers, and becoming Marshal of Jerusalem for Charles of Anjou.[110] James, who was certainly a liegeman of the kingdom,[111] also had fiefs in Caesarea in 1249, in Arsur between 1255 and 1269, in Scandelion in 1263 and perhaps in Nazareth in 1259.[112] The evidence provided by the charters is substantiated in the writings of the jurists. Philip of Novara, who drew attention to the problems resulting from conflicting loyalties to two lords, argued that since all fiefs were in the king's lordship and their holders were anyway bound to him by liege-homage there could be no fundamental conflict in this matter.[113] But the issue had resulted in much argument and Philip, himself a man of the Lords of Beirut, reported that 'it has sometimes happened that there have been quarrels and discord between the Lord of Beirut and his vassals' on the question.[114] A few years later John of Jaffa suggested that a vassal should support the lord to whom he had first made homage, but his treatment of the problem was so unsatisfactory that one feels that it had not yet been settled.[115] Perhaps it never could be.

The services owed by vassals to a lord were financial assets, saving him some of the expense of employing paid soldiers, officials and messengers, but they provided him with less than one might suppose. There seem to have been few of those additional rights for him which are known to historians as feudal incidents. I have for instance found no references in the law-books or charters to payments of relief – sums given to lords when vassals succeeded to their fiefs – and the silence of the sources leads me to suppose that reliefs were not paid.[116] Nor could a lord get much benefit from the wardship of rear-fiefs during minorities. In the Principality of Antioch as in Europe wardship came to be a profitable seigneurial perquisite,[117] but in the Kingdom of Jerusalem an older custom seems to have prevailed. If an heir was a boy under fifteen years old or a girl under twelve or unmarried, the wardship of the lands would be entrusted to the surviving parent or to the nearest relative on that side of the family through which the fief could be inherited; a parent would also have custody of the child, but the charge of an orphan would go to a friend of the family or to a relative who had no rights of inheritance: in his treatment of this Philip of Novara gave his readers a rhymed proverb:

> Ne doit mie garder l'aignel
> Qui en doit avoir la pel.[118]

It was only when there was no living parent or relative or when a widow refused to perform *service de mariage* for the wardship of her child's lands that the lord was justified in taking them over himself.[119] And though it is clear that lords did at times enjoy the profits of wardships, they[120] cannot have been a great source of income to them.

We have already seen that the performance of services and aids was important to the lords. And it is clear that they desired the services themselves, for there survives no evidence for the commutation of them for money payments in Palestine and there can be found only one example from the whole of Latin Syria :[121] of significance when it is considered that the commutation of village-returns for money was common. But the value of services must not be exaggerated, for the legal restriction on the proportion of a fief that could be sub-infeudated anyway limited the services at a lord's disposal and gave great importance to that part of his lordship he retained in his own hands.

3

THE DOMAIN IN THE COUNTRYSIDE

IN 1193 the Master of the Hospitallers confirmed, with some slight modifications, the rights to tithes that had been enjoyed in the fief of Margat in the Principality of Antioch by the local bishop. Since seigneurial revenues were titheable he detailed them: the returns from villages, mills, olive-presses, gardens and demesne lands; the profits from the town oven, the markets and other commercial offices: and the dues paid in the little port on local products, fermented and unfermented wine, sumach, almonds and figs, jars, pots and pitchers.[1] The sources of revenue on this list must have been typical of many fiefs and we can divide them into those in the countryside and those in the towns, although in a monetary economy, where even the revenues from villages could be estimated in terms of money,[2] there were not as far as the lords were concerned the differences we might imagine between agricultural returns and tolls levied on the passage of commerce. From fief to fief the proportion of lands as opposed to money-rents retained by a lord in his own hands varied, but most lords must have held many of the villages in their seigneuries, whether in compact blocks, as in the district of Shuf in Sidon, or scattered, as in Caesarea.[3]

Although there were a few isolated farms,[4] most of the rural population lived in villages where agricultural practices had changed little since late Roman times. The Franks called them *rustici* or *villani* and, although as in southern France villeinage seems to have been regarded as a feudal condition,[5] it is clear that like European serfs they were tied to their lands, unable in normal circumstances to leave or alienate them, and were treated in law no differently from their lords' other movable possessions.[6] For the purposes of reckoning the Franks assumed to be villeins all the descendants of those living in a village at the time of the siege of Antioch in 1098 by the First Crusade[7] and they drew up censuses so that they might know what inhabitants were subject to them, although the surviving lists are not very methodically compiled.[8] The acquirers of estates were sometimes given permission to scour the surrounding countryside for villeins living outside their villages.[9] Although lords might establish new native settlements[10] or themselves move villagers about from place to place,[11] the relationship between the villeins and their lands was normally so close that instead of a fraction of a village or some land in it a beneficiary could be given one or several villagers; and, although it is not always so specified in the charters, it is clear that the gift of villeins included not only their personal dues, but also their land and its returns.[12] The advantage for the beneficiary may have lain in the fact that villeins were granted together with their heirs and this kind of property could possibly increase in value, provided of course that the family involved did not die out, for it might in time acquire a larger proportion of the village lands as neighbouring families failed. Conversely, when in 1257 John of Jaffa reserved for himself in fourteen villages that he had promised to the Hospitallers,

> the villeins known to have been born in these places in the two first years after Ascalon has been restored to the Christians by treaty, that is to say those who will then be in the power of the Christians,

he was making an investment for the future.[13] The close identification of villeins with their lands would lead one to ask whether the village territories were divided among them according to *musha'*, a system still to be found in Palestine by which the fields are periodically redistributed among the peasants in proportions traditionally allotted to each family. But although recently this subject has been carefully studied no conclusive results have been obtained and it is not possible to say with any certainty that *musha'* was then practised.[14]

It is also impossible to make confident statements about the size of the native villages. Their populations varied widely, from for instance perhaps one family in each of two villages to about eighteen in a third, all being in the same district in 1243.[15] And the carrucate, the measure of land under cultivation, was not of a constant size: there were three different ways of estimating it, at least one of which was subject to local variations. The first type of carrucate was registered in the royal *secrete* or central financial

office and must have been introduced by the Latins, because it was
known as the Frankish carrucate. It was defined as follows:

> Each carrucate ought to be 24 cords long and 16 wide; and the cord
> is the ground covered by a man of medium height who takes 18
> paces with his arms outstretched

– we may therefore suggest that it was equivalent to 25–26 acres.
It was to be found throughout Palestine in rural areas, sometimes
in the middle of villages, but was applied only to comparatively
small pockets of land, perhaps fragments of demesne.[16] The
second was known as the Saracen carrucate. It was the amount of
land that could be ploughed in a single day by a pair of draught
animals, usually oxen, and it always seems to have been used for
measuring vineyards and olive groves, never specifically arable
lands.[17] The third type, which was and still is used to measure
cornfields, was one in which size was estimated by the amount of
grain that could be sown, but it could vary: near Tyre, for instance, it was that area of land that could be sown with nine *modii*
of corn; near Ascalon twelve *modii* were sown to a carrucate.[18]

A rural settlement was usually called a *casal*, although the word
villa had also been used in the early days.[19] Each *casal* had an inhabited nucleus around which stretched its lands, the boundaries
of which were carefully defined, being often marked with stones.[20]
The houses of the villeins, sometimes built for them by their
lords,[21] were low buildings, huddled together and probably
dominated by one belonging to the headman,[22] and near them
would be a cistern,[23] threshing floors and perhaps a mill and oven.
In some of the more important villages or in those which had been
made depots for the collection of revenues in kind from districts
there stood large warehouses and perhaps towers.[24]

Many villages contained vineyards and olive groves. In Palestine there had always been many olive-tree plantations, but wine
production became important under Christian rule and documents
of the period contain references to the planting and laying out of
vineyards and the building of terraces for them.[25] Vineyards and
olive groves tended to be grouped together[26] and were held in individual possession by peasants who, although they generally paid
higher rents for them than for the arable lands,[27] seem to have
been able to dispose of them by sale, presumably with their lord's
permission.[28] We are probably here faced by what are now known

as *hawakir* lands, the garden areas round the built-up centres which are held in individual possession and are much valued by villagers.[29] It was possible, as it is today, for members of another village community to hold some of these lands: in 1243 some of the owners of vines and olive groves in the village of Betheron near Tyre were not members of the community proper, for they had no share in the arable lands.[30] Some grapes were dried as raisins,[31] but wine was a main product and wine presses[32] and olive mills[33] were often referred to in the documents. Some *casalia* contained woodlands and there were occasionally to be found single trees of value like figs and carobs. There were also a few apple orchards, but these were not common.[34]

The arable lands stretched out around the centre. What evidence there is suggests that agricultural decisions were made for the whole village, presumably by the elders in collaboration with their lord.[35] It seems that a two-year crop rotation was practised, the lands being divided into those sown with wheat or barley in mid-November and those called collectively *garet*, half of which were sown with vegetables and half left fallow. In one district however part of the fallow land was sown with a crop like sesame that could be gathered in May. It is probable that a summer cereal crop was also sown.[36] Once the fields had been harvested they were combed for gleanings; and after threshing on the village threshing floors the harvest was shared out among the villagers themselves and between them and their lord.[37]

Attached to many villages there were *gastinae* and pasturages. The word *gastina* is derived from *gasta* or waste and has parallels in western Europe, but in the Latin East it was used to describe something often treated as an entity of some worth.[38] One can divide *gastinae* into at least three categories. First there was an important group of them in towns and it is clear that any houses on these were in a state of disrepair.[39] Secondly, and a larger class than has been supposed, there were independent properties in the countryside, two of which appear to have been pasturages.[40] It has been suggested that most *gastinae* were pasturages,[41] but one feature of this group of wastelands is the varied uses to which they were put: some were small plots of land;[42] some had buildings, probably ruined, upon them;[43] some were cultivated;[44] it was planned to convert one into a *casal*[45] and two others had been or were to become *casalia*;[46] another even had its own dependent *gastina*.[47] Thirdly there were those attached to *casalia*.[48] We can, first of all, establish that they were not usually the pasture lands, which lay round many villages,[49] for there are documents in which *gastinae* and pastures are mentioned together with reference to the same *casalia*.[50] One document referred to a group of *gastinae* attached to a village as having 'once been *casalia*' and there is evidence that there were others of this type,[51] although *gastinae* could be inhabited[52] and there are examples of deserted *casalia* which were not given this name.[53] It is probable that we are here being presented with evidence for practices still followed in the Near East. Most villages are built on high ground, often a long way from their low-lying territories, and for centuries it has been the custom for peasants to establish subsidiary settlements, known as *khirbats*, which they occupy for only short periods of the year in order to farm the more distant lands.[54] And, writing of judicial inquiries into the boundaries of properties, the jurists John of Jaffa and Philip of Novara bore witness to another feature of village life. In the course of centuries, as wells dried up and the ground upon which it lived became soured, a community would move round a fairly large district, leaving behind it ruined settlements, today also known as *khirbats*, the lands attached to which it would keep under cultivation. Both jurists seem to have regarded these as *gastinae*.[55]

A native village was a unit both of government and of economic exploitation. Government, expressed in jurisdiction, was profitable for a lord, because he had the right to enjoy the fines and confiscations taken from those who did wrong;[56] but the bulk of the revenues from a *casal* came in proportional rents paid out of the produce which do not seem to have imposed an intolerable burden on the villeins.[57] The ancient Muslim tax of *kharaj* continued to be levied on the arable lands, vineyards and olive groves. For arable lands it usually amounted to one-third or one-quarter of the harvest[58] and was collected in the following way: a lord or his agent would visit a village when the crops were brought in from the fields to the threshing floors; the piles of corn were divided in customary proportions between him and the peasants and, if the *casal* had several owners, between them as well; sometimes a further duty was charged on the share allotted to the villagers, sometimes small amounts were appropriated by the lord's officials.[59] Dues, varying between one-quarter and one-half of the produce, were owed on the vineyards, olive groves and orchards which, we have seen, were held individually by their tenants.[60] For every carrucate of arable land a peasant also paid three times a year a personal gift to his landlord called *exenia, presentatica, redditus personalis* or *monet*; throughout Palestine it seems to have taken roughly the same form, consisting of chickens, goats, eggs, cheese and wood.[61] Once a year villagers near Tyre gave their lord 3 chickens, 3 besants, 30 eggs and a *ratl* of cheese in rent for their houses [62] and this may be a variant of a possible tax on hearths in Transjordan [63] and of a poll-tax on non-Christians levied elsewhere in Palestine.[64] A duty, perhaps called *pascharium*, was taken on pasture lands [65] and near Acre a special charge similar to the Egyptian *mara'i*, was paid for the possession of goats, bees and it may be also sheep, being estimated according to the numbers of animals held by a peasant.[66] Other sources of income for a village proprietor were duties levied for the carrying of the harvests from the fields to the threshing floors and for the villeins' right to use the village cistern.[67] Villagers near Acre also paid *mensuragium*, a charge on the use of weights and measures in their transactions, and two levies called *gardagium* and *scenequie* about which nothing is known;[68] in *casalia* near Tyre straw was a perquisite of the lord's and a duty of one small chicken a carracute was paid by the villagers whenever they changed their seed-corn.[69]

In Egypt *kharaj* was often collected in cash at a standard rate, depending on the crop, for every unit of cultivated land.[70] In Latin Syria, where the payment of a money rent in place of labour services was envisaged as early as the 1120s in an agreement between the monks of Our Lady of the Valley of Josaphat and some villeins, the commutation of village returns for money seems to have become a common feature from the 1140s onwards.[71] There were also cases in which part of the returns were commuted: *kharaj* near Toron;[72] the dues on olive groves near Tyre and Margat;[73] the returns on vineyards and part of the *exenia* near Tyre [74] and also the *exenia* near Acre.[75] It is a sign of the developed state of the economy in the Latin East that such agreements, which were only just beginning to appear in the West, were usual.

One feature of Levantine agriculture gave Palestinian villages a markedly different character from those in Europe. It is well known that in a *casal* there was little demesne land, belonging directly to the lord and worked on his behalf by the boon work or

labour services of the peasants. This is not to say that there was
none. It is clear, especially from references to exemptions from the
payment of tithes on demesne possessed by religious orders, that
there were scattered pockets of it.[76] Treated as demesne could be
those village-lands belonging to lords that took the forms of
gardens, vineyards or sugar-cane plantations; and corn could be
sown in alternate years on the fields of sugar-cane.[77] There are
also a few examples of what appears to have been recognisable
demesne land of the European type: in 1168 the Hospitallers were
given the village of Avotha near Laodicea on condition that if
Aleppo fell to the Christians it would be returned to the donor
'save for the Order of the Hospital's own carracutes'; boon work
seems to have been performed on the same Order's lands in the
lordship of Margat; more important because it concerned a lay
fief in Palestine was a charter of 1213 by which the Lord of
Caesarea borrowed 1,000 saracen besants from the Hospitallers,
assigning to them as a gage of repayment three villages 'with the
peasants and all their appurtenances, except for my own carrucates
and the labour services of the peasants'; [78] and a parallel to this
may have been the work that seems to have been carried out by
peasants all through October on sugar-cane plantations at Casal
Imbert, north of Acre.[79] On the other hand it was stated in a
Venetian inventory of 1243 that villeins in the territory of Tyre
gave the commune one day's work for each carrucate they
possessed, 'just as the king's peasants are accustomed to do', and
a comparable reference in a charter of 1132 gave the canons of the
Holy Sepulchre two villages by the Sea of Galilee with the prince's
rights from the fisheries on that sea for eight days during Lent and
with boon work from the fishermen for *one day in the year*. The
Prince of Galilee must have received labour services on one day
out of eight, which suggests that one day's service was performed
weekly – a very light burden.[80] There also survive references to
the carriage by peasants of revenues in kind to storehouses and in
those villages where there were no demesne lands boon work may
have consisted only of the transportation of the lords' shares of
the harvest to collection centres, together perhaps with some
labour on roads and aqueducts.[81]

Demesne therefore, while not unknown, was to be found only
in certain localities and the labour services of most peasants were
minimal. This characteristic of Near Eastern agriculture meant

that one of the most important of the exemptions of the great religious houses – freedom from the payment of tithes on demesne – could not be generally applied. This in turn led to attempts to control agriculture, because tithes were also excused on the produce used by religious orders themselves from lands other than demesne: one can discern attempts to change the crops or to force villagers to alter the pattern of their production so as to provide revenues in kind which would qualify for this second exemption.[82] And the system made most landlords absentee *rentiers*. Of course they always had some interest in their villagers' activities and might use their authority benevolently: when in 1256 John of Beirut leased some *casalia* to the Teutonic Knights he laid down that the brothers were not to exact from the peasants more than was customary 'by the usages and customs of the land' and in 1257 John of Jaffa was planning to raise no revenues from the harvests of villages near Ascalon for two years after the territory had come again into Christian hands.[83] But although the jurists could envisage a vassal living in his fief – there is what seems to be evidence for residence on an estate in Galilee, while twelfth-century manor houses have been identified in a few villages, particularly around Jerusalem and Nablus [84] – the bulk of the land-owning class must have felt little need to visit their estates except at harvest time, for there was little or no land the exploitation of which was their direct concern. In an area in which the cities had always dominated the countryside the knights could live in great centres like Acre far from their rural properties. This must have been a major reason for the phenomenon of a town-dwelling feudal class.

In the absence of the lord each village seems to have been run by a council of elders, presided over by a headman called by the Latins a *rays*. In the medieval Islamic world the title of *ra'is* was given to one who had authority over a professional or religious corporation, a community such as the Jews, the quarter of a town, a village or even a clan; and in some twelfth-century Syrian towns he could be one of the most important officers. He is to be found representing the urban burgess population in its relations with higher authority, protecting the goods of inhabitants, overseeing the tax returns, leading the city militia, maintaining order and acting as a kind of mayor or provost of the merchants. In almost all its meaning *ri'asa*, which the Franks transliterated to *raisagium* or *raisage*, implied the office of an intermediary between government and governed, with responsibilities for discipline in the body over which its powers were exercised.[85]

The *rayses* were the heirs to a tradition that dated from before the arrival of the Franks and continued after their departure, for their successors are the *muhtars* of today.[86] They were theoretically chosen by their lords and held office at their pleasure,[87] but in the few cases in which we can see them faced by new lords, one seems to have been confirmed in his post and the others almost certainly were.[88] Local customs and the interests of both proprietor and tenants would have made the *raisage* one held for life and perhaps hereditary: at one village in the County of Tripoli the two *rayses* were brothers.[89] Once appointed or confirmed in office the *rays* represented the lord in the village, probably helping to levy the returns from the harvests: at a *casal* in the territory of Tyre he is to be found negotiating with his lord on how heavy in any year the *exenia* were to be.[90] He also represented the villagers in their relations with the village owner and can be seen coming before him on their behalf, bearing money and fruits of the land and trees as symbols of their produce.[91] He would have had an important say in the agricultural decisions taken by the village as a whole, for his commission gave him the task of supervising the farming.[92] He was almost certainly responsible for justice in the community and so must have had the right to take fines and confiscations on his lord's behalf.[93] He was presumably aided in everything by a council of village elders.[94]

Although no more free than the other villeins,[95] a *rays* enjoyed certain privileges in return for the trust of his lord, for he possessed more land than his fellow peasants, some of it freed from the usual obligations, and lived in a larger house. At Betheron, a village in the territory of Tyre about which many details are known, he owned several olive groves and a vineyard, had one-tenth of the arable land – at least twice as much as most other villagers – and held half of this land free from the payment of such returns as *kharaj* and *exenia*.[96] There are references to free carrucates in nearby villages and although they were not specifically assigned to *rayses* in the inventory that listed them it must be supposed that it was they who held them.[97] The *rays* of Betheron also owned a house. Its size is not known, but in 1184 a *rays* gave the Spanish traveller Ibn Jubair and his companions a party in a large room in his house, in 1254 the Master of the Hospital went into the largest house at Casal Robert as part of the ceremony of entering into corporal possession of the village and in the following year the Hospitaller Castellan of Mt Thabor did the same at a group of *casalia* in Galilee; presumably these were all *rayses'* houses, although this was mentioned only in the case of one village.[98]

In the countryside there were occasionally to be found villages that looked strikingly different from their neighbours. In place of a formless huddle of houses crowded on to high ground, there might be a planned settlement along a village street, with a tower, courthouse and Latin church.[99] Its inhabitants in fact were western colonists or their descendants and not serfs but free burgesses who could alienate their properties, although their landlord might enjoy pre-emption rights. The returns they paid, if not substantially different – perhaps slightly less burdensome – from those levied on native peasants, were regarded as rent not servile tribute and the community, with its own burgess court presided over by the lord's *dispensator* or *locator*, had a measure of autonomy.[100] There can have been little migration from Europe to Palestine after the territorial losses of the later twelfth century, but the colonial settlements established in earlier years did not entirely cease to exist. A *dispensator*, a lord's agent in the establishment of new villages of this type, was active in the Holy Land around 1200[101] and Casal Imbert, which had been founded by the king between 1146 and 1153, was still inhabited by burgesses a century later.[102]

A lord had other sources of revenue in the countryside. Of the dues from the saltpans that lined the coast we know little other than that they were profitable.[103] But near the cities and down on the well-watered lands between the sea and the hillsides there were gardens and sugar-cane plantations, and it was in these areas that were situated most of the mills. The gardens, often integral parts of the towns and under urban jurisdiction, will be referred to in the next chapter. Sugar-cane, a major product of Palestine, needed large quantities of water in its cultivation, and the plantations lay near aqueducts and rivers, connected to them by irrigation channels.[104] In the middle of the thirteenth century it seems that several varieties were grown on demesne near Casal Imbert; there, and also elsewhere, a two-year crop rotation was practised, corn being sown on part of the fallow land in alternate years.[105] When the cane was harvested it was cut into six-inch lengths, some to be sold raw,[106] but most to be converted into sugar, being crushed in the many presses standing amid the plantations, some of which were worked by water power.[107]

Although in villages and in the centres of towns there were horse-drawn mills,[108] the majority were hydraulically powered with horizontal rather than vertical mill-wheels, built in those localities where water was plentiful, several even using the same mill-pond. They were to be found at Syloe;[109] by the canals that ran from the great springs of the Ras al-'Ain near Tyre;[110] on the river Belus near Acre;[111] on the al-'Auja', the river of Jaffa;[112] and in the far north on the Orontes near Antioch.[113] They varied in size from those with only one millstone to those with four, it being a fairly easy matter to increase the number of stones provided one had an adequate water-supply.[114] We have very little information about the conditions under which mills were held. Near Acre two belonging to the Military Orders seem to have been run directly by the brothers and near Tyre in 1182 the king had retained possession of some mills, but in 1243 others in the same area, which were owned by the Venetians, were leased to millers.[115] We have some precious, though not necessarily relevant, evidence from the Principality of Antioch, where they could be held *in feodo villanie*. In one of the two surviving examples of this form of tenancy the possessor of it was a religious house, but the holding seems to have been regarded as heritable, although a tenant could be disinherited if its conditions were not fulfilled. Alienation was not permitted without the consent of the lord, to whom went half of all the revenues of the mill and the fishing rights attached to it. In one case expenses were shared by both parties, but in the other all expenses, even those resulting from a complete rebuilding if it became necessary, were to be met by the tenant.[116]

Water was of course scarce and therefore valuable: in 1160 the king was prepared to grant a fifth of the profits of certain sugar-cane plantations together with other privileges to a vassal in return for the right to draw off water from his stretch of the river Belus.[117] In those areas where the owners of mills, sugar-cane plantations and gardens were all seeking irrigation there was a natural tendency for disputes to arise. In 1235 the Templars and

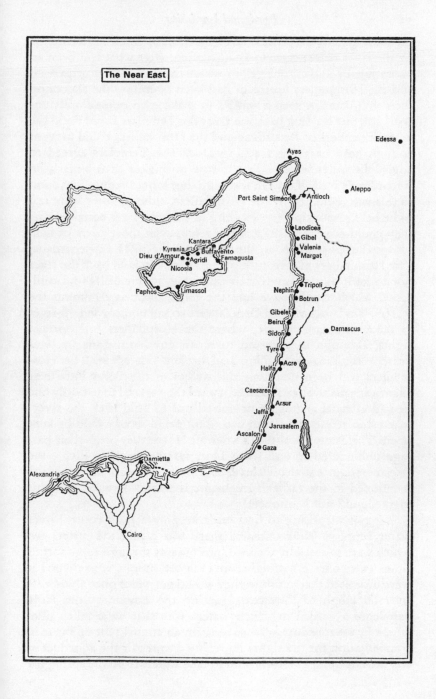

The Near East

Edessa

Ayas

Aleppo

Port Saint Simeon
Antioch

Laodicea
Gibel
Valenia
Margat

Kantara
Kyrenia
Buffavento
Dieu d'Amour
Agridi
Famagusta
Nicosia

Tripoli
Nephin
Botrun

Paphos
Limassol

Gibelet
Beirut
Sidon
Damascus

Tyre
Acre
Haifa

Caesarea
Arsur
Jaffa
Jerusalem
Ascalon
Gaza

Damietta
Alexandria

Cairo

the Hospitallers, the possessors of the mills of Doc and Recordane on the river Belus, came to an agreement after what had been an exceptionally violent quarrel, in which the Templars downstream and the Hospitallers upstream had been operating the sluices on their mill-dams in such a way as to make each other's mills unworkable: by holding back the river the Templars could flood the wheel chambers of Recordane and the Hospitallers could prevent enough head of water reaching Doc. The Templars agreed to adjust the water level so that it rose no higher than a mark on Recordane's wall; if it went too high they would reduce it as soon as this was requested by the Hospitallers, although they were not to be held responsible for flooding in winter. It was accepted that they could raise the banks of the river, even those parts of it in Hospitaller possession, to the height of the mark at Recordane. The Hospitallers in their turn promised not to hold back the river nor to let it pass through their mill only by one of its four mill-races, which would have had the same effect as damming the waters. The boats of both Orders were to sail unmolested up-river as far as the dam at Doc, where the Hospitallers had portage rights, although they agreed to repair any harm done by their vessels. By 1262 quarrelling had broken out again. The Hospitallers had been diverting the waters of the Belus into their sugar-cane plantations; thenceforward they agreed to use only one irrigation canal and again promised not to hold back the river: when Recordane was not in use all four mill-races would be kept open. The Templars agreed to permit Hospitaller boats their passage unhindered to and from Doc, nor would they divert the stream or dam it so that its level rose above the mark at Recordane mentioned in the earlier agreement; it was also stated that this mark should not be moved.[118]

It is not surprising to find lords keeping a tight control over water supplies. Near Caesarea there was a mill the waters for which were released by the lord, presumably through some sort of sluice gate, once a fortnight; in 1124 the monks who owned it were promised that in future they would get water once a week.[119] In 1166 Hugh of Caesarea, granting the canons of the Holy Sepulchre a garden in which waters rose that were taken elsewhere by an aqueduct, also gave them an annual rent of sugar in compensation for the rights he retained to repair the aqueduct at any time or build a new one and to take waters from the spring for the irrigation of sugar-cane plantations in one of his villages.[120] In 1256 a charter from Bohemond VI of Antioch contained a drawing of a cross-section of a water pipe to indicate the size the Hospitallers in Tripoli could use.[121] In the rich lands by the aqueduct that took the waters of the Ras al-'Ain to Tyre, one of the springs was shared in 1243 by the Venetians and the crown: the Venetians were allowed to draw off one-third of the waters and the king the rest, both parties contributing in the same proportion to the expenses of repairing the well and the aqueduct that led from it. In the same area the Genoese could tap the aqueduct for their own sugar-cane fields, but in 1264 Philip of Montfort, now Lord of Tyre, laid down that in times of drought water would be rationed out among those using the aqueduct by officers appointed by him.[122]

In his relations with the inhabitants of the country districts of his lordship a lord used agents, among whom the dragomans and scribes were of particular importance. The title dragoman was a corruption of the Arabic *tarjuman*, meaning interpreter, and indeed these officers were sometimes known as *interpretes*.[123] The Franks needed interpreters to transmit their commands to their Arab villagers; and at the time of their arrival in Palestine there existed in the Islamic legal system an official interpreter, the *mutarjim*, an assistant of the *qadi*, the Muslim judge, in his dealings with the many peoples under his rule.[124] It is possible that his office was taken over by the Christian lords who were themselves heirs to the *qadis'* jurisdictions.

In a lay lordship the dragoman seems to have acted as the intermediary between the lord and the *rayses* over a large area. We will see that the scribe gathered the revenues from the villagers and we must assume that the dragoman concerned himself with the administration of justice, the other basis upon which a lord's power rested. He rode through the villages under his control, presumably inspecting them, and we find one acting as an interpreter when the villagers of Casal Robert took oaths of fealty to the Master of the Hospitallers in 1254.[125] It is not clear what were the responsibilities of John and Samuel, *interpretes* of the king in the early years of the twelfth century or of the *interpres* Bernard, who witnessed an agreement in 1163 between the Templars and the Bishop of Valenia in the Principality of Antioch,[126] but two, John at Toron in 1151[127] and Guy at Arsur in 1261,[128] seem to have exercised authority throughout their respective lordships; and one, Peter, must have overseen an important subdivision of the lordship of Caesarea in 1135, being based at Cacho, where there was a castle and a burgess settlement.[129]

Another three dragomanates are even more interesting. In the course of the twelfth century much of the royal domain around Acre had been sub-infeudated. Some of the vassals acquired the right to have their estates supervised by their own dragomans, which presumably meant a corresponding lessening of the powers of a royal dragoman in Acre, if such an officer existed – there is no evidence for him. In 1160 King Baldwin III gave a knight called John of Haifa the castellany of Chastiau-dou-rei in fief with control of the surrounding countryside in which were nine villages. John was given the custody of the castle, provisions for himself and his horse when on campaign and the dragomanate and *scribanage* of the dependent villages. It is not clear whether he was to enjoy the profits of these offices himself or was to grant them out to rear-vassals,[130] but at any rate an individual dragomanate was in existence or had been created for the lands of the castellany and by 1183 this was perhaps held by another man called John.[131] Immediately to the east of Chastiau-dou-rei lay part of the fief of Geoffrey Le Tor, comprising fourteen villages, which by 1183 had been bought by Joscelin of Courtenay. Its dragomanate had been held by a sergeant of Geoffrey's called William who, the king now ruled, should be given another fief by Geoffrey in compensation for the loss of his office.[132] Some way to the south three neighbouring *casalia* made up a small fief for which in 1175 the king confirmed the dragomanate of a man called Barutus, in return for a payment of 225 besants to his immediate lord.[133] It looks as though the twelfth-century kings were allowing the dragomanate of the royal domain around Acre to be split up among the small fiefs held in-chief from them.

The majority of the dragomans whose names have survived were Latins, though John of Haifa and Brain, probably dragoman of the canons of the Holy Sepulchre, were native-born. Their status varied: John of Haifa and Peter of Cacho were knights;[134] William in the fief of Geoffrey Le Tor, Barutus in the fief of the Lady Joiette near Acre and Guy at Arsur were sergeants; most dragomans of religious houses seem to have been lay burgesses.[135]

On lay estates the dragomanate usually was held in fief as a ser-geantry and was fairly profitable. For every carrucate in a petty lordship near Acre the dragoman received from the villein owning it a *modius* of wheat and a *modius* of barley, and two *manipuli* of wheat and barley from the harvest piled up on the threshing floors before its division between the lord and the villagers; for every one hundred *modii* divided in this way, he could take a further six, although of grain of the poorer quality. He could requisition supplies for himself and his horse when travelling round the vil-lages. If his lord wished him to accompany him outside the fief he would be provided for, and if he lost his horse in service, he would be paid 15 besants as *restor* for its replacement.[136] The sergeant who held the dragomanate at Arsur in 1261 had a rent of 25 besants a year and the half-tithes of seven *casalia*.[137]

There survive many references in the charters to the scribes of lords. Of course a lord employed a heterogeneous collection of clerks,[138] local writers and, increasingly in the thirteenth century, Italian notaries-public to produce his charters, although he might have a chancellor of his own. But he had other servants who also called themselves scribes, although their title had a more technical meaning and seems to have been a direct translation of the Arabic *katib*, used of an official in the cadastral office in a Muslim state.[139] A treatise on the laws of the burgess court in Acre stated:

> If it happens that there is a Saracen or Frankish scribe in the lord's service in the *fonde* or the *chaine* or over any *casalia*, and that scribe robs the lord of his rights or conspires with merchants or villeins to rob the lord and divide the proceeds with them, or keeps for himself the dues paid in the *fonde* or the *chaine*; and he does this by false accounting or book-keeping . . . if that scribe can be proved guilty of this larceny, either by the evidence of his books or by that of the merchants, of allowing export without the payment of dues or of diminishing the half of the dues that ought to be given to the lord in favour of the other half or in favour of the third which is paid in cash,[140] without the knowledge of his *bailli* or the lord; or if he is found guilty in any other way or there is a situation in which the lord cannot find the rents he ought to get,

he should be hanged and, presumably only in the case of a royal scribe, all his goods ought to go to the king. This passage was as much concerned with officials in the *fonde* and the *chaine* – the markets and customs house – as it was with those in the country-

side, although it is clear that all these men were considered to
belong to the same class of officials.[141] John of Jaffa however provided more evidence about the scribe in rural areas. Writing about
a judicial inquiry into the demarcation of fiefs, he stated that a
scribe and sergeants should be provided by the lord to accompany
those drawing the boundaries 'to assemble the people of the
country'.[142] And a document of 1258 reveals that the oath of a
scribe was regarded in law as proof of the fact that the villein of
one lord had fled to the territory of another.[143] Although it is not
at all clear what is meant in the passage quoted above by the
reference to the payment by scribes to their lords of only half or
one-third of the dues, it may be deduced that scribes, among
whom were native-born men, were responsible for the collection
of the revenues and certain that they assembled the people of a
neighbourhood when a division of lands was to be made. In short
the scribe seems to have been a financial officer and collector of
taxes – perhaps combining the duties of Fatimid officers in charge
of the collection of the *kharaj* and the *jawali* tax on non-Muslims :
the *dalil*, *masih*, *ha'iz*, *khazin* and *hashir*.[144] Scribes are to be found
in the lordships of Arsur, Jaffa and Ascalon, Beaufort, Beirut,
Caesarea, Chastiau-dou-rei, Galilee, the fief of Geoffrey Le Tor,
Gibelet in the County of Tripoli, Haifa, Margat in the Principality
of Antioch, Nablus, Nazareth, Ramle, Scandelion and Tyre.[145] A
very high proportion of them were indigenous : fourteen, perhaps
sixteen, out of twenty-five. Some, especially the Latins among
them, were quite considerable persons, the holders of sergeantries
and members of local burgess courts, and one of the native-born
was the son of a man who was either a *bailli* or town-*rays*.[146]

Among them are to be found a group differentiated from the
rest by their title of *scribanus* as opposed to *scriba* or *escrivain*, although it is not at all clear that these titles were always precisely
expressed by the writers of the charters. It may be that the
scribanus differed from the *scriba* in that he held his office by feudal
tenure, although here the Muslim institution of *daman* or tax-farm
could have been taken over and converted into a western fief.[147]
One *scribanage* was held by a knight,[148] but all must have been
sergeantries : and indeed four *scribani* were sergeants. The *scribanus*
of Caesarea had a house, a threshing floor and a carrucate of land
at the village of Cafarlet; at this *casal* and at fifteen others he
enjoyed rents in kind which varied, although in general he took

specified amounts of the cuttings and gleanings left on the fields after the harvest and from every camel carrying the crops to the threshing floors; at two villages he took a proportion of the crop itself and at one he was paid a rent of 20 *modii* of wheat. Whether travelling inside or outside the Lordship of Caesarea he was provided with victuals – the same as would be given to a sergeant – and he was issued with barley, iron and nails for his horse, which his lord would replace by *restor* if he lost it.[149] The *scribanage* of the lands of Geoffrey Le Tor was exchanged for a fief at Manueth which was sold for 1,600 saracen besants by the *scribanus*'s grandson in 1231.[150] But in Arsur in 1261 the *scribanage* seems to have been worth less than a sergeantry, for to it were added certain moneys and rights.[151]

Six examples of *scribanage* survive, four and perhaps as many as five of the holders of which were indigenous. It has been suggested that the responsibilities of the dragoman and the *scribanus* became confused and that the offices were often held by the same man, but this assertion is not supported by the evidence. There is only one case of the dragomanate and *scribanage* being combined, in the grant to John of Haifa who, as has been shown, was given a hereditary castellany to which were linked the offices of dragoman and *scribanus*. The charter clearly separated them; John could doubtless have enfeoffed rear-vassals with them: by 1183 they seem to have been held by different men. The reference to them in the charter seems to have been rather an affirmation of John's semi-independence of the local seigneurial offices in Acre.[152] Elsewhere the *scribanage* was held on its own, as in the fief of Geoffrey Le Tor, where the *scribanus* in 1183 was a sergeant called Sa'id.[153] And these two examples suggest that in the royal domain around Acre the powers of the *secrete* as well as the dragomanate were being given to some of the small fiefs held from the king. Nablus, which had been another part of the royal domain, also had its own *scribanage*, held in *c*. 1180 by a knight called George.[154]

A curious and perhaps contrasting case concerns a certain George of Betheri, the holder of the *scribanage* of the village of Bethduras near Ascalon, which in 1176 was sold by John Arrabi to Constance, Countess of St Gilles, in a series of transactions that preluded its gift to the Order of St John. We have already seen that John Arrabi held the village from Balian, brother and vassal for it of Baldwin of Ramle, who in his confirmation expressly excluded from the sale the service owed by George of Betheri. In the following year the king, the Countess of Jaffa and Ascalon and the Lord of Ramle confirmed the sale for 250 besants of the *scribanage* itself by George to Constance of St Gilles, who was now free to give the village with all its rights to the Hospitallers.[155] There is no evidence that George was *scribanus* only over Bethduras and it is more likely that the rights of *scribanage* even over a single village were not the rear-vassal's, in this case John Arrabi or Balian of Nablus, to give or take away. They were rights belonging to the possessor of the *scribanage* throughout the territory – the Lord of Ramle or the Countess of Jaffa and Ascalon or, since he confirmed it and Bethduras was held from him, the king. George may well have been *scribanus* for the lordship or county or even part of the royal domain, with powers not only over villages in the hands of his lord, but also over those held by rear-vassals.

Outside the royal lands there are to be found *scribani* at Arsur and Caesarea. In 1261 the *scribanus* at Arsur was a man called Adam.[156] In Caesarea around 1200 the *scribanage* was held first by an uncle and then by his nephew, both native-born, and a document concerning them survives to illuminate the complications that could arise in an hereditary office and the application to it of the doctrine of *plus dreit heir aparant*. The *scribanus* John had died and, with his son in the hands of the Muslims, the *scribanage* was given to his nephew Soquerius (Sughir?) and the legitimate heirs of his body after a dispute for the office with a relative called George. But it was given on condition that if John's son was freed or a closer heir appeared Soquerius would renounce it.[157]

The subject here discussed raises the issue of the survival in Frankish Palestine of the old Muslim financial administration. The chief cadastral office in the kingdom was the *Grant Secrete*,[158] which obviously took its name from the Byzantine *sekreta*. The first evidence for it dates from 1160, when a *secretarius* seems to have been dependent on the chancery,[159] but it is likely that it had been in existence long before this. By the middle of the thirteenth century it had become a separate office, supervised by the seneschal, with its scribes differentiated from those 'in the royal household', probably the *camera*.[160] In it were registered the boundaries of fiefs and presumably the services owed for them, although possession of a territorial fief could only be proved in the High Court;[161] it listed *fiefs-rentes* and claims for payment could be proved by consulting its registers; it was responsible for paying *restor* for the replacement of horses lost or injured in the performance of military service, although these payments were overseen by the marshal;[162] to it were made accounts of the revenues collected by the royal agents, the viscounts, *baillis* and scribes;[163] it contained a record of the standard measurement of the carrucate and perhaps of the royal *modius* for reference.[164] It was therefore a financial office and department of registration like the Greek *sekreta* or the Muslim *diwan*, although the duties of collecting at least the urban revenues were assumed under the Christians by the courts. It looks as though it had duties like the Fatimid *bait* or *diwan al-mal*, the state treasury, combined with the functions of several subordinate offices like, as far as the country-side was concerned, the *diwan al-jaish*, overseeing *iqta*'s, the *diwan al-jawali wa'l mawarith al-hashriyya*, dealing with the poll tax on the recognised non-Muslim communities and estate duty, and the *diwan al-kharaj*, supervising the collection of village revenues.[165]

It is not easy to be precise about its personnel. A *Grant Bailli* of the *secrete* held office in Cyprus in the thirteenth century[166] and as early as 1140 in the Principality of Antioch there had been a *Magister Secretae*, whose department appears to have had registers dating from before the arrival of the Latins.[167] We have no know-ledge of the officer in the Kingdom of Jerusalem to whom the seneschal must have delegated responsibilities, but we know that the *secrete* was staffed by scribes and the names have survived of five men who possibly worked in it: Michael, who witnessed the gift of Chastiau-dou-rei to John of Haifa in 1160; Homo Dei, a landowner in Tyre before 1243 and probably indigenous; William, who witnessed the gifts of Casal Robert and some houses in Acre to the Hospitallers in 1254 and 1260 respectively; and perhaps Nasser and Poul (Paul) of Blanchegarde, both 'Saracen scribes', who witnessed a document in Acre in 1266.[168] Tantalisingly little is known of the local *baillis* who, according to John of Jaffa, were answerable to the seneschal and therefore presumably to the *secrete*.[169] Near Nablus in the twelfth century these seem to have had much the same duties as *scribani*,[170] but the title of *bailli* was granted to all kinds of officer and it may be that John of Jaffa was referring only to castellans, viscounts and royal lieutenants. It might be added that also called *baillis* were those agents put in charge of the collection of revenues from villages in some special circumstances, as when two lords had agreed to share the produce; besides collecting the harvests and selling them to raise cash, these men seem to have been able to draw their own living expenses from the returns.[171]

There survive no explicit references to *secretes* outside the royal domain, but there is good circumstantial evidence for them. Several lords had their own seneschals,[172] although there is no certainty that the powers of these officers were everywhere the same. The surviving census lists and the wording of a decree concerning a general tax imposed on the kingdom in 1183 suggest that fief-holders knew, or had the means of finding out, the numbers of peasants in their villages: the system of taxation to be used in 1183 was based on the population of *casalia*.[173] In 1243 the monasteries of Our Lady of Mt Sion and Our Lady of the Valley of Josaphat came to an agreement over the boundaries of certain lands in the territory of Tyre. They chose arbitrators who would consult their charters, but if the dispute could not be resolved by these means, the arbitrators:

> ought to have recourse to the *secrete* of Tyre and, if they cannot be certain after consulting the *secrete* of Tyre, they ought to proceed and arbitrate according to the usages and customs of the city of Tyre. And if by chance the matter concerning the said boundaries cannot be settled by ancient custom, the aforesaid arbitrators ought to have recourse to the *secrete* of Acre and according to what they find there are held to divide and measure the boundaries.[174]

The document is further evidence for the use of the *secretes* as places where were kept registers of land possession and the records of official land measurements, but it also reveals the existence of a second and local *secrete* besides the *Grant Secrete*, now in Acre. And although at this time the kingdom was divided into two separate areas of administration with the government of the imperial lieutenant over Tyre, Jerusalem and Ascalon unrecognised elsewhere, the wording of the agreement suggests that the *secrete* of Tyre had records stretching back further than the twelve years of imperial administration. But the most convincing evidence for the survival of other local cadastral offices is the existence of scribes in the lordships of Palestine. It seems to be a reasonable assumption that the central administrations of the great lordships were not unlike that for the lands of the royal domain, with its strong links with the Muslim past. More will be said in the next chapter about the bureaucrats who collected and accounted revenues in the ports and markets and their similarity, too close to be coincidental, to those in other eastern states. Here it has been suggested that in his relations with his villagers a lord also relied on agents inherited from his Muslim predecessors.

4

THE DOMAIN IN THE
TOWNS

PALESTINE'S economy was dominated by its towns, not only because they were markets for local produce,[1] but also because the ports among them were important stations on the international trade routes and were increasingly busy from the 1180s onwards, following the stability brought to the Near East by the conquests of Nur ad-Din and Saladin.[2] As a commercial centre Acre came in the thirteenth century to rival Constantinople and Alexandria. Its dealers handled every imaginable drug and spice:[3] from the East came aspic, brazil wood, cardamon, cassia, ammoniacum, arsenic and yellow arsenic, cloves, borax, cubebs, galengal, galega,[4] camphor and the much more rare and valuable root of camphor, gariophyllus, ginger, frankincense, lavender and spikenard, libanus, myrobalans, musc, sarcocolla, senna, terebinth, indigo, zedoary, aloe wood and above all cinnamon and pepper; from Europe and the Mediterranean basin came liquorice, blackcurrants, mastic and saffron. Acre was not only a great spice market, trading with Ayas in Cilicia and most of the Italian and south French ports; it also exported much of the sugar consumed in Europe, which was locally produced in large quantities and was sold in loaf or powdered form or in lengths of cane.[5] And it contained an important slave market,[6] where were sold prisoners acquired on military expeditions[7] and slaves brought in by the Italians.[8] By law no Christian of whatever denomination could be enslaved,[9] but at the turn of the years 1216 and 1217 a new Latin bishop wrote angrily that 'the Christians continually refused their Muslim slaves baptism, although these sought it earnestly and tearfully'. He claimed that he had persuaded the slave-owners to allow conversions, but the abuse continued throughout the century: in 1237 Pope Gregory IX wrote in the same vein to the prelates of Syria and the Military Orders, but by the following year he seems to have recognised the strength of the forces ranged against him for, although he ordered the Patriarch of Jerusalem to see that slaves should be able to hear regular sermons and be baptised if they so wished, he accepted that conversion would not automatically lead to liberty. Statutes issued by the Hospitallers in 1262 forbade local commanders to have slaves baptised without the Master's permission.[10] There is evidence for another grave abuse in a letter written by Pope Innocent IV in 1246 in which he informed the patriarch and his bishops that Italian merchants were sailing to Palestine from Greece with their ships loaded with Greeks, Bulgarians, Ruthenians and Wlachs, all Christian men and women, whom they would sell into slavery as Muslims: indeed this passing off of Christians as Muslims seems to have been common enough in the kingdom to have resulted in legislation.[11]

Besides spices, sugar and slaves Acre was an important market for other commodities. Through it passed dyes for Europe's booming cloth industry – myrobalans, saffron and indigo were dyes as well as drugs – and in it could be acquired henna, gall-nuts, lac and alum, the last presumably brought in from Asia Minor. It was also a centre for cloth itself and clothing materials: bords, hemp thread, buckram, cotton cloth, stitched clothes (especially elaborately worked garments from the northern Christian Principality of Antioch), camlets, samite,[12] Damascus thread and wool, besides shoes, boots, furs, leather tack and saddles, goatskins imported from Muslim lands, horse leather, ox and buffalo hides. To Nîmes from Acre went silk; to Acre from Naples came hemp. From Egypt on its way to Damascus came flax which was also sent to Savastro in Asia Minor. From Marseilles came cloth of all kinds, skins, tin and coral. Locally produced cotton, in its raw state or in wool or thread, was sent to Messina, Ancona, Chiarenza, Palermo, Barletta, Florence, Venice, Genoa, Marseilles, Nîmes and Montpellier. Local gardens and plantations sent to the markets almonds, chestnuts, walnuts, nutmegs and mace; apples, carobs, dates, figs both fresh and dried, pears, quinces (renowned for their medicinal qualities) and raisins; asparagus, capers, olives, onions and onion bulbs, rhubarb and sesame with its by-products sesame oil and tahina. From Naples came hazel-nuts;[13] to Ancona went honey. Merchants in Acre also dealt in precious metals: ivory, gold, both spun and in bullion, and pearls, which were exported to Barletta; and they handled clavellated ashes[14] which were a kind of crude potash, emery, copper, iron, glass (for the manufacture of which

Acre as well as Tyre was famous), goblets, pottery and blocks of marble from Muslim lands, bows, arrows and horses. Timber brought by Italians passed through the city on its way to the Muslim East.

Acre was itself a great consumer. Into the town came firewood to feed the baking ovens, domestic fires and bath-houses, straw for the basket-weavers, hay for the stables. On sale were fresh and salted meats, chickens of various kinds, geese, butter, wax, salted fish from Egypt and cheese from nearby Muslim villages and also from Apulia. From Apulia too came oil, meat and wheat, and the last commodity was also imported from Sicily and Cilicia: in the later thirteenth century the Latins were not self-supporting and came to rely upon Europe – especially Sicily and southern Italy – for even perishable foodstuffs.[15] And a great port needed wine – local wines from Nazareth, Le Saforie and Le Saffran, but others from Antioch and Laodicea as well as from Islamic lands and even imported from Messina, Naples and Marseilles. Some of these passed out of the city into nearby settlements like Haifa, Nazareth and Casal Imbert.

In spite of occasional areas of wasteland in them, Acre and Tyre had begun to grow rapidly in the 1180s, overflowing beyond their original walls,[16] and in the first half of the thirteenth century, in spite of at least one major financial crisis around 1220,[17] the whole area depended on them for its prosperity, a fact that discouraged neighbouring Muslim powers from attacking them.[18] The revenues drawn from the cities could be very large. The English chronicler Matthew Paris had heard from Richard, Earl of Cornwall, who was in the East in 1240–41, that Acre was worth each year 50,000 pounds of silver – it is clear that Matthew was referring to pounds sterling – to its ruler. Richard claimed to have been told this by the Templars and Hospitallers.[19] The sum may be exaggerated, but it is startling to find a contemporary believing that Acre alone provided rather more than the normal annual revenues of the Crown of England. It is not surprising that the Kings of Jerusalem should have tried to keep the profitable returns from commerce in their own hands. A twelfth-century law reserved the possession of ports dealing in international trade to the monarch, making it an offence for a lord to 'build a port in his land for ships and vessels and a road into paynim, to improve his land and diminish the rights of the crown'.[20]

At the same time the kings had maintained control of some highways. In 1161 King Baldwin III retained the right to levy tolls on caravans on their way between Egypt and Mesopotamia when he granted Oultrejourdain to Philip of Milly.[21] In 1184 no duty was levied at a customs house below the castle of Toron on merchants travelling with Ibn Jubair from Damascus, because they were going to the royal port of Acre; this suggests that the King's officials were stationed here, although Toron was not in the royal domain.[22] In almost identical passages in their lawbooks, Philip of Novara, writing of Cyprus, and John of Jaffa, writing of the Kingdom of Jerusalem, warned the knights conducting an inquiry into the boundaries of properties to make sure that the estates involved bordered on one another and that between them there was none of the land belonging to the 'lord' and called, according to Philip, *vaselico* or, according to John, *chemin reau*.[23] *Vaselico*, it has been suggested, was *Basilikos* or *Basilike ge* – the public land of the Byzantine empire – and this had been perfectly translated for the mainland as *chemin reau* in a reference to old public lands that had survived the Muslim conquest.[24] The association of *chemin reau* with waste in John of Jaffa's work – conforming to the Muslim use of the word *matruka*, meaning literally abandoned land, for public lands such as roads – is confirmed in charters where are to be found the phrases 'in viis et semitis' or 'chemins et hors de chemins'.[25] But if roads were treated as public lands – and therefore possibly subject to regalian right – it is not at all clear that by the middle of the thirteenth century the jurists believed them to belong to the crown. And the charters already mentioned reveal that the roads in a lordship were in the possession of its lord; indeed in a grant of 1257 of lands in his county John of Jaffa reserved the right of the roads to himself.[26]

It looks as though, in the same way as they had begun to mint their own coins, the thirteenth-century lords had usurped regalian rights over the roads. They had certainly ignored the prohibition against the building up of ports. Tyre of course was until the 1240s part of the royal domain, but it retained its commercial importance under Philip and John of Montfort.[27] Jaffa, for much of the period a crown apanage, was from the first a major point of disembarkation for pilgrims and under Prince Hugh in the 1120s it was also involved in commerce; a century later sea-trade linked it to Antioch and later still under John of Jaffa it seems to have been growing in importance.[28] Tyre and Jaffa may have been special cases, but in the 1160s the ports of Haifa and Caesarea were involved at least in local coastal traffic,[29] and charters to European merchants in the thirteenth century show certain fief-holders trying to develop their ports as trading stations. In 1234 a Lord of Haifa granted privileges to the Genoese.[30] But earlier, between 1221 and 1223, John of Beirut had given commercial rights to merchants from Genoa, Venice and Marseilles; already his markets were dealing not only in local products – pottery, wine, oil, corn, sugar, dyes, glass and soap – but also in commodities from further afield: silk, bombasine, wool and cloth, flax and linen, brazil-wood,[31] pepper, incense, spices, indigo, pearls and precious stones.[32] Beirut, which by the second half of the century had a flourishing colony of Genoese, was taking the first steps towards becoming what it now is, the most important port in the Levant.

It was as clear to the lords as it is to us that no port could develop its potential unless it was visited by foreign merchants and if possible by pilgrims too. Its geographical advantages as a terminus of the Asiatic trade routes would mean nothing if it was not visited by those capable of carrying to Europe the goods that had reached it overland from the East. The wealth of the lords depended on a through-traffic of commodities which could not flow without the regular arrival of fleets to take the goods away and it was western and oriental traders who would pay dues on the merchandise imported, exported and exchanged, while both they and pilgrims would spend cash in the shops and bazaars. In 1220 members of the hierarchy, writing to the West, blamed the kingdom's poverty on the fact that 'the returns from Acre and Tyre are reduced to nothing because pilgrims and merchants with their merchandise who were accustomed to come have not'; nor could the king get his money changed. It was the same point that the Master of the Templars made in 1261 when he wrote that 'in the absence from Acre of the Genoese and other merchants one cannot change money under usury or gage'.[33] In 1243 Bohemond V of Tripoli issued a charter to Montpellier, 'having regard for the good renown of the commune and the profit that can come to me and my lordship through their visits to the land'. The men of Montpellier guaranteed to send each year for ten years at least one ship of a specified size to Tripoli; if in any year the ship did not

CAESAREA. The citadel stood on the southern breakwater of the harbour. The three rounded apses of the cathedral can be seen in the southern part of the town.

arrive Bohemond was thenceforward to be released from his obligations.[34] In 1257 the Regent of Jerusalem and the High Court made a grant, admittedly political in that they needed support in the War of St Sabas, to the merchants of Ancona, conscious of 'the greater utility and manifest profit for the Kingdom'.[35] In 1277 Bohemond VII of Tripoli gave rights to the Venetians that were to last only as long as he and his heirs pleased and could be revoked at will.[36]

Though there was some shipping passing across the Mediterranean and down the Syrian coasts at all times of the year, it was in spring and autumn that the great fleets, the 'general passages', arrived from and sailed to the West. The purchasing power of the merchants and the pilgrims who arrived with them must have had the same indirect effect as that of modern tourists on an under-developed economy. And rulers showed themselves to be reluctant to absolve ship-masters of that part of the *terciaria* – a tax on a vessel's passengers and crew – that applied to pilgrims, probably because it was an important source of revenue.[37] But more important were the merchants from West and East who would fill the Palestinian ports at these times. Some of the communities of European merchants gained from the authorities important privileges, which can be summarised as being territorial or the gifts of quarters in the cities including administrative buildings, churches, public baths and ovens; jurisdictional or the rights of judging not only their own nationals, but also in some cases those living in their quarters; and commercial or the rights of entering, remaining in or leaving specified ports, the reduction or removal of entry, exit and sales dues and sometimes the possession of their own markets. The effects of these privileges on Latin Syria have in the past been misunderstood, for they did not always have the meaning attached to them by modern historians and very few communities enjoyed all of them at the same time. And although in the years following the conquest the Christian rulers were generous to western merchants, presumably to encourage them to come to Palestine and Syria, their attitude had changed by the middle of the twelfth century when they were already trying to cut back the gifts of their ancestors. This can be seen particularly in the successive grants concerning jurisdiction. In 1123, in return for their agreement to help capture Tyre, the Venetians had been given the right to judge, with the privilege of High Justice, their own merchants and other burgesses living in their quarters in the Palestinian towns, although it was laid down that Venetians must go to the royal court to make claims against men who were not fellow citizens and lived outside their quarter.[38] While there is no evidence for the rights granted at this time to the Genoese, they may have been similar.[39] But when in 1156 King Baldwin allowed the Pisans to have a court in Tyre, he reserved to his own jurisdiction cases concerning treason or death, 'according to justice and my rights'.[40] In 1168 King Amalric allowed the Pisans to have a court in Acre, but excluded from its jurisdiction all cases in which were concerned those who held possessions in the kingdom and all judgements involving High Justice.[41] At the same time there seems to have been a strong attempt made to reduce the privileges already enjoyed by the Italian communes, who were forced to cede some of their lands and rights to individuals or ecclesiastical institutions in order that others might take on the burden of defending them.[42]

Although it is dangerous to overstate the strength of the kings before 1187, many of them seem to have been pushing monarchs of a fairly conventional type, trying to exploit their rights and increase their power in practical terms. And these aggressive policies did not end with the disastrous loss of most of the kingdom to Saladin. It is true that jurisdictional rights were granted away in the period 1187–92 when Conrad of Montferrat and Guy of Lusignan were disputing the throne: the Pisans gained rights of High Justice and jurisdiction over all living in their quarters, and the Genoese the privilege that cases involving High Justice would be judged by their own and crown officials acting together.[43] But with Henry of Champagne one finds again the old attitude, although he had to bow to pressure from the Genoese: in 1192 he confirmed the rights in Tyre they had gained from Conrad of Montferrat and in 1195, it seems under threat from one of their fleets, he had to allow their court in Acre jurisdiction over all men living in their quarter.[44] He was however able to cut back the privileges of Pisa to the state in which they had been before 1187[45] and he made inroads into Venetian possessions and rights in the district of Tyre. He had claimed to judge those Jews who lived in the Venetian part of the city and a few years later King John imposed his jurisdiction over other native inhabitants of Venetian Tyre and seems to have refused to allow the commune to exercise

High Justice. Other rulers, among them the Emperor Frederick II, took an equally strong line, levying in Venetian Tyre taxes on Syrian dyeworkers and shopkeepers and using their courts to confiscate Venetian properties in the area on account of crimes committed by their tenants.[46] Even in 1243, after Tyre had been taken from the imperialists by baronial forces with Venice's help, the commune's claim to High Justice in its part of the city was not officially accepted, although it was sometimes able to exercise it in practice, and some of its properties in the surrounding countryside seem to have been irretrievably lost.[47] As late as 1277 the Lord of Tyre insisted in an agreement with the Venetians that they renounce any right to jurisdiction over his liegemen or burgesses who happened to live in their part of the city.[48] The laws of the burgess court of Acre, perhaps compiled in the 1260s, stated firmly that notarial letters of credit recognised in communal courts were not normally held to be valid in royal courts and that the communal courts had no jurisdiction in cases that involved High Justice or property disputes;[49] and in 1264 those convicted in the Genoese court in Tyre of a crime deserving death or physical punishment had to be handed over to the lord for the penalty to be carried out.[50] We will see that King Hugh was prepared to act quite firmly towards the Italians after his accession in 1269, although in the end his government suffered on account of his policies.

The rulers may have been able to force the issues because, although there were permanent groups of administrators and settlers living round their communal buildings, most of the European merchants only visited the great ports for a month or two in the year. Inventories of Venetian and Genoese properties in Acre, drawn up in 1244 and 1249 respectively, made reference to many houses and rooms which for most of the time lay empty and were leased at exorbitant rates only for the months when the passages arrived. One of these inventories enables an estimate to be made of the number of Genoese permanently resident in Acre: there do not seem to have been more than 70 householders and this might give a total of about 300 persons – or 1 % of the population of the city.[51] The great privileges applied largely to men who were themselves only temporary visitors to the Holy Land. And more than the pilgrims, indeed more than any other group, it was they who contributed to the prosperity of the kingdom in the thirteenth century, for their privileges also worked in favour of the grantors.

This can especially be seen when one looks at their commercial rights, which were naturally applied at those points in the passage of commerce at which dues were taken: in a port, at the gates of a town and in its markets. The privileges granted in connection with a port fall into three groups: general exemptions from all dues owing to the harbour officials, which often included freedom from levies on the re-export of unsold goods but were generally restricted to bona fide merchants from the European city involved and excluded taxes on pilgrim traffic;[52] partial exemptions;[53] and finally a right which seems to have been given only to the Pisans, who in 1187 were allowed to have their own agents to deal with their nationals in the ports and markets and at the gates of Tyre, Acre and Jaffa. We have already seen that the gains of the Pisans at this time were quashed in 1193, and in 1226–8 the port officials in Acre were certainly trying to enforce authority over them, but as late as 1286 their consul in Acre was believed to be still enjoying this privilege.[54] At the gates the same kinds of exemption were granted, although the loss in revenue for the governments may have been less. There were, we shall see, strong attempts to force the merchants to make some payment for those goods they brought in from or were exporting to Islamic countries, but the numbers of Europeans actually engaged in the traffic of merchandise along the western section of the trans-Asiatic trade route and organising caravans from Damascus and other Muslim centres to the coast must have been small. Rights in the markets again took much the same forms as those enjoyed in the ports and at the gates, although complete freedom from the market charges was less often granted – there is no evidence, for instance, that the Venetians were ever fully exempted.[55] One does also find general freedoms from which certain commodities or types of transaction were excluded;[56] general reductions of charges or reductions of dues on certain goods;[57] and privileges which were meant to apply only to one side of business transactions: freedoms from the charges either on sales or on purchases; not on both.[58] But it must be emphasised that whatever form a privilege in a market took it usually applied only to half the tax levied by a government since most tolls seem to have been shared by buyers and sellers. If an exempt merchant and a non-exempt had a business dealing – and most of the transactions in the markets must have been of this kind – the share of the duty owed by the man who was not privileged would still have to be paid. Even if complete exemption from sales tax had been granted to one group of traders, therefore, they had only to involve themselves in twice as many transactions or in deals in a particular commodity of twice the original value for the financial break-even point for the government to be reached. The lords of the Syrian ports clearly hoped – and that hope was surely realised – that the presence of European merchants would lead to an increase in business that would more than compensate for any revenue initially lost in inducements for them to come.

But some of the communities of European merchants and some religious orders[59] were also allowed to have their own markets, run by their officials and using their weights and measures. The first of these was granted to the Venetians in 1123:

> You may use scales of weight and measures of quantity in the following way. Whenever Venetians deal in their own goods with each other they ought to use Venetian measures. When Venetians sell their goods to other people they ought to make use of their own Venetian measures. But whenever Venetians purchase from foreign peoples other than Venetians, having paid the market tax, they ought to make use of royal measures.[60]

It will be noticed that this gave the Venetians in Acre the right to use their own weights and measures when dealing among themselves and with others, provided they were *selling* their goods. If, however, a Venetian wished to *buy* something from a non-Venetian he had to pay tax and use royal measures, in other words visit the royal markets. Although this clause was not repeated in the king's confirmation in 1125,[61] it seems to have set a standard followed in other privileges, for instance in those to the Pisans in Tyre, Jaffa and Acre and to merchants from Provence in Tyre granted by Raymond of Tripoli, Conrad of Montferrat and Guy of Lusignan: the Pisans were allowed to use weights and measures 'so that they can freely weigh and measure *among themselves* and for *strangers buying from them*'; the Provençals only for measuring in transactions among themselves.[62]

It is possible that the same sort of limited right was enjoyed in Tripoli by the Venetians, who in 1277 were allowed to establish a market under stringent conditions, among them one that obliged a Venetian to go with every man who had bought something owing 'two rights' from him in his own quarter to register the sale with the count's market officials.[63] It was also held in Tyre by the Genoese, who were permitted to use their own measures by Conrad of Montferrat in 1190,[64] and by the Venetians, who as owners of a third of the city certainly had markets.[65] On the other hand the Genoese never seem to have gained this right in Acre: no charter granting them such a privilege survives and the commercial writer Francesco Balducci Pegolotti did not mention them, although in his *Pratica* he made reference to the measures used by the Pisans and the Venetians; it is interesting to note that not only are there no references in contemporary material to a *unduq*, or enclosed market, in the Genoese quarter, but also that no foundations for one survive.[66] And the Genoese may have lost their rights in Tyre by 1264, for they then agreed to use the weights and measures of the lord and to pay him *mensuragium*, a payment on every deal estimated according to the quantity of merchandise involved.[67]

The recipients of the privilege of using their own weights and measures could sell the commodities they themselves had imported in their own markets, but to load their ships with cargoes for the return to the West they had to buy the goods coming to the Levant over the Asiatic trade routes in the royal or seigneurial markets where, even if they were freed from the sales tax, the other parties to the deals were probably not.[68] A loophole for them would have been to have gone themselves to the great Muslim centres, conducting caravans from and to the coast, exercising their privilege of free entry and bringing the uncharged goods into a port either for sale in their own markets free of dues or for shipping directly to the West. Alternatively their ships might have stopped off at a non-Christian port on the way to the Levant to pick up a cargo which they could dispose of in their own markets, using the Syrian town as a free commercial centre. To combat these methods, it seems that restrictions were imposed on them. Direct trading with the Muslim hinterland was discouraged or at least subjected to tax. In 1192 Henry of Champagne, confirming Genoese rights in Tyre, added that if

> they come by land to Tyre from any Muslim country and sell their merchandise in Tyre they will render the customary taxes. If indeed they do not sell they are held to pay no custom.[69]

In 1244 Marsiglio Giorgio, the leader of the Venetians in the East, complained:

> If any merchant of Venice wishes to go overland to Damascus or to any Muslim city and wishes to take any merchandise with him out of Acre he is forced to pay one *carat* for each besant ($4\frac{1}{6}$%) of its estimated worth.

and that:

> If anyone from Venice wishes to go to Damascus or to any Muslim country and buys merchandise and wishes to bring it to Acre by land, he must pay $9\frac{7}{24}$% if he wants to sell it in Acre,

unless he had come to an agreement beforehand with a royal official.[70] In 1264 the Genoese agreed to pay Philip of Montfort $2\frac{1}{12}$% on all goods exported or imported through the land gates of Tyre; but if they could not sell the goods they had taken out they were allowed to bring them back into the city without the payment of additional duty.[71]

The complaints of Marsiglio Giorgio also contained a reference to the government's attempts to prevent the Venetians from taking advantage of their privileges by shipping merchandise acquired in a Muslim centre directly to Europe. If a Venetian bought goods in Islamic lands and brought them to Acre

> and wishes to carry them to Venice, he pays $4\frac{1}{6}$%, unless he has previously come to an agreement with a royal official.[72]

And in 1243, in a charter from Bohemond V which otherwise reduced the dues payable by merchants from Montpellier, there was to be no reduction for those goods brought into Tripoli by land and then exported.[73]

Linked to these restrictions seems to have been one by which the rulers discouraged merchants from landing merchandise at one Christian port and bringing it overland to another. In 1244 Marsiglio Giorgio grumbled that:

> If any ship comes from Venice and applies at Tyre or any other city and the merchants wish to bring some of their merchandise overland to Acre they are charged $9\frac{1}{3}$%.[74]

In 1264 Philip of Montfort remitted the dues owed by the Genoese for bringing their goods overland to Tyre, if their ships had been wrecked or attacked by pirates off his lordship or that of

Sidon, provided that they let him or his lieutenant know: a clause which suggests that, as in Acre, a tax would otherwise have been paid.[75] These may have been attempts to prevent the Italians using the ports as free markets: certainly this is what Henry of Champagne seems to have been doing in 1192 when he bound the Genoese in Tyre to pay dues on any goods sold in the city markets which had been brought in by sea, if the ship in which they were imported had come from Barbary, Egypt or Constantinople by way of some other Islamic country.[76] In 1257 merchants from Ancona had to pay full dues on entry and sale if they imported into Acre taxable goods they had bought in Islamic lands. If these were not sold but re-exported, they would moreover have to pay the full export tax.[77] And in 1277 the Venetians were allowed to have a market in Tripoli on condition that rights in it were limited to Venetians and not to representatives appointed by them and that if a Venetian established a retail shop or bought corn, vegetables and oil in order to resell them he would pay the full market dues.[78]

The rulers in Latin Syria also seem to have discouraged their own subjects from buying goods in the exempt markets. They appear to have had no objection to oriental merchants, once they had sold their merchandise in the royal markets, going down to the European *funduqs* to acquire commodities to load their camels for their return home – the gate officials would of course tax what they took out of the city. But in 1277 the Count of Tripoli insisted that if the Venetians sold in their market to 'humble people' anything that owed 'two rights' to his officials in the *fonde* and fish-market they should themselves pay the tax owed by the purchasers.[79] A statute inserted into a list of dues to be taken in Acre commanded that all the indigenous inhabitants of the city should live round the *fonde en amont* – the royal markets – and not near the *fonde en aval* – those, it will be suggested, of the Italians –

> because otherwise the lord could not enjoy those rights it is established he should take from them.

The rights mentioned were the levying of dues, ranging from $12\frac{1}{2}\%$ to $4\frac{1}{6}\%$, on the purchases made in the *fonde en aval* by the natives and all villagers in the royal domain around Acre on the way back to the quarter where lay the *fonde en amont*. It seems that if locals went to buy in the Italian markets government officials would take a tax on what they had bought as they left the Italian quarters.[80] Between 1210 and 1225 King John exempted native Syrians in Tyre from port dues, thus encouraging them to live in his rather than in the Venetian part of the city, where they were not exempt.[81] Although the situation in Tyre was unusual in that the Venetians held one-third of the town in lordship, the king may also have been trying to discourage the indigenous population from using the Italian markets.

The rights of and limitations upon European merchants and the corresponding advantages for the rulers should now be clear. On arrival with a loaded ship in a Latin Syrian port, a privileged trader passed, with his merchandise untaxed, to the market of his own nationals where he sold it without paying dues on the sale to the town's lord. Merchants from the Muslim interior would come down to buy in the Europeans' markets, but they would be charged on what they had bought as they left by the gates of the city. Local people in Acre who did the same would be taxed on their purchases as they returned to the part of the town where they lived. And a western merchant could not buy goods to fill his ship for his return home in his national market, but would have to go up to that of the king or lord, to which were also directed those coming into the city from the hinterland with spices and other commodities. In the town markets a European merchant might well be absolved from the payment of his contribution to the purchase tax, but the man from whom he bought would not and the government could hope to receive at least half the toll. Should the westerner try to get round the obligation to buy in the town markets by involving himself in the trade between the Muslim cities and the coast, he would find that his privileges of exemption were of no avail and that he was subject to tolls. Having bought in the royal or seigneurial markets he could of course export his purchases to the West without the payment of custom dues. There is no doubt that the privileges he enjoyed were of real benefit to him, but his presence in the Latin East and the increased commercial business that resulted must have more than compensated, as far as the rulers were concerned, for the exemptions granted to him.

These conclusions are borne out by the fact that, although there was a continuing aggressiveness on the part of the rulers towards the European merchants' jurisdictional and territorial rights, there is little evidence for a similar attitude towards their genuine commercial exemptions.[82] Kings and lords continued well into the thirteenth century to make grants to them and to religious orders or reduce the dues they had to pay[83] and these grants were not carelessly made, for certain commodities were often specifically excluded from them. In 1183 the Venetians in Antioch had to pay dues on merchandise they sold in the markets;[84] in 1190 the Marseillais in Palestine were exempted only from port taxes and not from sales duty;[85] in 1202 the Pisans in Botrun were to pay a tax on every ship of theirs involved in the import and sale of corn;[86] in 1256 the Hospitallers in Tripoli could load and unload their ships with everything except soap and the charter granted to the Venetians in the same city by Bohemond VII in 1277 was hedged about by limitations.[87] There seem always to have been commodities on which rulers were reluctant to lose customs duties. In 1190 King Guy envisaged bans on the export of corn from Palestine;[88] in 1244 the Venetian Marsiglio Giorgio complained that his compatriots were forced to pay a tax on the horses and slaves they imported to sell in Acre and this is paralleled by what seems to have been an unsuccessful attempt by the Emperor Frederick II's officials to levy a toll on horses brought in by the Pisans before 1229;[89] in Acre and elsewhere duty was taken on the export of coins and precious metal for use in minting, although the Genoese in Tripoli were exempted from this in 1203.[90] In the 1250s the regent and the High Court unsuccessfully challenged rights claimed by Marseilles on the basis of forged charters.[91] It is clear that rulers did not entirely lose control over trade but that they knew that it was in their interest for European merchants to be encouraged to visit their ports.

A series of charters issued by John of Beirut in the early 1220s illustrate how a lord would set about building up a port. In November 1221 John granted a charter to the Genoese, giving them freedom from the harbour tax of *anchoragia* on all vessels that put into Beirut; exemption from dues on goods imported by them through the port and on their re-export – presumably if they could not sell them; freedom from purchase tax on their purchases in his market and from the *terciaria* levied on the ships into which these were loaded. It will be noted that the Genoese were not granted the right to have their own market nor were they given any exemption from customs duty on general exports. But John added

that they could have their own court with the same rights of jurisdiction as they had in the royal domain, confirmed their possession
of houses in the town and gave them permission to bathe once a
week in his own public baths. He renounced his rights to shipwreck if Genoese vessels were cast on the shores of his lordship
and he assured the Genoese that he would not take indiscriminate
action against their compatriots if he or his men suffered from the
piratical activities of Genoese corsairs. In May 1223 he confirmed
these privileges with important additions. Reiterating that the
Genoese could use his baths once a week, he added that on that
day no one else was to bathe there; he granted them an oven and
confirmed rights that they had 'in the woods of Beirut', which
suggests that a Genoese community was beginning to settle in the
town and that it had established a yard for ship-repairing. He
promised that the shipwrecked goods of the Genoese would be
safe and secure even if they had been carried in vessels other than
their own. Their commercial privileges were enlarged, but they
were also in some ways limited: all their ships, big and little, were
freed from *terciaria* and it was now stated that all they exported
from Beirut was to be exempt from dues, but pottery was specifically excluded from this and it was laid down that they must pay
charges for *mensuragium* on any wine, oil and corn bought by them.
In return for an extension of their privileges, therefore, the
Genoese had agreed to pay certain charges on purchases.[92]

A month after his original grant to the Genoese John issued a
charter to the Venetians. To them he also gave freedom from
anchoragia; exemption from import dues in the port, although here
there was no reference to any freedom for re-exported goods;
freedom from purchase taxes in the market of Beirut and from
terciaria on ships taking out the merchandise that had been bought.
John did not renounce shipwreck but said he would do his best to
save a Venetian ship, its crew and goods which were cast on his
shores; but like the Genoese the Venetians were promised that no
revenge would be taken against the compatriots of a pirate. In
granting them a court John was more specific than he had been to
their rivals, excluding from their powers of jurisdiction any exercise of High Justice. In June 1222 he granted them a new charter
allowing them to judge in their own court according to their own
laws, but explaining that he reserved High Justice in the same
way as did the king in Acre.[93] He now renounced his right to

shipwreck and clarified the earlier guarantee against indiscriminate punishments in cases of piracy by promising not to take steps against those merchants who came to Beirut. He granted an additional and important right: that the goods of Venetians who died intestate while in his lordship would not be confiscated by him, but would be handed over to their compatriots or, if there were none in the area at the time, would be held by him until he had learnt the wishes of the Doge. These rights, when taken together with the absence of any reference to communal property, suggest that there was at this time no Venetian settlement in Beirut. John also brought the commercial rights of the Venetians into line with those of the Genoese by granting the former the same privilege with regard to re-exports, but he extended their freedom from purchase tax by stating that no charge was to be made on any goods coming into his town by land or sea – and he listed them in an inventory to which reference has already been made, for it shows that Beirut was participating in the spice trade.[94]

In September 1223 John granted a charter to merchants from Marseilles, who were freed from import and export dues and sales and purchase taxes on those goods they brought in themselves. They were permitted to have their own court, although John reserved High Justice; there they could treat the complaints of other merchants against their fellow citizens.[95]

These charters of John of Beirut are important in two ways. They show the kinds of privilege a lord had to give to attract the European merchants whose presence was so necessary to the development of a port. But they also illustrate the care with which commercial rights were controlled and defined: while *terciaria* – scrupulously limited elsewhere – was given away, perhaps because little pilgrim traffic passed through Beirut, it is especially noticeable how in these grants, as in a comparable charter issued to the Genoese by a Lord of Haifa in 1234,[96] there is no question of western merchants having their own markets: they had to use those of the lord.

European traders made up only a part of the commercial community in Palestine. There were also those merchants who worked the oriental routes down which came the goods for the West. Many of these visited the cities with the spice caravans from Damascus,[97] but there were also agents of Muslim companies permanently resident in the Latin ports: partners in a trading

venture of the 1260s were four Damascenes and one man from
Mosul living in Tyre and Acre.[98] Subjects of the kingdom were
engaged in trade: merchants from Acre participated in the Champagne fairs[99] and were organised into the same kinds of commercial companies as were to be found in western Europe.[100] It is
clear moreover that there was a flourishing local trade up and
down the Syrian seaboard. Egyptian salt fish was imported into
Acre and Egyptian flax passed through that city on its way to
Damascus.[101] In the registers of a group of Genoese notaries
active in Ayas, Laodicea and Beirut there were references to eleven
separate sailings down the coast between February and June 1274
and to thirteen between February and December 1279.[102] Indigenous merchants seem to have played a significant part in this
local commerce. From the twelfth century there survives a safe
conduct issued on behalf of King Baldwin III to a native captain
who was trading between Egypt and Tyre and at about the same
time the traveller Benjamin of Tudela reported that Jews in Tyre
owned sea-going vessels.[103] In the thirteenth century there still
seems to have been an important Syrian trading community in
Tyre,[104] but the most impressive piece of evidence concerns a
company which appealed in 1268 to Genoa for compensation for
a ship of theirs taken by the commune's fleet off the Cilician coast
some five years before; the city government of Genoa agreed to
pay them no less than 14,900 Genoese pounds.[105] Involved as
partners and agents of this company, which seems to have been
organised from Mosul, were 23 men, all indigenous, of whom 6
resided in Ayas, 5 in Antioch, 2 in Tyre and 6 in Acre.[106] One of
them was a man called Saliba who was a burgess of Acre and,
although native-born, a Latin Christian. When in 1264 he was
dying he became a *confrater* of the Hospitallers and made a will
from which can be got some idea of his wealth. He referred to two
properties, a house in Montmusard, the suburb of Acre, which
had cost him 475 saracen besants and was left to the Order of St
John, and a vineyard, which had cost him 800 saracen besants and
was left to his nephews; he allotted 48 saracen besants for the
expenses of his funeral and for a priest to say Mass for his soul for
a year; 30 saracen besants for work on the walls of Acre and on a
church; 988 saracen besants and 10 royal pounds of Acre to his
family and 90 saracen besants to religious houses. These give
totals of 1,275 saracen besants invested in property and 1,156

saracen besants and 10 royal pounds of Acre in cash, but he also left all his other properties, unspecified, to the Hospitallers and these may have been considerable, because one of his daughters, to whom, interestingly, he had left nothing, was suing the Order for them in 1267.[107]

In the cities there were many others besides the merchants whose livelihood depended on commercial prosperity. At the lowest level were the servants of knights and burgesses, many of whom must have been indigenous;[108] labourers employed by agents of landowners or contractors to work lands – often some distance away – or to build houses and cisterns;[109] sailors;[110] porters,[111] cameleers and stable-owners.[112] There were also tradesmen, shopkeepers and stall-holders serving merchants and the local inhabitants and retailing goods they had bought in the markets like spices,[113] wine, oil and candles,[114] corn[115] and beans;[116] there were butchers,[117] cooking-pot makers,[118] goldsmiths,[119] cobblers[120] and curriers;[121] bread seems to have been sold in little stalls beneath gates and arches,[122] beer and wine not only in the markets but also in taverns;[123] in Jerusalem and probably in Acre too there were shops selling cooked meals.[124] Above all there were those who drew their living from the treatment or sale of the cloth brought mainly from France and Italy: tailors,[125] drapers,[126] dressmakers,[127] flax-dealers and rope-makers.[128] Craftsmen and retailers would work in streets specialising in their trades: in Jerusalem the street of the cooks was sardonically known as the Street of Bad Cooking;[129] in Tyre there was a street of goldsmiths and a street of butchers;[130] in Acre a street of cooking-pot makers and, as in Jerusalem, a *Parmentarie*, where were the tailors.[131] But there seem to have been no guilds : although the burgess laws of Acre contained regulations for goldsmiths, there is nothing to suggest that there was a guild for their craft controlled by the crown as there was in Cyprus by 1286.[132]

Trade could not have been conducted without money-changers and money-lenders: we have already seen how even the temporary absence of merchants would lead to anxieties about the difficulty of changing money. In Egypt and presumably also in Acre a great deal of business was conducted on credit,[133] and there were men in Palestine, above all in the Italian merchant companies and in the Military Orders, who could make use of facilities for the transmission of accounts to Europe, but traders also arrived with letters of exchange or with sums of money in one coin that they wanted changed for another.[134] In many towns the money-changers were gathered in special areas where they would be under the control of the lords: in Acre they had their tables along the main street and the royal customs house seems to have had some sort of control over the quality of the coin used.[135] Most of them seem to have been Latins, some being obviously prosperous and jurors of courts:[136] the names survive of only two, or perhaps three, native-born money-changers, one of whom can also be seen acting as a money-lender.[137] But there was an important group of Jewish money-lenders, unaffected of course by the laws concerning usury: in the twelfth century a Jew from Acre was acting in Egypt as an intermediary over a debt for Raymond III of Tripoli and his wife, Eschiva of Tiberias; and in the 1270s the impoverished Lady of Scandelion was heavily in debt to the Jews.[138]

The Palestinian ports contained fishing fleets. In spite of frequent shortages,[139] fishing was an important activity in Tyre and towards the end of the thirteenth century a fleet based in Acre was in the hands of families of Pisan origin.[140] There was also what might loosely be called industry, although it is possible that activities like the smelting of iron, which was mined in the Lordship of Beirut, were situated in the countryside.[141] The greater ports had arsenals, strips of sandy beach on which boats might be built and up which they would be dragged for careenage and repairs.[142] Most large towns seem to have had soap works[143] and tanneries, that in Acre being situated in Montmusard.[144] Some contained dyeworks: in the twelfth century Benjamin of Tudela had reported that engaged in this occupation were the Jewish communities in Lydda, Jerusalem, Bethlehem, Bethnoble, Jaffa and Le Petit Gerin.[145] But the most famous city for its dye was Tyre, where other indigenous peoples were involved in the works.[146] Tyre was also well known for its glass-manufacture in which its Jewish community participated.[147]

A town therefore provided its lord with income from many sources – rents on properties; taxes on persons, goods, shops and trades; revenues from public baths and ovens; dues from the port, the gates and the markets – and we must consider each of them in turn.

The Latins' inexperience of the complexities of urban life at the time of their arrival may have led them into that confusion with regard to the legal status of burgess properties which confounds the historian when he is first faced by it. One finds *borgesies*, houses and lands held by burgess tenure, in the rural colonial settlements and occasionally in native villages.[148] There was even one complete *casal*, La Fauconnerie near Acre, which was a *borgesie*.[149] But most properties of this sort were of course in the towns or just outside their walls, for an area of gardens and allotments around – perhaps to a league distant – was subject to the jurisdiction of the local burgess court.[150] The gardens, often with their own wells, cisterns and reservoirs,[151] were given over to the cultivation of fruit trees and herbs.[152] Not all the properties in and around a town however were subject to its burgess court: the houses in some of the quarters of the great merchant communities had passed under the jurisdiction of their own officers; all land and houses granted in alms to churches and religious orders were dealt with only by courts Christian;[153] some *borgesies* could be treated in the High Court as parts of fiefs;[154] and although for their properties in their own quarters or scattered through a town most of the indigenous householders seem to have been answerable to the *Cour des Bourgeois* rather than to their own tribunals,[155] there was, at least in the northern Christian states, a class of native urban householders who followed trades and even in one case a profession, but were treated as villeins.[156]

Borgesies should not be confused with censive lands – properties for which rents were paid[157] – for although the possessors of most *borgesies* paid rents in money and kind and could sub-let their properties,[158] there were heritages on which rent had been excused and others which were held as parts, though not integral parts, of fiefs in exchange for service,[159] even though a *borgesie* was never regarded as being held by feudal tenure unless a charter had specifically stated this;[160] conversely there were many lands leased out by religious institutions or by lords from their own estates that were not held in burgess tenure.[161] One may define a *borgesie* as being a property held by a tenant, either a knight or a burgess, who answered for it to his local *Cour des Bourgeois*.[162] It was hereditable, reverting to the lord only on the death without heirs of its possessor. Rent and burgess services were normally owed for it and the lord, through his court, retained preemption rights and demanded that any sale be registered:[163] it was sometimes specified that sales could only be made to other burgesses or at least not to knights or churchmen.[164] We shall see below that a charge was made by a lord for registration, but far more important to him must have been the rents collected from burgess properties, those accruing to him as a seigneurial right, as opposed to those from leases,[165] being probably known as *tallea*. In western Europe this word was used in a general sense to cover all feudal aids, although in England it became attached to servile dues. In the Latin East it can be found used in three contexts: as an imposition on the Church;[166] with reference to town-dwelling indigenous peoples in the Principality of Antioch;[167] and in the Kingdom of Jerusalem as the name given to the returns made to the king for burgess properties in the royal domain.[168] Its sense can best be seen in charters issued by the rivals Conrad of Montferrat and Guy of Lusignan when they were angling for Pisan support. In 1187, granting the Pisans rights in Tyre and future privileges in Acre and Jaffa, Conrad stated that 'the king can take *tallea* from the houses of Pisan burgesses that lie outside the Pisan honour – their quarter – if he receives this for all in the city'. When these rights in Tyre were confirmed by Guy in 1189 the Pisan privileges were increased by the substitution in this sentence of 'Pisans' for 'king' and 'for all the Pisans' for 'for all in the city'; and on the same day, with reference to Pisan rights in Acre, Guy was even more explicit:

> the Pisan consuls can collect *tallea* from the houses of Pisan burgesses outside the Pisan quarter when they wish to receive it for all, and the king cannot receive *tallea* from these houses, neither from Pisans nor from those whom they tax.[169]

This extraordinary extension of privileges did not last long,[170] but it is clear that *tallea* was a seigneurial due, levied on burgess properties in the royal domain, and presumably the same conditions were to be found in the fiefs, although no evidence for them can now be found.

There survives a reference to the payment by adult Jews of a capitation tax of one besant a year. We have already seen that a poll-tax was levied on Muslim peasants and it may be that under the Latins the *jawali* tax paid by the *dhimmis*, the Children of the Book, to Muslim rulers, was still levied on Jews, had been lifted from all Christians, but ironically had now been imposed on

Muslims.[171] A curious tax which was paid by pork butchers of 4 *denarii* for every pig killed, found only in Tyre and called *tuazo*, may also have been a survival from Fatimid times: its name appears to be linked to an Arabic word for ritual ablutions and one cannot imagine a Christian government initiating taxes on meat which was unclean only to Jews and Muslims.[172] All retail shopkeepers, whether owning or renting their shops and stalls, seem to have been subject to charges. These may have been a kind of *mensuragium* and certainly in Antioch the weights and measures used by retailers had seals fixed to them by officials,[173] but it is possible that we can see here a continuation of the Muslim *hilali* tax: license-fees paid to the state by shopkeepers, craftsmen and the owners of public baths, mills and ovens. The *hilali* tax was collected each month and it is significant that Syrian dyeworkers in Tyre paid 2 caroubles a month for each of their vats.[174] The tables of the money-changers provided revenue: in the Venetian quarter in Acre in 1244 there were twelve of them, returning to the commune rents varying from 4 to 41 besants.[175]

Perhaps also subject to *hilali* tax were the public baths and ovens which served the populated areas. The cities of Palestine seem to have been full of bath-houses. Early in the thirteenth century a Bishop of Acre wrote scornfully of lords who preferred baths to battles and he reported that some of them, who otherwise kept their wives in strict seclusion, allowed them to go under supervision to the baths three days a week.[176] Some decades earlier a Muslim who knew the Latin states well was astonished at the way the Franks brought their wives and daughters to the baths; and there is corroborating documentary evidence for his statement that one of the public baths in Tyre catered for mixed bathing.[177] The baths gave their possessors – knights, religious houses and merchant communes – good incomes: in 1243 three in Tyre provided the commune of Venice with 265 besants a year.[178] The bread ovens, placed in squares and at street corners, were even more profitable. In 1193 the oven at Margat seems to have returned an average of 150 besants a year. In 1243 two Venetian ovens in Tyre were returning 55 besants a year. In 1244 a Venetian oven in Acre was providing an annual rent of 150 besants, much more than the commune's houses, but rather less than its shops; and five years later the oven of the Commune of Genoa in Acre returned no less than 366 besants a year, more than anything else in the inventory of rents in which it is mentioned, more even than the Genoese garden and the total annual returns from houses.[179] Baths and ovens could be in private hands;[180] some may have been leased out; but others may have been managed for the lords by agents, like an oven in twelfth-century Jerusalem that belonged to the canons of the Holy Sepulchre.[181]

The rents and dues owed by householders, shopkeepers and tradesmen were probably collected by the agents of two courts, the *Cour des Bourgeois* and the *Cour des Syriens*. A *Cour des Bourgeois* was established in every place where there was a Frankish population of a reasonable size[182] and its rights, in the royal domain at least, were protected by the crown from the politically stronger High Court.[183] It exercised full jurisdiction, including High Justice, over all the non-feudal population and in all matters concerning property held in burgess tenure. And like most other courts it also seems to have been a financial office: in fourteenth-century Cyprus it collected the king's rents[184] and there is some evidence that burgesses in Palestine made their returns to their local courts.[185] There survives a compilation of laws and customs, apparently influenced from the same source as a twelfth-century Provençal *codi*, which was used by the burgess court in Acre and in its present form looks as though it had been put together in the 1260s.[186] It cannot be treated uncritically as evidence for the way these courts worked in the lordships but, although each had its own customs,[187] royal legislation was followed outside the royal domain as well as within[188] and it is probable that all had much the same procedures.

A *Cour des Bourgeois* – in Acre it may have met in a house in the suburb of Montmusard[189] – was presided over by an officer appointed by his king or lord on the advice of the High or seigneurial court and most commonly called a viscount, although he could also be entitled *bailli*;[190] in the twelfth-century city of Jerusalem the royal castellan sometimes doubled as president of the *Cour des Bourgeois*.[191] Viscounts also had police duties and patrolled the streets at night to arrest malefactors.[192] In the courts under their presidency sat burgess jurors – in Acre there were twelve.[193] The methods by which these men were appointed are not known, but in Acre successive generations of certain families, particularly the de Conches and the Antiaumes, were represented on the bench.[194] The jurors were important local figures, common counsellors and arbitrators in their neighbourhoods.[195] On appointment each of them took an oath: what form this took in Acre is not known, but certain clauses in the surviving burgess laws suggest that it cannot have been unlike that taken by the jurors in the Venetian burgess court in Tyre, who swore to make their judgements according to the customs of the land or, if there were none known to apply to the case before them, according to their consciences and never to reveal the secrets of the court.[196]

The procedure according to which they heard a case was somewhat different from that in the seigneurial courts. Although jurors were enjoined to give counsel to anyone who asked it of them, provided they were not actually sitting in judgement at the time,[197] all plaintiffs and defendants had to be represented by professional advocates, who were not jurors but in fourteenth-century Cyprus ranked as officers of the court.[198] On the other hand all witnesses gave their own evidence, being not, as in the High Court, represented by advocates.[199] Like the vassals in the High Court it was the jurors who were the judges: after a case had been heard the president would order them to reach a decision; they would withdraw and would later return to announce it in the same form as was followed in the High Court – as an *esgart*, *conoissance* or *recort*; the president would then pass sentence.[200] A great deal of their business naturally consisted of rather more mundane matters like the registration of changes in the possession of property. Here the procedure certainly varied slightly from place to place, but in Acre both parties would come to the court and the seller or donor would announce his act, promising to defend it in future and handing a staff, indicative of his possession, to the viscount who then passed it on to the new owner.[201] The court would make a charge for its registration: in thirteenth-century Acre and Tyre it took 1 mark from the seller and 3 besants from the purchaser; and in the Venetian court in Tyre the notary who drew up the charter and the *placier* each received a quarter of a besant.[202]

A viscount was assisted by subordinate officers. In fourteenth-century Cyprus his chief aid was the *muhtasib*, who, like his superior, undertook police duties in command of a band of sergeants, and also inspected the meat market and the shops of fish, bread and wine retailers for fraud.[203] But there survives only one reference to a *muhtasib* in the Kingdom of Jerusalem: a Venetian report concerning Tyre in 1243 stated that he had been established in the city by King John (1210–25). From the description given of him he would seem to have had duties corresponding to those of the Muslim judges of the same name who had jurisdiction in commercial matters, and, what is more, he is to be found, like the Mamluk *muhtasib*, collecting what look like *hilali* taxes.[204] In every royal town the king or viscount appointed a town crier who acted for both the seigneurial and burgess courts,[205] but whose office should not be confused with that of the *banier*, responsible for the publication of royal bans.[206] To every viscount and burgess court were attached sergeants, some of whom imposed physical punishment on offenders.[207] Among them was an important group of officers called *placearii* or *placiers*. It is possible that each *placier* was made responsible for a district within a town: the merchant communes gained the right to have their own in their quarters and in Acre the Venetians had at least two in 1244 and the Genoese three in 1250. *Placiers* seem to have been concerned in some way with the overseeing of property: one of them in Venetian Tyre gained something every time there was a sale, gift or exchange in court and another in Acre lived in the house where were stored Venetian building materials. To the office were attached perquisites, which may be why the salaries of the Venetian *placiers* in Acre were so low: in 1244 a room or apartment, 36 besants and a fresh suit of clothing each year.[208] *Placiers* were also policemen, for it was they who accompanied the viscount on his night tours of Tyre in the 1260s.[209] In the later years the burgess court of Acre also employed an official scribe. This had been decided in February 1251 at a meeting of the High and Low Courts and it was afterwards established that the burgess court should have official books in which would be recorded the details of all cases. The reforms were not immediately put into effect – indeed as late as 1260 the court was still making use of a public notary[210] – but certainly by 1269 it was employing a scribe and a record book and had in the meantime engraved its own seal.[211]

The *Cours des Syriens*, which were subordinate to the *Cours des Bourgeois*, had jurisdiction over all non-Latins. In law there were lines of demarcation between the various peoples in the kingdom which were based on religious belief and not on race: in the lawbooks the word 'nation' was synonymous with religion.[212] The first of these was between Christians and non-Christians. In those

cases in which non-Latins could be used as witnesses the testimony
of Muslims, Jews and Samaritans was treated as being of the least
value;[213] and Christians alone had the inherent right to personal
freedom, for none of them, whatever their sect, could be enslaved.[214] The second division separated Christians 'of the law of
Rome' from those of other denominations, who were generally
known as Syrians, although this word could be used with particular reference to the Jacobites.[215] The eastern Christians were
themselves graded by the courts according to the validity that
should be attached to their testimony – a Jacobite before a Greek
and a Greek before a Nestorian or Armenian – but anyway there
were only a few cases in which their evidence was acceptable: a
non-Latin could not bear witness in the High Court except to help
prove the age or genealogy of a Latin claimant or to provide evidence on the boundaries of estates; in the burgess courts he could
not give testimony against a Frank, nor indeed against anyone who
was not of his own denomination, although he could give evidence
directly to the viscount and jurors, who could then make use of
it themselves.[216] The refusal to hear in most cases the direct testimony of the native peoples in the seigneurial and burgess courts,
to which all important pleas were directed, had two serious consequences for them. They were denied entry into the ranks of the
feudatories and so into the ruling class, because obviously they
could not give a lord the service of *consilium* which was the consequence of homage, and they must always have been at a dis-
advantage in commercial and property cases.

This is not to say that they were deprived of justice, although it
is hard now to see quite how the competence of native or partially
native courts was decided. In Muslim states jurisdiction was exercised in five fields:[217] the judgements of the *qadi*, which might
be described as ordinary jurisdiction; *mazalim*, covering cases
beyond a *qadi*'s competence; *shurta* or criminal jurisdiction; *hisba*
or commercial jurisdiction concerning weights and measures,
fraudulent sales, litigation between neighbours and between em-
ployers and employees; and the judgements of the semi-
independent courts of the recognised non-Muslim communities of
dhimmis. In certain ways the links between the old Muslim and
new Frankish systems can be suggested: many of the duties and
rights of the *qadis* were taken over by the lords; some of the
powers of *shurta*, which had involved the policing of a town by

the *sahib ash-shurta* assisted by nightwatchmen, seem to have been assumed by the viscount and the *placiers*;[218] the *Cour de la Fonde* – about which more below – and the *Cour des Bourgeois* now imposed *hisba*, which under the Fatimids had sometimes been combined with *shurta*, but in Islamic lands was more commonly administered by the *muhtasib*. In two important ways however the Frankish legal system differed from its Muslim predecessor. The courts took upon themselves the powers of taxation, assuming some of the responsibilities of the Muslim *diwans*, and they dealt only with what were regarded as secular cases, since religious matters fell under the purview of ecclesiastical courts: there is evidence that even native Christian priests could plead privilege of clergy.[219] Muslims and Jews conceived of no such division in their jurisdiction – the *qadi* was a religious officer, making all his judgements according to Islamic law. There is in fact evidence for non-Christian religious tribunals in Latin Syria: rabbinical courts flourished in Acre and Tyre; and in Gibel in the Principality of Antioch there was in the 1180s a *qadi* who had authority over Muslims from a wide area around and was a close associate of the Latin prince.[220] But because there were also created special courts for the indigenous to which were directed supposedly secular cases, the Latins must have imposed on their non-Christian subjects a separation of jurisdictions into temporal and spiritual which would have seemed quite artificial to them.

The *Cours des Syriens* had been founded early in the twelfth century.[221] According to John of Jaffa:

> the people of the Syrians came before the king . . . and begged and required of him that he would see that they were judged according to the customs of the Syrians and that there should be for them a chieftain and jurors of a court and that by this court they should be judged according to their customs, concerning the quarrels that arose among them. And he authorised the said court.[222]

These 'customs of the Syrians' presumably antedated the arrival of the Franks and the very existence of the court must therefore have ensured continuity from, or rather the adaptation of, an earlier system of justice. The *Cours des Syriens* must have been the only lay courts in the kingdom in which religious decisions were still made, for their customs must have combined some of the traditions of the earlier *qadis* together with those of the tribunals of the *dhimmis*.

A *Cour des Syriens* was made up of an unknown number of jurors, presided over by a man known, like the village headman, as *rays*. His powers over his court were similar to those of the viscount in the *Cour des Bourgeois*: presumably therefore he was an officer appointed by the king or lord who chaired the court and gave it advice, but played no part in the decisions of the jurors on the cases before them. In this respect he must have been unlike a *qadi*, who had the sole responsibility for judgement. And although his court probably had the power to take fines and confiscations and perhaps helped to levy the taxes imposed on the native peoples, cases coming before it must have been limited to everyday disputes over personal rights, for any litigation that concerned burgess law or the judgement of which involved the forfeit of life or member was automatically transferred to the local *Cour des Bourgeois*.[223] The surviving references to the town *rayses* show them quite often to have been men of some wealth, householders and landowners; one was a fief-holder. Several appear as witnesses to documents and they must therefore have been Latin Christians, although ten of the sixteen known were native-born and only one, Guy of Nablus, can be said with any certainty to have been a Frank: his brother may have been a man called Amicus and his son was called Henry.[224]

In the thirteenth century it was believed that *Cours des Syriens* had been established in all the lordships as well as in the royal domain.[225] And although twelfth-century *rayses* can be identified only in Jerusalem,[226] Nablus,[227] Tyre[228] and Bethlehem[229] – of these only Nablus was outside the royal domain and it was at the time an apanage of the crown – the absence of references to seigneurial *rayses* may only be a consequence of the loss of the archives of the lordships, for they can be found outside the kingdom in Tripoli,[230] Antioch[231] and Margat.[232] In Acre there was by the middle of the thirteenth century no *Cour des Syriens*, for it had been absorbed by the *Cour de la Fonde*, responsible for the collection of market taxes and the judgement of commercial cases: its *bailli*, two Frankish and four Syrian jurors heard cases not only of debt, guarantees, the leasing of houses, sales and commercial dealings, but also those concerning:

anything that a Syrian or Jew or Muslim or Samaritan or Nestorian or Greek or Jacobite or Armenian has done. Know well that right judges and commands us to judge that none of the aforesaid peoples ought to plead in any court concerning any claim they make among themselves save in the *Cour de la Fonde*,

although cases of murder, treason and larceny, indeed all involving High Justice, were to be heard in the *Cour des Bourgeois*.[233] This curious situation may well have been confined only to Acre, where there is no evidence for a *Rays des Syriens* even in the twelfth century. This is what John of Jaffa seems to have reported[234] and although only one thirteenth-century *rays*, John Semes of Le Saforie, is known by name – and he may not have been one at all[235] – there is some slight evidence that Tyre continued to have a *Cour des Syriens*,[236] while the office of town *rays* survived in Nicosia and Famagusta in Cyprus throughout the fourteenth century.[237]

In commercial centres the departments which levied the dues on trade were the *chaines*, the city gates, the *fondes* and some individual markets. These not only collected tolls and market charges but also paid them out in money-fiefs and probably rendered accounts to the *secretes*: indeed nothing better demonstrates the sophistication of the Palestinian bureaucracy at this time than the way it was possible for a man who held a money-fief to create out of it a rear-fief[238] or make an eleemosynary grant to a religious order[239] which was paid not by him but by the office involved. The payments of rents and fiefs were made at fixed times in the year, the most common being quarterly,[240] although sometimes half-yearly and for small rents annual or even monthly returns were made.[241] In the markets of Tyre the financial year began on All Saints Day. In Jerusalem in 1171 and in Acre in 1198 the payments were made at Christmas, Easter, the Nativity of St John the Baptist and Michaelmas, but in 1177 the gate office of Ascalon made the fourth payment on the feast of St Remigius.[242]

The *chaine* or *cathena* was the chain stretched across a harbour entrance that could be raised in time of danger to prevent the entry of ships. Its name was also given to the port itself, or one of the ports, to the area of the town bordering on this port and to an office, in Acre in a *khan*-like building,[243] which combined several functions. At least from the reign of King Amalric it was a maritime court, known in Acre also as the *Cour de la Mer*, which in its judgements concerned itself with the law of the seas and cases arising out of mercantile contracts. Although any dispute over claims worth more than one mark went before the *Cour des*

Bourgeois, it is possible that the *bailli* and jurors – we do not know how many – of a *Cour de la Chaine* conducted preliminary inquiries into all matters before remitting major cases to the burgess court for judgement.[244] The *chaine* was also the body responsible for the running and upkeep of the port,[245] a department, as we have seen, accounting revenues and paying out rents[246] and a customs house. It is the last of these functions which is particularly relevant here, but we know very little about how it was organised: in the thirteenth century it was supervised by *baillis*, who were perhaps the same officers as the *custodes* of the port mentioned in an early document,[247] and it also employed scribes.[248] Its procedures however seem to have been so similar to those practised in Egyptian ports at the same time – and it is worth remembering that the royal *modius* of Acre was of exactly the same weight as the *ardab* of Alexandria[249] – that it is likely that, like other cadastral departments, its administration had been inherited from the Muslims.

In Egypt the cargo of a merchant ship entering a port was involved in the four processes of disembarkation, registration, storage and sale. On arrival the vessel was usually moored in the centre of the harbour and lighters ferried its cargo to the quays, while the captain paid a tax for the right to remain at anchor. The same kind of procedure seems to have been followed in the Latin Syrian ports. The arrival of ships outside Acre was signalled by the tolling of a bell and each was met by a small boat,[250] doubtless a pilot boat, which may have directed it either to a berth in the centre of the harbour – it seems that boats did not tie up alongside the ports of the city and barges must have carried cargo from them to the shore.[251] A port tax was levied on each ship, known as *anchoragia*, but it does not seem to have varied as in Egypt according to the size of the vessel involved.[252] In Egypt most goods, once disembarked, were inspected and registered for taxation on an *ad valorem* basis, that is a charge which depended on the estimated value of the commodity and was usually expressed as a percentage, although there were commodities, such as wine, oil and grain, which were always regarded as measurable, the duty on them being established according to quantity.[253] In the same way as in the Byzantine Empire,[254] nothing was levied until after sale in the market. Between registration and sale a cargo might be stored in warehouses at the port side. Registration of goods seems also to have taken place in the Latin Syrian ports: there is evidence from as early as the 1120s that officers on the quayside checked the goods of and took declarations from arrivals to find out if they were bringing in anything dutiable.[255] There also seem to have been facilities for storage.[256] And payment of duty on goods to be sold – as opposed to those brought in for personal consumption or for re-export by land – was probably made in the market together with the sales tax, although it must be admitted that the evidence here is ambiguous.[257] The entry duty itself varied: at different times in the thirteenth century it was 10%, 8% and $5\frac{1}{4}$%.[258] It is possible that some goods were sold on the quayside under the supervision of officials of the *chaine*,[259] but most must have passed out of their jurisdiction on leaving the port area for the markets.

Goods being exported from Egypt were inspected, taxed and ferried to their ship, which was also taxed; and the captain had to pay for an official authorisation to depart. The export dues were taken on the quayside and, unlike the entry charges, were estimated according to quantity, not *ad valorem*, although the bill finally presented, expressed in terms of a percentage of the value, might be in a form indistinguishable from an *ad valorem* account. In the Latin East the export charges were certainly taken by the *chaine* and were imposed even on re-exports that had not found buyers in the markets.[260] The office had its own weights and measures for estimating the quantity of goods passing through it,[261] but it is not clear that there was a consistent method of establishing the dues to be paid: a surviving list of charges made in the *chaine*, at the gates and in the markets of Acre and drawn up possibly in mid-thirteenth century contains commodities charged by quantity instead of *ad valorem* among both imports and exports and some exports taxable on an *ad valorem* basis.[262] In Egypt, in accordance with contemporary economic doctrine, a charge was taken on the difference between what a merchant had brought in and what he was taking out, if the value of the goods being exported was higher than that of the imports. It is possible that this was also payable in Acre, for in 1257 the High Court exempted merchants of Ancona from paying 'all the surplus which they ought to pay to the *chaine*'.[263] An additional harbour tax, the *terciaria*, was levied on the passengers and sailors in a ship.[264]

The other means of entering or leaving a city was of course through the land gates, and revenues from these were important

to the lords: when Bohemond IV gave the Hospitallers a gate in
the walls of Tripoli in 1196, he stated that they were not to allow
the passage of anything taxable through it.[265] Usually the gates
were administered separately from the markets, those of Jerusalem, Tyre, Beirut, Tripoli and Ascalon being run by their own
offices.[266] The absence of any reference in the documents to the
revenues of the gates of Acre is striking and, although it may be
that the market officials in Acre also levied the entry charges on
goods that came in by land,[267] it is possible that a famous passage
in Ibn Jubair's description of his journey through Palestine pro-
vides a solution to the problem. In 1184 Ibn Jubair travelled to
Acre from Damascus in company with some merchants. On
arrival he and his companions were taken to a *khan* at the gate of
which there were Christian scribes who made out their accounts in
Arabic. These examined the baggage of those who were not merchants to see whether it contained anything taxable, a procedure
similar to the inspection and registration we have already seen in
the port. Ibn Jubair noted that the '*diwan*' to which they belonged
was held in farm by a man honoured with the title of '*sahib*': all
that was taken by the scribes belonged to him and he in turn paid
a large sum to the government.[268] He was certainly not referring
to the *chaine*, for he had just come into the city by land, while
grants made on the revenues of the markets by the king, one of
them in the previous year,[269] and references in the thirteenth century to the *Bailli of the Fonde*, a royal official,[270] suggest that the
markets were not farmed either. It seems to be most likely that he
was describing the officials at the gates of Acre and that the
absence of references to grants made on their revenues by the king
can be explained by the fact that they were held in farm.[271]

Gate officials seem to have laid a charge on all imports as well
as exports and it appears that in Acre they would demand from a
man who was not exempt an oath that he was bringing in a commodity for his own use – if so he merely paid a passage tax.[272] For
imports that were to be sold in the town the duty owed at the
gates was probably deferred, to be taken in the markets at the
same time as the sales tax.[273] Exports were charged in much the
same way as were those passing through the *chaine*, some tolls
being estimated according to the quantity of the commodity involved[274] and for some goods an *ad valorem* duty being imposed.[275]

After entering a town either through the port or by the land gates a merchant and his merchandise would make for the markets. In Acre and some other towns the more important markets seem to have been under the jurisdiction of officials of the *fonde* or *funda*: this word and the linked *fonticum/fondicum* were corruptions of the Arabic *funduq*, itself a transliteration of the Greek *pandokeia*, and they were to be found in many of the countries bordering on the Mediterranean. In Latin Syria, however, *fonde* could mean at least four different things. It could refer to a building, a *khan*, built round a large open courtyard, in which goods were stored and in the upper stories of which there were lodging rooms for visiting merchants: the *funduqs* of the Italians in Alexandria and other Muslim centres were of this type.[276] It could be used of a market in a *khan*-shaped building that ought technically to have been called a *qaisariya*, although markets, of course, were often merely held in a square or open space.[277] Market *funduqs* could belong to an individual owner – an Italian commune in Acre for instance – or could be devoted to the sale of a particular commodity,[278] although in Egypt and doubtless also in Latin Syria specialisation was by no means strictly observed.

The word *fonde*, moreover, seems to have been applied often not to one but to a group of markets combined under a single administration. This can be the only explanation of the miscellany of goods listed in the middle of the thirteenth century as being sold in the *fonde* of Acre,[279] and incidentally it may help to make clear a reference in the statute already mentioned, which was clumsily inserted into the list, to two *fondes*, 'en amont' and 'en aval'.[280] The second of these phrases may have been used of the 'low' part of Acre lying by the *Port de la Chaine*[281] where were collected the Italian markets; and the *Fonde en aval* may be a collective reference to these. The *Fonde en amont*, which was clearly the royal *fonde*,[282] must have been a group of squares and markets in the vicinity of the *funda regis* mentioned in a document of 1188 and situated in the south-east part of the town, not far from the walls – there was in fact a reference to the 'platea publica civitatis' in this area.[283] Finally, *fonde* could refer not to the markets themselves but to their administration: the *bailli* and jurors of the *Cour de la Fonde*, which in Acre and probably elsewhere had no rights of High Justice but concerned itself with minor commercial matters, debts, broken sureties and the like; we have seen that in Acre the four native and two Frankish jurors also had jurisdiction over indigenous residents.[284] Linked to the court was an office, staffed by sergeants, auctioneers, scribes and measurers,[285] that may have supervised the work of the *coretiers* who oversaw individual markets,[286] levied tolls, accounted revenues and granted out money-fiefs and rents.[287] In Acre the *funda regis* of 1188, which from the one reference to it was clearly a single building, could simply have been a house situated at the centre of the markets, in which sat the *Cour de la Fonde*.

It has been suggested that the surviving list of the charges made in the *Fonde* of Acre is incomplete, because it covers by no means all the goods that are known to have been sold in the city.[288] But it is clear that throughout Latin Syria there were always markets administered separately from the *fondes*: in Antioch the tannery and the wine and fish markets;[289] in Laodicea the tannery and the markets for dyestuffs, certain oils and fruit;[290] in Gibel the cloth market;[291] at Margat the market for dyestuffs;[292] in Tripoli the meat market, soapworks, tannery and the markets for dyestuffs and fish;[293] and in Acre certainly the meat market[294] and probably also the tannery.[295] It is also possible that whereas in many towns most of the markets were gathered under one administration, in Tyre, the second city of the kingdom, all were semi-independent and the control of commerce may have resembled that of Damascus, with the markets under the general supervision of a *muhtasib*: it is noteworthy that the only mention of this official in the documents of Latin Syria is to be found with reference to Tyre between 1210 and 1243 and we have seen that he is here to be found functioning in much the same way as did the Damascene *muhtasib* – as a commercial judge and a supervisor of the markets.[296]

The crusader John of Joinville, describing the capture of Damietta in 1249, wrote that the Christians set fire to 'the *fonde* where were all the merchandise and all the goods that are sold by weight'.[297] In any market many of the commodities involved in commercial transactions were weighed on scales provided by the lord by measurers appointed by him.[298] In the *fonde* of Acre, and clearly also elsewhere, taxes were levied after the sale and were estimated *ad valorem* on a percentage basis. In the middle of the thirteenth century the duty payable varied, depending on the commodity, from $4\frac{1}{6}\%$[299] to 25 %. Of these charges the most important seem to have been $4\frac{1}{6}\%$, although this was almost certainly a transit tax,[300] $8\frac{1}{3}$%, 10%, $11\frac{5}{24}$%, probably the standard tax since it was called 'dreiture enterine', and 25%, this last being laid mainly on local vegetables and fruit: these seem to have been generally lower than the Egyptian *khums* of 20% and often higher than the Byzantine *kommerkion* of 10%.[301]

In Egypt there were two possible ways of levying the market dues, depending on the kind of business dealings used by the merchants. When man-to-man bargains were struck by the traders, a Master of the Markets fixed official prices in consultation with the chief merchants. The resulting price lists, often changed, were not directives – bargains would be struck as usual – but they established the theoretical value of a commodity which was the basis for the *ad valorem* tax on it.[302] The second method was that of the public auction, the *halqa*, which was not popular with the merchants but had by 1200 become the most usual way of transacting business.[303] All the lots of a given commodity would be auctioned together in the market by an official auctioneer. Levying the duty was simple, for the tax was merely taken off the top of the total proceeds of an auction before they were divided among the merchants involved. Both methods seem to have been used in Acre, where there is evidence for the employment of *vendours de la vile*, clearly public auctioneers.[304] But whatever method of sale was used it seems that in most cases, as in Egypt and Constantinople, the burden of the tax was shared, being split between the seller and the buyer, who each paid half.[305] It has already been pointed out that exemptions from purchase tax, therefore, could affect only half of the revenue collected by a ruler. In the administration of commerce and the way in which revenues were drawn from it the ports of the Latin Kingdom functioned in much the same way as did those of Egypt, the Byzantine Empire and other Near Eastern states.

It must be emphasised that western feudalism, according to the customs of which the Christian lords in Palestine inherited and held their fiefs, did not supplant but overlaid and was itself affected by the instruments of another ancient system of government. Whatever the political and jurisdictional changes in Palestine after the First Crusade the villages and ports continued to be organised as they always had been and were exploited on the lords' behalf by a fairly sophisticated bureaucracy, run on traditional, oriental lines. This had profound results. The Palestinian economy remained one based on money. The feudatories were absentee, town-dwelling *rentiers* who drew revenues from villages, in the agriculture of which they had little direct interest, and enjoyed *fiefs-rentes*. While trade flowed strongly through the ports and markets there was at least the possibility of great wealth for the lords, with their cadastral agents and commercial offices, and their revenues must have enabled them and their vassals to live the kind of leisured existence without which the emergence of an important school of jurisprudence is unthinkable: it was in the 1230s, during the period of greatest prosperity, that the baronial movement was at its height. But large profits were dependent on a flourishing through-traffic of goods passing between East and West and trade began to decline after 1250. The lords had always been faced by great expenses, for the burdens of the defence of the Holy Land rested heavily on their shoulders. And for their survival they relied on prosperity in a far more delicate way than did their contemporaries in the West. A European lord could get into debt, but provided he was prepared to retrench and tolerate some alienation of land he could recover. In Latin Syria, especially after 1260, even a temporary decline in revenues would so lessen a fief-holder's ability to defend his lands against an ever-present foe that it could well result in his annihilation. It is not surprising that the lords in the Kingdom of Jerusalem were always concerned to preserve their sources of revenue and that despite their ideals they appear so often to have opted in their politics for pragmatic choices that were more likely to leave their incomes and therefore their fiefs intact.

II

CONSTITUTIONAL CONFLICT

THE FATHERS OF
THE BARONIAL MOVEMENT

ON 11 July 1174 King Amalric died of dysentery, leaving a son Baldwin who was to prove himself to be intelligent and brave, but was at this time barely thirteen years old and already stricken with leprosy. It was during Baldwin's reign, punctuated by periods in which the king was prostrated by illness, that there appeared a party of nobles expressing for the first time ideas which were to dominate the politics of the kingdom for over a century. We are fortunate in having an account of the reign which, although it was prejudiced in favour of this group of barons, was written by an eyewitness closely involved in the events he described. The chronicler William of Tyre had been Baldwin's tutor – it was he who had first noticed his leprosy[1] – and after 1174 was chancellor, remaining near the centre of the stage until 1182 or 1183 when he was forced to retire to Rome.

Four days after his father's death Baldwin was crowned, but he was too young to rule himself. It may be that before he had died Amalric had nominated as regent Miles of Plancy, a relative of his from Champagne whom he had made his seneschal and to whom he had married the widowed Stephanie of Milly, Lady of Oultrejourdain; this was certainly believed at a later date in Genoa,[2] although the Palestinian sources contain no evidence that such had been Amalric's intention. Indeed a curious passage in the Chronicle of William of Tyre suggests that Miles arranged for the regency to be held not by himself but by the Castellan of Jerusalem, Rohard of Jaffa, who had played a significant part in affairs since the 1150s when as one of his vassals he may have attracted the attention of Amalric, then Count of Jaffa.[3] According to William of Tyre Miles, while keeping up the pretence of Rohard's superior position, in effect ran the kingdom, but a group of nobles, led by Count Raymond of Tripoli, took objection to his control of the government. It is noteworthy that from the first they looked for a lawful method of removing him. Raymond came before the boy king and formally claimed the regency himself, arguing that he was the richest and most powerful of the lords and that he was Baldwin's nearest relative, being the son of a younger daughter of Baldwin II; he seems to have suggested that it was because of this relationship that King Amalric had been regent of his county while he had been a prisoner of the Muslims between 1164 and 1172. Raymond was here proposing that the regency should automatically devolve on the *plus dreit heir aparant*, the nearest relative of the royal line present in the East, a concept that was to underlie a major theme in the constitutional history of the kingdom in the thirteenth century. We shall see that although the idea was far from being revolutionary – there are many western parallels – it was new as far as the Crown of Jerusalem was concerned. Raymond's position was strengthened, whether by accident or design, by the assassination in Acre of Miles of Plancy, who, it was rumoured, had been seeking support from the West; and at a full meeting of the High Court, which debated the matter for two days, Raymond was granted the regency. He was to hold it until the king came of age in 1177.[4]

The claims of Raymond of Tripoli are of great interest not only because he used arguments which were later to be elaborated by the jurists, but also because in William of Tyre's account of the discussions there is revealed a party of nobles with whom we are going to become very familiar. At its head was Raymond himself, a lord of the kingdom proper by reason of his recent marriage to Eschiva of Bures, the Lady of the great fief of Galilee, and it included Humphrey Lord of Toron and Reynald Lord of Sidon, two of the greatest fief-holders and the heads of old-established families, and Baldwin Lord of Ramle and his brother Balian of Nablus, the leading members of the house of Ibelin.[5] In 1174 therefore the three men who can be regarded as the progenitors of the baronial movement, Raymond of Tripoli, Reynald of Sidon and Balian of Nablus, can be seen acting together for the first time. It is conventional for historians of Latin Syria to regard them and their followers as the leaders of a native baronage which had now found its feet and during the next two decades represented the interests of the old-established settlers, seeking an understanding with Islamic powers and unwilling to participate in risky schemes proposed by aggressive and adventurous

newcomers like Miles of Plancy and Reynald of Châtillon.[6] This
is certainly the impression of their attitudes given by William of
Tyre, but it is worth asking whether we are being misled.

According to William, Miles of Plancy was an indiscreet, proud
and arrogant man who made certain of the barons envious and
worried because

> he ignored them and never convoked them and was always alone at
> the side of the king; he conducted the business of the kingdom with-
> out consulting the others, who were excluded from the king's
> entourage.[7]

To any constitutional historian of the twelfth century these words
have a familiar ring about them. As monarchy developed it tended
to take the conduct of affairs more and more into its own hands
and to use advisers of its own choosing – this had been no less true
of Amalric of Jerusalem than it had been of Henry I or Henry II
of England. To feudatories everywhere, increasingly banished
from the circles in which important decisions were made, their
service of *consilium*, which in the past had often been a burdensome
duty, became a precious right; the baronial movement in England,
for instance, seems to have seen the structure of the state in terms
of a natural order in which the counsellors of a king should be
those to whom birth and the feudal contract had given the rightful
duty of advising him. The arguments against Miles of Plancy
presented by William of Tyre sound very like those used against
the *novi homines* of the English kings, and it looks as though suspicion of royal counsellors drawn from outside the ranks of the
established baronage was at least an element in the thought of
Raymond and his supporters. If this is so, then in the narrative
that follows we must ask ourselves whether the circle round
Baldwin that included Reynald of Châtillon, Joscelin of Courtenay
and Aimery of Lusignan was made up of royalists rather than
militant adventurers.

There were however at least two other factors at work. It was
apparent to all that the kingdom was seriously threatened by a
resurgent Islam. The Franks were now faced by the union of
Egypt and Syria under Saladin, who gained control of Damascus
only four months after Amalric's death. There was obviously a
need for strong and experienced government and in these circumstances personal ambitions were bound to arise. Raymond of

Tripoli had real ability and in recent years has had a good press,[8] but a different picture of him is to be found in those sources which did not originate from among baronial sympathisers in Latin Syria. In the West he was almost universally condemned for the part he was to play in the 1180s.[9] The Muslims, with whom he was prepared to ally himself to further his designs, believed that he wanted power for himself[10] and this was also reported by a Genoese annalist, who wrote that he claimed to represent a more legitimate line of the royal house of Jerusalem than did the holders of the crown, because his mother, Hodierna, had been born while her father, King Baldwin II, was ruling over Jerusalem and there-fore had a better right than her sister Melisende, Baldwin IV's grandmother, who had been born while Baldwin II was still Count of Edessa: an argument that was historically erroneous but was based on the concept of the *porphyrogenitus* and very similar to what we shall see proposed on behalf of Isabella of Jerusalem in 1183.[11] In 1180 Baldwin thought that Raymond, acting with the Prince of Antioch, was out to seize the kingdom[12] and in 1181 or 1182 he refused him entry into the Holy Land because he had heard that he was planning to supplant him; it was only with difficulty that the count's supporters persuaded the king that his fears were groundless. At about this time Baldwin may indeed have been thinking of abdication and his envoys offered the crown to the Kings of England and France. In a passage of uncharacteristic vehemence William of Tyre reported that this crisis was a consequence of the schemings of the party round the king,[13] but we must be allowed to question whether Raymond was as blameless as William made him out to be.

The appearance of pretenders was a natural result of the physical decline of the royal line and Raymond of Tripoli was not the only one: in 1177 Count Philip of Flanders, representing the elder branch of the house of Boulogne to which the Kings of Jerusalem belonged, came East in what seems to have been the hope of gain-ing the crown.[14] Baldwin IV was incapable of having children and assured only of a short life, and although his sister Sibylla had a son, also called Baldwin, of her marriage in 1176 to William Long-Sword, the eldest son of the Marquis of Montferrat, it was clear by 1183 that this child was himself sickly and unlikely to attain manhood. The deaths both of the king and the child Baldwin would leave as heirs to the throne Baldwin IV's two sisters Sibylla and Isabella. Sibylla was a full sister and as such was his closest relative and the natural heiress. Her case had moreover the support of certain prestigious figures in the kingdom. Her mother Agnes's brother, the Seneschal Joscelin of Courtenay, titular Count of Edessa, became after 1179 a great landowner in Palestine, partly by reason of grants made to him by the king.[15] Reynald of Châtillon, the powerful Lord of Oultrejourdain, was an ally of the Courtenays for reasons that cannot now be established: his friendship for the Counts of Edessa may have dated from the time when he had been Prince of Antioch. These were later to be joined by the new Patriarch Heraclius, a worldly and rather ignorant cleric who openly paraded his mistress, known as the Patriarchess, round Jerusalem and owed his appointment in 1180 to Agnes's favour,[16] and by the Master of the Templars from 1185, Gerard of Ridefort, who had a long-standing personal grudge against Raymond of Tripoli.[17] Sibylla had in her favour, then, not only the normal rights of inheritance but also the support of a powerful group of nobles and Church leaders. It was this party which in the six years after his coming of age had been favoured by the king. His mother Agnes of Courtenay can be seen exercising great influence; Joscelin of Courtenay was granted important estates; Reynald of Châtillon was made the King's lieutenant during his first serious illness in 1177.[18] On the other hand Baldwin had consistently shown suspicion of Raymond of Tripoli, whose allies suffered. Although Humphrey of Toron's grandson and heir, who was also heir to Oultrejourdain, had been betrothed to the king's younger sister, he had been forced to surrender his fief of Toron and Chastel Neuf, which was granted to Agnes.[19] And William of Tyre failed to gain the patriarchate and was driven into exile.

Sibylla's first husband died in 1177 and in 1179 it was planned to wed her to the Duke of Burgundy. But at this time she was violently in love with Baldwin of Ramle, the elder of the Ibelins. Baldwin was captured by the Muslims in June 1179 and Sibylla contrived to send a message to him in Damascus, assuring him that she would ask her brother to allow them to marry once he was free. But when the Muslims, who demanded a ransom of 200,000 besants, released him he returned to Jerusalem to find that she wanted the ransom paid off completely before she would consider marriage. She said that she did not want her lands burdened with debts, but her feelings for him must have been cooling. Although Baldwin was given the money to pay his ransom by the

Byzantine Emperor Manuel, to whom he was related by marriage, he came back from a visit to Constantinople with his prospects gone. In his absence his son-in-law, Aimery of Lusignan, had persuaded Sibylla and Agnes that his own younger brother Guy was good-looking and ready for marriage and at their bidding had returned to France to fetch him. Sibylla at once succumbed to Guy's charms and with her mother's support persuaded the king to allow her to marry him at Easter 1180.[20] This story is curious above all because of the speed with which King Baldwin agreed to Sibylla's marriage to an unknown and relatively undistinguished knight at a time when the news of a breakdown in the negotiations with the Duke of Burgundy had not yet reached Palestine. It was rumoured that the couple were already lovers, but it should be remembered that at this time Bohemond of Antioch and Raymond of Tripoli were approaching the northern frontier with armed men and the king feared lest they wanted to seize his kingdom. It was later believed in the West that the Count of Tripoli wished to marry Sibylla himself, and it is possible that Baldwin had to act quickly to frustrate such a design.[21] Although he was brave – he showed this above all in 1189 – and was to be a success as ruler of Cyprus, Guy's early career in Palestine was disastrous, and appeared to justify the views of those of the nobles whose ideas were given voice by the chroniclers. To them he was a handsome but arrogant fool and a debauchee, scorned even by his brother Geoffrey.[22] Guy was thrust into a position for which he was unprepared. Criticised by jealous rivals and given no chance to find his feet, he had to learn by the experience of his mistakes. In the 1180s he aroused hostilities that were profoundly to affect the course of events over the next decade.

Early in 1183 the king, again desperately ill, was persuaded to give up trying to rule and to grant Guy the administration of the kingdom, only reserving for himself the city of Jerusalem and an annual rent of 10,000 besants. The feudatories were divided on the matter and while we need not attribute to those behind Guy the base motives ascribed to them by William of Tyre we know from his Chronicle what was the reaction of the members of Raymond of Tripoli's party: they did not believe that Guy was experienced enough for the task and they were worried by the ambitions of his supporters. What the High Court, or a section of it, thought was in fact quite irrelevant, for the king had every right to choose whomsoever he wished to be his lieutenant; but it may have been to appease the opposition that Guy was made to promise that while the king lived he would not aspire to the throne or alienate royal lands or change the castellans in royal cities and castles.[23] Guy now foolishly played into the hands of his opponents: he conducted a hesitant campaign against Saladin and he became angry when the king wanted to exchange the city of Jerusalem for Tyre. Baldwin, obviously deeply hurt, turned for the first time since 1177 to the baronial party and even Agnes came out openly against her son-in-law – perhaps in the circumstances there was nothing else she could do. Guy was removed from the *bailliage* and Baldwin reassumed power; on the advice of the barons – and especially mentioned by William of Tyre were again Raymond of Tripoli, Reynald of Sidon, Baldwin of Ramle and Balian of Nablus – he crowned Sibylla's son by her first marriage his co-ruler as Baldwin V, passing over her rights to the throne; the child was carried to his coronation by Balian of Nablus. Baldwin began to negotiate with the Church in the hope of finding grounds for the annulment of his sister's marriage[24] and he seems to have promised Raymond of Tripoli the regency in the event of his own death.[25] Guy retired to his county of Jaffa and Ascalon and although Jaffa opened its gates to Baldwin the town of Ascalon defied him. An attempt by the patriarch and the Masters of the Temple and the Hospital to intercede for Guy with the king came to nothing and Guy made his position worse by massacring some Bedouin near Ascalon who owed tribute to the crown. This senselessly vindictive act seems to have been the cause of the immediate appointment by the king of Raymond of Tripoli as his lieutenant, while Patriarch Heraclius was dispatched with an embassy to the West to offer Philip of France or Henry of England the overlordship of Jerusalem.[26]

Disappointment in, even hatred of, Guy had led Baldwin to take extravagant and illegitimate steps and Raymond and his supporters were ready to take advantage of them. But although the king, according to one account after a vote in the High Court, had promised Raymond the regency after his death, he had no right to do this. On his demise Raymond's lieutenancy would naturally lapse and the very precedent established for the choice of regent in 1174 would bar him from the regency now. Baldwin V's *plus dreit heir aparant* was Sibylla and she and Guy, who could not be countenanced as ruler, would succeed to the regency. The child moreover was himself sickly and in the event of his death Sibylla and Guy would inherit the crown. Some way of overruling their rights had to be found. Raymond therefore made certain conditions before he would consider holding the regency after Baldwin IV's death. He refused to have custody of Baldwin V, because he might be blamed if the child died before he came of age; Baldwin V was to be put into the care of his great-uncle Joscelin of Courtenay. Royal castles were to be entrusted to the Templars and Hospitallers. Raymond was to be repaid for expenses incurred during his regency; it was agreed that he should be given the Lordship of Beirut. But a final condition reveals something of the processes of thought behind the political moves being made, and how the count's supporters were developing an answer to their dilemma. Raymond had first suggested that if Baldwin V were to die before coming of age the regency should be given to his *plus dreit heir aparant*, presumably Sibylla, until the pope, counselled by the western emperor and the Kings of England and France, had decided which of the two royal sisters had the better claim to the throne. But there were protests at this – clearly if the inheritance was disputed so would be the regency – and Raymond agreed that he would continue to govern the kingdom until it had been decided who was the rightful heir.[27]

It is clear that Raymond's party now planned to prevent Sibylla's accession by throwing doubt on her position as *plus dreit heir aparant*. It was suggested that she was the daughter of an illegitimate and annulled marriage with Agnes, which King Amalric had been forced to repudiate before the patriarch would crown him, and that she had never been legitimised.[28] Only her sister Isabella, moreover, had been born to Amalric while he held the throne:[29] behind this argument might be seen the ideas of Isabella's mother, the Byzantine Maria Comnena now married to Balian of Nablus and thus closely allied to the baronial party,[30] proposing the prior claims of a child 'born into the purple'. But on his accession Amalric had insisted on the legitimisation of his children[31] and Sibylla had been enfeoffed with a royal apanage, while her young and inexperienced husband had been given the lieutenancy in 1183. And if Sibylla was illegitimate so then too were Baldwin IV and Baldwin V, both of them descendants of Amalric and Agnes. The dying king must have had an almost pathological hatred of Guy of Lusignan, since by permitting the questioning of his sister's legitimacy he was implicitly raising doubts about his own.

Baldwin IV died in March 1185 and Baldwin V in August 1186. The events that followed the latter death are well known. Joscelin of Courtenay persuaded Raymond of Tripoli to go to Tiberias while he sent the king's body to Jerusalem in the care of the Templars. He took possession of Acre and Beirut in Sibylla's name while she and her knights hurried to Jerusalem, where they were joined by Reynald of Châtillon. The Courtenays now held most of the royal domain and all Raymond of Tripoli could do was to summon the baronage to Nablus while Sibylla first buried her son and then, on the advice of the patriarch and Gerard of Ridefort, called the feudatories to attend her coronation, proclaiming publicly that the kingdom had escheated to her by hereditary right. The nobles at Nablus refused her invitation on the ground that by participating in her coronation they would break the oaths they had all made in the presence of Baldwin IV to follow Raymond of Tripoli; and inside Jerusalem they were supported by the Master of the Hospitallers who was forced only with difficulty to surrender his key to the treasury, one of the three needed to open the chest in which were the regalia. Sibylla's partisans had to improvise. In their view she was succeeding as rightful heiress, but, as they had taken the precaution of closing the city gates of Jerusalem to her opponents, a proper *collaudatio*, the open recognition of her rights of inheritance by all those at her coronation, would be lacking. They seem to have substituted for it the acclamation of the people of the city, to whom Reynald of Châtillon made a speech in which he emphasised Sibylla's rights as the *plus dreit heir aparant* and appealed for their acceptance. Sibylla was then crowned in the Church of the Holy Sepulchre by the patriarch and she herself crowned Guy, after Heraclius had formally renounced his rights in the matter by asking her to choose her own consort.[32] This revolutionary act caught the imagination of contemporaries,[33] but we should not be misled into thinking that Sibylla's accession was itself unconstitutional. It was far more in accord with convention than the arrangements made for Raymond of Tripoli's government and sworn to by the vassals in the last months of Baldwin IV's life.

Nor must it be supposed that Sibylla was opposed by a majority of the feudatories. Of the greater fief-holders only Joscelin of Courtenay and Reynald of Châtillon are known to have supported her, but these two men had great power at their disposal, and weight would have been added to Sibylla's cause by the adherence of the patriarch and the Master of the Templars. There must have been some vassals who would have found it difficult to commit themselves to one side or the other: William of Tyre in his narrative of earlier events implied that the feudatories were by no means unanimously behind Raymond of Tripoli.[34] The strength of the parties moreover would to some extent depend on the numbers of rear-vassals at their disposal, not only because of the military might they could command, but also because in theory at least the rear-vassals were members of the High Court and therefore had substantial political power. Sibylla and Guy controlled the County of Jaffa and Ascalon and the royal domain around Jerusalem; after subtracting the Ibelin vassals from the *servitia debita* of the county this gave them service from 91 knights. Joscelin of Courtenay could contribute a further 24 knights from his own lands and he was probably in possession of the fief of Toron and Chastel Neuf;[35] the service of Chastel Neuf is not known, but that of Toron without the rear-fief of Maron, which was in the hands of Humphrey of Toron,[36] was perhaps 15 knights. Joscelin moreover had secured for Sibylla the royal domain round Acre, providing either 76 or 80 knights, and the lordship of Beirut, with 21. Reynald of Châtillon could bring 60 knights from his fiefs of Oultrejourdain and Hebron. We do not know whether the Courtenays controlled the royal domain round Tyre, with 28 knights, but even accounting for absenteeism, minorities, the inaccuracy of the figures and sympathy for Raymond of Tripoli on the part of individual vavasours, we have already accounted for nearly half the total knightage of the kingdom. To it we should add vassals from the Templar lands, some of which, like the area around Saphet, may have somewhat diminished the contributions from baronial lordships. Against Sibylla, Raymond of Tripoli could provide 80 or 100 knights from his Principality of Galilee.[37] Baldwin of Ramle could bring in 40 from his lordship and his brother Balian 10 from Ibelin and between 81 and 85 from Nablus. The Hospitallers might have been able to provide service from some of their estates and Humphrey of Toron could call up 4[38] knights from Maron. So far we have a total figure that is smaller than that at Sibylla's disposal, but there remain the possible contributions of the episcopate – 16 knights – and of the fiefs of Darum, with 2 knights, and Sidon, Caesarea and Bethsan, which amounted to 100. The partisanship of the patriarch may have made the bishops reluctant to take sides and Reynald of Sidon, though indubitably a baronial supporter, had been married to Agnes of Courtenay and may have found himself in an embarrassing situation.[39] But even if he had brought his vassals to Nablus, the number of knights with Raymond would have been only slightly greater than those with Sibylla.[40]

The position of the feudatories at Nablus cannot have been as strong as their apologists later pretended and their reactions to the news of Sibylla's coronation are comprehensible once the nearly equal strength of the two parties is assumed. Baldwin of Ramle made a hysterical speech in which he threatened to leave the country to avoid being shamed by its loss, since Guy of Lusignan was a fool and would be 'led astray by the counsel of those who know nothing': a reference presumably to Reynald of Châtillon and Joscelin of Courtenay. Raymond of Tripoli pulled them out of their panic by suggesting that they immediately crown Isabella and her young husband Humphrey of Toron – desperate and unconstitutional advice that would have led to civil war – and he referred to his special relationship with Saladin, stating clearly that if need arose they could receive Muslim help. All agreed to crown Isabella and Humphrey, but that night Humphrey, perhaps hoping to recover the fief of Toron, fled to Jerusalem and submitted. His defection ended the rebellion and most of the feudatories made their peace, although Raymond of Tripoli retired to Tiberias to continue his resistance and Baldwin of Ramle made an unpleasant scene in Guy's presence before leaving for the Principality of Antioch. The revolt was over by late October 1186.[41]

With Muslim help and the scarcely disguised support of ex-partisans like Balian of Nablus Raymond held out in Tiberias until the following summer when, shocked at the annihilation at the Springs of Cresson of a combined force of Hospitallers and Templars by a Muslim army which he had allowed into Galilee, he came to terms with Guy at the intermediation of, among others, Balian of Nablus and Reynald of Sidon.[42] His reasons for refusing to make peace before this are interesting. He no longer challenged Sibylla and Guy's coronation, but complained that he had been dispossessed of Beirut which, it will be remembered, had been given to him to cover the expenses of the regency and had been seized by Joscelin of Courtenay in 1186; when Raymond's supporters had decided to submit to Guy they had promised to see that he was reimbursed.[43] But in spite of Raymond's protestations there seems to have been no question of an appeal to the High Court for judgement on the matter: Raymond of course had not yet paid homage to Guy and so that court could have no jurisdiction. And it is from the Muslims, who after all were close to Raymond, that we learn that Guy was demanding from him an account of the revenues he had received from the *secrete*: it may have been that the count had been guilty of maladministration.[44]

The story of Guy and Sibylla's assumption of power is not an edifying one. Sibylla's rights to the throne might have been unquestioned were it not for Guy's folly and the ambitions of Raymond of Tripoli. There can be no doubt however that it was in this crisis that the baronial movement began to be hammered into shape. And the aims of Isabella's adherents were not finally extinguished in the débâcle of 1186, for a movement, focusing not on constitutional issues but on the hereditary claims of the younger princess, was to grow as the years went by.

Political differences were put aside in the months that followed the disaster which befell the largest army ever put into the field by the kingdom at Hattin on 4 July 1187. In the late summer and autumn, as Saladin stormed through Palestine, confining the Christians to the city of Tyre on the coast and a few inland strongholds, the only concern of their leaders was survival. Under the pressure of events a commune, a sworn association of clerics, knights and burgesses, took over the government of Tyre,[45] but there seems to have been no challenge to the rights of Sibylla, absent in the north, and Guy, in a Muslim prison, although Raymond of Tripoli, Balian of Nablus and Reynald of Sidon had been among the few who had escaped from the Battle of Hattin.[46] Late in July or early in August Conrad of Montferrat, an ambitious, swashbuckling man who had already had an adventurous career in Greece, arrived in the Near East. Narrowly escaping capture by the Muslims when his ship put into Acre ignorant of its fall, he eventually reached Tyre.[47] The city was placed in his custody until, according to a Genoese source, the expected arrival of one of the kings of England, France or Sicily or the western emperor whom it was hoped were coming on crusade.[48] It has been suggested that this provision was influenced by the oath of 1183 according to which, it will be remembered, western rulers were to be involved in a decision upon the inheritance to the throne, but the new circumstances make this unlikely. With most of Palestine lost and a crusade expected, whatever was taken would not necessarily revert to the crown but could belong personally to the crusaders by the most absolute right of possession then known, the right of conquest: on 4 July 1190 at Vézelay the Kings of France and England decided to share their conquests with, it seems, no thought of an earlier possessor.[49] If therefore the King of Jerusalem wanted a certain title to his kingdom he must reconquer it himself, which explains Guy of Lusignan's daring attempt to take Acre in 1189. In 1187 it must have seemed unlikely that Guy or anyone else in the East would have the resources to reoccupy Palestine and the nobles in Tyre may well have realised that the attitude of the crusader kings towards the crown would be vital.

Conrad of Montferrat defended Tyre vigorously, but although at least as late as May 1188 he was recognising the kingship his own ambitions were perhaps reflected in his issuing of charters concerning other localities in Palestine over which he had no rights.[50] When Guy of Lusignan was released by Saladin in the summer of 1188 Conrad made public his personal views, referring to Guy, in a letter written in September to the Archbishop of Canterbury, as a man who had 'once been king'.[51] He would not allow Guy's brother Geoffrey entry into Tyre[52] and when in the following spring the king and queen themselves came before the city they found its gates closed to them.[53] There are several versions of the reasons Conrad gave for denying the crowned monarch admittance to a royal city. In one he claimed to have been received as lord of Tyre by the people while Guy was a prisoner of Saladin.[54] In another he argued that the city was his by right of conquest, presumably because his efforts had saved it: Tyre, he said, had been given to him by God.[55] In one of the less trustworthy chronicles he was reported to have claimed that Guy had lost the throne because he had lost the land,[56] and other contemporaries had heard that he had promised to surrender Tyre to whomsoever was the rightful king or heir to the kingdom, perhaps a reference to Isabella or to a decision on the throne to be made by the approaching crusaders.[57] At any rate it is clear that

Conrad believed that he now had personal rights over Tyre and would not recognise Guy's kingship.

Conrad does not seem to have been moved by anything more exalted than greed. It is indicative that, although he had the support of the Genoese and the Archbishop of Tyre, the Pisans and the Hospitallers, both of whom had originally helped him, went over to Guy. The Templars were opposed to him – they had consistently supported Guy – but at this time so were the feudatories of Jerusalem. As early as September 1188 Conrad was complaining of the opposition of the magnates and when in April 1189 Guy marched south to lay siege to Acre he was joined by the vassals; in the following autumn there are to be found with him Hugh and William of Tiberias, Geoffrey Le Tor and Balian of Nablus.[58] Guy's brave initiative and the support of the baronage for it tipped the scales in his favour. In September 1189 the crusading Margrave Louis of Thuringia persuaded Conrad to join the siege of Acre[59] and by 11 April 1190 Conrad had made his peace with Guy in return for the possession of Tyre, Sidon and Beirut. Of these only Tyre was in Christian hands, but the theoretical cession of the others is interesting: it is not to be supposed that the old Lords of Sidon were to be dispossessed of their lands if they came back under Frankish rule, but rather that a new super-fief, like that of Jaffa and Ascalon, was to be created in the north of Palestine.[60]

Sibylla had born Guy two daughters, but in the autumn of 1190 she and they died.[61] Isabella was now indubitably the heiress to the kingdom, but Guy believed that he could retain the crown as an anointed king who had received the homage of the fief-holders. In law it was doubtful if his rights could survive his wife's death and his coronation had been itself suspect because he had not been crowned by the patriarch and had not received acclamation from the feudatories. But it is clear that Isabella's chances of supplanting Guy were weakened not by objective legal considerations, but, like her sister four years before, by the character of her husband. Humphrey of Toron, though learned, was believed to be an effeminate and cowardly weakling, unfitted, in Conrad's words, to be king. He had antagonised his mother-in-law by being unwilling to let her see her daughter and he had alienated the baronial party by submitting so tamely to Sibylla and Guy in 1186.[62] Conrad of Montferrat now allied himself to Maria Comnena and a group of nobles led by Maria's husband, Balian of Nablus, and including Reynald of Sidon and Pagan of Haifa: their links with the men who had supported Raymond of Tripoli after 1174 and had gathered defiantly in Nablus in 1186 were emphasised by one hostile contemporary, probably a Templar, who wrote that had Raymond still been living he would have been one of their leaders.[63] They planned to have Isabella's marriage to Humphrey annulled and to marry her to Conrad; and they abducted her from her tent next to that of her husband in the camp before Acre. Many years later a witness called Hugh of St Maurice told a papal commission sitting in France that he had shared Humphrey's tent at this time and remembered Humphrey saying to him, 'Lord Hugh, I fear lest those who are with my wife will make her say something diabolical.' One of Humphrey's knights had come in to tell him that Isabella had been taken away. Humphrey had followed her and had said to her, 'Lady this is not the right way to your lodging. Come back with me'; but she, looking to the ground, had turned and gone another way.[64] Once she had her daughter in her power, Maria set out to persuade her to agree to be parted from Humphrey. Isabella, who seems genuinely to have loved her husband, at first resisted, but she was in the end borne down by her dominating mother's arguments: that Humphrey would never make a good ruler and would not be accepted as king and that anyway the marriage was invalid because she had been betrothed to him before the age of consent.[65]

The abduction caused a great stir in the Christian camp. There was general sympathy for Humphrey – indeed it is clear from the testimony given to the papal commission that the crusaders later believed their failure was a divine punishment for this sinful act – but at the time there was the conviction, fostered by the greater barons, that the parting of Humphrey and Isabella and her remarriage to Conrad was in the kingdom's interests: when Humphrey complained to what seems to have been a meeting of the High Court, most of those present argued that the needs of the crusade and the Latin settlement outweighed his rights. Conrad, meanwhile, had gained the support of the Bishop of Beauvais, a cousin of King Philip of France, and of the papal legate, Archbishop Albert of Pisa, who seems to have been hoping that his fellow citizens would be rewarded if Conrad became king. An ecclesiastical court was established which was asked to give judgement on three arguments: that Isabella had been too young when she had been betrothed; that she had not consented to the marriage; and that it had not been consummated. Humphrey strongly denied the last two allegations but, when challenged before the court to a duel by a visiting French crusader called Guy of Senlis, he was not prepared to take up the gage – in law he was quite right not to do so – and, persuaded by those opposed to him that he was not capable of governing the kingdom, abandoned his resistance. The legate then ruled the marriage to be invalid and on 24 November Isabella was wedded to Conrad. Deeply shocked by these iniquitous – and to us pathetic – proceedings, the Archbishop of Canterbury, who had represented in court the sick Patriarch of Jerusalem, excommunicated those concerned in the new marriage.[66] Even if both of Conrad's previous wives were dead – a matter of some doubt – the match was in canon law incestuous, because Isabella's sister had been married to Conrad's brother William Longsword, and bigamous, because the dissolution of her marriage to Humphrey was later established to have been illegitimate.[67]

As soon as she was freed from her ties to Humphrey Isabella seems to have formally required from the High Court the kingdom as rightful heiress. She was accepted and homage was paid her; and her first act was to return to Humphrey the fiefs of Toron and Chastel Neuf to which he had reasserted his claims in 1186.[68] But matters had not been finally resolved. The feudatories had accepted Isabella's claim, but she and Conrad had not been crowned, perhaps because the patriarch refused to recognise their marriage, perhaps because it was realised that the retaking of Palestine by the approaching crusaders would put them in the position to grant or deny their conquests to one or the other of the claimants for the throne. As far as the High Court was concerned it had given notice to the crusading kings that it no longer recognised Guy as king and that the fealty of the vassals was owed to Isabella,[69] but an outright clash was avoided because Guy remained before Acre while Conrad and Isabella went back to Tyre.

On 20 April and 8 June respectively King Philip of France and King Richard of England arrived before Acre. The presence of the two kings and the impending fall of the most important port in

Palestine encouraged the rivals to raise their claims once more. The Christian army was divided, Conrad being supported by Philip of France and his contingent, the barons of Jerusalem, the Templars and the Genoese; and Guy by Richard of England and his soldiers, Count Henry of Champagne, the Hospitallers and the Pisans: it would appear that the Military Orders and Henry of Champagne had switched sides.[70] Guy of Lusignan laid a formal complaint before the two kings, who agreed to adjudicate. This suited Guy, but to Conrad his wife was a legitimate heiress, the recognition of whom was a decision only for the High Court of Jerusalem, not visiting potentates. When Geoffrey of Lusignan appealed Conrad before the kings, accusing him of breach of faith, perjury and treason, Conrad refused to stand trial and left for Tyre. But he could not afford to overlook the crusaders' rights of conquest. Philip and Richard soon agreed not to keep their acquisitions but to give them all to the man whom they decided was rightful ruler, and they decreed that when Acre was captured the royal rents in the city were to be put into the custody of the Templars and Hospitallers until they had made their choice. Conrad seems to have realised that intransigence would get him nowhere and that it was important to see that his ally, Philip of France, acquired as much by conquest as did Richard. He was soon back in Acre, advising Philip on how to ensure a fair division of spoils.[71]

Acre capitulated on 12 July. On the 26th Conrad, advised by Philip, came before Richard and accepted his jurisdiction. On the following day both claimants formally asked for arbitration from the kings and the crusading army, Conrad demanding the throne of Jerusalem by right of his wife, Guy arguing that once crowned he could not be deposed. On the 28th Richard and Philip announced their decision, which was a compromise: Guy was to have the kingdom for the rest of his life, but no children of his were to have rights of succession; after his death Isabella and Conrad would inherit the throne. Meanwhile all royal rents were to be shared by the rivals; Guy's brother Geoffrey was to have the old royal apanage of Jaffa and Ascalon, and the precedent of the previous year was followed in the establishment of a new county for Conrad, made up of Tyre, Sidon and Beirut; if Guy, Conrad and Isabella all died while Richard was still in the East, he could dispose of the kingdom as he saw fit. On the following day Philip of France, against Richard's wishes, gave Conrad his half of Acre before returning home.[72]

Richard remained in Palestine and was ready to give Guy the territories he took. The policy now followed by Conrad and his partisans, who were not satisfied by the compromise, was to try to undermine Richard's campaign, while treating with the Muslims in the hope of bringing about personal accessions of territory that would be unaffected by Richard's rights of conquest. Conrad refused to help Richard, as did those French crusaders who had not left with Philip. He was treating with the Muslims in the summer – in July he was believed to be in league with them – and during the following winter he was negotiating with Saladin through Balian of Nablus and Reynald of Sidon, who were both seen in Jerusalem by one of Richard's emissaries. It was rumoured that he was not only discussing a treaty to cover his own county but was also trying to get from the sultan the grant of half of the city and Kingdom of Jerusalem. He was assassinated in April 1192 just before the ratification of a treaty between him and Saladin and later, in the final truce, the Palestinian barons seem to have received back their lordships directly from the sultan.[73]

Meanwhile, in February 1192 the Genoese and the French had tried to seize Acre for Conrad, who came down from Tyre, and it was the Pisans who saved the town until Richard's return. After a frustrating meeting at Casal Imbert, at which Conrad again refused to help the crusade, Richard presided over an assembly of the army which pronounced that he should be deprived of his rents,[74] but this was impossible to put into effect. It was becoming increasingly clear that Guy would never be able to rule the kingdom and, knowing that he must soon return to Europe, Richard called a second council of the crusading army which, considering that Guy had not been able to recover his share of the kingdom and that Conrad was abler than he was, begged Richard to make Conrad king. The failure of Guy to gain general acceptance and his own imminent departure forced Richard to agree, although he compensated Guy with the lordship of Cyprus. His emissaries announced to Conrad: 'Lord Marquis, the king and the Christian host at Ascalon has granted you the crown and kingdom of Syria. Come with your army, summoned by ban, and bravely conquer your kingdom.'[75] But although Conrad and his supporters had gained their ends, the assemblies of Richard's army, and parti-

cularly the second, show that at this time possession of the crown
de facto – and as far as the crusaders were concerned *de jure* –
derived not from hereditary rights, nor from a decision on these
rights by the High Court of Jerusalem, but from a choice made by
the crusaders, the conquerors, themselves.

Within a few weeks Conrad was dead, struck down in Tyre by
members of the Order of the Assassins.[76] The question of a husband for Isabella again arose and the choice fell on Richard's
nephew, Henry of Champagne. There are two different accounts
of the events leading up to his marriage, one told by a Latin
Syrian and the other by an English chronicler. To the Palestinian
writer it resulted from an initiative by Richard. On hearing of
Conrad's death he and Henry set out for Tyre, because they feared
lest the Pisans in that city would take advantage of the confusion
to reinstate Guy of Lusignan. On their arrival Richard persuaded
a reluctant Henry [77] to wed Isabella, promising him aid in the reconquest of the Holy Land and even offering him Cyprus, for
which Guy had not yet paid him all he owed. Henry married
Isabella and most of the feudatories, including the barons, swore
that his heirs would have precedence over those of Conrad; if this
promise was ever made – and it looks like a later addition inter-
polated perhaps for political reasons – it was never kept.[78] Richard
plays a very different part in an English chronicle, in which Henry
came to Tyre alone and was approached by the people, who
begged him to marry Isabella and receive the kingship. He replied
that he was willing, provided that to the 'election of the baronage'
he could add the assent of the King of England. Richard wanted
him to become king, but was concerned about so dubious a
marriage, for Humphrey of Toron was still alive. If Henry
accepted however, he promised to give him Acre and its rents,
Tyre and Jaffa and rights of jurisdiction 'over all conquered land'.
Henry, worried by his uncle's doubts, at first resisted the demands
of the feudatories, but when Isabella, who was beautiful, herself
sent him the keys of Tyre, he gave way and after the wedding took
possession of the kingdom.[79] It is impossible now to establish
which of these versions is correct – and it may be that neither is –
but at least it can be seen that Richard, as conqueror and therefore
disposer of Palestine, and the feudatories, as those who had to
accept a consort, were agreed on Henry as husband for Isabella.

The fascination of the years between 1188 and 1192 lies in the fact that there was in Palestine a peculiar constitutional situation. The lands reconquered by the Third Crusade did not automatically revert to the Kings of Jerusalem but could be held by their conquerors, who could grant them to whomsoever they wished: this explains Guy's efforts before Acre and Conrad's attempts to negotiate with Saladin behind Richard's back. After Sibylla's death the baronial party wished to marry Isabella to Conrad and to persuade Philip and Richard to recognise their rights. Richard's reluctance forced them to undermine his efforts to reconquer Palestine and to win over his army to Conrad's side. For all its understandable desire for strong government, the baronial movement at this time broke a good marriage and frustrated a crusade.

6

A SCHOOL OF FEUDAL
JURISTS

THE authors of the law-books of the middle of the thirteenth century acknowledged their debt to earlier jurists, but it would be a mistake to assume that all those with legal reputations were baronial sympathisers. Two of them, King Aimery and Bohemond IV of Antioch-Tripoli, were rulers and strong ones at that; another was one of the five imperial *baillis* of Cyprus; and the great jurists Balian of Sidon and Nicholas Antiaume were at times supporters of the Emperor Frederick II. Practising permanently in the Kingdom of Cyprus, moreover, where the courts applied almost the same laws as those of Jerusalem, were prestigious lawyers like the members of the family of Gibelet, the founder of which, Renier, had been in 1161 a burgess of Caesarea. By the early 1190s he had attached himself to Guy of Lusignan and followed him to Cyprus where he was raised to knighthood; when Aimery of Lusignan succeeded to the lordship of the island he sent him to Apulia to negotiate the grant of a crown from the western emperor. Renier, who died before 1205, was a devoted servant of the Lusignans and to later generations he had a great reputation for his wisdom and his ability in court.[1] Of his four sons, who themselves became involved in a legal wrangle over his estates after his death, Arneis 'had great knowledge and force in argument and was a good pleader'. A supporter of the Ibelins in the civil wars in Cyprus he was left by them in charge of the island in 1232 and in the following year negotiated the surrender of Kyrenia to the baronial forces.[2] William Viscount, who was born in the County of Tripoli, was 'the cleverest presenter of a plea of all the vavasours of his time' and an intimate of John of Beirut. He spoke on behalf of the child King of Cyprus when in 1231 an imperial fleet arrived off the island to demand the banishment of the Ibelins and in 1232 it was he who suggested the marriage of Isabella of Cyprus to Henry of Antioch, being a member of the embassy which arranged it.[3] On the other hand, William of Rivet the Young, another descendant of one of Guy of Lusignan's followers, was an opponent of the Ibelins and a supporter of the Emperor Frederick II in the civil wars. One of the five imperial lieutenants, he died in 1230, having fled to Cilicia after the fall of the castle of Dieu d'Amour. In spite of the hatred he felt for him Philip of Novara recognised his wisdom and his ability at public speaking.[4] Also practising in the Cypriot courts there were other knights, to us now only shadowy figures: Rostain Aimer,[5] Reynald Forson,[6] Paul of Nablus,[7] Philip Lebel[8] and William Raymond, who knew law well, although in 1233 he was given a lecture on it by John of Beirut.[9]

It is, nevertheless, true to say that most of the jurists were baronial in sympathy and practised at least part of the time in the courts of the Kingdom of Jerusalem. Early in the thirteenth century these courts were dominated by three men, whose reputations were to overshadow all their successors: 'the three wisest men', wrote a jurist, 'that I have ever seen on this side of the sea'.[10] Ralph of Tiberias was unquestionably the greatest of them and an inspiration to succeeding generations. The Socrates of the baronial movement, he seems to have written nothing himself, but it was believed that he had no equal. He was, wrote one who had known him well, 'the sovereign of cleverness in court cases and in speaking beautifully and highly'.[11] He seems to have had a naturally pedagogic bent. Philip of Novara recorded how he himself began to learn the law in a passage which shows Ralph, entering on the illness that would lead to his death, almost pathetically anxious to pass on his knowledge to a promising boy before it was too late.

It happened that I was at the first siege of Damietta (1218–19) in the service of my Lord Peter Chape and one day my Lord Ralph of Tiberias ate with him. After the meal my Lord Peter made me read to him from a romance. My Lord Ralph said that I read very well. Later my Lord Ralph was ill and my Lord Peter Chape, at his request, ordered me to read to him. This went on for more than three months and what should have made me very happy much displeased me. My Lord Ralph slept little and badly and when I had read as much as he wished he himself told me many things about the Kingdom of Jerusalem and about its customs and laws and said that I should remember them. And I, who feared him much, remembered everything.[12]

The reputation with later jurists of John, 'the Old Lord of Beirut', stood almost as high as that of Ralph, although he did not share the desire to teach. 'He taught me many things of his grace at my request,' wrote Philip of Novara, 'for he did not speak of the law willingly as had done my Lord Ralph.'[13] But great prestige attached to his legal decisions and in one case in 1233 his statement of a point of law seems to have been enough to end a plea.[14] Both Philip of Novara and John of Jaffa quoted him as their mentor and teacher; to Philip he had 'common sense and with knowledge and learning would act cleverly in and out of court'.[15] Balian of Sidon, the last member of the trio, was, wrote Philip of Novara, 'very wise and courteous and clever at law both in and out of court; and he loved wisdom and knowledge very much and was generous and vigorous'. Like those of Ralph of Tiberias and John of Beirut his legal arguments were repeated by Philip of Novara, who claimed to have been taught by him.[16]

These three great lords were at the centre of a circle of lesser lords, knights and burgesses. Among them was Geoffrey Le Tor, whose family had held important properties in and near Acre in the twelfth century; he was given a large fief in Cyprus by King Henry I and became chamberlain of that kingdom. He was used by the vassals as a messenger to Europe on two occasions which leads one to suppose that they had a high opinion of him. He was almost certainly the 'very good pleader and ancient knight' who was the author of one of the surviving law-books. Although occasionally expressing an independent view, his treatise was mostly a précis of that of John of Jaffa, completed in 1266, had some similarity to that of James of Ibelin, which was written in the 1270s, and in its treatment of the *bailliage* contained what seem to have been echoes of a dispute for the regency in 1264: we must assume that it was compiled when Geoffrey was an old man.[17] In this group too was a burgess of Acre called Philip of Baisdoin or Balduin, who flourished early in the 1240s, was a close adviser of Philip of Montfort and was known to Philip of Novara as a great pleader in court.[18] Also a burgess was Raymond of Conches, a member of a family perhaps originating from Marseilles and from the late twelfth century providing many jurors to the *Cour des Bourgeois* of Acre; it must have been among the most prosperous in the city. Raymond, himself a juror of the court, was known to be very wise and, unusually for a burgess, often went to plead in the

High Court of Nicosia.[19] Another important burgess family was the Antiaumes, a branch of which was admitted to knighthood in the thirteenth century. The family fortunes seem to have been founded by Raymond and Guy Antiaume in the 1190s.[20] Raymond was considered by Ralph of Tiberias to be the most learned of the burgesses[21] and his son Nicholas, a knight who lived in Acre, was one of the great lawyers of his day: like John of Beirut and Balian of Sidon his advice was sought and heeded in legal matters and he was admired by Philip of Novara. In 1225 he was one of those who accompanied Queen Yolande to Italy for her marriage to the Emperor Frederick II and he remained in her suite until her death. Perhaps because of his experiences in Italy he does not seem to have joined Frederick's opponents in the 1230s, but by 1243 he was supporting the baronial party, for after the accession of Alice of Cyprus to the regency he was one of those into whose custody Acre was granted by the High Court. He had died by 1249, but his career, like those of Renier of Gibelet, Philip of Baisdoin, Raymond of Conches, James Vidal and Philip of Novara, shows how the practice of law was a route to fame and status in the Latin East.[22]

This generation of the baronial movement was engaged in political struggles and perhaps this was why its literary output was less impressive than that of its successor. But if little was produced to rival the law-books of the 1260s there survives the old French Chronicle of Ernoul, which was used as a continuation up to 1229 of the Chronicle of William of Tyre and seems to have been based partly on the writings of someone who had been in the service of Balian of Nablus in the 1180s;[23] and a section of another continuation known as 'L'Estoire de Eracles', covering the years from 1229 to 1248, may have been composed at this time, although some of the passages in it are so like parts of the law-book of John of Jaffa that it may have been written by a member of the next generation.

We shall see that the events of 1243 marked a turning point in the history of the kingdom; and with most of the old leaders dead a fresh generation of jurists were now heading the baronial movement. They were men who had grown up and been blooded in the troubles of the 1220s and 1230s and most of them, like their predecessors, were Ibelins and their relatives. Balian of Beirut and John of Arsur were the sons of John of Beirut. Balian does not seem to have been much of a jurist,[24] but John of Arsur had some reputation as a lawyer and is to be found repeating arguments that he had heard used by his father.[25] More important than they, and certainly the best of all the legal writers, was John of Jaffa. Born in 1215, the son of John of Beirut's brother Philip and Alice of Montbéliard and probably raised in Cyprus where his father was bailli, he took part in the struggle against the imperialists: the wounds he suffered in 1232 at the Battle of Casal Imbert seem to have affected him all his life.[26] From quite young he was associated with the decisions of the great lawyers.[27] By 1229 he had, though still a minor, a fief in Acre, presumably inherited from his father,[28] and it must have been through Richard of Cornwall's treaty with Egypt in 1241 that he acquired the old Ibelin fief of Ramle.[29] By June 1247 he had been granted the County of Jaffa and Ascalon by the Regent Henry of Cyprus, a gift of doubtful validity which may be why he got papal confirmation of it:[30] we have already seen him stubbornly holding on to his exposed county in the 1250s and 1260s. One of the great fief-holders in the kingdom, a lieutenant of regents and a regent himself, John conducted his affairs with magnificence and display. Many years later his relative John of Joinville remembered his arrival in Egypt with the crusade of St Louis.

> He arrived most nobly of all, for his galley came painted below the waterline and above with escutcheons of his arms – *or* a cross paty *gules*. He had at least 300 oarsmen in his galley, each with a shield upon which were his arms; and to each shield there was attached a pennon on which were his arms beaten in gold. And as he approached it seemed as though his galley flew as the oarsmen drove it forward and it seemed as if lightning were falling from the skies at the sound made by the pennons and the cymbals, drums and Saracen horns.

And John of Joinville described how Jaffa was set out for Louis's visit in 1252: the count had prepared his castle so that it seemed to be

> a defensible town; for on each of the crenellations, of which there were more than 500, he had placed a shield with his arms and a pennon, which thing was beautiful to look at.[31]

John was more than a magnifico. His political activities show him to have been one of the cleverest of the barons and his law-book, still being compiled in its final form in the course of the year 1266, the last of his life,[32] is one of the most remarkable lay writings of the thirteenth century and ranks with Philip of Beaumanoir's *Coutumes de Beauvaisis*. Written with the grandiose aim of providing a guide for the conduct of lords and vassals in the courts, it was essentially a practical treatise, although John chose to consider each law in isolation, without any over-all theme or argument, and this led to some confusion and diffuseness. But he revealed himself as a man of independent judgement and great learning and his book is a monument not only to his abilities but also to the scholarly environment in which he moved.[33] We will see moreover that amid the practical details and personal opinions he put forward a view of political relationships which was in some ways similar to those found in other European baronial movements but was nowhere else expressed with more force and articulation. His political theories, reflecting a consensus of opinion in the baronial party which had developed over the years, were not new; but if Ralph of Tiberias was the vassals' Socrates, John of Jaffa was their Plato.

Close to the Ibelins, a vassal of Balian of Beirut as he had been of his father, was Philip of Novara. A Lombard, he was probably born about 1205 and he had travelled East by 1218 when he was a page of the Cypriot knight Peter Chape. He then entered the service of John of Beirut and until his death, perhaps late in the 1260s, was a devoted supporter of the Ibelins. He held a fief from them in Cyprus, where he settled, married and became an important figure in the island's affairs, being made one of the executors of the will of King Henry I.[34] He also had a fief in the Kingdom of Jerusalem.[35] He must have owed his success to his abilities as a lawyer: he was known to contemporaries as the best pleader in the East and his reputation was still bright in Cyprus a century later.[36] For us his fame rests on his history of the civil wars in Cyprus, written between 1243 and 1247 and revised in the following decade, which, though fiercely partisan and often extremely boastful, is still good reading – together with a fragment of autobiography it was inserted into the fourteenth-century compilation known as 'Les Gestes des Chiprois';[37] on his poetry, some of which survives incorporated into his history; on a moral tract, *Les Quatre Ages de l'Homme*, written in his old age; but above all on his law-book, the 'Livre de forme de plait'. The last work has come down to us in a form that presents all kinds of editorial problems and these were certainly not solved in the only published edition of it. It is clear that we have a private treatise on the practice of advocacy and the laws followed in the courts of Cyprus, arranged in a simple and logical way and expressed with clarity and precision, dedicated to Balian's son John of Beirut and written in about 1250, but revised, perhaps twice, in the 1260s when Philip must have been planning to bring out an expanded version.[38] The law-book, which influenced John of Jaffa, was not as original as John's: Philip tended to rely on the decisions of others and when he had to make a choice between conflicting earlier judgements he did so without giving reasons.[39] For all his prestige, he was not of the same social and political status as the Count of Jaffa and may have been reluctant to express too strong an opinion. But a surprising feature of the 'Livre de forme de plait', in view of the bragging in Philip's history, was his modesty: he strikes one as having been a real scholar, reluctant to give an opinion unless he was sure of it, and then always conscious that there might be contrary judgements of equal worth.

Outside the immediate circle of family and dependants was James Vidal, whose career has already been considered, and Philip of Montfort. Philip had some legal bent,[40] but although his mother was an Ibelin and he is to be found working closely with his cousins in the 1240s, the following decades found him and his son following their own path, independent of their fellow lords.

With Philip's death in 1270 the leaders of his generation were all gone: Balian of Beirut had died in 1247, John of Arsur in 1258 and John of Jaffa in 1266. Two Ibelins maintained their traditions. Balian of Arsur was the son of John of Arsur and was lieutenant for King Hugh at the time of the arrival in Acre of Roger of San Severino in 1277. James of Ibelin, a titular Count of Jaffa and probably the son of the great John[41], was chosen in 1271 to speak before the Lord Edward of England in Acre on behalf of the vassals of Cyprus, who had refused to serve their king outside the island, and was the author of a law-book, written on his deathbed in 1276, which was clear, methodical and based on that of John of Jaffa, although occasionally he took a divergent view.[42]

We have seen elsewhere how most of the leaders of the baronial movement were related by blood to one another or closely bound

by ties of marriage or vassalage. It is important to bear in mind
the family links between the leaders of the first and second
generations: Ralph of Tiberias was the stepson of Raymond of
Tripoli, John of Beirut was the son of Balian of Nablus and Balian
of Sidon the son of Reynald of Sidon. From the early thirteenth
century moreover we have evidence for the direct transmission
of ideas. John of Beirut admitted his debt to Ralph of Tiberias
and King Aimery.[43] Philip of Novara claimed to have learnt law
from Ralph of Tiberias, John of Beirut, Balian of Sidon, William
Viscount, Arneis of Gibelet, William of Rivet, Nicholas Antiaume
and Philip of Baisdoin.[44] John of Jaffa had sat at the feet of his
uncle John of Beirut, Balian of Sidon and Nicholas Antiaume
and knew the work of Philip of Novara.[45] It is clear that one is
faced here by a school of law, confined, it is true, to a small circle
of relatives and dependants, in which ideas and details of the
techniques of court practice were passed from generation to
generation.

Nothing in the sources for the history of the Latin kingdom is
more striking than the interest taken in the law by the Palestinian
nobility. William of Tyre had thought it worthy of note that
King Baldwin III had such a reputation for jurisprudence that
he was consulted on dubious matters by his barons.[46] In the
following century the authors of some of the continuations of
William's chronicle were themselves interested in abstruse points
of law, breaking off their narratives to describe, for instance, a
tricky case in the County of Tripoli that involved Ralph of
Tiberias or a change in the custom relating to the succession to
the Duchy of Burgundy.[47] Legal arguments occupied the time
of the leading lords out of court as well as in. Differing views by
Ralph of Tiberias, John of Beirut and Balian of Sidon on the
penalties to be imposed on a woman for neglect of the *service de
mariage* were expressed in discussion.[48] On another occasion
Nicholas Antiaume described privately to his son Balian and to
John of Arsur, Philip of Tyre and John of Jaffa a method of
defending a man against the charge of murder which had been
suggested to him by his father.[49]

> I have heard the Old Lord of Beirut speak (of the *assise* on the parti-
> tion of fiefs) many times [wrote Philip of Novara] and he said that
> if a man had a son who was only one day old and forty daughters
> they would have no rights of inheritance, for a daughter's rights

cannot take precedence over those of a son and the law was made for the advantage of the rightful heir. And my Lord of Sidon said that the law was made to deal with the situation in which there were several heirs, so that the lord could be assured of homage and service of the body; and the law did not specify *several male heirs*, but spoke only of *several heirs*. So a woman can inherit in those circumstances in which she can perform the services owed for the fief and the male heir cannot.[50]

In one passage in his treatise Philip of Novara described the qualities that in his view made a good pleader. He must, he said, be endowed with natural sense and subtle knowledge. By the first of these terms he meant not only that the aspiring lawyer should have native ability, but also that he should want to be a pleader – in other words enjoy what he did; that he should be of strong enough character to stand up bravely to opposition; that he should have the Grace to keep his soul from harm, because his position would expose him to much temptation; and that he must lead a life at least externally spotless, so that no one could accuse him of immorality. Subtle knowledge had two branches, wisdom and science, by the last of which Philip meant the ability to use logic.[51] The temptation Philip was referring to resulted from the prestige with which an able lawyer was regarded: that a man was a good pleader was the highest praise that he or John of Jaffa could award to any of their predecessors or contemporaries.

In considering the reasons for the interest in the practice of law and the prestige attached to it one must remember that in a state with a monetary economy, a comparatively sophisticated bureaucracy and a system of agriculture in which landlords had little direct concern in the cultivation of land, the lords lived in the cities, enjoying money-fiefs and village-rents and in close contact with merchants from Italian towns with traditions of secular learning, and with churchmen although they seem to have been extraordinarily reluctant to enter the spiritual life themselves or even to send their younger sons into the Church.[52] Ecclesiastical schools must have contributed to a scholarly ambience in the towns without which it is impossible to envisage the emergence of a school even of secular law or the production in less than a century of seven law-books and six other works. In 1179 the Third Lateran Council laid down that every cathedral should have a master and in 1215 the Fourth Lateran Council decreed that theology should be taught in every metropolitan church. These precepts were never properly carried out in Latin Christendom and certainly not in Palestine and Syria. But in 1103 a Master of Schools had been established in Jerusalem at the Church of the Holy Sepulchre;[53] there was another in Antioch from the 1180s onwards;[54] and there was a teacher attached to the cathedral of Beirut in 1133.[55] Of the higher studies, theology was taught in Acre by 1218, perhaps in response to the conciliar decree,[56] and canon and, it seems, civil law in Tripoli in the middle of the thirteenth century.[57] In Acre the Dominicans had a *studium* at which was taught oriental languages.[58] It is obvious that there was some church schooling in the Latin East; but on the other hand William of Tyre spent twenty years studying in the great schools of Europe, receiving an education he clearly could not get in Palestine, and there is evidence that in the thirteenth century his example was followed by others.[59] We know little of the way the sons of feudatories were educated. Some were brought up in the houses of religious orders,[60] but most lords may have followed the advice of Philip of Novara, who, believing that the rich should be literate, counselled the employment of good private tutors.[61] Learning in jurisprudence, however, must also have been grounded in practice in the courts, and three features of the system of justice in the kingdom contributed more than anything else to expertise and interest in it: the peerage, at least in theory, of all the feudatories; the use of *conseil*; and in the thirteenth century the absence of written legislation.

Every vassal who had made liege-homage to the king could sit in the High Court. At first, of course, it had been the immediate tenants of the king by virtue either of their great lordships or their minor holdings in the royal domain who had given him counsel in his court, but we have seen that one of the most important consequences of the *Assise sur la ligece* had been the widening of the membership of the court to include most fief-holders in the kingdom. We have also seen that it may not have been universal practice for rear-vassals to make liege-homage and anyway one could never assume that every meeting of the High Court was well attended. Presumably only a small group of knights were interested enough to come regularly, although it has already been seen how a lesser knight could, through regular participation, improve his status: Philip of Novara wrote of

vavasours, 'who were very wise and clever and good pleaders'.[62]
But important matters must have brought the feudatories flooding
in, while great lords could throw themselves, sometimes carelessly,[63] into litigation and would then pack the High Court with
their friends and dependants who would vote on their behalf.[64]

The High Court, at the apex of the feudal hierarchy, dealt with
cases that concerned the relationship between the kings as lords
and the *grands seigneurs* as vassals; some of these, like the debates
on the validity of claims to the regency, were matters of national
importance. But it was also the seigneurial court for all the lands
of the royal domain,[65] although it may be that in certain areas a
king, and also a lord in his seigneurie, could establish a permanent
judicial commission of three liegemen to deal with problems in
the laws relating to villeinage.[66] The High Court would consider
cases arising out of royal obligations towards and rights over
minor tenants[67] and, like any other lord's court, would confirm
the acts of lesser vassals who had no seals or courts of their own.[68]
In both its national and domainal functions it had to get through
much routine business, considering claims for lands,[69] witnessing
the exchange, donation or sale[70] and the taking of possession
of properties.[71] It might itself mediate in disputes.[72] It cannot be
emphasised enough that most of the business it dealt with and the
procedures it followed were the same as those in the ordinary
seigneurial courts. Throughout the feudal hierarchy there were
plentiful opportunities for a man who wanted to practise the
law; and a rear-vassal who had the inclination could spend much
time in the courts either of his lord or, if he was a liegeman, of the
crown, familiarising himself with the system. It was for the little
men as well as for the great that the jurists wrote their treatises:
to John of Jaffa not only the king and the lords, but also all the
vassals should have a knowledge of the laws they had sworn to
uphold.[73] Much matter in the law-books indeed was concerned
with purely technical questions: how to plead[74] and the importance
of using the right words;[75] how to protect one's witnesses;[76]
how to answer an opponent and test his evidence;[77] how to use
the law to one's own advantage.[78]

Some idea of the procedure in the feudal courts can be gained
from studying the descriptions of the jurists and the evidence
provided by the charters. The king or lord, his lieutenant or, in
the case of the High Court, the seneschal presided and the

presence of an additional two liegemen made a quorum.[79] A judgement was made not by the king or lord, who acted merely as president, but by the knights in attendance, who withdrew to reach their decision and returned to announce it to him.[80] This judgement was in theory *consilium*, but it was believed to be binding on the lord, who was subject like anyone else to his court,[81] because otherwise he would be failing openly to protect his vassal. The jurists had terms for the various forms their decisions could take. The word *esgart* was used of a judgement in the broadest sense: a *jugement* perhaps definitively ended a case; not an *esgart* but often ranking with one was a *conoissance*, an examination of the assertion of a pleader to see if it had merit *prima facie*; *recort de cort* was the witness of the court itself as to the validity of a statement concerning some past action, charter or judgement.[82]

The vesting of powers of judgement in the vassals was a commonplace in feudal states. What was a feature of court practice in the Latin East was the usage whereby one vassal, appointed by the president, aided another and even the king himself with *conseil*. In certain matters a man could conduct his own plea or act on behalf of his wife or a child,[83] but it was usually considered to be advisable for him to make use of the best counsellor he could find,[84] for in a case from the judgement of which there was no appeal arguments had to be presented with much care: it was customary indeed to end a plea or defence with a standard *formula* – a procedure known as *mettre retenail* – which permitted a man to raise his case again, not by appealing against a judgement already made, but by presenting his plea under a different aspect.[85] *Conseil* was a service like any other and a vassal was bound to perform it.[86] Normally a man presenting a case or making a defence would ask that he be assisted by the *conseil* of one or even two of his peers. A lord need not agree to the appointment of a counsellor who was not bound to him by homage and therefore under no obligation to attend his court, but while, in the case of the High Court, any liegeman in the neighbourhood could be requested by a pleader to act for him, provided he had not already been assigned to another, a lord must take care to see that one of the parties was not given a better adviser than the other.[87] The counsellor would intervene on behalf of his client with the correct requests and *formulae* and advise him on procedure and on how to reply,[88] but he could also speak on his behalf.[89] A king or lord would himself make use of *conseil* if he was involved in a dispute with a vassal; and when presiding over a case between two of his men, he would appoint a vassal 'to watch his words'; this man should be the best pleader present, for appeals on points of law might be made by either of the parties.[90] It must be emphasised that these counsellors were not professional advocates, who in the High Court represented only witnesses – though these could also have *conseil*[91] – but were feudatories. The knights therefore practised in the courts as legal experts as well as judges and the use of *conseil* led naturally to the emergence among them of a group of learned and experienced legal practitioners.

> The master of pleaders . . . has very great authority [wrote Philip of Novara] for by employing a clever pleader one can sometimes save and preserve in court one's honour and body, or one's inheritance or that of a friend; and through the lack of a clever pleader, when he is needed, one can lose one's honour, body or inheritance.[92]

The prestige of the pleaders grew after the disasters of 1187. According to the thirteenth-century jurists, the laws of Jerusalem, each magnificently written on a separate piece of vellum and sealed by the king, the patriarch and the Viscount of Jerusalem, had been kept in a box in the Church of the Holy Sepulchre which could be opened only in the presence of the king or his lieutenant and two vassals, the patriarch or the Prior of the Holy Sepulchre and two canons of the Holy Sepulchre and the Viscount of Jerusalem and two jurors of his *Cour des Bourgeois*. With the fall of the Holy City to Saladin the box and its contents, known as the *Letres dou Sepulcre*, were lost.[93] At one stroke the character of the law was changed: previously based on a *corpus* of written legislation, it became customary and so it was to remain until late in the thirteenth century, when a recorded element was provided unofficially by the law-books of the jurists and officially through a change in procedure in the courts. A description of the institution of this reform survives and reveals dramatically the chaos out of which the decisions of vassals were having to be made.

In February 1251 John of Arsur, lieutenant for the Regent Henry of Cyprus, called to the palace of the Lords of Beirut in Acre as many as he could of the liegemen who were in or near the city and the members of the local burgess court. To them he pointed out not only that the decisions they made were sometimes wrong, but also that the judges in court did not know as much as they should and, if a hearing had been adjourned, could not even remember the evidence originally presented, so that the pleaders had to make their cases all over again; it was not surprising that past *esgarts* had been forgotten by the time a court was asked to make *recorts* concerning them. He suggested that both courts should employ scribes who would write down in French in official books all the arguments put before them, including the pleas of both parties, and that no sitting should be closed until a recording of the proceedings had been made. Obviously thinking of the *Letres dou Sepulcre*, he proposed that the High Court's book be kept for consultation in the regent's palace, in a chest that could only be opened with three keys, one being held by the regent or his lieutenant and the other two by liegemen elected by the court. Philip of Montfort then rose and in a speech which is now hard to understand seems to have suggested that traditional *recorts* should still have precedence over the registers; this was agreed by the liegemen and burgesses present. It is clear that the courts were accepting that there should be compiled a body of recorded case-law to which reference could be made: an important step forward in legal practice which has many parallels elsewhere. By 1269 the burgess court was employing its own scribe, but the reform of the High Court was not put into effect for a long time, being put off in 1251 partly because of the bustle in Acre in connection with St Louis's expedition to Caesarea, and a scribe was not appointed until after 1286 when judgements as well as arguments were definitely recorded.[94]

The jurists writing in the middle of the century had to depend for their knowledge on custom and hearsay.

> The usages and laws of the Kingdom of Jerusalem [wrote Philip of Novara in answer to a question put to him] are not written down, nor are they made into canons, nor are they authorised by agreement, nor have they been since the land was lost.[95]

Elsewhere, in a passage that is echoed in John of Jaffa's law-book, he wrote that in his treatise he had described the laws according to his understanding, but with fear, because, although the lord of the kingdom and the vassals had sworn to keep them, we know them rather poorly, for they are known only by hearsay and usage; and we hold to be an *assise* that which we have seen used as one, saying that our understanding is that such is an *assise*; and sometimes, in a case concerning the sale of a fief or some other matter, one says that that *assise* was made, even though we do not know it at all well. But whoever says this with a clear conscience acccording to his understanding cannot do otherwise. In the Kingdom of Jerusalem they could make use of the laws much better and act on them more surely before the land was lost.[96]

The jurists' doubts as to whether they were describing actual laws or merely custom found expression in their law-books in the recurring phrase '*assise* or usage', so well known that even a pope referred to it on one occasion.[97]

These uncertainties led to an interest, even an obsession, with jurisprudence and an anxiety lest the old *assises* be completely forgotten: perhaps the first result of this, we shall see, was the 'Livre au roi'. Legal treatises, as their authors knew well, expressed no more than opinions and had not the force of law: Philip of Novara wrote that his book and those of others – perhaps he was referring to John of Jaffa – had no inherent value in court, where the views of the simplest and youngest knight could at times make even the expert change his mind.[98] But the law-books had value because in them were preserved the memories of experienced practitioners, especially those who had lived before 1187; again and again one finds in them references to and reliance upon the opinions of old men who remembered what had been done in the past.[99]

> I understand [wrote Philip of Novara] that he who claims something to be an *assise* ought to say that the *assises* are known and proved by custom; for one holds to be an *assise* that which is customarily used in the court and is said to be an *assise* and what one has heard and understood from the wise men who once were and who knew enough of the matters concerning the court.[100]

At a judgement in Cyprus the clinching argument seems to have been presented by John of Beirut, who said that he had heard a particular interpretation of the law given by King Aimery and Ralph of Tiberias, 'who knew the customs and laws and rights very well and were very clever and wise with natural sense'.[101] It was the pleaders and the jurists who moved in the circles in which the old laws were discussed and remembered and it was therefore to them that the confused and doubtful knights turned when sitting in judgement in the courts.

The constitutional ideas expressed by the feudatories in their law-books and chronicles were, like the law, affected by the loss of the *Letres dou Sepulcre*. Here again they had to rely on men's memories of the old *assises* and to supplement them they turned to historical writings of which there was a strong tradition in Palestine.[102] Some of their theories seem to have been based on a study of chronicles and documents, but objectivity, as we understand it, was not their aim; they were looking for support for their beliefs and precedents for their actions and, like every politician and historian since, they found them. The sudden disappearance of all written law, the reliance on memory and history contributed to the creation of a myth. The thirteenth century was a romantic age in which feudatories everywhere looked to chivalrous prototypes in the epics and romances;[103] and like all romantics they discovered in the distant past golden ages when feudal obligations were respected and the right order prevailed. The Palestinian jurists dated their mythological state to the early years of the twelfth century, but they gave it certain very unusual features, among them an origin based upon a contract of government and what might be called, in the broadest sense, a written constitution.

The political theories of the vassal-lawyers rested on a historical interpretation of the events which followed immediately upon the conquest of Palestine by the First Crusade. Their golden age was ushered in by this cataclysmic event during which the old orders both of the invaders and the invaded were overturned and a new system of government established. From the conquest all else flowed; and conquest – the acquisition of land as a gift from God – gave a man the most absolute right of possession he could have. Ideas of conquest had a particular relevance to the inhabitants of Palestine in the mid-thirteenth century, for they had been troubled by them since 1187. When lost lordships were reconquered the descendants of those who had held them expected, and were expected, to reoccupy them.[104] But their rights could conflict with the claims of visiting crusaders who would argue that lands taken by their armies were theirs to dispose of as they wished. After the fall of Acre to the Third

Crusade in 1191 the Latin burgesses found their old houses in the city in the hands of crusaders who claimed them by right of conquest. The burgesses appealed to Philip of France, who had already agreed with Richard of England not to keep any of the lands they had taken. The two kings accepted that those burgesses who could prove past possession by charter or testimony should have the right to return to them.[105] But we have already seen that the conquests of Richard and Philip had given them great political power and it is possible that the same rights accounted for the influence enjoyed by visiting crusaders like Richard of Cornwall in 1241 and Louis of France between 1250 and 1254. During the invasion of Egypt by the Fifth Crusade, King John of Jerusalem had been given 'the lordship of the host and of the conquests it would make, save for the shares allotted to those who participated in the conquest'. This had been disputed by the papal legate Pelagius, who claimed whatever was taken for the Church, and although John later gained from the pope the promise that all future conquests in the Near East would be absorbed by the Kingdom of Jerusalem, St Louis clearly regarded Egypt as his own personal possession after the capture of Damietta in 1249.[106]

To the jurists Palestine had been conquered by the First Crusade and was therefore a possession held by the most absolute of rights. But to whom did the rights of conquest belong? Not, in their view, to the Church, although the crusade had been preached by Pope Urban II and was his instrument: John of Jaffa stated twice that the kingdom was held from none but God, adding that the king 'owed no man or woman homage or service or any other returns', and in the 1270s the royal procurators stated before papal judges that 'the pleas of the Kingdom of Jerusalem belong in no way to the Roman curia'.[107] The jurists saw the crusade as a kind of mass migration over which there had been no true leader, not even those participants like Godfrey of Bouillon, Robert of Normandy or Raymond of St Gilles who were great figures in the West: indeed a translator of the Chronicle of William of Tyre inserted a passage in which the crusaders from each locality elected their own captains for the march to the Holy Land.[108] The author of a continuation of that chronicle succinctly expressed the idea of a leaderless migration in reporting a speech supposedly made by Balian of Sidon in 1231. 'When this land

was conquered it was by no chief lord, but by a crusade and by
the movement of pilgrims and assembled people.' These words
were echoed by John of Jaffa, to whom the city of Jerusalem
had been 'conquered . . . by the pilgrims who had moved
themselves to come and conquer her'.[109] It followed that by
conquest the Holy Land belonged neither to the pope, nor to a
king, but to God and the people: in the hour of the fall of the
city of Jerusalem sovereignty had belonged to the mass of the
migrants.

In the eyes of the jurists there then followed a conscious act by
which Godfrey was chosen as ruler of the new state. 'When they –
the people – had conquered (the land),' Balian of Sidon is supposed to have said, 'they made a lord by agreement and by
election and they gave him the lordship of the kingdom.' The
same idea was expressed by the writer of a genealogical treatise
on the baronial families in the East and by John of Jaffa, although
he modified it by giving the powers of election, more accurately,
to 'the princes and barons'.[110] Of course, the idea that Godfrey
had been elected by his future vassals was bad history, for he had
been chosen not by the ordinary participants on the crusade, the
subjects-to-be of the kingdom, but by a small group of leaders,
only one of whom, Tancred, was to remain in Palestine.[111] It is
however worthy of note that in William of Tyre's Chronicle, to
which the jurists had access, there was included a charter issued
eleven years after the conquest by Godfrey's brother Baldwin, in
which it was stated that after the capture of Jerusalem,

> it pleased the clergy and the Counts Raymond of St Gilles, Robert of
> Normandy, Robert of Flanders, Tancred and other leaders, *with the
> whole multitude of the Franks,* that the most pious and merciful Duke
> Godfrey, my dearest brother, should rule.[112]

Of course these words could never have meant to Baldwin that
Godfrey had been elected ruler by his subjects, but it is permissible
to see in the document a basis for the jurists' belief. To them
kingship in Jerusalem stemmed from a deliberate act by which the
people renounced their possession of Palestine to a lord chosen
by them. In other words, they held to the idea that their state
originated in a contract of government.[113]

It must be emphasised that the theory that kingship originated
in contract would not in itself have limited a ruler a century later –

indeed social contract concepts have been used in support of absolutism. We have seen that the vassal-lawyers believed that the kings held their crown directly from God and it was recognised that all the territories in the kingdom belonged in the last resort to them by proprietary right.[114] Much has been made of the way John of Jaffa consistently referred to the ruler of Jerusalem as *chef seigneur*, chief lord, as though he believed that the king had no powers other than those of a feudal suzerain. In fact this does seem to have corresponded to John's views, but no such conclusion can be drawn merely from his use of that phrase; for all his adult life there had been no resident king, only regents, and it is clear that he used the term only because it could be applied to both types of ruler.[115] Nor must we fall into the trap of supposing that Godfrey of Bouillon's successors were elected, save in the most formal sense. The High Court did have the formal right to accept a claimant as its true king, but the exercise was genealogical rather than democratic. It was what was believed to follow on from the contract of government, rather than the contract itself, which provided the bases for the limitations supposedly binding on the crown.

John of Jaffa wrote that once Godfrey had been elected he chose, with the advice of the patriarch, the barons and the wisest men, a committee to look into the customs of other lands. He had the committee's report read to the patriarch and others,

> and afterwards by their counsel and agreement he collected those writings which seemed to him good and he made *assises* and usages which should be held and maintained and used in the Kingdom of Jerusalem, by which he and his men and his people and all other manner of people . . . in his kingdom should be governed, kept, held, maintained, tried and judged by right and reason.[116]

In the speech put into Balian of Sidon's mouth there was the same emphasis on legislation by agreement and on the fact that the ruler was as bound by the laws as was his people:

> and afterwards with the agreement and at the *conoissance* of the wise men they made statutes and *assises* which they wished to be held and used in the kingdom for the safety of the lord and other people and to maintain right.[117]

The earliest laws therefore were made by the *conoissance* of Godfrey's court and it followed that the legislation of his successors would have no validity unless it was made in the same way: indeed one twelfth-century law was regarded as being of no worth because it had been made by a king 'without the counsel of his vassals and his burgesses of the city'.[118]

John of Jaffa continued his account of the establishment of the legal system by describing the foundation by Godfrey of the courts, again 'with the common agreement of the lord, his vassals and burgesses'.[119] And in an extraordinary passage, the ideas in which are to be found echoed in other works, he wrote not only that amendments and additions to the original laws were made by the counsel of the subjects, but also that messengers were sent to Europe to inquire into various legal systems, while for several years the High Court was assembled at Acre at the time of general passages, and visitors to the Holy Land were interrogated about the customs of their countries, in order to find out if any of them were suitable for Palestine.[120] This account of the early legislation was not accepted by all the feudatories, some of whom, represented in the 1260s and 1270s by Hugh of Brienne and James of Ibelin, believed that the colonists had brought with them the customs of France and that one should look to France for precedents which were lacking in Jerusalem.[121] But John of Jaffa, at least, seems to have been positing not only a contract of government, but also a comprehensive body of law drawn up in writing after the invasion by the conscious deliberation and agreement of both ruler and ruled. In his mind the *Letres dou Sepulcre* had become more than a *corpus* of law; they had become, in so far as they dealt with the relationship between ruler and ruled, a kind of lost constitution.

'Then (the people),' Balian of Sidon is supposed to have said, 'swore to hold to the laws and they made the lord swear; and from that day to this all the lords who have been over this kingdom have so sworn.'[122] To the jurists each king was limited by the oath he had taken to hold to the laws of his ancestors and to make judgements through his courts, an oath sworn not only by him but also, as we have seen, by the vassals and rear-vassals. After a king's death the rightful heir should come before the assembled High Court and lay his claims before it, demanding homage from the vassals and promising in general terms to behave towards them as a lord should. The members of the court, his future vassals, would withdraw to discuss his claims and once they recognised his right to inherit he would take the oath before receiving their homage and fealty. According to John of Jaffa, he promised to defend the Church, widows and orphans; to hold to the usages, customs and *assises* that were ordained and maintained in the kingdom; to preserve the gifts and charters made by his ancestors and, if there was any dispute over them, to see that it was determined by the judgement of his court; and to render justice to all.[123] This oath, or one like it, was demanded of Hugh of Antioch-Lusignan by the High Court in 1269.[124] By that date, of course, John of Jaffa's law-book had been written, but there may have been early precedents for it: certainly in 1100 Baldwin I had sworn some sort of oath on his acceptance as king.[125]

The coronation, which after the loss of the city of Jerusalem usually took place in Tyre, followed a common European *ordo*.[126] At the start of the ceremony the *coronandus* took a second oath, this time to the patriarch, the text of which survives in four versions: a copy of the promises made by Aimery in 1198 preserved by the canons of the Holy Sepulchre; an early thirteenth-century variant in an *ordo* which was in the possession of the cathedral of Tyre and so may have been used at the coronation of John of Brienne in 1210 and at those of his successors who were crowned in Palestine; a fragment which has some resemblance to Aimery's oath and was added in the thirteenth century to a ritual belonging to the canons of the Holy Sepulchre; and a description of the ceremony in John of Jaffa's law-book.[127] Aimery's oath contained a reference to new customs which must reflect special circumstances in 1198, but the three variants with ecclesiastical provenances give a fairly consistent picture in which the king-elect's promises concerned only the Church: he swore to preserve its canonical privileges, its franchises and the laws relating to it, to be the helper and defender of the patriarch and all persons and to protect ecclesiastical possessions. The oath reproduced by John of Jaffa contained three further promises, not concerned with church rights: to protect widows and orphans, to respect ancient custom and all the charters and laws of royal ancestors, particularly those of Amalric and Baldwin IV, and to give justice to all according to these ancient customs and laws. It has been suggested that John was confusing the oath sworn to the patriarch with that sworn to the vassals,[128] but he was so conscious of the importance of the promises that it is unlikely that he would not have been clear in his own mind about them. It is possible that he was eager to show that the crown was limited by the consequences of the commitments made to the vassals at the start of a reign and so felt it necessary to add them to the oath made to the patriarch as well.[129]

The laws which the king and his vassals had sworn to obey were the bones and sinews of the feudal body politic described by the jurists, the centre-piece of which was of course the contract made by the king not only with his tenants-in-chief, but also in consequence of the *Assise sur la ligece* with all fief-holders. The purpose of feudal law was to define the terms of the contract and provide for possible infringements of it. The proper place to discuss this and therefore the laws covering it was the king's court. When John of Jaffa wrote that the king's coronation oath bound him to act according to the law and through his court if properly requested for justice,[130] he meant that judgements on the contract belonged not to the king as one of the parties to it but to a properly constituted court, made up of the royal vassals who were in a special relationship with their king and with each other because of the homage they had all paid. It was for this reason that the king was bound by the decisions of his court and was himself, as a matter of course, answerable to its *esgarts*.[131] Above all, he could take no steps against the body or fief of a vassal – thus acting contrary to his obligations of protection and maintenance – without first asking for his court's judgement on the matter.

> The lord cannot put a hand, nor have a hand put, on the body or fief of his man unless it is by the *esgart* or *conoissance* of his court.[132]

John of Jaffa was arguing a case, but there is support for his opinion in no less a source than the 'Livre au roi', written between 1198 and 1205. This law-book has attracted much attention, because it was the earliest and because it was the only one which seems to have been written for a monarch. It has been described as if it were a kind of bridge between the documents of the strong twelfth-century monarchy and those of the thirteenth-century baronial 'oligarchy', containing a royal rather than a baronial viewpoint.[133] In certain chapters, it is true, it reveals a concept of royal power more exalted than anything to be found in the later treatises. It opened with a strong statement on the king's rights and the royal domain.

Know well . . . that the king is held to increase and not to diminish the rights of the crown in his kingdom.

The vassals were committed to prevent improper alienations of the royal domain-lands, which is why no gift of a king had validity unless it was witnessed by them.[134] The 'Livre au roi' defined only vaguely the rights of king and vassals that resulted from the contract made between them,[135] whereas a feature of the baronial law-books was the elaboration of these rights. It reproduced an *assise* of Baldwin III, which will be discussed below, referring to royal prerogatives and listing those circumstances in which a king could dispossess a vassal of his fief without judgement.[136] But it is an exaggeration to call it a treatise on behalf of the monarchy. It carefully described the rights of the barons in their fiefs, including that of High Justice,[137] and it firmly stated – directly contradicting the *assise* of Baldwin III – that a vassal could not be arrested by his lord unless he had been judged by his peers in court.

> If by chance it happens that a liegeman or liegewoman acts wrongly towards his lord in any way, right judges and commands one thus to judge that the king has no power legally to lay hands immediately on his liegeman. . . . He ought to send for his other liegemen . . . and according to what his peers have judged him worthy of so can the king or queen command that immediately justice be done to him, if he so wishes. But if it happens that the king or queen does not act in this way, but lays hands on the liegeman or his wife without *esgart* of court and does him shame or beats him or cuts off any of his limbs, right judges that first of all the monarch has done wrong and denied God, because he has broken faith with his man and has acted disloyally, so that broken too are the loyalties by which he is held to all his men.[138]

In other words, his contract with his vassals was automatically annulled. The evidence provided by the 'Livre au roi' suggests that, however mythical the background they created, the jurists' views of the crown's obligations under contract were based on long-standing custom.

The need to judge a man by the decision of his peers and to legislate through counsel bound the crown in practice as well as in the imaginations of the jurists. But it must be emphasised that while this gave the High Court great powers, these powers were

directly linked to those of the crown; and if the kings weakened
then so did their court. It could no more interfere in the day-to-
day running of the great fiefs than could they. And the long
absence of a resident monarchy from 1225 to 1269 paradoxically
limited its field of action, for in those periods in which the
kingdom was governed by vassal-regents and lieutenants, which
was most of the time, it had, in theory, no authority to hear
seigneurial cases: it was deprived, in other words, of most of its
normal business.[139] And when a king was present in Palestine
what bound him to the decisions of his court, giving a customary
relationship with his vassals – it was no more than that – its life-
force, was an element that even John of Jaffa could not define.
'Between lord and vassal,' he wrote, 'there is only faith'; and
elsewhere:

> Many times have I heard . . . my Lord my uncle (John of Beirut)
> and other wise men say and many times have I been in court where
> I have seen and heard this . . . that pleas are perilous and should be
> avoided; and above all those between a lord and his vassal. For
> between them is faith.[140]

But ideas of fidelity were vague and open to several interpretations. The baronial view of them, moreover, presupposed a
non-existent constitutional situation in which the king had no
specifically kingly rights other than those accruing to him as a lord
at the apex of the feudal hierarchy, enjoying only those rights
which stemmed from his contract with his vassals. If a king were
to hold another opinion about his position or if he were simply
to refuse to be bound by customary practice, lectures to him on
faith would have little effect unless they were backed up by
sanctions. The constitutional history of the kingdom from 1198
to 1231 was to be overshadowed by the theories evolved by the
jurists on this matter and by their attempts to enforce the sanctions they believed were at their disposal.

THE ASSISE SUR LA
LIGECE

IT is easy for the historian of medieval government to over-simplify the ideas men had of monarchy in the twelfth and thirteenth centuries. One can read into the institution of kingship political theories that were present, if at all, in embryonic forms, giving more significance than is their due to signs of an elective or hereditary monarchy and to the limitations upon as well as the rights of kings. Kingship in the High Middle Ages was an amalgam of elements that had never been separately analysed because the theoretical foundations upon which it was based were only just coming to be considered. It was at the same time hereditary and elective or nominative – that is to say that kings succeeded one another because they were related, but also because of the choice of their subjects or nomination by their predecessors. The monarchs were heirs to the public rights of the Roman principate or Germanic theocracy, but they were also bound by feudal contract and by custom. The historian must also recognise that the Kingdom of Jerusalem was a state in some ways unlike those with which he is familiar. Partly because of the near-independence of the great fiefs from royal control the central organs of government were apparently primitive; but we have seen that a close inspection reveals a fairly sophisticated bureaucratic machine collecting and accounting revenues both in the royal domain and in the fiefs and inherited by king and barons alike from the system of government that had existed before the First Crusade. Historians, rooted in European history, have assumed wrongly that in Latin Syria there was no developed administration because one of the usual reasons for its appearance in the West, the drive towards centralisation, was absent.

Like all medieval monarchies kingship in Jerusalem contained within itself an inherent conflict between two contradictory principles. Public rights, the factured remnants of the universal

government of pre-feudal rulers, were those held by a king as
sovereign, over and above his privileges and duties as a chief
lord contractually bound to his vassals. As sovereign rather than
as suzerain a King of Jerusalem legislated for his kingdom, even
if bound to take counsel before issuing *assises*, and, as the defender
of the Church and the Faith, issued bans calling out to war not
just the feudal host, but in time of emergency troops also
provided by cities, churches and monasteries, and even a
levée en masse of all able-bodied male subjects.[1] As sovereign he
enjoyed regalian prerogatives that in the middle of the twelfth
century can be identified as the rights to possess all major ports,
to monopolise the minting of coins,[2] to levy shipwreck[3] and to
approve the appointment of bishops.[4] The theory of *regalia*,
reflected in the adoption by the kings at their coronations of the
vestments of Byzantine emperors,[5] was best expressed in an
assise, perhaps issued by King Baldwin III,[6] which was incorporated into the 'Livre au roi'. This law described twelve types of
case in which, it said, a man could be dispossessed of his fief by
the king *without esgart* of court. They covered particularly violent
breaches of the feudal contract, those matters which seem later
to have been regarded as apparent treason:[7] armed rebellion;
taking legal action against the king; plotting to poison him and
his family; deserting him in battle to be captured by the Muslims;
entering into possession of a fief with the help of Muslim forces
against the will of the king and without the *esgart* of the High
Court; reneging, leaving a fief and becoming a Muslim; alienating
or renting property to Muslims without royal permission; and
refusing to obey a lawful command of the king. One clause
covered a felony, the forging of coins, and two the infringement of
royal prerogatives, the construction of a port and a road from it
into the hinterland and the minting of money.[8]

An eminent historian has shown how this *assise* is an early
example of a law on regalian right.[9] But it is not easy to understand how a king could ever disinherit the guilty without *esgart*
of court. It has been pointed out that the only reference to this
appears in the rubric to the *assise*: it is not mentioned in the body of
the law.[10] It conflicted not only with much of the 'Livre au roi',
but also with a king's private obligations, for, as we have already
seen, a feudal king, with the duty to protect and maintain his
vassal, could not in theory act against that man's life, honour or

fief without proof of breach of contract, judged in the seigneurial court by the other vassals. And in 1132 an early accusation of *crimen majestatis* was dealt with in the conventional way in the High Court.[11] It was of course impractical for a king always to wait for the long and clumsy processes of law before taking action: when faced by treason or rebellion he often had to act first and ask questions afterwards. This was recognised by the English baronage as late as 1191 and indeed by one of the best of the Eastern jurists in the middle of the thirteenth century, although he was referring only to very special circumstances; and in Palestine in the early thirteenth century it was apparently quite common for lords to treat arbitrarily those responsible for breaches of *service de mariage*.[12] But it was the occasional manifestations of *vis* and *volentia* that vassals were determined to reduce as much as possible, if not entirely prevent.[13] And while the idea of *crimen majestatis* survived into the thirteenth century,[14] it is noteworthy that when John of Jaffa dealt with apparent treason, not only did his account show clearly that to him it could not result in arbitrary confiscations by the crown, but also from his list of treasonable activities was expunged every reference to regalian prerogatives: to him treason consisted only of direct infringements of the feudal contract; and conversely for him the crown had in this respect no regalian rights.[15]

The fact is that by the end of the twelfth century the regalian rights had been whittled away and in practical terms had become almost non-existent: the lords had begun to develop their ports and mint their own coins; shipwreck had been granted to them by King Amalric; and interference in episcopal elections was forbidden by the papacy in the 1190s.[16] Two cases from the early years of the thirteenth century show how impotent even as feudal lords could be kings who were otherwise capable of fairly strong government. Between 1198 and 1205 Beatrice, the elder daughter of Joscelin of Courtenay and part heiress to his extensive lands, married, against the wishes of King Aimery and therefore in breach of her *service de mariage*, a German count called Otto of Henneberg. This violation of the feudal contract does not seem to have affected the couple's right to dispose of most of their lands to the Teutonic Knights, although it is true they did not do this until after Aimery's death.[17] Some years later King John held a court at which Bernard of Beirut, Lord of

Blanchegarde, killed one of John's relatives who had spoken 'grossly' of the inhabitants of Palestine. Bernard then left for Tripoli, with no one daring to stop him.[18] While of course such events could occur in the West one cannot imagine an Angevin or Capetian king failing to take any subsequent action; and Bohemond of Tripoli, Aimery's contemporary, took strong steps against a lord who had married an heiress without his permission.[19]

It is, however, possible to exaggerate the weakness of the kings. Their public rights may have been dormant, but their constitutional position was to say the least ambiguous and could be exploited by those of them who were strong-willed, because they had other sources of strength. However peaceful were the frontiers, the kingdom was surrounded by enemies whom the Christians had every reason to fear. Their optimism in the mid-twelfth century with their grandiose plans for the capture of Egypt was replaced, after the territorial losses of 1187-9, by a caution in military matters that infuriated visiting crusaders who did not have to live with the problems facing the Latin settlers[20] and declining confidence was reflected in charters of lease or in agreements on the division of revenues by the use of clauses to cover contingencies in which the peasants rebelled or Muslim troops devastated or permanently occupied the properties involved. These are to be found in documents issued in the northern Christian states from before 1187,[21] but in the Kingdom of Jerusalem itself they only appear in 1234 and thereafter are common and ubiquitous;[22] from 1248 onwards, and especially as fear of the Mongols grew, the loss of Acre itself was envisaged.[23] The threat from Islam and the Mongols, increasing in the 1240s and 1250s and particularly after the accession of Baibars to the government of Egypt in 1260, imposed on the Latin settlement a constant drain on its resources and led to the emergence of over-powerful and semi-independent institutions committed to its defence, but it also gave moral force to the kings as the state's natural defenders. The great rulers of the twelfth century were all active soldiers and so in the thirteenth were Aimery, John of Brienne and Hugh of Antioch-Lusignan. Military insecurity tended to act in a ruler's favour.

Kingship was also assisted by the wealth of the royal domain. Even in the thirteenth century, after the loss to the Muslims of Jerusalem and the rich agricultural lands round Nablus and the passing of Jaffa and Tyre into baronial hands, the crown retained Acre; and everything that has been written of the baronial domains applied with greater force to this port and its district, much richer than they were. The royal domain provided the kings with a means of exercising patronage in the appointments to castellanies and *bailliages* and of rewarding supporters with money-fiefs. But above all it gave them personal wealth and therefore a certain independence. The narrative that follows would be incomprehensible if it were not realised that it was possible for a ruler to act out his own, rather than his vassals', conception of what monarchy was.

Faced by rulers who desired to exercise powers beyond those authorised by feudal contract and sometimes were in the position to try to do so, it was understandable that the jurists should have set out to provide their peers with a legal means of enforcing their interpretation of a king's obligations. They did this by glossing in their own way the great twelfth century law that has already been mentioned, the *Assise sur la ligece*. 'Among the other statutes and *assises*, there is this *assise*, that the lord cannot and ought not to disseize his man without *esgart* of court,' Balian of Sidon was supposed to have said in the 1231.[24] He was clearly referring to the *Assise*, which, according to John of Jaffa, 'lords and men ought to take the most trouble to know'.[25] The treatment of it by the vassal-jurists of the mid-thirteenth century was probably based, as we shall see, on views expressed by Ralph of Tiberias in 1198 and it contains all the best elements in their thought: it appears in their law-books as an equitable law based on historical precedent which had been subjected to a logical though original elaboration. We have already considered some of their conclusions: that the *Assise* strengthened the king by linking to him by direct homage the rear-vassals, who had to support him even against their own lords in certain circumstances, and by giving these minor knights the right to sit in the High Court with the greater tenants, about whom they could complain; and that further it provided a king with the machinery for taking action against a lord who tyrannised his vassals.

But to the jurists the *Assise* worked not only for the crown but also against it. The law had come into existence because of an act of wrongful dispossession by a Lord of Sidon and it underlined the condition of homage that there were no occasions on which a lord could act against a vassal without formal trial. There can be no doubt that although they rested their inflexible approach to disseizin on the obligations of the crown under the feudal contract itself, they saw in the *Assise sur la ligece* confirmation of the legality of their attitude: indeed the connection between the *Assise* and freedom from arbitrary dispossession was so close that a leading historian has suggested that King Amalric, who issued it, was tacitly but deliberately abrogating the *assise* of Baldwin III which gave him the right to disseize without trial in certain cases.[26]

The jurists' interpretation of the *Assise* provided the vassals not only with a legal basis for resisting arbitrary acts by a king, but also with the means by which to do so; and here again they merely applied to the crown the methods by which a vassal defended himself against a local lord. They argued that when a lord failed in his duties towards his vassal there were four options open to the wronged man. One of these, appeal to the king, was obviously not relevant when the dispute was with the monarch himself, but the other three were applicable to lords and the king alike: the vassal could solemnly conjure his lord, demanding justice according to the law from him; he could withdraw his own service; and he could conjure his peers, requiring their aid to make the lord hold court.[27] When the king was involved, this last step meant an appeal to the High Court and we have seen that to the jurists the *Assise sur la ligece* had underlined the common bond of all knights as peers linked together by the liege-homage they had made to the king and committed to aid one another against the encroachments of royal power.[28] In a case of injustice the wronged vassal would ask his peers to demand of the king that he be allowed to stand trial in the High Court or, if the knights heard that one of their number had been imprisoned, they could take the initiative and require a court-hearing. This demand was essential, for they could do nothing if the man was not prepared to stand trial.[29] Should the king refuse to try the vassal in the High Court or carry out the terms of an *esgart*, his vassals had two courses open to them. If their peer had been deprived of his fief or imprisoned, they could use force to restore the fief to him or release him from jail, provided the king did not personally occupy the fief or stand before the prison door, in which circumstances force must be discontinued, because no one could raise his hand against the person of his lord, whatever he might have done.

When unable to use force, or in cases in which physical methods were not applicable,[30] the vassals would solemnly 'all together and each individually' withdraw their services from the king.[31]

The jurists' treatment of the *Assise* is impressive. While recognising the special powers enjoyed by a monarch directly linked to the rear-vassals and able to appeal to them over the heads of the tenants-in-chief, it also provided the formal means by which all fief-holders could resist a king who forgot his obligations to them. In the feudal utopia they constructed in their law-books, with its emphasis on the reciprocal obligations of crown and vassal, the *Assise* provided the jurists with an essential mechanism: the sanctions at the disposal of an oppressed feudal class, the means of bringing a recalcitrant king back into a true relationship with his subjects. But as it turned out this elaborate constitutional check proved to be impractical. The final sanction, the withdrawal of service, could only have been effective in a dreamland in which all feudatories acted always in unison and a ruler was dependent solely on their services. In other words, for their 'perfect' feudal ideas to succeed the jurists needed a 'perfect' feudal state, and this the Kingdom of Jerusalem definitely was not. The weaknesses in the baronial interpretation of the *Assise sur la ligece* will become apparent as we consider its development from the moment when it was first proposed by Ralph of Tiberias.

In the late summer of 1198[32] King Aimery of Jerusalem was nearly murdered as he was riding along the sea-shore near Tyre – probably to the south, in an area scattered with the ruins of the classical city, past the port known to the Ancients as the Egyptian Harbour. Four[33] German knights threw themselves upon the king, severely wounding him while his unarmed companions fled back to Tyre. The Germans then made for Acre. It was clear that they were members of a large company of German crusaders who had been in the East for the past year but were already beginning to depart for home. Conrad of Querfurt, Bishop of Hildesheim, who was one of their leaders, started a search in which three of them were found lodging with the Templars and were publicly executed; the fourth was never discovered. Meanwhile Aimery was carried to his palace in Tyre and doctors were fetched from Acre to tend him. He seems to have recovered quickly.

One of the most puzzling things about this assault was that it was apparently without motive. While one might well ask what part in it had been played by the Templars, Aimery was convinced that behind it lay the jealousy of the baronial house of Galilee and particularly of Ralph, although his complicity was never proved. Ralph's subsequent behaviour arouses some suspicions, but it must be said in his favour that relations between his family and the German crusaders had been bad. On their arrival in September 1197 the Germans had behaved with such brutality towards their hosts that Hugh of Tiberias, Ralph's brother, had advised his peers to put their women and children under the protection of the Military Orders.[34] It was the Germans too who had been partly responsible for a major disappointment to Ralph. In the same month Henry of Champagne had perished in a bizarre accident: stepping backwards out of a window in the castle of Acre, he had fallen to his death in the ditch below, dragging after him his dwarf, who had vainly tried to save him by grabbing at his clothing.[35] At a meeting of the Christian leaders, called to decide on a new consort for Isabella of Jerusalem, Hugh of Tiberias, supported by a party of barons, had put forward his brother, but Ralph's candidature had been rejected, it seems on the advice of the Templars and the Hospitallers, because he was not rich enough. It was then that Conrad of Querfurt had proposed Aimery, who was now King of Cyprus by grant of the western empire and had recently become a widower. The suggestion was accepted, not without opposition from Patriarch Haymarus who argued that Aimery and Isabella's marriage would transgress canon law: his brother had been married to her sister; and it might be added that Humphrey of Toron was still alive. But the patriarch changed his mind, probably in return for concessions to the Church, and in January 1198 he crowned Aimery and Isabella in a ceremony of great magnificence.[36] The leaders of the German crusade were not therefore natural allies of the Falconberg family; and if Ralph was guilty then the four would-be assassins must have been acting as individuals.

King Aimery was nearing the end of an extraordinary career. The second son of Hugh of Lusignan, Count of La Marche, he had been born into a family already involved in the crusading movement. He arrived in Palestine before 1174, for King Amalric paid a ransom to release him from imprisonment in Damascus,[37] but it was after Amalric's death that he began to play an important part in the affairs of the kingdom. He had become one of the lovers of Agnes of Courtenay, the new king's mother,[38] and he seems to have been made Chamberlain of Jerusalem, which must reflect his close personal relationship with the royal family, since this was the most intimate of the great sergeantries.[39] He secured his position by marrying Eschiva of Ibelin, the daughter of Baldwin of Ramle,[40] and on the death of Humphrey of Toron in 1179 he was granted the constableship of the kingdom.[41] Aimery's arrangement of the marriage of his brother Guy to Sibylla of Jerusalem was a great political achievement, the culmination of a period in which he had made use of his intimacy with the king's mother to further his career, against the interests even of his own father-in-law who, it will be remembered, had hoped for Sibylla's hand. He was now closely linked to the political group that was to polarise around Sibylla as the prospect of Baldwin IV's early death became more certain.

The accession of Sibylla and Guy to the throne in 1186 found Aimery, still constable, at his brother's side.[42] Captured at the Battle of Hattin, he was released in the summer of 1188 at the same time as Guy,[43] by whom he stood in the dispute for the crown that followed,[44] laying claim to the County of Jaffa and Ascalon after the departure for France of his elder brother Geoffrey, who had been granted it in 1191.[45] With Guy in Cyprus but still ambitious for the throne,[46] it is not surprising that Henry of Champagne should have doubted the constable's loyalty. Aimery does not seem to have performed homage – this was argued by Henry and he is not to be found in the witness lists to his charters – and a major row between the two men broke out in the first half of 1193. The Pisans, who had received great privileges from Conrad of Montferrat and Guy of Lusignan, were at this time supporters of the latter, for whom, it was believed, they wished to seize Tyre. Henry heard confirmation of these rumours and he wanted anyway to reduce the strength of the Pisans in Palestine, especially because some of them had been involved in piracy along the Syrian coasts. When their leaders only half-heartedly carried out his orders to put a stop to this, he exiled them saying that he would hang any he found in the kingdom. Aimery intervened on their behalf, but Henry turned on him, accused him of plotting with the Pisans to put Guy back on the throne and threatened to hold him prisoner until Guy surrendered Cyprus to him: he had inherited the rights of Richard of England in the East and Guy had not yet paid Richard all he owed for the island. Aimery replied that Henry had no right to arrest a vassal and his constable, but Henry, refusing to recognise the constableship which, he said, had been granted by a king whose rights were not acknowledged, held Aimery in the citadel of Acre. In fact the constableship dated not from the reign of Guy of Lusignan, but from that of Baldwin IV, although no doubt it had been renewed by Guy; and Henry's case may not have been particularly strong, for Aimery must have made homage to Isabella even if he had not to him. He was certainly admonished by the Masters of the Temple and the Hospital and the barons for arresting one of his men without trial, and although he persisted in denying that Aimery was his vassal he followed their advice and released him at once. Three days later Aimery left for Cyprus after surrendering the constableship and the fief of Jaffa, both of which were granted to the young John of Ibelin, the son of Balian of Nablus and Maria Comnena. In May 1193 Henry imposed his terms on the Pisans, annulling all the privileges granted to them by Conrad of Montferrat and Guy of Lusignan.[47] Although we find Aimery putting forward the kind of argument he was to deny when king in 1198, we can discern here for the first time two features of his later career, his legal ability, perhaps developed during his years as chamberlain and constable[48] and demonstrated in his carefully worded answer to Henry's threats, and his popularity with the nobles in spite of his long association with his brother.

Guy died late in 1194[49] and, since Geoffrey of Lusignan had returned to France, Aimery succeeded to the lordship of Cyprus. His government of the island does not directly concern us here; but his improvement of the domain and his acquisition of a crown from the western emperor showed that he had real qualities as a ruler.[50] He made peace with Henry of Champagne, recovering the County of Jaffa and betrothing his three sons to the three daughters of Henry, who renounced his claims to Cyprus.[51] Aimery's ability must have influenced the decision of the High Court in 1197 to accept him as consort for Isabella, but it was a remarkable tribute to a man who, after all, had supported Guy of Lusignan against Raymond of Tripoli, Conrad of Montferrat and

Henry of Champagne and had betrayed his father-in-law Baldwin of Ramle.

The adventurer had become a sage. His later reputation was that of a king who governed Cyprus and Jerusalem wisely and knew the laws and customs better than other men, having memorised many of them; only Ralph of Tiberias was believed to have been more learned.[52] The king certainly shared the anxiety of the feudatories lest the lost laws be completely forgotten and he may also have sensed a possible danger to the crown if its past record of legislation was obliterated. He thought of establishing a commission of two men under his presidency to codify what was remembered of the law and he wanted Ralph of Tiberias to participate as well. It is unlikely that Ralph flatly refused to serve on the commission – it would have been a service required of him as a vassal – but it is very possible that his quarrel with the king intervened before the commission met.[53] At any rate he played no part in the compiling of a treatise on the laws.

The 'Livre au roi' seems to have been the result of the commission's work.[54] It is short and seems to deal with specific issues of contemporary significance. The concern for the position of the queen-heiress and her consort, the rights of inheritance of her children and the regency in the event of her death were an obvious commentary on the conditions in the kingdom and the constitutional troubles of the past two decades. The chapters devoted to military organisation, services and fiefs perhaps answered the needs of the Latins in a period of reconquest. Other issues can be discerned, although their immediate relevance now escapes us: relations between knights, burgesses and mercenaries; the High Court and the king; rights of barons in their baronies; the status of sick and aged knights; the debts of knights and bans of the crown. We have already seen moreover that while one must be careful not to exaggerate the royalism in the 'Livre au roi' there was expressed in certain chapters a concept of monarchical power more exalted than that to be found in later treatises: above all there was included the *assise* of Baldwin III in which the king was permitted to dispossess a man of his fief without formal judgement in court for certain crimes, including apparent treason and *lèse-majesté*. It has already been suggested that the inclusion of this *assise* is curious, for it was uncharacteristic of the laws of the kingdom and against trends in twelfth-century feudal society;

it should be remembered that one of its clauses was being consistently broken by Aimery's reign without the prosecution of those involved, for seigneurial coins were being minted. This might throw doubt on the very existence of the law itself, or at least on the phrase in the rubric justifying disseizin without *esgart*, were it not for seemingly specific references to it made by Aimery in 1198 and by Richard Filangieri in 1231, about which more below. An alternative explanation of its inclusion in the 'Livre au roi' comes to mind: that it was an archaic, half-forgotten piece of legislation introduced, like so much else in the book, to answer a contemporary need.

It is hard not to relate this to the constitutional crisis that arose after the attempted murder of the king. During his convalescence Aimery became convinced that Ralph of Tiberias was responsible for the attack upon him.[55] Convoking a full meeting of the High Court, he announced that Ralph

> had acted disloyally and like a traitor and he would have treated him as a traitor if he had not been his vassal. And he ordered him to leave his land within eight days.

If he was found in the kingdom from that time on things would go badly for him.[56] This speech is not easy to interpret. The significance of the reference to Ralph's vassalage is not clear; nor did Aimery intend, at least as reported, to confiscate Ralph's possessions. It is certain however that he announced in the High Court the fact of Ralph's apparent treason, although it was never proved, and then banished him without *esgart*.[57] One cannot fail to be struck by the fact that this action, for which there could be no justification other than in the *assise* of Baldwin III, was carried out by a man who was known to have a profound knowledge of the law and took pains to perform it 'in his full court': in the particularly solemn surroundings in which an *esgart* would naturally have been made. Aimery's promulgation of Ralph's banishment looks like a trial of strength with reference to the *assise* of Baldwin III, an attempt to re-establish a right to act without *esgart* in certain circumstances.

It might have succeeded were it not that it involved a man every bit as remarkable as the king. Ralph, Lord of Tiberias by March 1198,[58] was one of the four sons of Walter of Falconberg, Prince of Galilee, and Eschiva of Bures. After his father's death his mother had married Raymond of Tripoli, so that Ralph and his brothers were the stepsons of the leader of the baronial dissidents in the 1170s and 1180s. Ralph fought at Hattin and escaped from the battle with his stepfather.[59] In October 1187 he was in Tyre with Conrad of Montferrat,[60] but after Guy of Lusignan's release he joined the king before Acre,[61] and seems to have acted as Humphrey of Toron's counsel when the latter complained to the High Court of the abduction of his wife.[62] By January 1194 he had been made seneschal and he therefore held the most important of the great sergeantries, representing an absent king, regent or lieutenant in the High Court and presiding over the *secrete*. He was seneschal for nearly thirty years and, although in exile for much of the time, must have gained an unrivalled experience of court procedures and the working of the administration.[63] His appointment to this prestigious post may be evidence for his growing reputation in jurisprudence, for at the time he cannot have been aged more than thirty: we have seen that by the middle of the thirteenth century he was regarded as the finest jurist there had ever been in the kingdom.

It does not really matter whether he was guilty or not of plotting Aimery's death. The important thing is that he evolved a method of defending himself in which the main themes of the later interpretation of the *Assise sur la ligece* can already be discerned: the argument that the law underlined the absolute necessity for a judgement in court in a case concerning the relationship between a lord and his vassal; what has aptly been called the 'Estate of Nobility',[64] in which all vassals were peers, bound to give each other mutual assistance; and the withdrawal of service from a lord who refused to permit a decision by *esgart*. Ralph's achievement was that he applied a law originally covering a lord's treatment of his vassals to the actions of the king himself. First he formally asked his peers to demand from Aimery *esgart* by the High Court. At what seems to have been the subsequent meeting of the court he solemnly read out a version of the *Assise sur la ligece*, thus clearly placing it in contradiction to the *assise* of Baldwin III or whatever law Aimery regarded as justifying his action. He addressed the king, pointing out that he had been banished without *esgart* or *conoissance*; this was illegal as long as he was willing to stand trial, to the judgement of which he formally submitted himself; he was reported as having said that he was prepared to defend himself in a judicial duel against anyone who cared to accept his challenge, from a kitchen scullion to the king himself. He emphasised that, as his lord, Aimery was bound to give him justice by calling on his fellow vassals to conduct an *esgart*. Aimery refused, whereupon Ralph solemnly demanded of his peers that they do him right. After they had replied that they were willing to assist him he left the court while the vassals tried to persuade the king to grant him a trial, threatening to withdraw their services from him until he agreed to their request. The king being obdurate, they solemnly withdrew their services from him after 'great words' and informed Ralph of their action, offering to maintain him in his rights. Thanking them, he told them that he would nevertheless leave the kingdom: the king felt so strongly about him that he could not stay and would not have done so even had he held in fief thirty realms. He left within the eight days, but the knights did not immediately return to the service of the king, because Ralph had suffered on account of the stand he had made. They may not have resumed their services until 1200.[65]

Ralph went to the County of Tripoli, where he was given a fief by Bohemond IV who himself was 'very wise and clever at the science of law both in and out of court'.[66] In 1204 Ralph supported the rebellion of Raynouard of Nephin and in an impossible situation decided to renounce his lands. This involved a complicated piece of court procedure and some legal wise-cracking which both he and Bohemond seem to have enjoyed.[67] Accompanied by his brother Hugh he then travelled on to Greece,[68] but soon afterwards King Aimery died and by July 1207, with John of Beirut the Regent of Jerusalem, he had returned to Acre.[69] Philip of Novara's compelling portrait of him before Damietta on the Fifth Crusade has already been referred to, but he was now ill – indeed Philip's account suggests that he knew he was dying – and although he was back in Acre by the end of May 1220 he must have died soon afterwards, for he was never again mentioned in the chronicles or the witness-lists to charters.[70]

The evidence for the dramatic meeting of the High Court in 1198 dates from half a century later, but it is to be found in the books of men who knew several of the chief participants well and it can therefore be followed with some confidence.[71] Faced by an attempt on the part of the king to act arbitrarily, perhaps with reference to an old law, Ralph had taken up an *assise* which must have been known to all because the make-up of the High Court had been affected by it. He had applied it to the actions of the crown in such a way as to provide himself and his peers not only with the justification for, but also with the means of, resistance and with the sanctions that could legally be brought to bear in a case of this kind. He was the first of the true lawyer barons but his career has a constitutional significance as important as his influence on legal practice. At the same time one cannot pretend that his use of the *Assise sur la ligece* had been very effective. The king had flatly refused to grant him an *esgart* and nothing had made him change his mind. He had found it necessary to leave the country, even though he had argued that this was a voluntary action, and he had not returned until after Aimery's death. The High Court however had withdrawn its services as a body and it may have been the idea of its members acting in concert which persuaded the jurists that Ralph's interpretation of the *Assise* was an effective means of resisting an autocratic king.[72] Certainly the precedent of 1198 was consciously followed thirty years later when the issue again arose.

In August 1225 Isabella, known to her contemporaries as Yolande and the heiress to the throne of Jerusalem, was married to the Emperor Frederick II in the cathedral of Acre, the Archbishop-elect of Capua acting as the emperor's proxy. She was subsequently crowned queen and a fortnight later embarked for Brindisi, where she went through a second marriage to Frederick, this time in person. Three years before, when King John, regent since his wife's death in 1212, had left for the West to seek help from the pope and arrange his daughter's marriage, it had been Hermann of Salza, the Master of the Teutonic Knights, who had suggested the match. The pope had supported it, for the union of the empire and Jerusalem would strengthen the Holy Land, to the aid of which the emperor, for a long time committed to a crusade, would soon be leading an important expedition. John's status after his wife's death must never have been defined for him and he had hoped, perhaps like Guy of Lusignan because he was a crowned king, that he might continue to rule Jerusalem for the rest of his life. He had been encouraged in this by Hermann of Salza, but on the wedding day Frederick demanded from him all the rights of the crown, together with moneys recently granted by the King of France for use in the Holy Land. John could only give way and, as relations between him and Frederick worsened when he learned that the emperor was unfaithful to his daughter, he left for Rome to complain to the pope.[73]

Frederick had acted immorally and unattractively, but as the consort of a crowned queen he had constitutionally an arguable point of view. He adopted the title of King of Jerusalem, which from now onwards appeared on all his charters immediately after that of Roman Emperor; he demanded and received homage from the small group of knights who had accompanied Yolande to Italy, among them Balian of Sidon and Nicholas Antiaume; and he sent the Bishop of Melfi to Palestine to receive on his behalf the homage of the rest of the vassals.[74] His character and thinking are now almost impossible to describe. The views of his contemporaries and later historians alike have been coloured by his bitter quarrel with the papacy, which certainly influenced the course of events in the East. It may be – though I am inclined to doubt it – that in Europe he was a Roman autocrat, the *stupor mundi*, basing his rule on Roman law, and that he was unconventional, even cynical, in his personal beliefs. But at least on his crusade and in his relations with the kingdoms of Cyprus and Jerusalem one is faced by a man who had a strong will and was capable of ruthless and arbitrary acts, but was motivated by conservative ideas, determined to enjoy what he took to be established imperial or royal rights, and although these rarely coincided with the baronial interpretation of law and custom it does not follow that they were indefensible.

He took a very long time before he could be persuaded to carry out the crusading vow that he had made in 1215, but no one could deny that his vow had been spontaneously made or that once determined to fulfil it he took the project seriously. It was of course for an emperor the performance of a sacred duty as the defender of Christendom. To some of his predecessors the corollary had been that the defence of the 'Christian Republic' was the responsibility of the emperor alone, whose function a pope usurped whenever he initiated a new crusade. But there are no signs that Frederick shared this view. In the Treaty of San Germano of July 1225 he renewed his crusading vow in an agreement with the pope, the terms of which, it has been said, were unique in their harshness. He agreed to act as an agent of the papacy and pledged the resources of his empire to the limit of its capacity. His preparations were detailed and thorough and he was ready to depart by the middle of August 1227, the time specified two years before.[75] Just after putting to sea, however, he fell ill, had to return to land and himself did not set out again until the following May. This delay had two important consequences. First, he was excommunicated by Pope Gregory IX for, among other things, failure to fulfil his vow, although his illness seems to have been genuine. Gregory's reaction was, as far as the crusade was concerned, quite unjustifiable, but it is clear that what worried him far more was Frederick's violation of papal claims in Sicily.[76] It is worth while remembering that excommunication removed from Frederick his protected status as a crusader and therefore freed the pope from the obligation to defend his lands in his absence and that what followed the emperor's departure was a papal invasion of southern Italy. And there can be little doubt that apprehension about Gregory's intentions made the emperor more anxious to conclude his expedition and he was therefore in a weaker position in the East than he might otherwise have been, while a sense of urgency may have led him to try rashly to impose his will on his political opponents without proper preparation. Secondly, the main body of his crusade had left Palestine before he ever reached it. When he eventually arrived it was at the head of a small company, estimated at between 40 and 100 knights. To increase his forces he had to hire mercenaries and for that he needed money which he now had to raise in the East itself.[77]

Frederick's policy towards Cyprus seems to have had two aims: to establish what he believed to be his rights as suzerain – the Kings of Cyprus were vassals of the empire – and to finance his crusade from the revenues that should, he argued, have accrued to him during a minority. King Hugh had died in January 1218 when his son Henry was only just over seven months old. The child's mother Alice was recognised by the Cypriot knights as regent and she made Philip of Ibelin, John of Beirut's brother, her lieutenant.[78] The acceptance of Alice as regent for Henry was prefectly in accord with Eastern practice, but there was a developing custom in Europe by which a king or lord had wardship of a vassal's lands in a minority. This, we have seen, was not generally followed in the laws of Jerusalem which were applied in Cyprus, except when there was no near relative to enjoy the wardship, but since Cyprus was a vassal state of the empire it was not unreasonable for Frederick to claim that it should follow imperial custom and that as Henry's liege-lord he should have the wardship of his lands until he came of age – incidentally he accepted the Cypriot reckoning that a man attained his majority at fifteen years. He asserted his claims in several letters to Alice, reminding her that she held the regency only at his pleasure.[79] Then in 1225 Henry, now only eight years old, was crowned by the Ibelins and their supporters. This act was accepted by the pope, who intervened with Frederick on Henry's behalf,[80] and in itself it did not affect whatever rights of wardship Frederick claimed. But it was done without the permission of the emperor, who stated with some justice that Henry could receive his crown only from him,[81] and it may be that the Cypriots feared lest he would take advantage of some technical matter to replace the child with another king and carried through the coronation to establish Henry's rights to the throne without qualification. Whatever their motives one cannot but see that the Cypriot nobles, or rather an influential group of them, had ignored the emperor's claims to the *bailliage* and had flouted his rights by crowning his vassal without his knowledge or licence.

On Philip of Ibelin's death in 1227 it is possible, though not certain, that his place as Alice's lieutenant was taken by his brother John of Beirut. If Ralph of Tiberias was the mentor of the later jurists, John was their hero. A half-brother of Queen Isabella, he had been Regent of Jerusalem for her daughter Maria of Montferrat from 1205 to 1210 and until his death in 1236 he was to be the leader of the opposition to the emperor. His character is as hard to read as that of his great enemy. He was a man of taste – the décor in his castle of Beirut greatly impressed one visitor – but it was perhaps fortunate for his later reputation that nearly all the evidence for his life comes from sources written by members of his family or dependants, for elsewhere are to be found hints of over-ambition and of corruption.[82] His supporters portrayed him as a perfect nobleman, chivalrous and honourable, wise and moderate, who was forced into an impossible situation by his opponents. There are reasons for distrusting this portrait, for by no means all the Cypriot knights aided him in his struggle with Frederick,[83] while in Palestine too there was a strong group of men who were prepared to stand by the emperor, even after his deposition in 1245.[84] John must have been a magnificent orator, even though his greater rhetorical exploits, his speeches to the emperor in 1228 and to the Bishop of Sidon in 1233, survive as reported by Philip of Novara who may well have embellished them. He inspired devotion in his followers and he was a learned and articulate lawyer.

Before Frederick's arrival in Cyprus his crusading army had crumbled away, he had been excommunicated by the pope and his lands were in danger; his claims as overlord of Cyprus had been ignored by the nobility in power, but the small size of the force he now led meant that he would want to exercise what rights he could on the island to further his plans in the Orient. It may be that he intended to use against the Cypriot lords those methods which he had applied with conspicuous success against the nobility of southern Italy, although there is evidence that he took care not to show his feelings at this time.[85] There was moreover a faction, perhaps large, in the Cypriot knightage which had been antagonised by the Ibelins. Its leaders went to meet the emperor at sea and, significantly pointing out how useful Cyprus could be to his crusade, complained bitterly of the way they had been treated.[86] It is noteworthy that as soon as he arrived in Limassol in July 1228 Frederick borrowed 30,000 saracen besants from the Lord of Gibelet.[87] And he now demanded by right of the empire the wardship of the king and kingdom and the homage of Henry and the Cypriot feudatories. Homage was paid him, but only after a long debate in Nicosia, where were gathered the Ibelin party with the young king. John of Beirut was advised to go straight 'in the service of God' to Syria, where he would be served as lord: it seems that it was suggested that he should lead an independent crusade, so that as crusaders his property and that of his followers would be protected by the Church. His reply, as reported by Philip of Novara, dwelt on the shame that would reflect on him and his friends if they did not aid the emperor in the reconquest of the Holy Land.[88]

Accompanied by two of his sons and by other knights of Cyprus, John brought the young king to Limassol. Frederick received them well, ordered them to dress in brightly coloured clothes – they were still in mourning for Philip of Ibelin – and invited them to a banquet, during which there occurred one of the best-known scenes of the thirteenth century. Before it had begun Frederick had brought 3,000 armed men, most of them presumably hired with the Lord of Gibelet's money, into the castle and some of these filed into the hall as the last course of the meal was served, while the Cypriot guests uneasily pretended not to notice them. Frederick had arranged the tables and seating carefully, so that all the feudatories could hear what passed between him and John, who was placed next to him. As soon as the soldiers had entered, he turned to John and demanded of him the surrender of his fief of Beirut, which, he said, was not held by right, and the profits of the revenues of the *bailliage* and *regalia* of Cyprus for the ten years since the death of King Hugh, 'for this is my right according to the usage of Germany'. It has already been suggested that the second of these requests was reasonable from Frederick's point of view; and the homage just rendered to him had established without doubt that he was rightful lord of the island. There is, moreover, evidence that he suspected the Ibelins of corrupt administration.[89] But he must have weakened his position by raising at the same time the question of Beirut, for he had not yet been received as Regent of Jerusalem and therefore had no powers in that kingdom. John rightly argued that if he was to be accused of wrongful possession of Beirut, then this was a case only for the High Court of Jerusalem. On the Cypriot rents he claimed that neither he nor his brother had enjoyed them, for they had gone to Alice, and he firmly stated his right to trial on this matter in the High Court of Cyprus. After a bitter public wrangle it was agreed that he should allow twenty of his followers, including his two sons present, to join the emperor's company as hostages for his appearance at the Court of Jerusalem, while he promised to serve Frederick on the mainland. It is odd that there was no reference made in this agreement to the revenues of Cyprus: Frederick may now have realised that his demands could not reasonably be made of John, but only of Alice.[90]

It is also curious that against the advice of his collaborators Frederick made no attempt to watch the movements of John and his followers. On the same night, after a discussion during which two of the Ibelins' fiercest partisans, John of Caesarea and Anceau of Brie, suggested assassinating the emperor, a proposal that John indignantly rejected, the Ibelin party made for Nicosia, from where they made sure of the island's fortresses, and when the emperor approached they withdrew to the castle of Dieu d'Amour. In all this they carefully observed their own ideas of legality: John emphasised that as vassals his followers must not raise arms against Frederick's person,[91] and he could claim that, whatever the emperor might desire, the castles should be in the hands of the High Court during a minority. On the other hand Frederick, after the failure of his carefully staged piece of theatrical display at Limassol, had not behaved arbitrarily: he had not seized John's person, the hostages had been surrendered to him voluntarily – although the baronial writers claimed that he ill-treated them – and he had agreed to take the case of Beirut to the High Court of Jerusalem. A reputation for toughness had certainly preceded him,[92] but he cannot at this stage be accused of anything more than a ham-handed and bullying attempt to impose his own view of his suzerainty.

With the threat of a papal invasion of southern Italy,[93] worry about the possible course of events back home would have made Frederick want to continue with his crusade. Some of the more moderate Syrian leaders began to mediate between the emperor and his opponents. An agreement was reached in which John of Beirut and his followers promised fealty to Frederick as liege-lord of their king – presumably this would outlast Henry's coming-of-age – provided that the duty to pay such fealty had been laid down in the original treaty between King Aimery and the Emperor Henry VI. They agreed to serve Frederick in Palestine and they recognised him as suzerain of Cyprus, but they refused him the *bailliage* because this belonged by right to Alice. In practice, however, they allowed him the rents and the custody of the child king, to whom they promised to surrender the castles. The emperor was to appoint liegemen from Cyprus to guard them until Henry came of age. Frederick returned the hostages and swore to allow the king to receive in person the castles and the kingdom. Alice's rights therefore, after a formal recognition, were ignored and in return for control of the island Frederick had agreed to a compromise in accordance with Cypriot law.[94]

On 3 September he set sail for Palestine, after trying to establish suzerainty over the Principality and County of Antioch-Tripoli, presumably as regent-to-be of Jerusalem. He demanded fealty from all the vassals of Bohemond IV and it was only by feigning sickness that the prince was able to escape before he was forced to comply.[95] In Palestine Frederick seems to have had a change of heart with regard to Cyprus, probably in the euphoria that followed his acquisition of the city of Jerusalem.[96] In April 1229 he sent one of his officers, Stephen of Cotron, to the island with a force of Italians to impose his regency and take possession of the fortresses and revenues. Some members of the baronial party fled from Cyprus and those Cypriots serving on the mainland with the emperor became uneasy, although John of Beirut discouraged them from doing anything rash. Then, before he left Acre on 1 May, the emperor farmed out the *bailliage* of the island to five of the leaders of that section of the nobility which was opposed to the Ibelins. He placed mercenaries at their disposal; others they hired in Acre. In Limassol he married the child-king by proxy to Alice of Montferrat and he ordered his five lieutenants to disinherit the Lord of Beirut and his followers, making them swear that they would not permit them to re-enter Cyprus.[97] It seems that it was in the spring of 1229 that there came the turning point in Cypriot politics, for Frederick now broke his side of the agreement he had made in the late summer of 1228: he entrusted the fortresses not to liegemen but to his own officers; he took over the *bailliage* and then farmed it out to five of his own supporters; and he ordered them to take action against certain of the vassals with no reference to the High Court. These acts were to lead to civil war and they were profoundly to affect relations between Frederick and the feudatories on the mainland, many of whom had fiefs in both states.

By his marriage to Yolande Frederick had become King-consort of Jerusalem. As such he had received the homage of the vassals; with Yolande he had issued charters for the kingdom and had appointed lieutenants to rule on his behalf: Odo of Montbéliard in 1225 and Thomas of Acerra in 1226.[98] His three predecessors, Henry of Champagne, Aimery and John of Brienne, had been comparatively strong rulers, but he seems to have determined to act even more firmly than they. In 1226-8 and 1231 his lieutenants Thomas of Acerra and Balian of Sidon were trying to restore what were believed to be royal rights over the *chaine* in the face of opposition from Italian merchants.[99] Frederick himself attempted to reduce the power of the Templars, who reacted violently to his acquisition of Jerusalem and were by the spring of 1229 in open revolt. He tried to seize their castle of Chastel Pèlerin and he later besieged their house in Acre.[100] And even before his arrival in Palestine he seems to have decided to bring its baronage to heel. He claimed to have heard much of John of Beirut before coming East,[101] and the appointment of Thomas of Acerra as his lieutenant in 1226 is evidence that he knew what he was up against. At the Diet of Capua in 1220 he had formulated his policy towards the south Italian nobility. Royal rights were to be re-established to the state in which they had been under the Norman kings: by the Law of Privileges all grants of the last thirty years were declared null and void; all castles and fortified places erected by the vassals in the same period were to be surrendered to him or razed to the ground, for the right to castellate was a royal prerogative; no rear-vassal was to be created, no feudatory was to marry and no child was to inherit a fief without his consent. Two years of campaigning followed at the end of which the resistance of the lords was broken. Thomas of Acerra had been a captain of the imperial forces and it has been remarked before that his appointment to the lieutenancy of Jerusalem cannot have been a coincidence.[102] It suggests that the emperor was hoping to pursue the same policy in Palestine as he had in Italy, a policy, it must be emphasised, which had been characterised by a kind of *quo warranto* approach to privileges and rights, being firmly based on the supposed powers of earlier kings. It is no surprise to learn that Thomas of Acerra was feared by the people of Palestine and that it was wondered what his appointment presaged of Frederick's intentions.[103]

But the emperor's constitutional position in the Kingdom of Jerusalem was not that of a King of Sicily. No regent could legally exercise authority until he came in person to receive it and with Yolande's death, the news of which reached Acre in the summer of 1228, his rights lapsed in law until he himself arrived in Palestine to claim the regency for the son, Conrad, born to his wife just before she died. In the meantime the High Court appointed Balian of Sidon and Odo of Montbéliard as regents for Conrad.[104] While he was in Cyprus, therefore, Frederick had no rights recognised in Jerusalem although he later believed, like Guy and John before him, that he had acquired an inalienable right to rule. On his arrival in Acre he was received as regent and homage was made to him.[105] He was to remain in the Holy Land until the following May, but, apart from letters written by Frederick himself, Hermann of Salza and the patriarch for propaganda purposes and the partisan accounts in the baronial histories, the documentary evidence for his visit is scanty: there survive only fifteen charters, two of which date from October 1228, twelve from April and one from May 1229.[106] Of the feudatories of Jerusalem Balian of Sidon and Garnier L'Aleman witnessed every charter and Odo of Montbéliard and John of Beirut fourteen of the fifteen, but the charters are dated too closely together into two groups for this to have much significance. It is clear, however, that Frederick's stay in Palestine fell into two periods: the time of the crusade proper, culminating in the acquisition of Jerusalem by treaty in February 1229; and the following months in which the emperor seems to have begun a campaign against the nobility which ended in his humiliation.

The events of the first period are too well known to need repeating in detail here. Even before his arrival Frederick had begun to treat with the Muslim powers, particularly Egypt. There were precedents for the acquisition of lands by treaty from the infidel: Conrad of Montferrat has already been seen trying to arrange the return of part of the kingdom to the Christians in the 1190s and various offers made by the Egyptians in the course of the Fifth Crusade had been seriously considered and supported by influential elements in the Latin army, if in the end they had been turned down.[107] In the winter of 1228-9, in spite of the fact that he had been excommunicated by the pope and had with him an unimposing army, Frederick persuaded the Sultan al-Kamil of Egypt to surrender Jerusalem to him by a mixture of the threat of force and skilful negotiation, undertaken by Balian of Sidon and Thomas of Acerra. He gained the Holy City, except for the Temple area, and Bethlehem, a corridor of land from Jerusalem and Bethlehem by way of Lydda to the coast at Jaffa, Nazareth and western Galilee, including the castles of Montfort and Toron, and those parts of the hinterland of Sidon that were still in Muslim hands.[108] On 17 March he made a ceremonial entry into Jerusalem and on Sunday the 18th he solemnly wore the imperial crown in the Church of the Holy Sepulchre: the emperor, the defender of Christendom, had showed himself performing his God-given task; as a second Heraclius he had brought Jerusalem back into the Christian fold.[109]

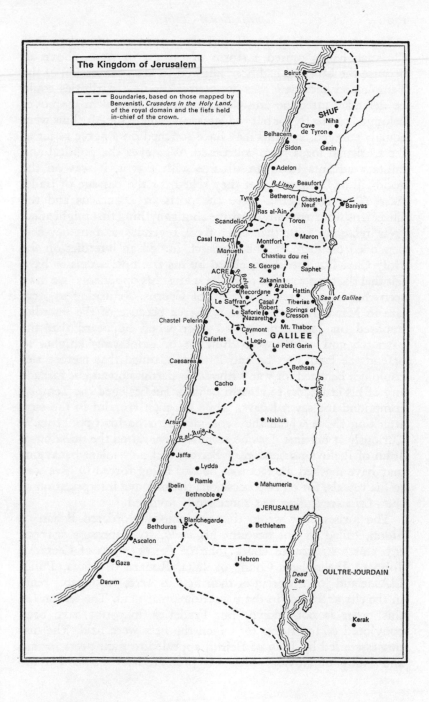

The Kingdom of Jerusalem

- - - - Boundaries, based on those mapped by
Benvenisti, *Crusaders in the Holy Land,*
of the royal domain and the fiefs held
in-chief of the crown.

Beirut

SHUF

Cave Niha
de Tyron
Belhacem
Sidon Gezin

Adelon

R. Litani

Beaufort

Betheron

Tyre Chastel
Neuf
Ras al-Ain Baniyas
Toron
Scandelion

Maron
Casal Imbert
Montfort
Manueth
Chastiau dou rei

St. George Saphet

ACRE
Belus Zakanin I
Haifa Docl Arabia Hattin
Recordane
Le Saffran Casal Tiberias Sea of Galilee
Robert
Le Saforie Springs of
Nazareth Cresson
Chastel Pelerin
Caymont Mt. Thabor GALILEE
Cafarlet
Legio Le Petit Gerin

Caesarea
Bethsan
R. Jordan
Cacho

Arsur Nablus
R. al-Auja

Jaffa
Lydda
Ibelin Ramle Mahumeria
Bethnoble
JERUSALEM
Blanchegarde
Bethduras Bethlehem
Ascalon

Hebron
Gaza
OULTRE-JOURDAIN
Darum
Dead
Sea

Kerak

The treaty with al-Kamil and the return of Jerusalem into Christian hands caused a storm of protest in Acre, above all because the Muslims had been allowed to keep possession of the Temple and because it was doubted if the new territories could be defended after the crusade's departure. Jerusalem moreover belonged not to Egypt but to Damascus, where the Muslims were equally enraged, and this may have touched on a nerve as far as the Christian lords were concerned. Whatever the political and military advantages of an alliance with Egypt, it was on the goodwill of Damascus that they relied for the passage of trade. Acre, Tyre and Beirut were the ports of Damascus and the Christians were naturally sensitive about anything that might affect their relations with that city: their revenues and money-fiefs depended on them.[110] The patriarch hurled an interdict on the Holy City. But Frederick, elated by his triumph, seems to have felt that the time was ripe to strike against his opponents: we have seen that he now seized control of Cyprus. Returning to Acre late in March his anger, already fierce because of the interdict imposed on Jerusalem, boiled over when he heard that the patriarch and others were thinking of employing knights to defend the land after he had left. He claimed that mercenaries could not be hired for war without his permission and he forbade any of his crusaders to remain behind. He besieged the Templar compound for several days, while his men ran riot in the city, attacking those whom they considered to be his opponents.[111] Curiously at no time does he seem to have raised the question of John of Ibelin's possession of Beirut; and his violent behaviour may have masked the fact that he was being forced to give way to his vassals, for on two occasions the baronial interpretation of the *Assise sur la ligece* was successfully invoked.

The jurists later wrote that the emperor ordered Balian of Sidon, called in one account his *bailli*, to dispossess without *esgart* or *conoissance* of court John of Beirut, John of Caesarea, John of Ibelin later Count of Jaffa, Rohard of Haifa, Philip L'Asne and John Moriau of their fiefs in Acre, presumably rents in the city and lands in the royal domain around. The reason for this order is not known, but Frederick may not have been convinced of the rights by which the fiefs were held. The dispossessed, led by John of Beirut, appealed to their peers for aid and Philip of Novara, who was present, later wrote that the

Assise sur la ligece was read out at a meeting of the High Court, many of whose members had seen Ralph of Tiberias invoke it thirty years before. For the first time however the knights seem to have made use of what was believed to be another sanction open to them under the *Assise*, for they restored the fiefs to their peers by the use of physical force, an action presumably based on the precedent of the royal campaign against Gerard of Sidon in the 1160s.[112]

The second case concerned a dispute over the Lordship of Toron and Chastel Neuf, which the Teutonic Knights had claimed as a possession of the late Joscelin of Courtenay, much of whose domains they had acquired.[113] Frederick, who favoured the brothers as his staunchest supporters, seems to have been genuinely mistaken about rights, for theoretical lordship over Toron, it will be remembered, had been returned to Humphrey in the 1190s. The Teutonic Knights' claim to it was challenged by Alice of Armenia, who was able to prove that she had an hereditary right to it through her mother, Isabella of Toron. A meeting of the High Court, at which John of Beirut played a large part, ruled for Alice, but Balian of Sidon, again called by the jurists Frederick's *bailli*, produced letters from the emperor forbidding him to put her into seizin. According to John of Jaffa, who was in Acre at the time although too young to be in the High Court, the vassals, acting as had their ancestors in 1198 and in accordance with their interpretation of the *Assise sur la ligece*, solemnly withdrew their service from the emperor, stating that they would only serve Frederick again when he agreed to carry out what the court had decided by *esgart*.[114]

The references to Balian of Sidon as the emperor's *bailli* have led historians to suppose that these disputes took place after Frederick's departure in May 1229, when Balian was left as one of his representatives. But the term *bailli* is a vague one, being used of any lieutenant of a ruler, and it looks as though Balian had been appointed Frederick's *bailli* in Acre while the emperor was in southern Palestine, because the second case occurred, according to John of Jaffa, while Frederick was in Syria, and indeed it was referred to in one of Frederick's charters.[115] Toron was returned to Christian hands in February 1229 by the terms of the treaty with Egypt and Frederick did not come back to Acre until 23 March. We may therefore date the withdrawal of service

to the period 18 February–23 March 1229 and, since the two
quarrels are linked in the law-books, we may assume that the
forcible re-possession of fiefs, which it is otherwise not possible
to date, took place at about the same time.[116]

John of Jaffa wrote that after a period, with the will and
authority of the Princess of Armenia and the vassals, the liegemen
re-entered Frederick's service.[117] Evidence survives to show that
this marked a baronial victory. In a charter Frederick recounted
how he had assigned Toron to the Teutonic Knights, but Alice
of Armenia, 'coming into our presence', required it by hereditary
right. She was prepared to come to the High Court to prove her
claim and, appearing within the allotted time, showed sufficiently
that Toron should belong to her. And so 'we had this land
restored to her *according to the esgart of our court*'. The Teutonic
Knights were granted other estates and rents in place of Toron.[118]
This charter is one of the series dating from April, almost certainly from the second half of the month, and witnessed by the
baronial leaders, the presence of whose names must mark their
return to Frederick's service. It is clear from it that the emperor
had been forced to accept *esgart* of the High Court on the matter
of Toron. The vassals' withdrawal of service had been successful;
and if the forcible reseizin of the Ibelin fiefs took place at the
same time, then this underlined the extent of Frederick's failure
in his treatment of the feudatories of Jerusalem. The fact is that
he was not strong enough. He was disturbed by news from the
West and anxious to leave, and he had at his disposal only a small
force of crusaders together with mercenaries for whom he had to
find pay; and a number of these had been dispatched to Cyprus.

His impotence may also have been revealed in another way.
The patriarch reported that in March he was disposed to leave
behind Thomas of Acerra as his lieutenant and this appointment
seems to have been made, for in April Thomas witnessed two of
his charters as *bailli* of the kingdom.[119] Although Frederick had
every right to leave as his lieutenant whomsoever he wished, the
appointment of Thomas had been reversed by the time of his
departure. Philip of Novara told how the emperor tried to leave
Acre secretly on 1 May, but on his way down to his galley was
recognised and pelted with offal by the butchers and old women
who lived around the meat markets. Hearing of this John of Beirut
and Odo of Montbéliard rushed after him, stopped the disgraceful

scene and hurried on to the shore. The emperor had already embarked, but in a low voice informed them that he left Balian of Sidon and Garnier L'Aleman as his *baillis* and this he seems to have confirmed a day or two later in Tyre, where he was joined by Balian and Garnier themselves.[120] Although Balian had shown himself to be a faithful agent of imperial policies, the circumstances of the appointment of these two liegemen, made at the last moment in 'a low voice', suggest that it was against Frederick's wishes and that his decision to make Thomas his lieutenant had attracted such resistance that he had been forced to withdraw it.

The first part of Frederick's stay in Palestine had ended in triumph with an imperial crown-wearing in the Church of the Holy Sepulchre, but the second, although it was marked by his seizure of power in Cyprus, could scarcely have been more humiliating for him. At least once, and probably twice, he had seen his wishes overruled by the application against him of the *Assise sur la ligece*; and he probably had to rescind the appointment of a lieutenant whose post was in his gift. His sojourn in the East had four main consequences. His treaty with Egypt led him to become a protagonist of a continuing alliance with that state at a time when it could damage a delicate relationship with Damascus upon which seigneurial economies relied; the conflict in Cyprus remained a running sore, poisoning his relations with his vassals in Jerusalem; he seems to have become even more determined to impose his will in some way on his recalcitrant subjects in Palestine, but their success had firmly implanted into the minds of the baronial leaders the value of their interpretation of the *Assise sur la ligece* and convinced them that by means of it they could resist any attempt by a ruler to infringe what they believed to be their rights. They forgot that Frederick had been in an exceptionally weak position and the *Assise* remained in their minds the bulwark of their freedoms, even after it had become obvious that it was not the panacea they believed it to be.

The emperor's departure left Cyprus on the verge of civil war. The Ibelin party refused to recognise the rule of the five *baillis*, who had to extort money ruthlessly from the people in order to fulfil their commitments. Their seizure of the fiefs of the emperor's opponents led John of Beirut to fit out and lead an expedition from Palestine which defeated the imperial forces before Nicosia on 14 July 1229. The *baillis* and their supporters withdrew to the island's three most important fortresses, Kyrenia, Kantara and Dieu d'Amour, holding out in the last two until the summer of 1230. Peace followed, in which they surrendered the castles and the king to the Ibelins, towards whom they swore to bear no enmity in future. Cyprus was now controlled by the baronial party, but Frederick did not yet consider himself beaten. Having come to terms with the pope at San Germano in July 1230, he prepared a strong force which sailed for the East in the autumn of 1231. When the main body of the imperial fleet arrived off Cyprus, its captains sent a message to the king, demanding the banishment of the Ibelins. Henry being still a minor, William Viscount replied on his behalf, refusing to countenance such an arbitrary act against royal vassals.[121]

The events in Cyprus were bound to inflame feelings on the mainland in the interval between Frederick's departure and the arrival of the imperial army: in 1230 it was intended to send Philip of Novara to the rulers of the West, to complain to them of the behaviour of the emperor and his followers in the Latin East.[122] In February 1231 the pope had to issue a warning to the Templars, who were building up their forces in Palestine in spite of the prohibition of Frederick's lieutenant, presumably either Balian of Sidon or Garnier L'Aleman, and were thought to be intent on violating the treaty with Egypt.[123] But Frederick's position as regent and perhaps his rapprochement with the papacy may have made his opponents reluctant to commit themselves too publicly against him. The High Court turned down a claim for the crown put forward by Alice of Cyprus. Alice was unpopular because of the way she had behaved as *bailli* of the island in the 1220s, but she was the daughter of Isabella of Jerusalem and Henry of Champagne and was next in line for the throne after Conrad. She presented herself in Acre as the *plus dreit heir aparant*, implying that Conrad's right had lapsed. It is possible that she rested her argument on a custom, later described by John of Jaffa, that nothing should escheat to a man who did not come to claim it; and the timing of her plea suggests that she was proposing that the fact that Conrad had not come East within a year and a day of Yolande's death had lost him his title.[124] But her claim was ruled to be inadmissible. The members of the High Court replied that the vassals of Jerusalem had made homage to Frederick as regent for his son – presumably they believed this answered her case – and therefore could not recognise her, but they determined to ask the emperor to send out Conrad within a year, promising to 'guard him as lord', although they did not specify what they would do if he did not come. Their message to Frederick was delivered by two knights, both fief-holders in Acre; one of them was the baronial supporter Geoffrey Le Tor, but the other, a Flemish knight called John of Bailleul, seems from his later activities to have been an imperialist. Frederick gave them a non-committal answer and he never sent Conrad to the East.[125]

In the autumn of 1231 the leaders of the baronial party had warning of the approach of the imperial armada from a spy in the crew of a galley belonging to the Teutonic Knights. John of Beirut and his followers hurried to Cyprus and were at the king's side when the fleet came to anchor. The force was under the command of the imperial marshal Richard Filangieri, but Richard himself was following on some days behind the main body and the captains do not seem to have felt strong enough to attempt a landing. After the king had refused to banish the Ibelins they sailed on and disembarked their forces before the city of Beirut, which was surrendered to them by its bishop. They settled down to invest the citadel and when Richard joined them he pressed on with the siege.[126] This attempt to dispossess a vassal of his fief by force was the act that set in motion the train of events leading to the establishment of the Commune of Acre, but it is worth asking whether it was undertaken in accordance with Frederick's instructions or was rather a move made on the spur of the moment by the captains of the imperial army before Richard Filangieri's arrival. Richard was later to say that he was following Frederick's orders[127] and the emperor may well have wanted John to be dispossessed of Beirut, for he had had little satisfaction on the matter in 1228. Although it may have been told to make a demonstration against Cyprus on the way, the imperial fleet was clearly destined for Palestine: the emperor had told the pope that he was sending an army to the aid of the city of Jerusalem[128] and he wanted Richard to replace Balian of Sidon and Garnier L'Aleman as his lieutenant in Acre. But it is hardly credible that either he or Richard would have been so foolish as to order a blatant attack on the lands of a vassal at the start of a new *bailliage*.

Whether on his arrival Richard was or was not surprised to

find his army besieging Beirut, he made formal approaches to Frederick's vassals. From Beirut he sent to Tyre, ordering the city, which was part of the royal domain, to surrender to him and he was obeyed, perhaps on the command of Balian of Sidon.[129] A short time afterwards he came to Acre with a small company and on his arrival assembled all the knights and burgesses in the city. John of Beirut and his friends were absent in Cyprus but to those who attended Richard read a Golden Bull from Frederick, addressed to all in the kingdom and informing them that he had sent Richard to be his lieutenant 'to maintain right and justice and to guard in their rights the great and the little and the rich and the poor'. He then assured the assembly that he was 'prepared to act by the counsel of the wise men of the land'. Were it not for the siege of Beirut, nothing here, except perhaps the occupation by a lieutenant of the citadel of Tyre, conflicted with the baronial view of Richard's duties and the author of an account of his reception commented on the acceptability of the imperial letters of appointment. Richard was later to send part of the imperial fleet to winter in the port of Acre, which suggests that he believed that he had control of the city. Whatever was later said, the feudatories seem to have recognised him as *bailli* and probably took some oath to him: otherwise they could scarcely have demanded an ending to the siege of Beirut in the way they did.[130]

It seems that a formal request was made of Richard in the High Court by Balian of Sidon. The speech put into Balian's mouth by a chronicler is one of the most famous of all the barons' statements and in no other passage in the sources is their view of the relations between crown and vassal so well expressed: that because of the circumstances of the conquest of Palestine by the First Crusade and the election of Godfrey of Bouillon as ruler the kings had a special relationship with their vassals; that among the laws they had sworn to obey was one forbidding them to dispossess their vassals without *esgart* of court; that John of Beirut was the emperor's man and that Richard Filangieri, who was Frederick's lieutenant with the duty of guarding the land and maintaining the rightful heir – evidence that he had been accepted as *bailli* – had dispossessed John of the city and fief of Beirut and was besieging his castle without previously having sought *esgart* or *jugement*; that in consequence Balian, on behalf of the vassals, required Richard to withdraw from Beirut so that John could be put back in seizin of it, because no action could be taken unless John were summoned to trial in the High Court according to the usages of the Kingdom of Jerusalem; and that if by the *esgart* of the court John was found to be guilty of wrongful possession of the fief, Balian committed the vassals to help Richard to dispossess him.[131]

Richard answered that he would take counsel with the captains of the imperial host before giving a reply, but on his return to Beirut he continued to press its castle hard. And he informed two emissaries from Acre that he was an imperial servant, bound to follow the orders of the emperor, towards whom everyone knew how John of Beirut had behaved: he seems to have been suggesting here that John had committed apparent treason and was perhaps referring to the *assise* of Baldwin III. If they could not accept what he was doing, he added, they should apply directly to the emperor for a ruling.[132] In fact Balian of Sidon, Odo of Montbéliard and Garnier L'Aleman may have hurried to Italy to confer with Frederick,[133] but if they did so it is clear that they got no satisfaction from him and that they were back in the East early in 1232. Meanwhile, John of Beirut presented himself before the King and the High Court of Cyprus. In the most plausible version of his speech he reminded the king of their blood relationship and of the way his family had helped to preserve the crown, begging him and all others present 'as my brothers and dear friends' to come in person with all their power to relieve his castle.[134] The king and his vassals agreed, although the imperial supporters among them deserted at the first possible moment and were later to reoccupy Cyprus on Frederick's behalf. Early in 1232 the Cypriot force passed over to Puy du Connétable, south of Tripoli. Part of the army disembarked and, with the fleet sailing alongside, marched down to Beirut.[135]

By this time a commune had been established in Acre. After hearing of Richard Filangieri's reply the vassals had met to discuss the matter. The wisest of them, according to a chronicler, saw that there was no hope for them unless they were bound together by an oath to guard and maintain their rights and the laws and franchises of the kingdom. In Acre there happened to be a confraternity dedicated to St Andrew and chartered perhaps by Baldwin IV and Henry of Champagne, which of the many bodies of this kind in the city was unusual in that its membership was not limited to those of one nationality or sect but was open to all. An institution with an unrestricted membership, in which knights and burgesses could be bound by a common oath assuring mutual security, suited the vassals' purposes. So barons, knights and burgesses assembled and sent for the confraternity's counsellors and charters. These were read out and the majority of those present solemnly swore themselves in as members.[136]

The Commune of Acre, which is what resulted from this enlargement of the Confraternity of St Andrew, had its own bell, probably hanging in the cathedral church of the Holy Cross. It had officers, the chief of whom was mayor: John of Beirut was chosen to be the first holder of this office in 1232. The mayoralty may have been renewable each year, because in 1233 John was re-elected. In his absence he may have been represented by a deputy mayor: in 1233 John of Caesarea. There also were consuls and captains, who were perhaps military leaders.[137] At first sight the commune seems to resemble similar bodies in the West, particularly in Italy, but it was in fact quite unique, unlike even the two previous Syrian communal experiments at Tyre and Antioch.[138]

It has already been said that membership was open to any freeman willing to take an oath binding himself to the other members in the preservation of their rights. By so doing he participated in a body which regarded itself, and was regarded by others, as a corporation representative of the community of the Kingdom of Jerusalem.[139] While the vassals in Acre were of course fief-holders in the royal domain, the adherence of the greater lords brought representatives of the lordships into the commune as individuals and it could claim support in much of the territory in Christian hands in 1231. But one should be careful not to accept too uncritically its view of itself. The vassals in the royal domain of Tyre and the burgesses and knights of the city of Jerusalem had accepted the rule of Richard Filangieri and seem never to have recognised the commune; in the early 1240s there was an important group of burgesses within Acre who were ready to lend aid to an attempted *coup d'état* in the emperor's favour; and Frederick had powerful supporters in Palestine until his death in 1250.[140] However much the leaders of the commune might have liked to regard themselves as representing the whole country in its relations with the regent, they clearly did not. The commune, moreover, was ephemeral. After 1236 there survive only two references to it, one in an obscure letter of 1241, the other a passing mention in a report of 1243 by the chief Venetian administrator in the East.[141] It never obtained a charter from the crown which might have given it a permanent form and it seems to have been disbanded with the coming of age of Conrad in 1243 and the ending of Frederick's regency.

It was unlike the communes in the West in that it never seems to have acquired administrative functions, although these have been attributed to it in the past. It has been seen as taking over the administration of the city of Acre, thus providing the burgess population with a further opportunity to participate in city government.[142] But this is probably in error, because the Viscount and jurors of the *Cour des Bourgeois* are to be found still exercising jurisdiction in two documents of 1232, when the communal movement was presumably at its height.[143] An alternative argument has been proposed by one of the finest historians of the Latin East. To him the commune stemmed from the basic political needs of the kingdom in 1231. In calling together the knights and burgesses to hear his letters of appointment, 'a novel and revolutionary' action, Richard Filangieri was appealing over the heads of the High Court directly to the populace. The barons needed some answer to this appeal for popular backing and they were moreover faced by a problem resulting from their reluctance to recognise Richard's *bailliage* and his hostility towards them. Without the authority of a *bailli* the High Court could not be convoked and without convoking the court the *Assise sur la ligece* could not be applied in the matter of Beirut. Richard would not and the old *bailli*, Balian of Sidon, could not call together the High Court for such a purpose. The answer for the barons was the commune to which all, knights and burgesses, could be bound, and which could replace the High Court in the government of the country, or at least of those parts of it which did not recognise Richard, until 1243 when the High Court was 'revived'. This argument suggests that the commune was not only an attempt to win popular support for the baronial party after a blatant appeal to the burgesses by Richard Filangieri, but also that in a situation in which the *Assise sur la ligece* could not legally be invoked it took over government from the *baillis* and the High Court for twelve years.[144]

When however Richard Filangieri assembled in Acre the

knights and burgesses he was doing nothing revolutionary. It is true that there is no evidence before 1231 for the *Cour des Bourgeois* joining the High Court in the discussion of constitutional matters, but there had been a long and close association between the High Court and the burgess courts of Jerusalem or Acre on legal and feudal matters and they had often met together during the twelfth century.[145] And surely there cannot have been anything particularly striking about a lieutenant asking for support from the burgesses in the royal domain – which is all that Richard seems to have been doing. Far more revolutionary than this had been the right of the king, established in the previous century under the *Assise sur la ligece*, to demand fealty from freemen *outside* the royal domain. Nor can one agree that there was any doubt over Richard's *bailliage*. It is true that John of Jaffa, making no reference at all to Richard Filangieri, wrote later that Balian of Sidon and Garnier L'Aleman, the imperial appointees in 1229, remained *baillis* until Garnier entered the Order of the Knights Templar and was replaced by Odo of Montbéliard and that, although Balian died in 1239, Odo continued to hold the *bailliage* until Conrad came of age in 1243.[146] But this account, written after the events, seems to have been special pleading, a justification for past actions by pretending that Richard's lieutenancy had never existed. We have seen that it is probable, on the contrary, that Richard was accepted as *bailli* by the High Court and it seems that the problem facing the baronial party in 1231 was not whether he was rightfully in office, but how to resist him once he had been lawfully appointed.

The failure of a *bailli* to convoke the High Court moreover did not in itself nullify the use of the *Assise sur la ligece*, which, as interpreted by the vassals, was the very instrument to be wielded in a case in which a ruler had refused to hold trial. And, in spite of the fact that Richard Filangieri never authorised its convocation, there is some evidence for the High Court, or at least an assembly of liegemen, continuing to meet in Acre throughout the period, whatever the doubts about its validity. It was called together early in 1232 to hear John of Beirut's appeal for help to relieve his castle.[147] When in 1233 the Bishop of Sidon arrived with letters from Frederick II appointing Philip of Maugustel his *bailli*, Balian of Sidon and Odo of Montbéliard 'assembled the liegemen in the Church of the Holy Cross'.[148] When Conrad came of age in

1243 and there was an attempt to appoint a new *bailli* the 'liege-men assembled' to discuss the matter.[149] It should be remembered that we would anyway expect to find little evidence for the High Court in these twelve years, because in the absence of a king or hereditary regent there was in fact little that it could legally do.[150]

If the commune had taken over the government we should find its chief officers acting in place of the High Court and the *baillis*. But we have seen that the liegemen continued to meet apart from the other 'communards' and there is no evidence to suggest that the *bailliage* was considered to have ceased to exist. John of Jaffa's account of the *bailliage* in the 1230s may have been in error, but it shows that he did not believe that it had been supplanted. And it seems that neither Frederick nor the leaders of the commune thought that in Acre the *bailliage* had been replaced by a new instrument of government. It is indeed impossible to see how the commune could have 'governed'. It could not settle feudal matters, for these came under the purview of the High Court; it had no jurisdiction, for it was not a court; it could not discuss foreign policies, which were customarily dealt with by a larger body, containing representatives of the Church; it never seems to have had the right to collect royal rents and revenues. In other words it had none of the attributes of government.

An examination of its known actions supports this view. In 1232 John of Beirut led its members down to the port of Acre to seize the ships of the imperial fleet that had been sent to winter there by Richard Filangieri.[151] In 1233 John of Caesarea summoned it to arms by the ringing of its bell to prevent Philip of Maugustel from being received as lieutenant.[152] In the summer of 1235 its leaders were planning to launch an attack on Tyre,[153] and in the mid-1230s their representatives were negotiating with papal emissaries or at the papal curia on the future position of Frederick's lieutenants.[154] In 1243 members of the commune attended a parliament called to discuss the claims of Alice of Cyprus to the regency.[155] It is only in this last appearance that it can be seen as anything more than an agent of resistance to the emperor, but it played no greater part at the parliament than did other non-knightly institutions, for the right of deciding whether Alice's claims had validity belonged only to the liegemen. The commune seems to have been a body the sole *raison d'être* of which was resistance to the emperor, and this explains why it is not to be found after 1243: with Conrad of age there were now other ways of opposing the object of its animosity.

If the commune was not an instrument of government but was merely a means of resisting Frederick II and his lieutenants, it may well be asked why a baronial movement which had already provided itself with an elaborate method of opposing arbitrary acts by a ruler should have resorted to such a measure, one moreover that by enlarging the class of those bound to one another must have been repugnant to it. The seizure of the city of Beirut, the siege of its citadel and the refusal by a lieutenant to discontinue what amounted to dispossession without *esgart* created a situation to which *par excellence* the *Assise sur la ligece* applied. In fact it is clear that the *Assise* was invoked shortly after the establishment of the commune. It will be remembered that in a case of arbitrary disseizin by a lord there were three options open to the injured vassal: he could conjure his lord, he could withdraw his own service or he could conjure his peers who, if his case had justice, would either put him forcibly back into possession of his fief or would solemnly withdraw their own services from the lord. Balian of Sidon, speaking for the vassals, had formally required Richard Filangieri to raise the siege of Beirut and in his speech as it is reported there seems to have been a reference to the *Assise sur la ligece*.[156] Richard had refused this request. The next move was for John of Beirut to conjure his peers and this he did. After crossing over from Cyprus early in 1232 he sent a letter to Acre. It has been suggested that this letter was sent to the commune, but in fact John wrote 'au comun des homes de la terre'. In thirteenth-century texts the word 'homes', as opposed to 'gens', was often used of vassals. John was writing here not to the commune, but to the vassals of Jerusalem in general, and this conclusion is supported by a statement in a chronicle that the letter was 'read in the palace of Balian of Sidon where most of the *men of the emperor* were gathered'. The letter demanded that these vassals put John back into possession of Beirut by force.

> Lords, I would let you know that a foreign people from another land have overrun me and have seized and taken my city and my land and have besieged my castle, so that I cannot come to you nor send any of my men, for they are enclosed and besieged in my castle. For which reason I would let you know my need by these

letters, in which I summon and require you as my brothers and my friends that you *maintain me in right according to the usages and customs of the Kingdom of Jerusalem* and that you help me retake and deliver my city, castle and land.[157]

The reaction to this clear request under the *Assise sur la ligece* was in sad contrast to those of 1198 and 1229. The vassals were divided as to what to do, but a strong party of 43 knights, including John of Caesarea, who promised fiefs to those who would lend support, Rohard of Haifa, Geoffrey Le Tor and Geoffrey of Estraing, who was later to be Lord of Haifa, rode north to John's aid. Meeting him not far from Beirut they encamped while Balian of Sidon and Odo of Montbéliard, the Patriarch of Jerusalem, the Archbishop of Caesarea, the Masters of the Templars and the Hospitallers and the leaders of the three Italian communes tried unsuccessfully to make peace between them and Richard Filangieri. The imperial forces could not be dislodged, but John of Beirut, satisfied that his castle could hold out, came to Acre, where in April the commune was assembled in the cathedral of the Holy Cross. John himself now solemnly entered the Confraternity of St Andrew and was appointed mayor.[158]

The failure of John's supporters to relieve Beirut was therefore closely followed by a re-assembly of the Commune of Acre and the election of John as its first mayor. The association of these events is surely significant. It cannot be denied that the *Assise sur la ligece* had been a failure. The vassals of Jerusalem had shown themselves incapable of putting John back in possession of his fief by force; and had he and his peers solemnly withdrawn their services their action would have had little effect, because Richard Filangieri had a strong force of his own Italian soldiers and could survive without them. The situation in 1231–2 exposed an inherent flaw in the baronial interpretation of the *Assise*. The power of its sanctions depended on the opposition of a weak king and if the ruler had a mercenary army at his disposal, 'foreign people' as John of Beirut called them,[159] there was no method by which it could be made effective. It became an empty formality.

This must have been clear to the vassals in Acre in the autumn of 1231; and the attempt to apply the *Assise* after the creation of the commune may reveal a difference of opinion between them and

John of Beirut, who was in Cyprus at the time and may have insisted on trying to carry out the law on his arrival in the following year, an action that those who had been on the spot since Richard's coming knew would be worthless. Their 'only salvation'[160] had been to evolve an alternative method of resistance, one that would bind to them not only the knights but also as many freemen as possible, and so they had created a sworn association dedicated only to resistance to the emperor. It is important to emphasise their essentially negative approach. The commune was not an organ of government or administration, but merely an instrument of resistance, established in circumstances in which the *Assise sur la ligece* was worthless. Even here it can be overestimated: it never represented all the kingdom, nor even all those in Acre, and it had no successors, except perhaps for the short-lived Commune of Tripoli.[161] The idea of national as opposed to feudal resistance was not enshrined in the writings of the later jurists, who continued to treat the *Assise* as if it were the cure of all ills. One cannot avoid the conclusion that the establishment of the Commune of Acre, so soon after the successes of 1229, marks a failure of the vassals' ideas and exposes the weakness that lay at the root of their political thought. And the sorry collapse of the *Assise* – it was never again applied in the Kingdom of Jerusalem – reveals something of the great jurists who wrote a quarter of a century later. Neither Philip of Novara nor John of Jaffa mentioned the events of 1231–2[162] and we have seen that to John the *bailliage* of Richard Filangieri never existed. Both used much ink in describing what we know was a cardboard fortification of their interests and their treatment, impressive as it remains, is further evidence that they related their constitutional ideas to a political state that existed only in their dreams.

8

THE BAILLIAGE

EVEN before John of Beirut had tried to make use of the *Assise sur la ligece* in 1232 another legal and constitutional issue, the powers that could be exercised by a *bailli*, had begun to attract the attention of the leading vassals. In the Kingdom of Jerusalem the title of *bailli* was given to many who held executive powers, including minor officials in the royal domain and the lordships, administrators in the Military Orders and particularly those who presided over the administration in the absence of the king. But it was not a very accurate term even when used of the last of these groups, because it was given indiscriminately to those chosen to rule in times of minority or when the heir to the throne had not come to Palestine to be crowned, and to those whom established kings and regents appointed to take their places temporarily while they were out of the country. A differentiation can be made by referring to members of the first class as regents and to members of the second as lieutenants. Practical necessity forced the jurists to consider the powers of both these types of men: in the 1230s the vassals were engaged in a conflict with Frederick II over them; and there was in fact a resident or properly crowned monarch in Palestine for only eleven of the first seventy years of the thirteenth century. The lords were to become adept at making use of the law on the *bailliage* to suit their own political purposes.

In the course of time the jurists came to distinguish six kinds of regent, different not only in the conditions under which he was chosen, but also in the rights he possessed: the parent of a minor; the relative of a minor; the relative of a king who had come of age but had not yet been crowned or come East to receive homage; the parent and the relative acting on behalf of a regent who was himself a minor; and finally a vassal appointed to the regency by the High Court. To all these types of regency except the last the principle of the *plus dreit heir aparant* was applied.

The laws governing regency seem to have been based on the precedent established in 1174 by Raymond of Tripoli. It will be remembered that Raymond claimed the *bailliage* for Baldwin IV, arguing that he was the richest and most powerful of the lords and also that he was Baldwin's nearest relative; in fact Baldwin's sister Sibylla was of age and a nearer relative, but she was as yet unmarried and may therefore have been regarded as ineligible. Although Raymond's suggestion, supported by a reference to Amalric's regency in his own county, that the *bailliage* should go to the nearest relative was reflecting a common enough practice in Europe, the way he introduced it as only one of his arguments and the fact that there was a long debate on the matter in the High Court suggest that he was proposing something quite new as far as the kingdom was concerned. At a plenary session of the High Court his claim was accepted[1] and it must have been on this that the authors of the 'Livre au roi' and John of Jaffa based their statements of law. To them a regency belonged first to the child's surviving parent;[2] after the death of Queen Maria in 1212 her husband John of Brienne was regent for their daughter Yolande[3] and in 1228 the Emperor Frederick II was accepted as regent for his son Conrad.[4] If the child had no surviving parent the regency went by right to the nearest relative, male or female, of the blood royal, in other words to the immediate heir. But to enjoy the regency the parent or near relative must come personally into the High Court to claim it: we have seen, for instance, that Frederick II was not recognised as regent for Conrad until his arrival in Acre.[5] The presence of the regent-to-be was needed so that his personal relationship with his subjects could be established, but it did not give the High Court any elective powers, for a parent or near relative had an absolute right to the office. The High Court however could be called upon to decide for one of two relatives who disputed their relationship to the minor and it would choose a regent from among its own members when there was present in Palestine no blood-relative with rights of inheritance.[6] When Queen Isabella died John of Beirut, her half-brother – but not of the royal line – and already her lieutenant, stayed on as regent.[7] On the news of Queen Yolande's death in 1228 the office of her lieutenant Thomas of Acerra lapsed and the High Court chose to be regents Balian of Sidon and Odo of Montbéliard, after John of Beirut and John of Caesarea had refused to take up the office.[8]

Every regent took an oath on entering into the *bailliage* and the promises made by him, according to John of Jaffa, fell into three groups. First he would dwell on the rights of the man he was representing, promising to maintain him and to guard and defend the kingdom for him and his children, while accepting that the fortresses would be overseen and their castellans appointed by the High Court. Secondly he would make promises of great importance to the vassals, swearing to maintain and preserve the gifts and charters of previous kings, to determine any dispute over his own gifts and charters by *esgart* or *conoissance* of the High Court and to govern men by the same *esgarts* and *conoissances*: the reference to the issuing of charters must only have been included at the reception of a parent or relative. Thirdly, the regent would make some more general commitments, promising to maintain justice and the good usages, customs and *assises* of earlier rulers.[9]

William of Tyre wrote that in 1174 Raymond of Tripoli received from the High Court 'procuratio et potestas'.[10] By *procuratio* William presumably meant full powers to act in place of the king and by *potestas* the executive but not the sovereign authority. But what rights had this kind of regent in practice? According to later writers he received homage saving the rights of the child, his contract with the vassals lapsing as soon as the minor came of age or personally entered into the kingship. For this reason any infringement of a lord's rights, like the refusal to perform the act of homage or *service de mariage* were punishable by the confiscation of the fief involved only for the period of the *bailliage*, for once it was over the acts of a regent no longer had any force; and to John of Jaffa it followed logically that the vassals need not enter even into a temporary and restricted contract with a regent.[11] In practice the position of the regents does not seem to have been quite so severe, for parents of minors and the near relatives of absentee, uncrowned kings were usually given homage.[12] It must be assumed that, unless the regent was a parent, he had not the custody of the person of the minor. This was in accordance with the laws governing the wardship of fiefs and it will be remembered that in 1184 Raymond of Tripoli refused to take personal guard of Baldwin V.[13] To John of Jaffa the royal fortresses should be put under the supervision of the High Court, which would appoint their castellans; without its *conoissance* a regent could not even send in provisions.[14]

Parents of a minor had one right denied to all other regents, perhaps because they too had been crowned as consorts, perhaps because they could have no personal interest in the royal domain since they could not inherit it. Gifts made by them were considered to be of permanent validity, provided that their charters were witnessed by the men of the High Court. Their right to issue charters however lapsed and privileges from them had no worth, unless countersealed by the heir, as soon as the minor came of age, even before he was crowned and had received the homage of the vassals.[15] On the other hand the gifts of near relatives and changes in tenure within the royal domain had worth only as long as their *bailliages* lasted and in a series of charters from 1249 to 1261, by which lords made grants out of lands they possessed in the royal domain, there are to be found clauses which covered the possibility of the refusal of the 'rightful lord', and even in one instance a future *bailli*, to recognise them.[16]

Special powers however seem to have been accorded to those near relatives who were regents for an absent and uncrowned king who had nevertheless attained his majority: Conrad from 1243 to 1254 and Conradin in 1267 and 1268 were of age, but never came to Palestine to be crowned. There seems at these times to have been an emphasis on the seigneurial rights of the regents which does not occur elsewhere. Although she used the conventional title of *baiulla*, Alice of Cyprus 'entered into the lordship' in 1243, was 'the most rightful heir present to have and hold the lordship of the kingdom', 'held and used the kingdom as Lady' and 'was received as Lady'.[17] In 1246 Henry of Cyprus, who had the use of the seal of the kingdom,[18] 'took the lordship' and 'held it and used it as lord', entitling himself as *seigneur* in his charters. Although we shall see that this may have been the result of a papal grant, it is clear that the title was not simply one to be held by him personally, but would have been used by any near relative who was regent at the time.[19] In 1268 Hugh of Antioch-Lusignan asked the High Court for the 'homages, returns and services that ought to be made to a lord of this kingdom'.[20] These regents therefore enjoyed personally the revenues and services of the crown and one case suggests that they could also preside over judgements in feudal cases. The villages of Arabia and Zakanin, in the royal domain near Acre, made up a small fief which in 1174 had been given to a knight called Philip Rufus. Philip's daughter, Isabella of Bethsan, sold them to the Teutonic Knights in 1234, but the sale was arranged so as to take the form of an eleemosynary gift. It was confirmed as such by Richard Filangieri, the Emperor Frederick II and Isabella's grandson and heir, John Barlais.[21] In about 1250 the brothers' rights were challenged by Aimery Barlais, John's brother, who appealed to Henry of Cyprus. Henry cited the Teutonic Knights to appear before him and when they refused to come, pleading clergy and stating that even though he was the lord of the kingdom this was a matter for an ecclesiastical court, he pronounced them to be contumacious and granted Aimery a charter of possession. Meanwhile the Teutonic Knights had put the case before the papal legate and it devolved on appeal to the papal curia. Here Aimery's procurator argued that

> since the said *casalia* were once held in fief of the Kingdom of Jerusalem, the Teutonic Knights could be called to answer a plea over them before the king (of Cyprus) as lord, even if they were no longer fiefs. Since (Aimery) had made a plea over these villages as concerning a fief, the brothers, once cited, ought to have presented themselves before the man who had summoned them in order at least that there be a *conoissance* to decide whether the case fell under the (regent's) jurisdiction.

The procurator of the Teutonic Knights replied that in his first plea Aimery had accused the brothers not of an infringement of the law concerning fiefs but of forcible occupation. And he added that since the villages had been given as an alms-gift they were now subject to ecclesiastical jurisdiction and the brothers were not held to respond to a plea about them before the regent, for they did not recognise themselves as feudatories for them and a case only answered to feudal jurisdiction when both the parties involved recognised the jurisdiction of the same lord. He would accept neither that there had been a legal hearing on the matter nor that Henry's charter was valid. The curia found for the Teutonic Knights, but they had already reached agreement with Aimery's brother Amalric, who received the fief in exchange for the payment of a large sum to them. He promised to get Henry of Cyprus to confirm the agreement.[22] It is quite clear that the Teutonic Knights recognised that the regent's court could hear feudal cases, but pleaded that they were clergy and that the villages of Arabia and Zakanin had passed under the jurisdiction of courts Christian. One can be sure that had they considered that

Henry had no powers to settle a matter concerning a feudal inheritance they would have said so.

But while a regent of this type could preside over decisions in some feudal matters, there were also doubts about the validity of his grants. We shall see that Alice claimed to be barred from making judgements concerning the acts of past kings; and some of the charters which contain clauses covering the possible annulment by future monarchs of alienations within the royal domain refer to gifts made by Henry. The position was in fact very delicate legally and constitutionally. While the custom that no wardship of a fief could be granted except in the presence of a minor[23] did not concern the crown – Frederick was received as *bailli* in 1228 without his son being present – there was the law, already mentioned, which laid down that once the heir to the kingdom had come of age, although not yet crowned, a regent's acts had no validity unless countersealed by him.[24]

Between 1258 and 1267 the regency was held by a relative who was himself a minor. Homage to his *baillis* involved the reservation of the rights not of one but of two heirs and the presence of the minor regent seems to have been regarded as necessary for it to be performed. When Isabella of Cyprus and her husband Henry of Antioch claimed the *bailliage* in 1263 the High Court refused to grant them homage or fealty because the minor was not present.[25]

A regent who was a vassal elected by his peers in the absence of any relative was considered to be exercising a kind of lieutenancy.

> One does not [wrote John of Jaffa] call *baillis* only those to whom the kingdom can escheat (the near relatives). Both mother and father are *baillis*; and all those who are *in place of the lordship* are *baillis* and ought to swear to the liegemen the aforementioned oath.[26]

The term 'in place of the lordship' can be found used of Odo of Montbéliard, John of Arsur and Philip Chamberlain during their regencies.[27] The vassal-regents could assemble the High Court, but under them it could make no decisions on matters, like a man's body, fief or honour, that directly involved his relationship with his lord; and in 1257 the pope was called upon to issue a ruling because of property disputes concerning the Church that had arisen partly because the regent 'cannot make decisions about the royal domain'.[28] This must have meant a moratorium on all feudal and seigneurial cases and would have left the High Court with very little to do. But in practice the vassal-regents seem to have been able to break the letter of the law, for one finds them sometimes issuing charters concerning fiefs in the royal domain.[29]

The second type of *bailli*, the lieutenant, represented the person of the king or regent when he was out of the country or indisposed and he is therefore comparable with the English Chief Justiciar. The lieutenancy can be studied at a fairly early stage of development during the reign of Baldwin IV, whose leprosy meant that at times he was incapable of government. When in 1177 Reynald of Châtillon was confirmed as 'procurator' of the kingdom and its army, Count Philip of Flanders had himself already turned down the offer made by a parliament of

> *potestas* and free and general administration of all the kingdom, so that in peace and war, inside and outside the kingdom, he would have full jurisdiction over both small and great and complete authority over royal treasures and rents.[30]

These powers, particularly the right to full jurisdiction, seem to have been unusually wide for a lieutenant. More in accord with later practice, and apparently similar to the office held by Reynald of Châtillon, was the lieutenancy granted to Guy of Lusignan in 1183. Baldwin made Guy 'procurator', with general and free administration and fealty, though apparently not homage, from the vassals, but with no rights to change the royal castellans or alienate portions of the royal domain.[31] From this we might say that during Baldwin's reign a lieutenant represented the person of the king in executive, but not in sovereign affairs.

By the thirteenth century it was accepted that a king or regent could choose a lieutenant to administer the whole or part of the kingdom during a temporary absence. But although the nominator need answer to no one for his choice, there were certain limits to his power of appointment. He must obviously have already been received himself in Palestine: after Yolande's death Frederick II could choose no lieutenant before his arrival in Acre and in 1243 the Hohenstaufen attempt to make Thomas of Acerra *bailli* was rejected by the High Court, because Conrad had not yet come out in person to be crowned.[32] And the vassals in the High Court could have some indirect power over the appointments. We have already seen that Frederick had to change the disposition he had made on his departure in 1229 and the resistance to the choice of

Philip of Maugustel in 1233 will be discussed below. The liegemen played a large part in the election of John of Beirut as Isabella's lieutenant in 1205 [33] and in 1248 Henry of Cyprus appointed John Fuinon on the advice of Philip of Montfort.[34] A glance at a list of those who held the lieutenancy will show how the names of members of the nobility predominate and a striking comparison can here be made with the holders of the great sergeantries.[35] For most of our period baronial figures are to be found as constables, but surprisingly few important lords held the seneschalcy and the marshalsy was in the hands of lesser knights. The powers of the great officers could of course easily be displaced by the appointment of lieutenants who would supersede the seneschal in the High Court and the constable in the army. The lieutenancy was by far the most important office in the kingdom and it was natural for the vassals, and particularly those of the baronial party, to try to keep it in their hands or in the hands of sympathisers.

An interesting case which illustrates their attitude concerned the *bailliage* of Cyprus in *c.* 1226. On the death of King Hugh I in 1218 his widow Alice had taken the regency for her son, Henry I. Bowing to the will of many of the nobles and perhaps to the last wishes of her husband she had appointed Philip of Ibelin as her lieutenant. But she and Philip did not have a happy relationship. After she had left Cyprus to marry in Tripoli the future Bohemond V she sent orders that Philip, who wanted to resign, be replaced by a knight called Aimery Barlais, an opponent of the Ibelins and later to be one of Frederick II's five *baillis* on the island. There are two versions of the story of his appointment and the reactions to it. In one, Alice wrote that:

> since she was regent for her son, by her desire and full will, without any pressure and for no reason other than that she had desired it, she had put and established in her place her uncle Philip of Ibelin and she does not wish him to hold the office any longer. So she orders and commands you, as her vassals, to be no longer subject to him nor to do anything for him and to receive in his place Aimery Barlais.

It can be seen that this was an accurate description of a nominator's rights. But Philip claimed that on Alice's orders the oath originally taken by him as *bailli* had specified that he was to remain in power until the child-king came of age: it is noteworthy that he did not contradict Alice's description of her powers but argued that his was a special case. Everyone supported him except for one knight who said that he recognised no *bailli* but Alice – by this presumably implying that Philip was usurping her authority – and he was set upon and killed by Philip's relatives and friends. In the other account, there was again no denial of Alice's rights to appoint Aimery, but members of the High Court made such aggressive speeches that Aimery departed.[36] Both accounts of the crisis, foreshadowing events on the mainland in the following decade, show how, although the vassals had no legal authority to reject a lieutenancy, a determined group of them could in practice make things impossible for the appointee.

A lieutenant represented the person of his nominator: in 1241 the vassals were prepared to swear to guard and save him in his *bailliage* and obey him as though he were the regent himself. So although homage was not paid him it is clear that some sort of oath was taken to him. In his turn he swore to preserve the rights of the man he was representing and the king, if these were two different persons, and to govern all in accordance with the usages, customs and *assises* of the kingdom.[37] It must be presumed that like vassal-regents and seneschals no decisions could theoretically be made in the High Court under his presidency concerning the feudal relationship between lord and vassal, but there is evidence that he supervised the collection of royal rents[38] and commanded the army in time of war.[39] In the 1230s the pope seems to have believed that he could 'ordain castles and officials',[40] but this may have been inaccurate. In 1231 Richard Filangieri had taken possession of the castle of Tyre without opposition and after 1277 Roger of San Severino, in the quite unique circumstances of his *bailliage*, is to be found appointing officers.[41] But Richard Filangieri was the lieutenant of a regent, not a king, and we have seen that technically the supervision of fortresses in time of regency ought to have belonged to the High Court. There is also an example of a king appointing to subordinate offices at the same time as he chose a lieutenant.[42]

It has often been said that the government of the Kingdom of Jerusalem in the middle of the thirteenth century was oligarchic: that under the regents and lieutenants it was not in the hands of any individual ruler but was controlled by a group of lords and ecclesiastical leaders. This is not strictly true, for although the powers attached to the various forms of *bailliage* were limited they were real. It is clear however that all *baillis* had to act in close collaboration with the High Court over which they presided, not only in routine business like the confirmation of sales and gifts in the royal domain, but also in other matters: in 1233, for instance, Odo of Montbéliard and a number of knights witnessed an agreement between the Templars and Hospitallers and the city of Marseilles; in 1252 Henry of Cyprus, in the presence of his lieutenant John of Arsur and the High Court, allowed the Hospitallers to make two gates in their compound in Acre, in effect creating a new public street; and in 1258 an important treaty, regulating the relations of the three main Military Orders, was witnessed by the *bailli* John of Arsur, the patriarch and some of the liegemen.[43] *Baillis* and the High Court might be involved in acts of higher policy such as the making of treaties with other powers, for instance a special agreement with the city of Ancona in 1257, which will be described, made by John of Arsur 'with the assent and will of the liegemen' and negotiated for the High Court by Stephen of Sauvegny.[44] But generally this kind of subject was discussed in what might be called a parliament, a much larger assembly than the High Court. After 1243 one finds regularly included in it representatives of the Italian communes and the burgesses and confraternities of Acre. Great significance has been attached to the participation of freemen in these meetings, which has been seen as marking a stage in the emergence of a Third Estate, analogous to the rise of the Commons in England.[45] But the parliaments in Acre had their own development and in the century before 1243 one finds four kinds of assembly to which were called members of the High Court and representatives of other institutions.

The first has been mentioned in an earlier chapter. There were times when the High Court and the *Cours des Bourgeois* of Jerusalem or Acre met together to witness legislation or charters.[46] Secondly, the knights sometimes joined visiting crusaders to decide the strategy and tactics to be used on a military campaign: examples of such meetings in Acre took place in 1148 at the time of the Second Crusade, in 1197 when it was decided to attack Beirut, in 1217 during the Fifth Crusade to plan a raid into Galilee, and in 1250 after St Louis's release from Egypt.[47] Crusaders might also

become involved in legislation: we have seen that the jurists
believed that in early times the laws had been amended in the
light of information provided by visitors to the Holy Land. At
least once in the twelfth century the knowledge of a crusader had
been used in deciding a point of law[48] and in 1271 Edward of
England was called upon to judge whether the liegemen of Cyprus
owed their king service outside the island.[49] Thirdly, there
occasionally took place what seem to have been particularly
solemn assemblies of the liegemen, together not only with the
bishops, a few of whom were members of the High Court by
virtue of their fiefs, but also with the papal legates and the
Masters or representatives of the Military Orders. These meetings
– one of them was called by William of Tyre a *Curia Generalis* and
by his translator a *Grant Parlement* – were usually convened to
consider three matters: the choice of consorts for the queens, relations with the Muslims and the need to appeal to the West for
help. One finds them asking Philip of Flanders to take control of
the government in 1177, deciding to offer overlordship to a
western king in 1184, offering the hand of Isabella of Jerusalem to
Aimery in 1197 and asking Philip of France to choose a husband
for Maria of Jerusalem in 1208.[50] Representatives of the Military
Orders also seem to have attended discussions on the making of
peace or war with the Muslims[51] and in the middle years of the
thirteenth century parliaments of this kind must have been responsible for the letters sent to the West in the names of the papal
legates, *baillis*, bishops, leaders of the Military Orders and liegemen:
it is clear that these considered themselves to be representative of
all the people resident in the Holy Land.[52] Fourthly, two twelfth-
century parliaments, held in Nablus in 1166 and Jerusalem in 1183
and certainly attended by burgesses, discussed granting the king
general taxes for the aid of the kingdom, a matter with which the
rise of the Third Estate in Europe was everywhere intimately
connected.[53]

There were therefore traditions for the holding of parliaments
and precedents for the attendance of freemen before 1243. After
that date the parliaments to which the burgesses were called took
place only on seven occasions. Present besides the *bailli* or king
and the liegemen of the High Court were in 1243 bishops, the
leaders of the Venetian and Genoese communes, the Master of the
Templars and perhaps representatives from the other Military

Orders, the leaders of the Commune of Acre and the confraternities;[54] in 1258 Templars, Hospitallers and Teutonic Knights,
representatives from the Italian communes and 'the Spaniards' –
either Catalans or the Confraternity of St James;[55] in 1264 the
papal legate, the Masters of the Military Orders and delegates
from the Italian communes and the confraternities;[56] in 1268
jurors of the *Cour des Bourgeois* of Acre, the papal legate, members
of religious and Military Orders, the leaders of the Pisan and
Venetian communes and the confraternities;[57] in 1276 bishops,
Hospitallers and Teutonic Knights, Pisans, Genoese, members of
the confraternities and burgesses from Acre; and perhaps on a
second occasion in the same year the bishops, the Master of the
Hospitallers and the leaders of some of the Italian communes.[58]
The composition of an assembly in 1277 cannot now be established.[59] Five of these meetings, those of 1243, 1258, 1264, 1268
and 1277, were concerned with the *bailliage*, either as regency or
lieutenancy. One or perhaps two of them, those of 1276, were
convoked in an atmosphere of political crisis when King Hugh
was threatening to leave Palestine for Cyprus. It will be noticed
that none considered taxation or the financial needs of government. Apart indeed from a levy on the Church to cover repairs to
the walls of Jerusalem in 1243,[60] there were no general taxes imposed in the thirteenth century.

The matters discussed in the thirteenth-century parliaments
were not, therefore, those which customarily concerned burgesses. On appeals to the West the lead was usually taken by the
Church. Decisions on questions of peace or war were the prerogative of the rulers, kings or regents, and the parliaments were
advisory, although the vassals themselves would doubtless make
such decisions in their lord's absence, since they were the defenders of the kingdom when he was not present. The choice of
consorts for heiresses and the recognition of the hereditary claims
of regents were matters that properly belonged only to the vassals,
because they alone could accept the man or woman to whom they
would owe homage. This is brought out clearly in contemporary
descriptions of the parliaments that recognised the regents. In
1268 a claimant 'spoke to the men of the High Court of Jerusalem
who were there assembled', in the presence of the others at the
meeting [61] and parliaments of this kind seem to have been conducted as if they were normal meetings of the High Court, with a

lofty disregard for the other participants. In 1243 Philip of Novara acted as counsel for Alice of Cyprus in the usual way; [62] and the claims presented by Hugh of Brienne and Hugh of Antioch-Lusignan in 1264 made reference only to judgements of the High Court and were couched in the language of pleas before that body. [63] In 1243, 1264, 1268 and probably also in 1258 the liegemen of the High Court withdrew after the formal arguments had been made to reach a verdict on their own, and any debate seems to have taken place only among themselves. And they then appointed one of their number to announce their decision formally to the assembly: Philip of Novara did this in 1243 and James Vidal in 1268. [64] Those present who were not vassals seem to have played no active part, in 1243 agreeing 'by their silence'; [65] and if, like the Hospitallers, Genoese and Spaniards in 1258, they did not agree with the verdict there was nothing they could do other than refuse to put it into effect. [66]

It might well be asked why burgesses and churchmen were called to these parliaments at all. Of course the support of the prelates was important, not only because the Church was rich and influential, but also because the backing of Rome was increasingly needed as the threat from Islam increased; the brothers of the Military Orders were great landowners and they had also shouldered a major share in the defence of Palestine; the Italians contributed to the kingdom's defence and their presence and therefore their goodwill was economically essential; many of the burgess confraternities played a significant military role – of the eight whose names have survived seven seem to have been committed to the defence of the Holy Land – and they should be seen as participating in the parliaments for much the same reasons as did the Military Orders rather than as representatives of the burgess population; the majority of them seem anyway to have drawn their members from foreign visitors and not from subjects of the kingdom. [67] The jurors of the *Cour des Bourgeois* of Acre represented only the burgesses in the royal domain of Acre, not the freeman population of the kingdom, but they included some of the richest men in the city. It looks very much as if the attendance at the parliaments of the burgesses and members of non-feudal institutions had more of a political than a constitutional importance and one can understand why at least their tacit agreement to major constitutional decisions was wanted. Of course had the kingdom survived longer the role of the burgesses in the parliaments might have become active rather than passive; and had there been renewed attempts to levy general taxes – it is extraordinary that this was never tried after 1183 – then burgesses, outside as well as within the royal domain, might have become represented. As it was even those who witnessed the proceedings had no say in them and any power they exercised, though doubtless real, was indirect.

It was during the long period of regency that the Mamluks took over the government of Egypt and the Muslim resurgence began. Baibars acquired the sultanate in 1260 and by 1269 he had made some of his most important conquests: in Palestine he had taken Jaffa, Arsur, Caesarea, Saphet and Beaufort; Acre was hemmed in by his forts; in northern Syria he had destroyed the great city of Antioch. The settlement faced the greatest threat to its existence since the days of Saladin and this at a time when there was a decline in the revenues from commerce as the trade routes moved northwards. The 1260s was a decade in which the kingdom needed strong government, but it was one in which the special weakness of the rule provided by the *bailliage* was revealed. We shall see that the king was Conradin, a child in Europe, and the regent was Hugh, a child in Cyprus. For Hugh the appointed regents – to one of whom homage was not even given – were either for most of the time residents of Cyprus, being represented by lieutenants, or they were vassal-regents. Neither lieutenants nor vassal-regents could call on the normal feudal services. Although the government cannot be said to have made any great mistakes, and indeed one of the *baillis*, Geoffrey of Sargines, had a good reputation among his contemporaries for the strength of his rule,[68] one gets the impression that without a suzerain there was little consistent direction, few active initiatives and only intermittently aggressive leadership. The trouble with the government of the *baillis* was not that it was bad, but that it was essentially negative.[69]

The conflict between the vassals in Acre and Frederick and Richard Filangieri had begun in 1231 over a case of dispossession without trial. But the founding of a commune and its rejection of Richard's government transformed the dispute into one over the powers of the lieutenancy and the rights of Frederick to appoint men to represent him. After his election as mayor John of Beirut spent some days in Acre, collecting troops and concluding an alliance with the Genoese who were also opposed to imperial policies. He seems to have planned to threaten Tyre in order to draw the emperor's army away from Beirut. As expected, Richard ordered his troops back to protect Tyre and Beirut was reoccupied by John's eldest son Balian who came down on it from the north. John returned to Acre with the Patriarch of Antioch, who was suspected of being in league with Richard Filangieri, although in fact he seems to have been carrying out a papal commission to mediate between the two sides. A small force, in the ranks of which was the King of Cyprus, was left at Casal Imbert to guard the road to Tyre. It was surprised by Richard on 3 May and, although the king was hurried away, the survivors had to be relieved by troops from Acre led by John of Beirut, Balian of Sidon, Odo of Montbéliard, John of Caesarea and Rohard of Haifa.[70] Victory at Casal Imbert belonged to Richard, but six weeks later the balance was redressed in Cyprus. In March the failure of the knights' attempt to loosen the Lombard hold on Beirut had encouraged the Cypriot imperialists to return to the island, where they overran the strongpoints which had been denuded of their garrisons: only Buffavento and Dieu d'Amour held out against them. After the Battle of Casal Imbert they were joined by Richard Filangieri, but the Ibelins and their allies, selling fiefs in Palestine to enable them to carry on the war, followed the marshal to Cyprus and on 15 June annihilated the imperial forces at Agridi. Kyrenia was to hold out for ten months, allowing Richard and his chief supporters to escape, but with its fall in 1233 the civil war in Cyprus was over.[71]

Both sides were now exhausted and the honours of war were even. Beirut was again in Ibelin hands, but Richard Filangieri was firmly in control of Tyre. From now until 1243 the aims of the Commune of Acre seem to have been to preserve Acre's independence of Richard's government, while looking for an opportunity to dislodge him from Tyre. This amounted to a refusal to recognise his lieutenancy and it should be emphasised that the baronial position was legally a precarious one. In the eyes of the vassals Richard was a man who was prepared to act with no regard for the laws; he was committed to bringing the Ibelins, and especially John of Beirut, to heel; while he was in control no feudatory could feel secure in the possession of his fief. But

Frederick had been perfectly entitled to appoint him *bailli* and there was no precedent for a situation in which the ruler and his lieutenant, backed by a strong mercenary force, were determined to act against the vassals' wishes. It seems that while in practice Balian of Sidon and Odo of Montbéliard continued to be recognised as *de facto baillis* in Acre they could not, and at this time did not, claim to be imperial lieutenants *de jure*. And the feudatories in Acre showed that turn of mind which we have already seen in their writings. They ignored the real state of affairs and acted as though Richard's appointment and their acceptance of him had never taken place.

On 23 July 1230 Frederick and Pope Gregory had come to terms in the Treaty of San Germano. On 12 August 1231 the pope wrote to Frederick, recognising for the first time his title as King of Jerusalem and approving the appointment of Richard Filangieri as his lieutenant. He agreed to ask the bishops in Palestine to receive Richard well, but he wanted it made clear that Richard was to be Frederick's personal representative and not a legate of the empire, to which Jerusalem was not subject. The emperor ignored this proviso.[72] Early in 1232 the pope must have known that Richard had not had a good reception, for in the early summer Patriarch Albert of Antioch was trying to mediate and was presumably following papal orders.[73] On 17 June Gregory, who had already ordered Patriarch Gerold of Jerusalem to promote Frederick's rights, admonished him for assisting the rebels. On 7 July he wrote again. Fearing for the safety of the Holy Land torn by dissension, he ordered Gerold and representatives of the Templars and the Hospitallers to come to Italy on the coming passage – the following August or September – or the next after that – April 1233 – to inform him of the state of affairs. Five days later he told Frederick that he had summoned these men from the East and asked for safe-conducts for them.[74]

By the end of July Gregory's anxieties seem to have been growing. He wrote to Gerold on the 25th and the 26th, ordering him to come and to see him without delay – Frederick had promised a safe-conduct – but forbidding him, if he could not make the journey, to use his legatine powers, because it was being said openly that he was behind the rebellion.[75] On the 26th he also sent letters to the Patriarch of Antioch, the Military Orders and the hierarchy of the Province of Jerusalem. To the Patriarch of

Antioch, whom he made papal legate in the absence abroad of Gerold, he expressed surprise that the men of the kingdom should have rebelled against Frederick, for it was said that they had no real grounds for complaint. Nevertheless, pointing out that the emperor had given him a free hand in the matter, he told Albert to discuss with the Christian leaders, including the Hospitallers and the Templars, ways by which 'the nobles of the aforesaid kingdom, the citizens of Acre and others' could be brought back to fealty and devotion to their ruler. He ordered the brothers of the Military Orders and the prelates to assist the Patriarch of Antioch on his mission.[76] So far the pope seems to have favoured Frederick; and early in 1233 he demanded that John of Beirut release a certain Haymo of Aquino, probably a relative of Thomas of Acerra who must have been captured after Agridi, and ordered the Patriarch of Antioch to excommunicate John if the man was not freed.[77] But if in 1232 the emperor had allowed him to try to bring about peace, the following year was one in which Gregory seems to have been content to let Frederick try out a plan of his own, for in June 1233 he was forbidding the Patriarch of Antioch to use legatine powers outside his province: a sign that he was not prepared to permit any ecclesiastical action at present.[78]

A scheme for breaking the deadlock may have been formulated by Frederick and his advisers in Italy late in 1232.[79] The emperor was now prepared to be conciliatory in three ways: he issued a general pardon, from which however it seems that John of Beirut was excluded; in return for a theoretical recognition of Richard's status he would accept that Acre should be administered by its own *bailli* independently of Tyre; and, while wishing to retain Richard Filangieri as his lieutenant in Tyre, he was ready to appoint a vassal of Jerusalem to the *bailliage* of Acre. His choice was a knight of Tyre called Philip of Maugustel, who was accused by the Ibelin partisans of having a homosexual relationship with Richard. The Bishop of Sidon, who was on his way out to Syria, was entrusted with the emperor's proposals. Arriving in Acre before April 1233, he presented letters to Balian of Sidon and Odo of Montbéliard, a recognition that it was they who were in control, and they assembled a meeting of the liegemen in the cathedral of the Holy Cross. John of Beirut, his nephew the future Count of Jaffa and many of his party were in Cyprus, but John of Caesarea hurried up to Acre from his fief. The imperial letters of appointment were read, but before oaths to the new *bailli* could be taken John of Caesarea rose to his feet. Recalling how Frederick, Balian and Odo had sworn to uphold the laws and customs of the kingdom and indeed how all, especially those who had lordships, were bound to maintain them, he claimed that the emperor was breaking the law, because he was trying to undo by letters what had been done in court. He argued, in other words, that in order to change a lieutenant Frederick must come to Syria and personally carry out the change in the High Court.[80]

It must be said at once that John of Caesarea's argument was of very little worth. Except for the doubtful precedent of the resistance to the appointment of Aimery Barlais in Cyprus in the 1220s, there was nothing in the customs or laws to support it and better jurists than he had been prepared to accept Philip of Maugustel. In May 1259 Queen Plaisance was to come from Cyprus to give the *bailliage* to Geoffrey of Sargines,[81] but before 1233 the feudatories had already accepted from afar two changes in the lieutenancy with the appointments of Thomas of Acerra in 1226 and Richard Filangieri in 1231, however much they might pretend that the latter had been received only in Tyre; in Acre they had recognised, admittedly illegally, the replacement as *de facto bailli* of Garnier L'Aleman by Odo of Montbéliard and in 1241 the leaders of the commune were themselves to beg the emperor to appoint Simon of Montfort as *bailli*, at a time when they cannot have expected him to travel out to Palestine to announce his choice.[82] It looks as though John had found a legal expedient – and not a very good one – for refusing to recognise as lieutenant a friend of Richard Filangieri, and this is confirmed by what followed. His speech seems to have been ignored and the liegemen present prepared to take their oaths to the new *bailli*. Always a violent man, John at once ordered the ringing of the bell of the commune and the Confraternity of St Andrew rushed to arms. In the riot that followed Balian of Sidon, Odo of Montbéliard and the Bishop of Sidon, who had taken refuge in the episcopal palace of Acre, might have been murdered had not John protected them.[83]

John of Beirut, who had been engaged in the siege of Kyrenia, crossed over to Acre where he was confirmed in office as mayor of the commune, to which all oaths were renewed. He met the Bishop of Sidon who read him a letter in which the emperor suggested a compromise in the differences between them. John

was to go to any place in which Frederick's authority was recognised and was to say: 'I put myself at the mercy of the emperor as
my lord.' In practice this would have put John in an impossible
position and would have been regarded by everyone as surrender.
In a speech of great power, at least as reported by Philip of
Novara, he told the bishop a fable of a sick lion who to cure himself had to eat the heart of a great stag. Twice his treacherous
schemes failed, but in the end the poor beast was taken and killed.
While it was being skinned Reynard the Fox took away its heart
and ate it himself, but when accused of this misdeed he lied his
way out of punishment, saying that the stag could have had no
heart, for otherwise it would not have walked into such a trap.
John compared Frederick to the lion and himself to the stag:
twice deceived he refused to be ensnared a third time and to put
himself in peril of death.[84] It was a proud speech, but neither it
nor the solemn renewal of oaths to the commune could hide the
fact that the opposition to the appointment of Philip of Maugustel
was doubtful in law.

The failure of the plan to make Philip of Maugustel a *bailli* does
not seem to have made Frederick any less conciliatory. He may
well have been hoping that a new papal initiative would succeed
where he had not and was therefore anxious to make things as
easy as possible for the ecclesiastical mediators, for it seems that
he legitimised the position in Acre of Odo of Montbéliard, who in
October 1233 is to be found witnessing an agreement between the
Templars and Hospitallers and the city of Marseilles as *bailli* 'for
the lord emperor'.[85] Pope Gregory now had a plan of his own,
which had been worked out by the Patriarch of Antioch and the
Master of the Teutonic Knights.[86] They had suggested that both
sides agree to return to the *status quo*: that moment in 1231 when
Richard Filangieri had been accepted as *bailli*. The rights of
Frederick and Conrad were to be restored and the citizens of
Acre were to be subject to Richard and other *baillis* appointed by
Frederick in his son's name. These lieutenants would have charge
of the royal castles and officials, would collect rents and exercise
other rights which by ancient custom belonged to the crown. The
nobles were to dissolve the commune, taking down its bell and
removing the consuls and captains who had been appointed since
the discord arose. The Church would support the agreement, imposing ecclesiastical sanctions on all those who broke it. But

while everything that had happened since 1231 was to be forgotten, Frederick would not pardon John of Beirut, whom, on 7 August 1234, the pope sternly counselled to offer the emperor satisfaction, although he promised to use his influence on his behalf.[87]

By March 1234 both sides seem to have accepted the compromise provisionally and the emperor and the pope confirmed their assent to it in writing.[88] But it proved to be difficult to get further agreement from the commune. On 8 August Gregory, anxious because the truce with Egypt would expire in 1239 and the time for a new crusade was beginning to draw near, informed the Military Orders, the hierarchy, 'the barons of Jerusalem and the citizens of Acre' that he was sending to the East the Archbishop of Ravenna to put the compromise into effect. The archbishop was authorised to excommunicate opponents of it and the Church in Palestine was to help him in every way it could.[89] The mission was a failure and the archbishop excommunicated the leaders of the commune, placing the city of Acre under an interdict.[90] By 28 July 1235 the pope had heard that there was a possibility that the commune would launch another attack on Tyre. He forbade John of Beirut and the people of Acre to take such an action against the emperor and at the same time told the Military Orders to help Richard Filangieri maintain Frederick's rights.[91]

So far it had been the commune, not Frederick or the pope, who had been intransigent. But now, perhaps in the late summer of 1235, its messengers arrived at the papal court. The pope, fearing, he said, lest the barons in Acre would turn away from Rome to another Christian denomination, had annulled the Archbishop of Ravenna's excommunication and interdict – later Frederick seems to have regarded this as a turning point in his relations with the papacy and the commune[92] – but he also ordered the leaders in Acre to send representatives to him. The vassals were persuaded to obey by the ubiquitous Hermann of Salza and they sent two knights, Philip of Troyes and Henry of Nazareth, whom the pope thought had full powers of procuration although this was later to be denied. These men were definitely at Viterbo in February 1236, but it seems that they had already arrived some time before 22 September 1235, when Gregory wrote a long letter to Frederick. He recounted all that had happened since 1234 and he informed the emperor that acceptable terms had been negotiated between the representatives both of the commune and of Frederick himself. Frederick's ambassadors had said that they could not proceed without referring back to their master and Gregory therefore forwarded a draft of the treaty. It was not unlike the previous compromise, but it contained important additions. All oaths taken to the detriment of Frederick and Conrad were to be abjured and fealty to them was to be renewed; on the other hand the emperor's lieutenants were to be obeyed, 'saving the *assises* and the ancient and approved customs of the kingdom'. Richard Filangieri was to be restored to the *bailliage* by the following February by Frederick's letters of appointment, but freed from all suspicion, which presumably meant that first there would be an investigation into his behaviour, and, because of the animosity felt for him in Acre and the fear with which he was held, other *baillis* would administer the kingdom in the interval. In a reference to Cyprus, the pope ordered Frederick to come to a working relationship with the king, even if he could not impose his authority on him. On the same day Gregory informed Hermann of Salza of the provisional agreement.[93]

The winter was taken up with further negotiations, with Hermann taking over from Peter of Vinea as Frederick's representative. On 19 February 1236 Gregory was able to inform the Teutonic Knights in Acre of their obligations under the final agreement. Two days later he wrote officially to the emperor, Odo of Montbéliard, Balian of Sidon, John of Caesarea, the Hospitallers and Teutonic Knights, the people of the kingdom and the Bishops of Chieti and Acre. The treaty he described contained even more safeguards for the vassals than that of the previous year. While Frederick and Conrad would have all their rights restored and the *baillis* appointed by them would have the supervision of royal fortresses and officials and the administration of royal revenues and other rights belonging by ancient custom to the crown, obedience to them in these matters would be saving the ancient *assises* and approved customs of the kingdom. The commune would be dissolved and those consuls and captains appointed since the discord arose would be removed; oaths of fealty to Frederick and his son would be renewed and Richard Filangieri would be restored to the *bailliage*; but because of the suspicion with which he was regarded by those in Acre another man would administer the kingdom until the end of the following

September, put into office by Richard himself, with the advice of
Odo of Montbéliard. Then Prince Bohemond of Antioch-Tripoli
would be appointed *bailli* with Frederick's authority and he,
having been sworn in according to custom, would hold all the
rights and possessions of the crown, including the city of Tyre,
although the citadel of Tyre would be garrisoned by the Teutonic
Knights on Frederick's and Conrad's behalf. If the Prince of
Antioch could not for any reason hold the post Frederick would
institute Odo of Montbéliard as his *bailli*; and if before Conrad
came of age a lieutenant had to be removed by reason of infirmity,
maladministration or other just cause, the emperor would replace
him with another liegeman of Jerusalem. He would receive all
those in the kingdom into his grace; but John of Beirut, his sons
and nephews, especially John of Caesarea and John of Ibelin,
later to be Count of Jaffa, although assured of full safety within
Palestine, were not to be accorded any security by him outside.
He guaranteed to proceed against them and other vassals according to the laws of the land if he had any complaint of them. The
pope promised to see that the agreement was enforced by the
Church and on 23 February he ordered the Archbishop of
Nazareth and the Bishop of Acre to release anyone excommunicated during the dispute.[94]

It might have seemed as though the commune's intransigence
was now being rewarded. Richard Filangieri was in practice to be
bailli no longer and the Ibelins' security was assured, if only in
Palestine. But when Philip of Troyes and Henry of Nazareth
returned to Acre they were met not with praise but with fury.
Accused of treachery and false-dealing they were nearly harmed
physically. It was said that in negotiating a shameful peace they
had exceeded their instructions and it was denied that they had
received powers to conclude an agreement without referring back
to Acre. This violent reaction is not easy to understand, but it may
be that two clauses in the treaty were unacceptable. We have seen
that it was believed by the jurists that the administration of royal
castles in a minority should be undertaken by the High Court,
although Richard Filangieri had been surrendered Tyre in 1231.
That citadel would now be held by the Teutonic Knights, which
left the fortress of Acre to be overseen by Frederick's *baillis* and it
may have been felt that the terms of the treaty were too specific
to be nullified by the saving clause which was included. And if in

the future there would be some change in political conditions in
Cyprus the fact that the Ibelins were to be treated as outlaws outside Palestine could have made it difficult for them to visit the
island where were many of their possessions. The vassals in Acre
decided to act together with the King of Cyprus in sending a
messenger to explain to the pope why the treaty was not acceptable. King Henry now joined the commune and it was agreed to
send to Viterbo Geoffrey Le Tor, who crossed the Mediterranean
in a Genoese ship, carrying presents for the pope and cardinals.
Gregory, whose relations with Frederick were worsening, received
him well. According to a baronial source, he too felt that the
treaty favoured Frederick too much and claimed that Philip of
Troyes and Henry of Nazareth had agreed to it against his own
wishes. He accepted the refusal of the commune to ratify it,
promised the aid of the Church and asked the Military Orders, the
Italian communities in Acre and the city government of Genoa
to lend aid to the King of Cyprus and the Kingdom of Jerusalem.[95]

Whatever Gregory's ill-will for Frederick this seems to have
been an extraordinary *volte-face* and one would doubt the account
in a partisan chronicle were it not for what was implied in the
later complaints of the emperor against the pope.[96] And it is
certainly true that the great peace plan of 1236 came to nothing.
The Commune of Acre continued in being, although the death of
John of Beirut in the same year – a death which was magnificently
described by Philip of Novara[97] – seems to have deprived the
movement of its driving force. In the eyes of the vassals in Acre
Odo of Montbéliard carried on as *bailli* after the death of Balian of
Sidon in 1239,[98] but Richard Filangieri maintained his administration of Tyre and his supervision over Jerusalem. For the next few
years, marked by the arrival of the crusading expeditions of
Thibaut of Champagne and Richard of Cornwall, the kingdom
remained divided.[99]

In a treaty he made with Egypt in 1241 Richard of Cornwall
greatly extended the area of land under Christian control, but he
favoured Frederick's policy towards Egypt and his constitutional
claims.[100] After fortifying the castle of Ascalon he handed it over
to Walter Pennenpié, the imperial *bailli* in Jerusalem; and Ascalon
was later garrisoned on the emperor's behalf by the Hospitallers,
who were also on his side.[101] Richard seems to have persuaded the
baronial leaders to sue the emperor for peace. A letter survives,

written on 7 June 1241, from Balian of Beirut, Philip of Montfort, John of Arsur and Geoffrey of Estraing, the Lord of Haifa, which, it has been suggested, was sent to Richard for his use in mediation with the emperor on their behalf. It contained four proposals: the emperor should pardon all 'the misdeeds' of the baronial party; he should appoint as *bailli* Simon of Montfort, Earl of Leicester, who was in the East at that time, and this appointment would be observed until Conrad himself came of age, travelled to Palestine or chose a replacement; Simon would be *bailli* of the whole kingdom, presumably controlling both Tyre and Acre, and he would take an oath to guard the rights of Frederick and Conrad and to govern all in the land in accordance with the laws and customs of Jerusalem; the subjects would swear to obey him and would surrender to him the bell, consuls and captains of the commune, save for those officers – presumably the counsellors of the Confraternity of St Andrew – who had been appointed before the emperor became regent.[102] These terms are in many ways reminiscent of those rejected in 1236, although Simon was obviously not to be replaced before Conrad came of age, was acceptable to the vassals and his powers were not specified; nor was there any reference to the outlawry of the Ibelins. On the other hand the vassals in Acre admitted that they had acted wrongly; they accepted that the emperor had the right to appoint a representative without himself coming to the East; they suggested for the post a man who was not himself a liegeman of Jerusalem; and they agreed to the dismantling of the commune. The circumstances in which this letter was sent are not known and nothing came of it, but its contents suggest that in the summer of 1241 the leading vassals were prepared to give way.

It may have been that they felt they were losing support in Acre, for in the following spring Richard Filangieri, with the aid of the Hospitallers and a powerful group of burgesses, almost took the city by surprise. Quick action by Philip of Montfort, the only member of the baronial party present, saved the situation. He called out the Genoese and the Venetians and Richard fled back to Tyre. Balian of Beirut and John of Arsur hurried up from their fiefs and Odo of Montbéliard came from Caesarea with the Templars and the knights of the kingdom. The Hospital in Acre was besieged for six months and from an obscure reference in one of the accounts it seems that the indigenous inhabitants of the city also rose, although it is not clear which side they were supporting. A leader of the movement in the emperor's favour was William of Conches, a member of one of the most important burgess families in Acre, and Richard's supporters seem to have entered into a *conjuratio*, similar to that of 1231 which resulted in the commune, to restore him to power. One gets the impression that the numbers involved were not small.[103]

In the following year, 1243, Conrad came of age and in law the whole situation changed, for Frederick's regency must now lapse. For twelve years the vassals had been trying to nullify the acts of an opponent who had legality on his side. Their leaders in 1243, Balian of Beirut, John of Arsur and John of Ibelin, the future Count of Jaffa, had been brought up in an atmosphere of hatred and bitterness. Their background and experiences did not lead them to trust either the father or the son; and a strong Hohenstaufen monarchy would threaten their semi-independence in their lordships and their usurpation of royal prerogatives like the minting of coins and the exploitation of international trade. Frederick's long-standing alliance with Egypt, which had helped to draw the Hospitallers on to his side in the 1230s and was renewed by Richard of Cornwall in 1241, was inimical to their commercial interests. At a time such as this when Cairo and Damascus were bitter rivals they would have been reluctant to endanger their relations with the chief entrepôt in Syria. It is not surprising that soon after Richard's departure they should have entered into negotiations with Damascus and overturned the treaty with Egypt;[104] and a potential threat to their revenues from trade would have bolstered up the political reasons for resisting government from Sicily. They would probably have opposed the Hohenstaufen whatever had happened.

But now, for the first time, Frederick himself began to move away from a position based on strict constitutional principles. Even after Conrad had come of age he continued to grant rights in Palestine[105] and went on entitling himself king and dating his charters by his regnal years in Jerusalem.[106] And until February 1251, when he must first have heard of his father's death, Conrad called himself not king, but 'heir to the kingdom'.[107] Frederick may have been reviving the view, held by Guy of Lusignan in 1191 and perhaps by John of Brienne in 1225, that a king-consort, once given homage, remained ruler *de jure* until his death.

Of course this question had never properly been settled, but custom to the contrary had already been enunciated by the writers of the 'Livre au roi'[108] and Frederick and Conrad must have known this, since in 1225 Frederick had refused to allow John of Brienne to continue to rule. That the Hohenstaufen knew that they were putting forward something uncustomary is clear from the way they proceeded. Conrad sent letters to the High Court of Jerusalem formally announcing that he was of age and proposed to appoint Thomas of Acerra as his lieutenant.[109] These letters seem to have referred only to Conrad's kingship and in so far as they made no mention of Frederick's must have been deceitful. Although Thomas, who never entered the kingdom but spent some years in the County of Tripoli, was entitled 'our *bailli*' in a charter of Conrad's of 1244 and Frederick referred to him vaguely as '*bailli* of the King of Jerusalem and legate of the sacred empire', Pope Innocent IV did not doubt but that he represented Frederick not Conrad.[110] In 1243 therefore the vassals were presented with a constitutional issue in which the emperor was putting forward a case that was doubtful in law. He had ventured on to the ground on which they were best able to make use of their ingenuity and learning. It looks as though he played straight into their hands.

What now happened was described by four contemporaries, three of whom we know to have been participants in the events, and their accounts complement one another in a remarkable way.[111] The vassals replied to Conrad's letters that while they would guard the land for him until his arrival they would accept none of his representatives until he himself had come to his kingdom and had been received personally as king. A second meeting of the High Court ruled formally that now Conrad was of age his father was no longer regent and, after both John L'Aleman of Caesarea and John of Ibelin, later Count of Jaffa, had refused the regency, granted it to Odo of Montbéliard. It seems that there now appeared to be a real chance of taking Tyre, for Balian of Beirut was in touch with some of its citizens who were willing to rise against the imperial garrison. But he and his closest confidants, Philip of Montfort and Philip of Novara, doubted the legality of such a move: the knighthood of Tyre were bound by homage to the emperor and had accepted the rule of his officers – this seems to suggest that it was known that Frederick intended to continue to rule – and there was no precedent for the vassals in one royal district taking possession of another against the wishes of those in it. It was at this point that Philip of Novara made a suggestion, or later boasted that this is what he had done, although his legal expedient may have been the product of long discussions: it had always been known when Conrad would come of age. He proposed a gloss on the laws of the regency, although he took care to express it in terms of established legal practices. 'It is,' he said, 'the custom in the Kingdom of Jerusalem that the *plus dreit heir aparant* should hold the royal inheritance by right until the most rightful heir arrives': in fact there was no such custom, for no similar situation had ever before arisen. Philip claimed to have then pointed out, as if it were not clear to everyone, that Alice of Cyprus, the second daughter of Henry of Champagne and Queen Isabella and Conrad's great-aunt, was present in Acre and as the *plus dreit heir aparant* ought to hold the kingdom. He suggested that the High Court be assembled so that she could require the lordship of the kingdom, for once she had been accepted as regent Tyre could be taken quite legally if its knights refused to recognise her. Accordingly Balian of Beirut and Philip of Montfort sent him to see Alice and her husband Ralph of Soissons, who agreed to the plan and to the convocation of the members of the High Court, together with the leaders of other institutions in the kingdom. Philip acted as Alice's counsel[112] and was called in to advise the liegemen of the High Court when they withdrew to consider their verdict; he boasted that people joked that in this case he had made the plea, the response and the judgement. Odo of Montbéliard, who argued that Conrad should once more be formally requested to come to his coronation before anything was done, was overruled, Balian of Beirut and John, later Count of Jaffa, being prominent among those for Alice, and the official decision of the vassals seems to have been that she be given the custody of the kingdom, saving Conrad's rights, because he was not present and never had been.

Tyre fell to the forces from Acre in June 1243 and Jerusalem seems to have been occupied soon afterwards. At about the same time the vassals and the Templars entered into an offensive alliance with Damascus, aimed against Egypt, that extended Christian rule over the Temple area in the Holy City.[113] The vassals' constitutional victory therefore was accompanied by what must have seemed to have been a diplomatic triumph, although it aroused Egypt and led directly to the loss of Jerusalem and the annihilation of a Franco-Damascene army at Gaza in 1244. It is in the description by a Venetian present of the parliament at which Alice's claims to the regency were discussed that one finds the last reference to the Commune of Acre.[114] It must have been disbanded soon afterwards. The vassals had now found another, more legal and probably more attractive, means of preventing the imposition upon them of Hohenstaufen rule. This they had done by formulating a new legal maxim: that a king who had reached his majority but had not come East to be crowned and to receive homage was to be treated as though he were still a minor.

The regency of Alice was obviously something of an experiment. Homage and service were paid her, saving Conrad's rights,[115] but restrictions seem to have been written into a secret agreement with the baronial leaders which was drawn up by Philip of Novara and Philip of Baisdoin. One of its conditions, in accord with the baronial view of the *bailliage*, was that until Conrad arrived Balian of Beirut and Philip of Montfort should have custody of the royal fortresses. But Alice does not seem to have expected them to occupy the city of Tyre, although they defended their action by claiming to be moved by the precedent of a regent's usurpation in 1210 of the lands of the heirs to the Principality of Morea in Greece.[116] Alice's weakness is further revealed in the report of the Venetian Marsiglio Giorgio. In answer to his demand that Venetian privileges be restored Alice replied that anything disturbed by a previous regent could be corrected; but if Marsiglio was referring to the acts of past kings, then nothing could be done, because she herself 'was not legitimately in possession of the kingdom, but Conrad was'.[117] It is no wonder that her husband soon left Palestine in disgust, because his power seemed to be 'no more than that of a shadow'.[118]

The regency of Alice's son Henry of Cyprus, who succeeded her in 1246,[119] was challenged by Melisende, the widow of Bohemond IV of Antioch-Tripoli, who, as the only surviving daughter of King Aimery and Queen Isabella, was more nearly related to Conrad. She appealed to the pope who in 1249 told his legate Odo of Châteauroux to investigate the matter and, if she had told the truth, to put her into the *bailliage*, providing this could be done without scandal.[120] Rome had no jurisdiction in the matter and nothing more is heard of it, although it foreshadowed the claims for the throne of her daughter Maria in 1269. Henry seems to have been the only regent to call himself Lord of Jerusalem in his charters. Of course this title reflected ideas of the powers, already described, of a near-relative who was regent for an uncrowned king, but it is also possible that it was used because of a grant made by Pope Innocent IV.

At the Council of Lyons on 17 July 1245 Innocent formally deposed Frederick, releasing from their oaths all bound by fealty to him.[121] As far as the Kingdom of Cyprus was concerned the effect of this decree was to free King Henry from his obligations to his suzerain and this was confirmed by the pope in March 1247. But Innocent went further: taking Cyprus under his protection and mindful of an assertion of Henry – perhaps a reference to the rule in the twelfth century of Isaac Comnenus – that in the past Cyprus had been independent, he decreed that the island was to have no secular overlord.[122] The Kingdom of Jerusalem needed different treatment, for Frederick's opponents had since 1243 refused to recognise that he had any rights there. Within a few days of Frederick's deposition Innocent granted commercial rights to the Guelf merchants of Ancona not only in Sicily, which was a papal fief, but also in Jerusalem. In 1248 and 1250 he confirmed the privileges – some of them fraudulent – of Marseilles in Palestine and in 1247 he stated that neither Frederick nor his sons were to be recognised as king or emperor.[123] But he continued to recognise Conrad as heir to the kingship in spite of all the difficulties between them.[124] At the same time he did not wish the Hohenstaufen to enjoy any effective power in the East and he took steps to isolate those institutions and groups among whom there was still sympathy for the Ghibelline cause; these included the Hospitals of St John and St Mary of the Germans.[125] In 1247 and 1248 he ordered the Patriarch of Jerusalem to annul the ecclesiastical exemptions accorded to the Pisan Church in Acre because of the commune's adherence to the emperor and to forbid the Pisans to fly imperial standards on their ships and place them in their churches.[126] In 1247 he wrote to the faithful in Palestine, asking them to assist the Church and to lend no support to Frederick, and in May 1248 he ordered churchmen, brethren of the Military Orders, barons and people to see that none of those who favoured Frederick or Conrad brought about a change in the lordship of the

kingdom, by which he presumably meant depriving the Regent
Henry of his rights, and to take steps to drive Thomas of Acerra
from the County of Tripoli.[127] By this year however support for
the Hohenstaufen may have been collapsing, for in July the pope
informed the hierarchy of Jerusalem that Odo of Châteauroux, the
papal legate appointed for the crusade of Louis of France, had
been given powers to absolve the many adherents of Frederick's
cause who had been excommunicated.[128]

Since Innocent was trying to prevent Conrad from exercising
effective authority in the Holy Land while at the same time recognising his rights to the kingship, the vassals' interpretation of the
conditions for a regency and their refusal to allow Frederick or
Conrad to reign *in absentia* exactly suited his purposes. In April
1247, a month after he had freed Cyprus from imperial suzerainty,
he addressed Henry for the first time not only as King of Cyprus
but also as Lord of Jerusalem and asked him to reform the state of
the Holy Land.[129] In June he wrote again to Henry and to his
lieutenant in Palestine, Balian of Beirut, encouraging them to
persevere in this task and to make peace between the supporters of
the Church and its adversaries, who were, he reminded them, also
their enemies.[130] In the same year Balian of Beirut, his family,
dependants and goods, were taken under papal protection and he
was given the privilege of exemption for three years from excommunication by anyone except a papal legate or the bearer of a
special mandate from the Holy See: Balian may have needed
support against Frederick's adherents.[131] In 1253 the same privileges were granted for five years to John of Jaffa, to whom the
pope gave two additional rights: John could not be called to
answer a court action outside the Kingdoms of Jerusalem and
Cyprus without a specific papal command – one is reminded of
John of Beirut's fears in the 1230s – and he and his family were
licensed to hear mass even in times of interdict.[132] These privileges, without parallel as far as ordinary laymen in Palestine were
concerned,[133] suggest that John was now Henry's lieutenant or at
least that he was being threatened by followers of Conrad.

Henry's regency is also remarkable for the grants made to some
of the greater lords. The nobles were of course his natural allies
against Frederick and Conrad and it is not surprising to find them
receiving substantial rewards for their support and perhaps also
for their rejection of the claims of Melisende. It will be remem-

bered that the High Court had refused to allow Alice of Cyprus to
take custody of the royal fortresses of Acre and Tyre and of the
city of Tyre, which had been handed over to Balian of Beirut and
Philip of Montfort: there is evidence that Balian held Tyre and
Philip and Nicholas Antiaume shared the guard of the citadel of
Acre.[134] But on Henry's accession Philip was given Tyre and this,
almost half of the royal domain, was to pass to his descendants.[135]
Before his death in 1247 Balian of Beirut was given by Henry an
important fief in the royal domain round Casal Imbert and in 1253
the regent confirmed the estate in the possession of Balian's son
John: it had been granted to supplement the Lordship of Beirut
and no additional service was owed for it.[136] By June 1247 John of
Jaffa had received the County of Jaffa and Ascalon, vacant because
of the death of Walter of Brienne in an Egyptian prison.[137] This
reckless alienation of royal lands suggests that Henry needed the
lords' help and recognition: perhaps Balian of Beirut and certainly
his son John made homage to him for Casal Imbert.[138] If anyone
gained from the new interpretation of the laws of the regency and
the dispute between the empire and the papacy in the 1240s it was
the baronage of Jerusalem.

Henry died in 1253 and in the absence of a rightful heir to the
throne the High Court appointed first John of Arsur and then
Philip Chamberlain as regents.[139] But in May 1254 Conrad himself
died, leaving as his heir a child called Conradin whose rights as
King of Jerusalem were recognised by the pope.[140] The crown
was again in a straightforward minority and it must have been for
that reason that the regency changed hands. Late in September the
High Court made John of Jaffa regent,[141] but the need to defend
his county forced him to give up office in 1256 and John of Arsur
was chosen to replace him.[142]

In 1258[143] political expediency once more gave a new twist to
the tortuous course taken by the laws of the *bailliage*. For nearly
two years the Italian communes in Acre had been at war with one
another, a conflict sparked off by a dispute between the Venetians
and the Genoese over some property belonging to the monastery
of St Sabas, but inflamed by their commercial rivalries in the
Eastern Mediterranean.[144] The inhabitants of Acre, among them
the Pisans who had supported Genoa but went over to the
Venetians in 1257, found themselves inexorably drawn on to one
side or the other. Most of the feudatories under John of Arsur,

who had first tried to mediate, favoured the Genoese[145] and in
August 1257 the High Court came to an agreement with Ancona,
another ally of Genoa, granting its merchants in Acre commercial
rights and property in return for the aid of 50 armed men for two
years. All Anconitans were held to help the regent as far as they
could and he promised that their city would be indemnified for
any damages sustained and would be included in any future truce.
The treaty was negotiated by Stephen of Sauvegny and subscribed
to by some of the most important vassals in the kingdom: besides
John of Arsur himself, Philip of Montfort, a staunch supporter of
Genoa, the Lords of Caesarea and Haifa, James of La Mandelée,
Thibaut of Bethsan, Simon of Malembec, Balian Antiaume and
John of Flori.[146]

But on this matter the lords of Palestine were not united. The
names of John of Jaffa, John of Beirut and Julian of Sidon are
notably absent from the list of adherents to the treaty. Julian of
Sidon seems to have had little interest in politics,[147] but John of
Jaffa, for reasons now obscure, had been opposed to the Genoese
from the start of the War of St Sabas, when he had been regent,
and he and John of Beirut,[148] with the support of the Templars,
now exploited the laws of regency to bring about a switch in
alliances. Conradin's nearest heir in the East was claimed to be
the child King Hugh of Cyprus who was the son of Henry and
Plaisance, the sister of Bohemond of Antioch-Tripoli. After
Henry's death Plaisance had married Balian, John of Arsur's son,
who should have had the co-regency of Cyprus. She seems quickly
to have changed her mind and sought an annulment: the marriage
was within the prohibited degrees. Balian naturally had resisted
this and there was at the time much ill-feeling between Plaisance
and Bohemond on the one side and John of Arsur and his son on
the other.[149] At the instigation of John of Jaffa and the Templars,
Hugh was brought to Acre by Bohemond and Plaisance and on
behalf of his nephew the prince summoned the liegemen to meet
in parliament together with representatives of the Italian communes, the Military Orders and the confraternities. He asked them
to give Hugh fealty as their rightful heir and lord. Although the
parliament was divided, with important voices both for and
against the proposition, Hugh's claim was practically unassailable
in law and was in the end accepted by the liegemen, the only men
whose votes mattered.[150] The Regent of Jerusalem was now him-

JOHN II OF IBELIN, LORD OF BEIRUT.   Seal attached to a
charter of 1261.

self a minor and in this extraordinary situation exactly the same rules were applied to the choice of a regent for him as would have been followed in an ordinary minority, except that it was the *bailli*'s relationship to Hugh that was important and not her relationship to Conradin. John of Jaffa's legal training may be discerned in the way a loophole for opponents was neatly covered. According to a law, which had in fact never been applied to the crown, the ward of a minor should bring the child to court with him when he wished to be granted the *bailliage*. With Hugh present Plaisance, as his surviving parent, had to be accepted as his regent, although she was only a distant relative of Conradin.[151] No sooner had she been received than she ordered the feudatories to turn against the Genoese and support the Venetians.[152] John of Arsur seems to have given in gracefully. He was reconciled with Bohemond and when Plaisance returned to Cyprus he was again left in command as her lieutenant.[153] On his death he was succeeded by Geoffrey of Sargines.[154]

The acceptance of Hugh, resulting in a regency in minority for a kingship in minority, was a particularly subtle political manoeuvre, truly worthy of John of Jaffa. For the purpose of changing the balance of power in Acre during the War of St Sabas John had exploited the law so as to force the vassals to renege on an earlier alliance and accept the far from attractive prospect of the regency of a child. There seems to have been surprisingly little opposition, except from Philip of Montfort,[155] to the change in policy towards Genoa.

Plaisance died in September 1261 and it seems that in the absence of a near relative the High Court made Geoffrey of Sargines regent for Hugh.[156] In 1263 Hugh's aunt Isabella of Cyprus came to Acre with her husband Henry of Antioch to claim the *bailliage* as her nephew's heir. We have seen that the fact that Hugh did not come with her led to her being accorded only a restricted rule by the High Court.[157] Her husband acted as her lieutenant, but when she died in 1264, probably in the second half of the year, Geoffrey of Sargines may have been reappointed regent.[158]

In July 1264 Pope Urban IV, who three years earlier had himself been Patriarch of Jerusalem, wrote to the leaders in the kingdom, including the *bailli* Henry of Antioch, Geoffrey of Sargines, John of Jaffa and John of Beirut, imploring them to bring to an end the internal discord that was endangering the Holy Land and ordering them to make peace among themselves before the arrival in the East of the crusade that was being planned.[159] The reasons for this letter are obscure: there may have been differences in Palestine over the policy that should be followed towards the growing threat from Islam or over the High Court's refusal to make homage and fealty to Isabella and Henry. But whatever the pope's motives the problems faced in the kingdom were exacerbated on Isabella's death, because two contenders for the *bailliage* now presented themselves, both claiming to be the heir of Hugh of Cyprus. The first was Isabella's son, Hugh of Antioch-Lusignan, but she had had an elder sister Maria, long dead, whose son Count Hugh of Brienne claimed the regency by right of primogeniture. The details of the claimants' debate before the High Court survive and show how, for all their quotations from previous cases, there was no precedent for their situation.[160]

On the surface Hugh of Brienne's case seemed a good one. Primogeniture was recognised for the transmission of the crown and as the son of the elder aunt he was after the king himself a scion of the senior branch of the Cypriot royal family. This was the basis of his case,[161] which his opponent could not shake with the specious argument that since Maria had died before her brother King Henry nothing could have escheated from him to her.[162] Hugh of Brienne pointed out that nothing had escheated to Isabella either.[163] More serious was a precedent involving the *bailliage* of Cyprus. On Plaisance's death Hugh of Antioch-Lusignan had claimed the regency as King Hugh's *plus dreit heir aparant* after Isabella, who waived her rights. Hugh of Brienne had been present at the meeting of the High Court of Cyprus which had accepted Hugh of Antioch-Lusignan as *bailli* and he had not put forward a counter-claim because, he said in 1264, he had a great respect for Isabella who had brought him up and so did not want to oppose her son.[164] This turned out to have been foolish because the decision of the Cypriot High Court certainly strengthened Hugh of Antioch-Lusignan's case; but it did not completely undermine Hugh of Brienne's position, especially because part of his rival's argument was that foreign examples should not be taken as being relevant to court decisions in the Kingdom of Jerusalem.

Hugh of Antioch-Lusignan's main argument was one over

which some doubts must remain. Whereas the Count of Brienne tended to stress his relationship to his grandmother Alice and his uncle Henry, he emphasised that the important issue was their relationship to the child on behalf of whom one of them would be regent.[165] Both being related to Hugh of Cyprus in the same degree of consanguinity, he suggested that the custom should be followed which applied, he said, to the situation in which two cousins were left to inherit a fief last held by their common grandfather; here the elder of the two, irrespective of the branch of the family to which he belonged, was treated as being more nearly related to the last possessor of the fief. This clever argument was repeated in the works of John of Jaffa and Geoffrey Le Tor,[166] but the custom upon which it purported to be based was not known to Hugh of Brienne, who quoted precedents to the contrary from Cyprus and France, nor had it been known sixty years earlier to the authors of the 'Livre au roi';[167] it is possible that it appeared in the law-books of John and Geoffrey in consequence of this very case. Hugh of Antioch-Lusignan also claimed that it was relevant that his mother had been the last in seizin of the *bailliage*, suggesting therefore that claims to the regency could be strengthened by the claimant's relationship to the last holder of it.[168] This was obviously bad law, as Hugh of Brienne pointed out.

> The *bailliage* does not escheat nor can it escheat to a son or daughter of him who held it, unless the son is the nearest relative or the most rightful heir on that side of the family by which the *bailliage* descends of him who holds the regency on behalf of the heir to the crown.[169]

Hugh of Antioch-Lusignan seems to have realised the weaknesses of this second plea and quickly dropped it.

The cousins presented their cases before a parliament. After hearing them the knights of the High Court recognised that Hugh of Antioch-Lusignan's claim was in accord with the law and that he should be received as regent because he was older than Hugh of Brienne.[170] It is true that the laws governing the *bailliage* were not the same as those applying to inheritance to the throne – the regency was not heritable and right to it had to be proved again every time the need for it arose – but the decision was also a recognition that, if both Conradin and Hugh of Cyprus died, Hugh of Antioch-Lusignan was their heir and so, by denying a claim based on rights of primogeniture, it established a new precedent for the transmission of the crown. It is hard not to suspect that the vassals were moved to this by the fact that as Regent of Cyprus Hugh could command funds and troops to put at the kingdom's disposal. Hugh of Brienne remained in Palestine for another three years but he did not give up his claims: after the death of the child-king Hugh, he challenged Hugh of Antioch-Lusignan's accession to the throne of Cyprus, and although he never claimed the throne of Jerusalem, being in Armenia in 1269, many years later he was still fighting for what he considered to be his lawful inheritance.[171]

In 1267 Hugh of Cyprus died and Hugh of Antioch-Lusignan claimed and received his throne. In November Conradin, who had just come of age and had returned from Germany to Italy to recover what he believed were his rights, was deprived of the Kingdom of Jerusalem by Pope Clement IV.[172] Conradin's majority and papal opposition to him, but surprisingly not his deposition, can be seen to have had effects in Palestine. With the death of the King of Cyprus, Hugh of Antioch-Lusignan's regency of Jerusalem had anyway lapsed and in April 1268 he came to Palestine, this time demanding from a parliament the regency for Conradin. He also asked for the lordship: once again there was an absentee king who had reached his majority and had antagonised a pope. Homage was paid to Hugh and it was agreed that he should enjoy the royal rents and services.[173] He made Balian of Arsur his lieutenant.[174] Then on 29 October Conradin was beheaded in Naples and the elder line of the royal house of Jerusalem was extinguished: in the words of the chronicler known as the Templar of Tyre, the crown 'returned to the line of the mother of his father'.[175] Hugh crossed over to Acre in the late summer of 1269 to claim it as Conradin's heir. At first he was accepted, but he was soon faced by a very strong challenge. His aunt Maria of Antioch was the daughter of Melisende, child of Isabella of Jerusalem's marriage to Aimery, and she was therefore a member of a more junior line of the House of Jerusalem. But she was of an earlier generation, for she was Isabella's granddaughter while Hugh was only a great-grandson and she was therefore nearer by one degree of consanguinity to Conradin – or rather to Yolande, who had been the last in seizin of the throne. Her mother, it will be remembered, had put forward a similar argument in the 1240s when challenging Henry of Cyprus for the *bailliage*.

Maria, aged over forty and unmarried, was not a very attractive candidate [176] and she seems to have handled her case badly, but her claims made good law. They were obviously based on the precedent established by Hugh himself and the High Court in 1264 and confirmed in 1268: that primogeniture did not apply to the inheritance of the crown, the only relevant criterion being that of consanguinity. She seems first to have raised the question at Tyre at a meeting with Hugh arranged by Philip of Montfort and the Military Orders. The High Court was then convoked in the presence of both claimants and a clerk read out a formal plea in which she described her ancestry to prove that she was the *plus dreit heir aparant* of the last monarch in possession of the throne. In this she recognised that neither of the Hohenstaufen kings had actually held the kingdom, whatever their theoretical rights, and that it was necessary to trace her relationship to Isabella, the grandmother common both to her and Conrad.[177] Once her formal claim had been made Hugh, having asked her if it reflected her own views, rose and addressed the High Court. He took up and, it seems, deliberately misrepresented her arguments on the question of seizin, stating wrongly that she had tried to suggest that Conrad had been the last king in possession of the throne. He agreed that the crown should go to the person who showed himself to be the closest relative of the last in seizin, but claimed that both Henry and Hugh of Cyprus had been in possession of the kingdom as regents; and he could then easily show that he was their nearest heir. And he argued irrelevantly that the fact that neither Maria nor her mother had been recognised as heirs before told against her. He therefore blatantly and crudely falsified Maria's case and used himself an erroneous treatment of the law of succession, simply returning to the weakest part of his plea of 1264.[178] So false was his position that in 1324 his grandson could only suggest that the High Court had decided in his favour because he was male. 'This *conoissance* . . . is clear demonstration that the usage of Jerusalem is such, that male heirs . . . inherit the kingdom before female heirs who are nearer.'[179]

It may have been obvious to Maria that her case was not going to be accepted by the High Court; or perhaps she was already in league with Charles of Anjou and so did not want anything to be finally settled. At any rate she now reacted in an apparently foolish way. As the liegemen were preparing to withdraw to consider the two arguments she abruptly left the meeting without making any reply to Hugh or pressing her claim, a point noticed by James Vidal when he came to speak on the vassals' behalf. He told Hugh that the High Court had sent three of its members to invite her formally to hear its answer, but she had refused to return; he went on to say that, on what they had already heard, the liegemen saw no reason for withdrawing the offer of kingship already made to Hugh: an answer which implied that Maria's case had failed because it had not been properly presented, rather than because it was inherently invalid, but which only showed that the vassals were prepared to ignore a precedent they had themselves established in order to be governed by the candidate whom they considered would make a better ruler, a man of intelligence, as Philip of Montfort informed the Sultan Baibars.[180] James Vidal presented Hugh with a document containing, he said, the tenor of an oath, presumably that described in John of Jaffa's law-book, which the lords of the kingdom were accustomed and ought to make to their vassals. After swearing it Hugh received the homage of the knights and fealty from the confraternities and other institutions,[181] before being crowned in Tyre by the Bishop of Lydda on 24 September.

Maria pursued her claim in three ways. She demanded coronation of the Patriarch of Jerusalem but, ignoring her, he gave the Bishop of Lydda authority to crown Hugh.[182] On the day of the coronation a clerk and a notary, acting on her behalf, challenged it aloud and then quickly fled from the cathedral.[183] Meanwhile, with the support of the Templars, she had appealed to Rome, where her case was being heard in 1272, for on 13 April Pope Gregory X assured her that any use made of the title of King of Jerusalem in letters sent by him to Hugh would not prejudice the issue. On 24 October he informed the Archbishop of Nazareth and the Bishops of Bethlehem and Baniyas that the case had been opened at the curia and ordered them to cite Hugh to appear in person to answer Maria's charges or send a procurator with all the relevant documents within nine months. They were to let him know the date on which Hugh had been cited.[184] Preparing his case the king seems to have had an account of the proceedings drawn up, together with those on the *bailliage* of 1264 and 1268,[185] and he sent procurators to the pope, who was now at Lyons: they were included in the kingdom's delegation to the Council, which consisted of the Archbishop of Tyre, the Bishop of Paphos, the seneschal John of Grailly, the Hospitaller William of Corceles, James Vidal and Enguerrand of Jorni.[186]

Before the papal judges they denied that the curia had any jurisdiction in the matter, for the only court competent to hear the case was the High Court of Jerusalem. Meanwhile the Templars seem to have suggested that Maria sell her rights to Charles of Anjou, King of Sicily, who was ambitious to extend his power throughout the lands bordering on the Mediterranean. It is not clear at what date approaches had been made. Charles had had a representative in Acre as early as 1259,[187] and once he had received the crown of Sicily in 1266 his interest in the East grew.[188] It is possible, though perhaps unlikely, that Maria's challenge for the throne had all along been made with the knowledge that her rights would eventually be assumed by him. Negotiations may have begun almost as soon as Hugh had been crowned, for in 1269 the Muslims knew that the King of Jerusalem was frightened of Charles's ambitions.[189] But for some reason it was decided, possibly in 1276, to remove the case from the curia before Maria completed the sale of the kingdom. To the joy of Hugh's procurators she therefore accepted the argument that Rome had no jurisdiction and begged the ecclesiastical judges to quash the case, stating that she was too poor to carry on with her plea.[190] What followed is not clear, although it may be that the papal judges agreed to the withdrawal of the action and that it was afterwards reopened by Charles, who managed to get a quick decision in his favour: certainly when Maria sold Charles her rights to the kingdom the transaction took place in the presence of curial officials and with the approval of the pope. Charles gave Maria an annual rent of 4,000 *livres tournois* and a further 10,000 saracen besants a year from the revenues of Acre. His charter of March 1277 contained the fascinating but probably false statement that Maria, herself too poor to press her claims, had offered the kingdom to many princes before Charles and they had all refused it.[191] But the whole affair is extraordinary. Maria's claim was better than Hugh's and the papal curia obviously thought so – the pope himself had been in Acre at the time of his elevation and must have known of the background to Hugh's accession – but there was no precedent for the sale of the crown to a stranger. The transaction was in breach of the rigid laws of inheritance in Jerusalem and it must

have been repugnant to the feudatories with their ideas of a contract of government stemming from the election of Godfrey of
Bouillon as ruler.

Between 1269 and 1277 Hugh was *de facto* King of Jerusalem.
He was absent in Cyprus for most of the time and when he
stormed out of Palestine in 1276 he claimed that he had been unable to govern the land because of the insubordination of some of
its more powerful institutions.[192] It is true that in 1275 he had not
been able to enforce *service de mariage* from Isabella of Beirut, who
was supported by the Templars and by the Sultan Baibars.[193] But
in fact Hugh does not seem to have had any less power than had
his predecessors fifty years earlier. He may have insisted on his
jurisdiction over Italian property outside the communal quarters.[194] He was certainly determined not to sanction automatically
the alienation to the Military Orders of the lordships of Sidon and
Arsur that had taken place during the years of regency.[195] The
family of Montfort still held Tyre, but there was no question of
the new king recognising their lordship as a matter of course.
Henry of Cyprus's gift to Philip of Montfort was invalid on
Hugh's accession[196] and it is known that Philip feared lest he
would wish to re-possess such an important part of the old royal
domain. He came to an agreement by which the king's sister
Margaret was married to his son John. Hugh granted Tyre to
John as a *fié de conquest* and confirmed that the heirs of this marriage would inherit it; if the marriage was barren Tyre would
escheat to the crown, at which time John's other heirs would be
paid 150,000 saracen besants in repayment of the expenses Philip
had met in refortifying the city. No child was born of the match,
but on John's death in 1283 Hugh, now recognised only by part of
the kingdom, was clearly hard put to find the 150,000 besants. He
put John's brother Humphrey in possession of Tyre on condition
that the city and lordship would be returned to him if he could
find the money within six months. He died before the term had
elapsed, but in 1289 Tyre escheated to the crown on Humphrey's
death and King Henry granted it as an apanage to his own
brother Amalric.[197] The agreements over Tyre show that while
the king was prepared to compromise, he refused to treat a major
alienation of royal domain as a *fait accompli*. And the care with
which the Lord of Tyre had to tread is revealed in an agreement
made by John of Montfort with Venice in 1277: a clause laying

down the procedures to be followed when privileges were disputed specified that before any arbitration John should seek royal licence; and his title of Lord of Tyre was accompanied by the modifying statement that he was called this according to usage generally observed in those parts and that this should not be taken as prejudicing any rights.[198] Under Hugh the powers of the crown may even have increased. Two instruments of government found in James of Ibelin's law-book were new, since they were not mentioned in the writings of John of Jaffa. James referred to a council – it was treasonable to reveal its secrets – and a method of summoning vassals to service by letters 'on which will be (the king's) seal', which suggests the use of a privy seal rather than the great seal.[199] The development of an inner council, a great advance in government, and the use of a privy seal may both have been imports from the Cypriot administration – certainly there was a small council in Cyprus in the fourteenth century. But whatever their origins it looks as though they were introduced by Hugh and this suggests that he was trying to improve the system of royal government.

Although since 1225 the powers of the crown had not been drastically reduced and royal government may even have advanced in the early 1270s, the strength of Hugh's rule may have aroused antagonisms and it was also the case that the king was not everywhere recognised as legitimate. The two main narrative sources for his reign were hostile to him, the writer of one of them going so far as to describe him as 'Hugh of Lusignan, who called himself King of Jerusalem and Cyprus'.[200] The other, written by a man close to the Templars, reported that Hugh deserted Palestine in 1276 because he knew that Maria had sold her rights to Charles of Anjou and that Charles was sending out Roger of San Severino to be his lieutenant; he did not want to be in Acre when Roger arrived.[201] In fact the sale was not completed until the following March and Roger did not arrive in the East for a year, but we have seen that the Muslims had known that Hugh was worried about Charles's ambitions long before this and it may be that news of the negotiations and anxiety about the course of events in France and Italy were at least partly responsible for his hurried departure in 1276. He became involved in a bitter quarrel with the Templars over the *casal* of La Fauconnerie, a *borgesie* bought by them without his permission: they may have been demonstrating that they did not recognise him as king.[202] In October he departed for Tyre in a rage, leaving behind him no officials to administer the kingdom in his absence and complaining that it was impossible for him to govern the land not only because of the dispute over La Fauconnerie, but also because of other quarrels he had had with religious orders, communes and confraternities. A parliament in Acre begged him not to leave at so unpropitious a time, but the Templars and the Venetians, who also seem to have denied his kingship, ostentatiously disassociated themselves from this request, proclaiming their indifference as to what he might do. The air of crisis was heightened by rioting by native client-confraternities of the Hospitallers and the Templars, although it was said by one hostile witness that the trouble in the streets was deliberately whipped up in an attempt to create chaos in which the king could return, restore order and put down his opponents. The patriarch, the Master of the Hospitallers and the captain of the French garrison in Acre led a delegation to Tyre, where the king had assembled the High Court. He could not be persuaded to return, although he agreed to appoint administrative officials and to leave Balian of Arsur as his lieutenant. Then he left for Cyprus.[203]

In September 1277 Roger of San Severino arrived in Acre with six galleys. Presenting himself as Charles of Anjou's representative, he brought with him letters from the pope, Charles and Maria of Antioch, which were read at a parliament. They informed the liegemen that Maria had been granted the Throne of Jerusalem by the sentence of the Court of Rome and that she had sold her rights to Charles, who was now their king and lord; at the same time an ecclesiastical lawyer preached in Acre on the validity of Maria's claim.[204] But although supported by the Templars and Venetians[205] Roger, it should be emphasised, had no rights in law whatsoever. Charles's claim to the kingdom was without precedent, and even had he been accepted he could not appoint a lieutenant without himself coming to the East to be received as king. There was only one course open to the feudatories if they were to remain true to their constitutional principles. They must reject Roger's pretensions, discuss Charles's rights and in the meantime appoint a *bailli* of their own. But this was the course they avoided. Balian of Arsur, who may have been ill for he died in the same year, resigned the *bailliage* and left the citadel of Acre, which was immediately occupied by Roger. The vassals in the

High Court put up a little more of a fight. Roger several times demanded homage: the title of vicar-general he had been given presumably empowered him to enter into the feudal contract on Charles's behalf. Instead of questioning the right of the King of Sicily to make such an appointment or of Roger to make such a demand, the feudatories merely replied that having made homage to Hugh of Cyprus they could not submit themselves to Roger until they had Hugh's permission to diffidate themselves in the customary way. They sent messengers to Cyprus but Hugh steadfastly and quite rightly refused to give any answer to such a preposterous proposal. In the end Roger threatened to exile them from the land, their fiefs and possessions if they did not render him his due as the representative of a man who had received the kingdom from an heiress recognised as rightful by the wisest judges in Christendom. It would have been thought that gross threats of banishment and disinheritance, reminiscent of those of Aimery, Frederick II and Richard Filangieri, would have roused some of the old fire in the vassals' bellies. But all the liegemen did was to ask for some respite until a final party of emissaries had returned from Cyprus. Roger was persuaded to agree to this by the Master of the Templars, but the messengers had no satisfactory response from Hugh and so the liegemen made homage to Roger after he had been sworn in as *bailli*. He then appointed his own officials to the administration.[206]

Angevin government was to collapse and Lusignan kingship was to be restored in 1286; and the lords of two of the most important seigneuries, John of Tyre and Isabella of Beirut, refused ever to recognise Roger.[207] But the behaviour of the other liegemen in 1277 needs to be explained. What had happened to the constitutional principles to which these pusillanimous weaklings were the heirs? The baronial ideals cannot have already been forgotten, for only ten years had passed since the days of John of Jaffa and constitutional issues were to be raised again in fourteenth-century Cyprus. Four reasons may be given for the knights' wretched performance. First, Rome was against them and, although the disapproval of Gregory IX had not deflected John of Beirut and his followers from their path in the 1230s, the kingdom was now weaker and correspondingly more dependent for its survival on papal support. Secondly, the loss through alienation or Muslim conquest of the fiefs of Sidon, Jaffa, Arsur, Caesarea and Galilee and the decline in the general commercial prosperity must have had profound economic effects: in the 1230s the lords had been rich, but now they were growing poorer. Thirdly, Hugh himself had a dubious claim to the throne and the tergiversations of the last decade may have demoralised a group as self-righteous as the vassal jurists. Finally and most importantly, Roger of San Severino had arrived with a military force and was supported by the Templars and naturally by the French troops permanently garrisoned in Acre, who made up one of the most effective small armies in the East. They had been established by St Louis and their leaders had played an increasingly important part in internal politics; and Charles was the uncle of the King of France.[208] Like Richard Filangieri in 1231 Roger of San Severino had military strength at his command and had little need of the vassals' services. Against him the armed resistance of the knights would have been useless in the circumstances and positively dangerous at a time when the Mamluks were at their most powerful. The hallowed and rusty sanctions allowed by the jurists in their feudal utopia were again quite unworkable. John of Tyre and Isabella of Beirut could retire to their fiefs and hope to preserve them from Roger's government, but the rest of the vassals, having nowhere to go, could only submit and accept a *bailli* whose appointment broke every rule their ancestors had devised. Although the western settlers were to hold out in Palestine for another fourteen years, the triumph of Charles of Anjou and Roger of San Severino in 1277 marked, in a sense, an awakening: the end of the vassals' dreams.

CONCLUSION

At one point in the research for this book I thought I was going to be able to rehabilitate the Palestinian feudatories and rescue them from the traditional view that they were quarrelsome and short-sighted. Now I am not so sure. The Kingdom of Jerusalem was able to hold out against the might of the Mamluks and the Mongols until 1291, longer than did most of the smaller Asiatic states, although there were reasons for this modest achievement that were beyond the control of the Latin settlers, above all the fact that the Mamluks and Mongols themselves were constantly at war with one another. But one cannot help feeling that the settlement could have been more permanent if it had been given strong government and if the Frankish lords had not themselves been so unmanageable. The donnish pedantry of their leaders, their refusal to compromise on some issues and their mantling of political actions in self-justificatory and sometimes spurious legal terminology must have infuriated those outside their circle who had to deal with them. It would be different if one could portray them as romantic idealists to whom principles were more important even than survival. But if they thought it necessary they seem to have been quite prepared to exploit their own laws or overturn them for political ends. They had many qualities but they were not very likeable. At the same time however their western cousins would have shrunk from the problems with which they had daily to deal. Without the international resources of the Military Orders they had to bear the brunt of the defence of Palestine. Before 1244 their wealth, founded on the prosperity of their ports and markets and a fairly efficient bureaucracy for the exploitation of their assets, meant that for them this was not too great a burden. But later, as trade declined and Muslim aggressiveness increased, the pressures on them must have become nearly unbearable. After 1250 constitutional ideals became a luxury they could no longer afford and it is not surprising to find them becoming inconsistent in their search for acceptable government.

Their political theories place them on an extreme wing of the European baronial movement, unwilling to concede effective public rights to the crown against which they evolved an elaborate and original method of defending themselves. They based their ideals on a mythological and unreal history of the founding and early legislation of the kingdom, and in their treatises they tried to interpret the laws of Jerusalem in such a way as to correspond to their fantasies: they had an impossible, utopian dream which in the end influenced nobody but the Latin Cypriots, whose state was to fall to the Turks in the sixteenth century.[1] Their ideas were not always very effective, but are, nevertheless, extremely interesting, not least because they exemplify what could happen to views of the state common to feudatories everywhere, and reflected in *Magna Carta*, if they were allowed to develop in a circle whose traditions and way of life encouraged a study of the law, and in an alien environment where a monetary economy and an advanced administration widened the gap between feudal theory and practice. Perhaps the greatest monument to the western settlers in Palestine, finer even than the cathedrals and castles still dominating the landscape, is the law-book of John of Jaffa, which, for all its pedantry and long-windedness, is one of the great works of thirteenth-century thought.

LIST OF ABBREVIATIONS

AOL	*Archives de l'Orient latin*
BEC	*Bibliothèque de l'École des Chartes*
HPM	*Historiae patriae monumenta*, ed. iussu regis Caroli Alberti, 20 vols so far (Turin, 1836 ff)
MGH	*Monumenta Germaniae historica inde ab anno Christi quingentesimo usque ad annum millesimum et quingentesimum auspiciis societatis aperiendis fontibus rerum Germanicarum medii aevi*, ed. G. H. Pertz *et al.* (Hanover/Weimar/Berlin/Stuttgart/Cologne, 1826 ff.)
MGHS	*MGH Scriptores in Folio et Quarto*, 32 vols, 1826–1934
MGHS rer. Germ.	*MGH Scriptores rerum Germanicarum in usum scholarum separatim editi*, 61 vols, 1840–1937
PL	*Patrologiae cursus completus. Series Latina*, publ. J. P. Migne, 217 vols and 4 vols of indexes (Paris, 1844–64)
PMAQ	*Peregrinatores medii aevi quatuor*, ed. J. C. M. Laurent, 2nd ed. (Leipzig, 1873)
QFIAB	*Quellen und Forschungen aus italienischen Archiven und Bibliotheken*
RHC	*Recueil des historiens des croisades*, ed. Académie des Inscriptions et Belles-Lettres (Paris, 1841–1906)
RHC arm.	*RHC Documents arméniens*, 2 vols, 1869–1906
RHC Lois	*RHC Lois. Les Assises de Jérusalem*, 2 vols, 1841–3
RHC Oc.	*RHC Historiens occidentaux*, 5 vols, 1844–95
RHC Or.	*RHC Historiens orientaux*, 5 vols, 1872–1906
RHDFE	*Revue historique de droit français et étranger*
RIS	*Rerum Italicarum scriptores*, ed. L. A. Muratori, 25 vols (Milan, 1723–38)
RISNS	*Rerum Italicarum scriptores. Nova series*, ed. G. Carducci *et al.* (Città di Castello/Bologna, 1900 ff.)
ROL	*Revue de l'Orient latin*

NOTES

PREFACE

1. They were edited, very badly, by Comte A. A. Beugnot as 'Les Assises de Jérusalem ou Recueil des ouvrages de Jurisprudence composés pendant le XIIIe siècle dans les royaumes de Jérusalem et de Chypre', in *RHC Lois*. For the 'Livre des Assises de la Cour des Bourgeois' I have used the edition by E. H. Kausler, *Les Livres des Assises et des Usages dou reaume de Jérusalem*, i; except on a few occasions, clearly signified, when Beugnot's edition is more useful.

2. The last practitioner of this school of historians was J. L. La Monte, *Feudal Monarchy in the Latin Kingdom of Jerusalem, 1100–1291*.

3. M. Grandclaude, 'Liste d'Assises remontant au premier royaume de Jérusalem', *Mélanges Paul Fournier* (Paris, 1929).

4. J. Richard, *Le royaume latin de Jérusalem*, pp. 61–79; J. Prawer, 'The Assise de Teneure and the Assise de Vente. A Study of Landed Property in the Latin Kingdom', *Economic History Review*, ser. 2, iv (1951); J. Prawer, 'Les premiers temps de la féodalité du royaume latin de Jérusalem', *Tijdschrift voor rechtsgeschiedenis*, xxii (1954); J. Prawer, 'La noblesse et le régime féodal du royaume latin de Jérusalem', *Le moyen âge*, lxv (1959); J. Prawer, 'Étude sur le droit des Assises de Jérusalem' *RHDFE*, sér. 4, xxxix–xl (1961–2); J. Prawer, *Histoire du royaume latin de Jérusalem*, i, pp. 463–503; C. Cahen, 'La féodalité et les institutions politiques de l'Orient latin', *Oriente ed Occidente nel Medio Evo* (Accad. naz. dei Lincei, Rome, 1957); H. E. Mayer, 'Das Pontifikale von Tyrus und die Krönung der lateinischen Könige von Jerusalem', *Dumbarton Oaks Papers*, xxi (1967). Prawer takes the view that the apogee of royal power was reached in the reign of Baldwin III (1143–63) and that the reign of Amalric (1163–74) saw the beginnings of its decline.

5. Prawer, 'La noblesse', *passim*. Perhaps here too should be mentioned an important study of the rise in the twelfth century of the greatest of the baronial families: W. H. Rüdt de Collenberg, 'Les premiers Ibelins', *Le moyen âge*, lxxi (1965).

6. J. L. La Monte, 'The Communal Movement in Syria in the Thirteenth Century', *Haskins Anniversary Essays*; J. Colson, 'Aux origines des assemblées d'Etat – L'exemple de L'Orient latin', *Revue des études byzantines*, xii (1954); J. Prawer, 'Estates, Communities and the Constitution of the Latin Kingdom', *Proceedings of the Israel Academy of Sciences and Humanities*, ii (1966); J. Richard, 'Pairie d'Orient latin. Les

quatre baronnies des royaumes de Jérusalem et de Chypre', *RHDFE*, sér. 4, xxviii (1950); H. E. Mayer, 'On the Beginnings of the Communal Movement in the Holy Land: The Commune of Tyre', *Traditio*, xxiv (1968); H. E. Mayer, 'Zwei Kommunen in Akkon?', *Deutsches Archiv*, xxvi (1970). These and other historians have also written works on specific problems in social and economic history to which I will make reference elsewhere.

7. See R. Röhricht, *Geschichte des Königreichs Jerusalem*; R. Grousset, *Histoire des croisades et du royaume franc de Jérusalem*, iii; S. Runciman, *A History of the Crusades*, iii; H. E. Mayer, *The Crusades*; Richard, *Le royaume latin*; Prawer, *Histoire*, ii.

8. I have taken one very dangerous course. I believe that it is sometimes justifiable to make use of a forged charter if it is contemporary or nearly so. A forgery is of course no evidence that the organisation for whom it was made enjoyed the estates or privileges it purported to grant; but on the other hand it would have been of no worth to the forger if the *formulae* used in it had no correspondence with actual conditions. I have, of course, drawn attention to the very few occasions on which I have used a forgery in this way. There has just been written what will become a classic work on Palestinian forged charters. H. E. Mayer, *Marseilles Levantehandel und ein akkonensisches Fälscheratelier des 13. Jahrhunderts* (Tübingen, 1972).

9. See M. Grandclaude, 'Classement sommaire des manuscripts des principaux livres des Assises de Jérusalem', *RHDFE*, sér. 4, v (1926), pp. 418–75 *passim*.

10. Edited under the titles *Chronique d'Ernoul et de Bernard le Trésorier* and 'L'Estoire de Eracles empereur et la conqueste de la Terre d'Outremer'. A good general summary of the relationships between these narrative histories and the problems concerning their authorship can be found in C. Cahen, *La Syrie du Nord à l'époque des croisades et la principauté franque d'Antioche*, pp. 20–5.

11. See P. Richter, 'Beiträge zur Historiographie in den Kreuzfahrerstaaten', *Mitteilungen des Instituts für österreichische Geschichtsforschung*, xiii–xv (1892–4).

PART I: LORDS AND LORDSHIPS

CHAPTER 1 FEUDALISM IN PALESTINE

1. Ralph of Tiberias in Philip of Novara, 'Livre de forme de plait', p. 544. See John of Jaffa, p. 401. On the death of a fief-holder, his children – but only they – could enter into possession of his fief imme-

diately, without first informing the lord. John of Jaffa, pp. 231, 261; James of Ibelin, p. 461; Philip of Novara 'Livre', p. 494.

2. *Cartulaire général de l'ordre des Hospitaliers*, ed. J. Delaville le Roulx, no. 2985.

3. J. S. C. Riley-Smith 'Some lesser officials in Latin Syria', *English Historical Review*, lxxxvii (1972) pp. 18, 24.

4. A. L. Poole, *Obligations of Society in the XII and XIII Centuries*, p. 61.

5. See Riley-Smith, 'Some lesser officials', pp. 15–26.

6. Poole, pp. 57–9, 62 and *passim*.

7. John of Jaffa, pp. 411, 413–14.

8. 'Livre au roi', p. 613; Philip of Novara 'Livre', p. 542; *Cart. gen. Hosp.*, no. 2985; 'Inventaire de pièces de Terre Sainte de l'ordre de l'Hôpital', ed. J. Delaville Le Roulx, *ROL*, iii (1895) no. 321; Richard, *Le royaume latin*, p. 130. See also *Cart. gen. Hosp.*, no. 787; 'Eracles' ii, p. 192.

9. John of Jaffa, p. 300; Philip of Novara 'Livre', p. 542. This was unlike England; see Poole, p. 59.

10. *Cart. gen. Hosp.*, nos. 480, 1996 (see also nos. 2576–7), 2985; *Tabulae ordinis Theutonici*, ed. E. Strehlke, no. 16; and probably *Codice diplomatico del sacro militare ordine gerosolimitano*, ed. S. Pauli, i, pp. 288–9.

11. James of Ibelin, p. 459; Philip of Novara, 'Livre', pp. 486, 502. See also 'Inventaire de l'Hôpital', no. 321.

12. To many grants seem to have been added the obligation of *restor*, or compensation made by the lord for the loss of a horse or beast of burden while performing service. La Monte, *Feudal Monarchy*, pp. 120–1, 152. See *Cart. gen. Hosp.*, nos. 480, 2985; *Cod. dipl. geros.*, i, p. 288; R. Röhricht, 'Amalrich I., König von Jerusalem', *Mitteilungen des Instituts für österreichische Geschichtsforschung*, xii (1891) p. 493.

13. See John of Jaffa, pp. 218, 253, 255; Philip of Novara, 'Livre', p. 519.

14. See for example *Tab. ord. Theut.*, no. 7; *Cart. gen. Hosp.* nos. 786, 1156, 1174, 2670, 3684.

15. J. Prawer, 'Etude de quelques problèmes agraires et sociaux d'une seigneurie croisée au XIIIe siècle', *Byzantion*, xxii (1952) pp. 21–4.

16. B. D. Lyon, *From Fief to Indenture*, *passim*; see pp. 6–16 for the arguments for the use of the term *fief-rente*.

17. See *Cart. gen. Hosp.*, nos. 480, 2985; *Cod. dipl. geros.*, i, pp. 241, 288; John of Jaffa, pp. 383–4; Philip of Novara, 'Livre', p. 515; also 'Livre au roi', pp. 626, 628, 631.

18. *Cart. gen. Hosp.*, nos. 480, 754, 2985; *Tab. ord. Theut.*, no. 9; *Cod. dipl. geros.*, i, pp. 241, 248, 288; *Chartes de la Terre Sainte provenant de l'abbaye de Notre Dame de Josaphat*, ed. H. F. Delaborde, no. 38.

19. John of Jaffa, p. 253; Philip of Novara, 'Livre', p. 519.

20. 'Eracles', ii, p. 224; *Ernoul*, p. 311; also *Cart. gen. Hosp.* no. 2985.

21. John of Jaffa, pp. 218, 273–4, 388; 'Livre au roi', p. 625; Philip of Novara, 'Livre', p. 531. See *Tab. ord. Theut.*, no. 9. These seem to have been paid in one sum a year.

22. *Cart. gen. Hosp.* no. 144 (p. 117); *Cod. dipl. geros.*, i. p. 241; John of Jaffa, p. 424. See also 'Inventaire de l'Hôpital' no. 321.

23. John of Jaffa, p. 274; *Tab. ord. Theut.*, nos. 4–5, 7–9, 13–14, 17, 19, 53, 63–4, 98; 'Fragment d'un cartulaire de l'ordre de Saint-Lazare en Terre Sainte', ed. A de Marsy, *AOL*, ii (1884) nos. 28–9; 'Sankt Samuel auf dem Freudenberge und sein Besitz nach einem unbekannter Diplom König Balduins V', ed. H. E. Mayer, *QFIAB*, xliv (1964) p. 70; *Historia diplomatica Frederici secundi*, ed. J. L. A. de Huillard-Bréholles, iii, p. 117; 'Quatre pièces relatives à l'ordre teutonique en Orient'. *AOL*, ii (1884), no. 3; *Cart. gen. Hosp.* nos. 311, 437, 1031–2, 1684, 2001–2, 2143, 2280 (pp. 594–5); 'Un diplôme inédit d'Amaury I, roi de Jérusalem, en faveur de l'abbaye du Temple-Notre-Seigneur (1166)', ed. F. Chalandon, *ROL*, viii (1900–1), p. 312; *Les Archives la Bibliothèque et le trésor de l'ordre de Saint-Jean de Jérusalem à Malte*, ed. J. Delaville Le Roulx, no. 52; *Urkunden zur älteren Handels- und Staatsgeschichte der Republik Venedig*, ed. G. L. F. Tafel and G. M. Thomas, no. 299 (p. 377). See also *Assises d'Antioche*, pp. 40–2; *Cart. gen. Hosp.*, nos. 390, 526, 3047; 'Frag. cart. St-Lazare', no. 27.

24. John of Jaffa, p. 257.

25. *Cart. gen. Hosp.*, no. 2985: one fief in Arsur was the subject of dispute. For other examples, see *Cart. gen. Hosp.*, nos. 144 (p. 117), 390, 754, 3047; *Cod. dipl. geros*, i, pp. 241, 248, 288; *Chartes de Josaphat*, ed. Delaborde, no. 38; *Tab. ord. Theut.*, nos. 7, 9; *Urkunden Venedig*, no. 299 (pp. 375–9).

26. *Tab. ord. Theut.*, nos. 14, 16–17, 53, 98; *Hist. dipl. Fred. secundi*, ii, p. 533.

27. *Cart. gen. Hosp.*, no. 144 (p. 117); *Tab. Ord. Theut.*, nos. 4–5. See also *Cart. gen. Hosp.*, no. 202 (p. 156).

28. See J. S. C. Riley-Smith, 'Historical Introduction', Ibn al-Furat, ii, p. xvi; also John of Jaffa, pp. 270–4.

29. Geoffrey Le Tor, p. 436.

30. John of Jaffa, pp. 215–16. The authors of the 'Livre au roi' (p. 607) stated that royal fortresses could not be alienated to the Church.

31. John of Jaffa, p. 399; Geoffrey Le Tor, p. 440. See John of Jaffa, pp. 397–8; *Tab. ord. Theut.* no. 11; *Cartulaire de l'église du Saint-Sépulcre de Jérusalem*, ed. E. de Rozière, no. 100; *Cart. gen. Hosp.*, no. 2581; also *Tab. ord. Theut.*, no. 103; Prawer, 'Les premiers temps', pp. 413 ff.

32. J. S. C. Riley-Smith, *The Knights of St John in Jerusalem and Cyprus*, pp. 456–9. See *Hist. dipl. Fred. secundi*, iii, p. 119; *Tab. ord. Theut.*, no. 99; *Cod. dipl. geros.* i, p. 206.

33. *Tab. ord. Theut.* no. 100.

34. *Cart. gen. Hosp.*, nos. 311, 317, 391, 783 (p. 495), 2856. For the service owed by the Italian communes, see *Urkunden Venedig*, no. 41 (p. 93); 'Liber iurium reipublicae Ianuensis', no. 477; *Cod. dipl. geros.*, i, pp. 159–60.

35. 'Livre au roi', p. 624.

36. See John of Jaffa, pp. 312–16, 397–9; Philip of Novara, 'Livre', p. 455; also *Cart. gen. Hosp.*, no. 168; *Cart. du St-Sépulcre*, no. 60.

37. By word of mouth, if the vassal was present in court, or by the lord's *banier* or by three other vassals representing the court or by letters. John of Jaffa, pp. 42, 138, 253, 258, 338, 342–5, 348–52, 359; 'Livre au roi', p. 643; Geoffrey Le Tor, pp. 438, 448; James of Ibelin, pp. 463, 467; Philip of Novara 'Livre', pp. 520, 529, 555. The summons had to be issued in court. John of Jaffa, pp. 348–9.

38. John of Jaffa, pp. 259, 358–9, 362–4.

39. *Cart. gen. Hosp.*, no. 3047 – a document issued in 1269. For *service de cors*, see also Röhricht, 'Amalrich I,' p. 493; 'Quatre pièces teut.', no. 3.

40. See *Cart. gen. Hosp.*, no. 2902 (p. 861).

41. John of Jaffa, pp. 343, 347, 353; 'Livre au roi', p. 626. See also *Tab. ord. Theut.*, no. 2. One problem, which seems only to have become acute when there was a dispute over service in the Holy Land between the King of Cyprus and his knights in 1271, was whether the summoning to service beyond the frontiers could be made solely at the wishes of the king: in other words as an expression of his will. The eventual decision in 1273 seems to have been that this indeed was the case. 'Document relatif au service militaire', pp. 427, 430; 'Eracles', ii, pp. 463–4.

42. Philip of Novara, 'Livre', p. 541.

43. John of Jaffa, pp. 345–6. To James of Ibelin (p. 454) a knight should bring with him a 'cheval' (war-horse) and 2 other 'chevauchures'. But there were probably different local practices: in Arsur the knights had to bring 4 'chevauchures' and many of the sergeants 2; one sergeant in Caymont also brought 2 horses: in Tyre a vassal brought 3 horses and esquires. *Cart. gen. Hosp.*, no. 2985; *Tab. ord. Theut.*, no. 14; 'Inventaire de l'Hôpital', no. 321. One tenancy in Tripoli specified service for half a year. 'Les Porcellets de Syrie', ed. F. Benoit, *Congrès de Marseille* (1929), no. 1.

44. *Cart. gen. Hosp.*, nos. 783 (p. 495), 2985; *Recherches géographiques et historiques sur la domination des Latins en Orient*, ed. E. G. Rey, p. 40. The reference to the defence of a town or castle in John of Jaffa (p. 342)

was concerned with the defence of a lord's body, rather than with castle-guard.

45. John of Jaffa, pp. 263–7, 279–80, 348, 359–69; Philip of Novara, 'Livre', pp. 558–60; 'Livre au roi', pp. 626–8; James of Ibelin, p. 467. See *Cart. du St-Sépulcre*, no. 77; J. Richard, 'Le statut de la femme dans l'Orient latin', *Recueils de la société Jean Bodin xii: La femme, 2e partie*, pp. 378–80. It might be worth mentioning here that in the County of Tripoli service at sea was also demanded. *Memorie storico-diplomatiche di Amalfi*, ed. M. Camera, i, p. 204; *Regesta regni Hierosolymitani*, comp. R. Röhricht, no. 754.

46. John of Jaffa, p. 347; also pp. 73, 253, 352; and below, pp. 132–3.

47. 'Livre au roi', p. 625; John of Jaffa, pp. 24, 225, 358, 411, 422–7; Philip of Novara, p. 519; Geoffrey Le Tor, p. 449; James of Ibelin, p. 464; *Tab. ord. Theut.*, nos. 5, 10, 13, 16, 21, 100; *Cart. gen. Hosp.*, nos. 1156, 1174, 3684; 'Quatre pièces teut.', no. 3; 'Inventaire de l'Hôpital', no. 321. See *Cart. gen. Hosp.*, no. 787.

48. 'Livre au roi', p. 641; John of Jaffa, pp. 356–7, 358, 375, 378; James of Ibelin, p. 455; Philip of Novara, pp. 539, 540. See also John of Jaffa, p. 218; James of Ibelin, p. 463. On the greater fiefs the companions would be commanded by a rear-vassal.

49. John of Jaffa, pp. 422–7. See R. C. Smail, *Crusading Warfare*, pp. 89–90.

50. Philip of Novara, 'Livre', p. 543; John of Jaffa, p. 422.

51. John of Jaffa, p. 423; *Tab. ord. Theut.*, no. 21.

52. *Cart. gen. Hosp.*, no. 2985. Cf. John of Jaffa, pp. 422–3.

53. *Cart. gen. Hosp.*, nos. 1156, 1174, 2670, 3684.

54. 'Livre au roi', p. 630; John of Jaffa, pp. 284–5; *Tab. ord. Theut.*, nos. 4–5, 7, 9–10, 13–14, 21–2, 100; *Cart. gen. Hosp.*, no. 2985. 'Quatre pièces teut.,' no. 3; 'Inventaire de l'Hôpital' no. 321. But 300 besants a year were paid in Tripoli in place of service. *Cart. gen. Hosp.*, nos. 1156, 1174, 2670.

55. 'Livre au roi', p. 630; John of Jaffa, pp. 284–5. See Philip of Novara, 'Livre', pp. 530–1.

56. *Cart. gen. Hosp.*, nos. 59, 354, 491, 495; *Cart. du St-Sépulcre*, nos. 56, 60, 65; *Chartes de Josaphat*, ed. Delaborde, no. 32. See also *Cod. dipl. geros.*, i, p. 206.

57. Jerusalem: *Reg. Hier.*, nos. 43, 52, 76b, 79–80, 130, 391; John of Jaffa, p. 423. Nablus: John of Jaffa, p. 424. Acre: *Reg. Hier.*, nos. 115, 130, 293, 367; John of Jaffa, p. 425. Oultrejourdain: *Reg. Hier.*, nos. 365b, 454, 551, 587, 595, 628. Haifa: *Reg. Hier.*, nos. 341, 377, 594. The knightage of Antioch looks very Greek. See *Reg. Hier.*, *passim*.

58. *Tab. ord. Theut.*, no. 105; 'Documents et mémoires servant de preuves à l'histoire de l'île de Chypre sous les Lusignans', ed. L. de

Mas-Latrie, iii, pp. 662–8; 'Gestes des Chiprois', pp. 782, 787; 'Deux chartes des croisés dans les archives arabes', ed. C. Clermont-Ganneau, *Receuil d'archéologie orientale*, vi (1905), pp. 4, 9–11. See also *Tab. ord. Theut.*, no. 40.

59. John of Jaffa, pp. 186–7; and see p. 123; James of Ibelin, p. 459; Philip of Novara, 'Livre', pp. 483, 488; 'Livre au roi', pp. 617–19. See the *Assise* of Belbeis according to which a knight involved in a siege need not perform service where his horse could not carry him. 'Gestes des Chiprois', p. 721; also Prawer 'La noblesse', pp. 53–5; Riley-Smith, *Knights of St John*, pp. 236–9.

60. John of Jaffa, pp. 188, 300–1.

61. Philip of Novara, pp. 486, 502.

62. John of Jaffa, pp. 297–9; Geoffrey Le Tor, p. 450; Philip of Novara, 'Livre', p. 500.

63. See below, p. 29 and Riley-Smith, *Knights of St John* pp. 324–8; Smail, *Crusading Warfare*, pp. 93–4.

64. John of Jaffa, p. 260. For dubbing, see M. Bloch, *Feudal Society*, pp. 312 ff.

65. 'Annales de Terre Sainte', pp. 445–6. See also 'Gestes des Chiprois', p. 715. For a reference to the 'age of knighthood', see *Cart. gen. Hosp.* no. 144 (p. 117).

66. Ernoul, p. 175; 'Eracles', ii. p. 70. See John of Jaffa, p. 260.

67. Ernoul, loc. cit., 'Eracles', loc. cit. For the family of Antiaume, see below p. 124.

68. But a sergeant who challenged a knight, accusing him of murder, would be dubbed a knight himself before the duel. James of Ibelin, p. 459; Philip of Novara, 'Livre', pp. 486, 502.

69. Philip of Novara 'Livre', p. 538. See Prawer, 'La noblesse', p. 49.

70. Philip of Novara, 'Livre', pp. 538–9; 'Livre au roi,' p. 633; John of Jaffa, pp. 223–4. See E. Meynial, 'De quelques particularités des successions féodales dans les Assises de Jérusalem', *RHDFE*, xvi (1892), pp. 408–19. As late as the 1180s Humphrey, the heir to the fiefs of Toron and Oultrejourdain, was made to renounce Toron on his marriage to the king's sister. See below, p. 105.

71. 'Livre au roi', pp. 633–4; John of Jaffa, pp. 223–4; Geoffrey Le Tor, p. 439. See also the example of Shuf in the lordship of Sidon described below, p. 33.

72. Philip of Novara, 'Livre', pp. 538–40. Anjou of Malembec was also a fief-holder in Cyprus: *Reg. Hier.* 1049 (Guillinus de Malenbec). Thomas of St Bertin is not to be confused with his better-known descendant. For Walter of St Bertin, see *Reg. Hier.*, nos. 846, 1149.

73. John of Jaffa, pp. 284–5; Philip of Novara, 'Livre', pp. 553–4; Grandclaude, 'Liste d'Assises', p. 335.

74. Geoffrey Le Tor, p. 448.

75. John of Jaffa, pp. 372, 399; Philip of Novara, 'Livre', pp. 530–1. See for example *Cart. du St-Sépulcre*, no. 60; *Cart. gen. Hosp.* nos. 603, 606–7, but also no. 1231.

76. John of Jaffa, pp. 63–4, 216–17, 288–9, 301, 398–9; Geoffrey Le Tor, pp. 449–50; James of Ibelin, p. 464; Philip of Novara 'Livre', pp. 500–1, 532. See *Chartes de Josaphat*, ed. Delaborde, no. 43; *Tab. ord. Theut.*, nos. 41, 53, 56; *Cart. gen. Hosp.*, nos. 495, 1996 (see also nos. 2576–7). In certain circumstances the exchange of fiefs was permitted. John of Jaffa, pp. 286–7; Geoffrey Le Tor, p. 460.

77. Philip of Novara 'Livre', pp. 543–4; John of Jaffa, pp. 217–19, 401; 'Eracles', ii, pp. 230–1.

78. John of Jaffa, pp. 217, 218, 220–3, 234, 235, 308–9; James of Ibelin, pp. 460, 461; Philip of Novara, 'Livre', pp. 504, 537, 545–6.

79. For a native sergeantry, see *Cod. dipl. geros.*, i, p. 288.

80. 'Livre au roi', p. 630; John of Jaffa, pp. 224–31; Geoffrey Le Tor, pp. 435–6, 442. See Philip of Novara, 'Livre', pp. 503–6; and below, p. 219.

81. See especially Philip of Novara, 'Livre', pp. 539–40.

82. Homage had to be performed within a year and a day of inheriting a fief and within forty days to a new lord. *Ligece* had to be made to the king within a year and a day. James of Ibelin, pp. 455–6; Geoffrey Le Tor, pp. 437–8; John of Jaffa, p. 305. But this may also have been covered by the *Assise* of a year and a day, for the inheritor of property had to take possession of it within this time-limit. Prawer ('Assise de Teneure', p. 84) believed that to the thirteenth-century jurists this *assise* no longer applied to fiefs. But see John of Jaffa, pp. 63–4; Philip of Novara 'Livre', pp. 484–5, 554, although admittedly they were referring to burgess heritages which were parts of fiefs. See also *Tab. ord. Teut.*, no 3 (p. 4).

83. Geoffrey Le Tor, p. 436; 'Documents relatifs à la successibilité au trône et à la régence', p. 406. See 'Gestes des Chiprois', p. 725; also, for instance, *Chartes de Josaphat*, ed. Delaborde, no. 14; *Tab. ord. Theut.* no. 53; *Hist. dipl. Fred. secundi*, ii, pp. 533–4.

84. Philip of Novara, 'Livre', pp. 542–3; 'Documents relatifs à la successibilité, pp. 408, 409. See 'Livre au roi', pp. 629–30; John of Jaffa, pp. 225–7. For Stephen of Sancerre's visit, see Runciman, *Crusades*, ii, pp. 392–3.

85. John of Jaffa, pp. 107–9. See 'Livre au roi', p. 632.

86. 'Livre au roi', pp. 620, 621, 627, 631; Philip of Novara 'Livre', p. 545; John of Jaffa, pp. 131, 175–6, 279–82.

87. R. R. Reid, 'Barony and Thanage', *English Historical Review*, xxxv (1920) pp. 161–8; R. Boutruche, *Seigneurie et Féodalité*, ii, pp. 264–7.

88. John of Jaffa, pp. 417–19. See 'Gestes des Chiprois', p. 819.

89. John of Jaffa, p. 30.

90. John of Jaffa, p. 280. See James of Ibelin, p. 467. Cf. Reid, 'Barony', p. 163.

91. Richard, 'Pairie', pp. 72–80. See also J. Richard, 'Les listes des seigneuries dans "Le Livre de Jean d'Ibelin". Recherches sur l'Assebebe et Mimars', *RHDFE*, sér. 4, xxxii (1954) pp. 571–2. Perhaps Philip of Montfort played some part in this: he was believed to have been one of the twelve peers of France. See below, p. 19.

92. John of Jaffa, pp. 24, 27, 28, 30, 31, 214, 216, 422.

93. John of Jaffa, p. 418.

94. Philip of Novara, 'Livre', p. 526, and see pp. 481, 514, 517, 527 (Sidon), 531–2, 538, 541, 542 (Henry Le Buffle), 565, 566. Of course Cyprus, with which Philip was mainly concerned, had no great territorial lordship similar to those in Palestine. For other references to 'riches homes', see John of Jaffa, pp. 150, 320 (Sidon), 334; Geoffrey Le Tor, p. 435; 'Livre des Assises des Bourgeois', p. 239.

95. James of Ibelin, p. 457 – but see also p. 467; 'Livre des Assises des Bourgeois', p. 346; Geoffrey Le Tor, p. 448; 'Eracles', ii, p. 475. For Geoffrey Le Tor, see Richard, 'Pairie', p. 80.

96. *Sacrorum conciliorum nova et amplissima collectio*, ed. G. D. Mansi, xxi, col. 266; *Chartes de Josaphat*, ed. Delaborde, nos. 5, 26; *Cart. gen. Hosp.*, nos. 116, 139, 173, 411, 422; *Cart du St-Sépulcre*, nos. 34, 56, 59, 62, 67; 'Frag. cart. St-Lazare', no. 31; 'Liber iurium', no. 363; *Documenti sulle relazione delle città toscane coll'Oriente cristiano*, ed. G. Müller, nos. 23–5, 31 (p. 37), 32 (p. 38); Mayer, *Marseilles Levantehandel*, no. 4 (p. 183).

97. *Chartes de Josaphat* ed. Delaborde, nos. 14, 20; *Cart. gen. Hosp.*, nos. 74, 77, 94; *Cart. du St-Sépulcre*, no. 123. See also *Cart. gen. Hosp.*, no. 198.

98. *Documenti delle citta toscane*, nos. 23–5; Mayer, *Marseilles Levantehandel*, no. 4 (p. 183).

99. *Cart. gen. Hosp.*, no. 1996. The named witnesses were Odo of Montbéliard, Garnier L'Aleman, James of La Mandelée, Aymar of Layron, Monabeu and Nicholas Antiaume.

100. *Cart. gen. Hosp.*, nos. 82 (p. 77), 144; *Cart. du St-Sépulcre*, no. 93.

101. *Cart. du St-Sépulcre*, no. 56; and see nos. 59, 62.

102. *Cart. du St-Sépulcre*, nos. 54–5, 57.

103. William of Tyre, p. 1008. He usually referred to the lords as 'principes': an interesting title, with all that it implied concerning independent jurisdiction.

104. William of Tyre, p. 1111.

105. 'Eracles', ii, pp. 64–5.

106. 'Livre au roi', pp. 608, 609, 617, 634; and see pp. 622–3.

107. 'Eracles', ii, p. 305; *Thesaurus novus anecdotorum*, ed. E. Martène

and U. Durand, i, col. 806. See also *Tab. ord. Theut.*, no. 52; 'Gestes des Chiprois', p. 667.

108. 'Tractatus de locis et statu sancte terre ierosolimitane', p. 157; James of Vitry, 'Historia', p. 1074. The chroniclers seem to have used 'baron' in a general sense until well into the thirteenth century. 'Eracles', ii, pp. 8, 26–7, 32, 154, 309; 'Gestes des Chiprois', pp. 658–9.

109. *Reg. Hier*, nos. 92, 414, 447–8, 583.

110. *Reg. Hier*, nos. 92, 131, 336, 414, 447, 479.

111. *Reg. Hier.*, nos. 1205, 1247, 1249c.

112. *Reg. Hier.*, nos. 1056, 1297a, 1322, 1370–1.

113. *Reg. Hier.*, nos. 89, 100, 102a, 112–13, 137a; Rüdt de Collenberg, 'Les premiers Ibelins', pp. 452–3.

114. *Reg. Hier.*, nos. 1245–6.

115. 'Chartes de Terre Sainte', ed. J. Delaville Le Roulx, *ROL*, xi (1905/8), no. 1.

116. *Reg. Hier.*, nos. 1205, 1217, 1220, 1253, 1256–7, 1265, 1300.

117. *Reg. Hier.*, nos. 986, 1253, 1256–7, 1300. Several other fiefs had seigneurial officers, but the only others to have had marshals seem to have been Nazareth (*Reg. Hier.*, no. 1280) and Arsur (*Reg. Hier.* no. 1302).

118. *Cart. gen. Hosp.*, no. 2810; 'Quatre titres des propriétés des Génois à Acre et à Tyr', ed. C. Desimoni, *AOL*, ii (1884), no. 4 (p. 225). It is noteworthy that John of Jaffa, who claimed (pp. 417, 419, 422) that the seigneurie of Ramle was subject to his county, also styled himself its lord. 'Documents et mémoires de Chypre', iii, p. 647; Pope Innocent IV, *Registre*, no. 6463; 'Annales monasterii Burtonensis', p. 368.

119. Francesco Amadi, p. 187. See 'Quatre titres des Génois', no. 4 (p. 229). For the twelve peers of France, see C. Petit-Dutaillis, *L'Essor des États d'Occident*, pp. 30–1, 247; Bloch, *Feudal Society*, pp. 334–5.

CHAPTER 2 LORDS, LORDSHIPS AND VAVASOURS

1. Pope Clement IV, *Registre*, no. 673.

2. 'Les lignages d'Outremer', p. 448; Rüdt de Collenberg, 'Les premiers Ibelins', pp. 433–74. The popular name of Balian was in fact a variant of Barisan.

3. 'Gestes des Chiprois', pp. 678–9.

4. J. L. La Monte, 'The Lords of Sidon in the Twelfth and Thirteenth Centuries', *Byzantion*, xvii (1944–5) pp. 185–90; J. L. La Monte,

'The Lords of Caesarea in the Period of the Crusades', *Speculum*, xxii (1947) pp. 147–8.

5. John of Jaffa, p. 422. A variant reading of John of Jaffa, p. 420 (n. 15) gave Haifa as a rear-fief of Caesarea.

6. William of Tyre, p. 629; and see p. 759; *Cart. gen. Hosp.*, no. 621.

7. La Monte, 'The Lords of Caesarea', pp. 155–6. Margaret's first husband had been Hugh of Tiberias.

8. Grousset, *Histoire des croisades*, ii, pp. 840–50.

9. For Oultrejourdain, see 'Étude sur un texte latin énumérant les possessions musulmanes dans le royaume de Jérusalem', ed. P. Deschamps, *Syria*, xxiii (1942–3) pp. 88, 89, 91.

10. See the genealogical table in C. de Fresne Du Cange, *Les familles d'Outre-mer*, ed. E. G. Rey, p. 379. For the marriage of James, see 'Annales de Terre Sainte', p. 456.

11. Du Cange, *Les familles*, pp. 302–3.

12. Their common ancestor was Bouchard of Montlhéry, Count of Corbeil.

13. 'Doc. rel. au service militaire', p. 434.

14. John of Jaffa, p. 24.

15. The Lords, for instance, of Caesarea. ('Les lignages', p. 457), Beirut ('Abrégé du Livre des Assises de la Cour des Bourgeois', p. 246), Tyre ('Gestes des Chiprois', p. 813) and Odo of Montbéliard (*Itinéraires à Jérusalem*, ed. H. Michelant and G. Raynaud, p. 136).

16. If J. Prawer and M. Benvenisti ('Crusader Palestine') are right in their identification of the village of Boussaih. The lordship did not correspond to the Muslim district of Sidon, which seems to have lost Kafr Kifa, now in the lordship of Tyre. See *Reg. Hier.*, no. 134.

17. See *Tab. ord. Theut.*, no. 110.

18. *Urkunden Venedig*, no. 299 (pp. 370, 375); *Cart. gen. Hosp.*, no. 2688; 'Eracles', ii, p. 394.

19. M. Benvenisti, *The Crusaders in the Holy Land*, pp. 130–5; *Cart. gen. Hosp.*, nos. 2753, 3047.

20. Benvenisti, pp. 14, 132.

21. See below, pp. 67 ff.

22. For the Council of Nablus, see Prawer, 'Les premiers temps', pp. 419–21, although I am certain he would not agree with my interpretation of Jerusalem's early feudal history.

23. 'Livre au roi', p. 634. See also *Cart. gen. Hosp.*, no. 3071.

24. See John of Jaffa, pp. 419–21. For seigneurial courts before 1187, see 'Chartes de Terre Sainte', ed. Delaville Le Roulx, no. 1; *Cart. gen. Hosp.*, nos. 603, 621, 819; 'Sankt Samuel', p. 69; 'Frag. cart. St-Lazare', no. 4. For seals, see G. Schlumberger, *Sigillographie de l'Orient latin*, pp. 39–64; F. Chandon de Briailles, 'Bulles de l'Orient latin', *Syria*, xxvii (1950), pp. 286–8; F. Chandon de Briailles, 'Le

droit de "coins" dans le royaume de Jérusalem', *Syria*, xxiii (1942/3), *passim*.

25. 'Livre des Assises des Bourgeois' p. 82 (see 'Livre des Assises des Bourgeois', ed. Beugnot, p. 47). But see *Documenti delle città toscane*, nos. 23 (p. 27), 24 (pp. 28–9), 25 (pp. 30–1), 31 (p. 37), 32 (pp. 38–9) in which the Pisans were freed from the payment of shipwreck throughout the kingdom. The lords, who were also not to impose new dues on the Pisans, must have been persuaded to agree to this.

26. G. Schlumberger, *Numismatique de l'Orient latin*, pp. 108–29; Ibn al-Furat, ii, pp. 42, 192; Abu-Shamah, v, p. 203.

27. 'Livre au roi', p. 609; John of Jaffa, pp. 254, 303. See *Cart. gen. Hosp.*, no. 180.

28. See below, pp. 111 ff.

29. 'Eracles', ii, p. 34.

30. 'Eracles', ii, p. 198; and see p. 346.

31. Ibn al-Furat, ii, p. 131.

32. Ibn al-Furat, ii, pp. 43–4, 53, 77–8, 90–1, 107. For Jaffa in the 1250s, see below, pp. 30–1.

33. Ibn al-Furat, ii, pp. 89–90, 103, 129; but see pp. 133–4.

34. Ibn al-Furat, ii, p. 164; and see pp. 104–5, 113, 135.

35. Ibn al-Furat, ii, pp. 157–8. The lords made their own treaties with the Muslims: for example, see Ibn al-Furat, ii, p. 154; al-Maqrizi, ii, A, pp. 213–21; *Itinéraires à Jérusalem*, pp. 255–6.

36. Riley-Smith, *Knights of St John*, pp. 55–7, 67–8, 463–5.

37. 'Annales mon. Burtonensis', p. 494.

38. 'De constructione castri Saphet', ed. R. B. C. Huygens, *Studi medievali*, ser. 3, vi (1965) p. 384. Early in the 1240s Saphet contained 50 brother knights, 30 brother sergeants, 50 turcopoles, 300 crossbowmen, 820 workmen and 400 slaves. See also 'Annales mon. Burtonensis', p. 494; *Codex epistolaris Rudolphi I*, ed. M. Gerbert, p. 67; Pope Nicholas IV, *Registre*, no. 1357; James of Vitry, *Lettres*, p. 99; Pope Alexander IV, *Registre*, no. 1939; 'Lettres inédites concernant les croisades', ed. C. Kohler and C. V Langlois, *BEC*, lii (1891) pp. 55–6; *Cart. gen. Hosp.*, no. 2727; Riley-Smith, *Knights of St John*, pp. 439–43.

39. *Cart. gen. Hosp.*, nos. 938–9, 954, 972, 990; *Tab. ord. Theut.*, nos. 28, 35, 44; *Hist. dipl. Fred. secundi*, ii, pp. 534–5, 537, iii, p. 128; 'Annales mon. Burtonensis', p. 494.

40. *Cart. gen. Hosp.*, no. 207.

41. *Cart. gen. Hosp.*, no. 258; William of Tyre, pp. 837–8. See Riley-Smith, *Knights of St John*, p. 72.

42. *Cart. gen. Hosp.*, no. 302.

43. *Cod. dipl. geros.*, i, p. 63. See Baha' ad-Din, p. 299.

44. *Cart. gen. Hosp.*, no. 783 (p. 492).

45. *Tab. ord. Theut.*, no. 40.

46. *Tab. ord. Theut.*, nos. 108–11, 114–15; 117–18: especially no. 109. See also *Cart. gen. Hosp.*, nos. 2688, 2693.

47. According to the authors of 'Eracles' (ii, p. 445), 'Gestes des Chiprois' (p. 752) and 'Annales de Terre Sainte' (p. 449), Sidon was sold; but the gist of a passage by Philip of Novara ('Livre', pp. 530–1) seems to be that it was leased. For the negotiations with the Hospitallers, see *Cart. gen. Hosp.*, no. 3029 (p. 33).

48. 'Gestes des Chiprois', pp. 752, 775.

49. See P. Deschamps, *La défense du royaume de Jérusalem*, pp. 225–6.

50. 'Gestes des Chiprois', p. 752. Julian later became a Templar and died a brother of St Trinity. 'Eracles', ii, p. 467.

51. Riley-Smith, *Knights of St John*, pp. 133–4. For its refortification in 1241, see 'Gestes des Chiprois', p. 728; 'Annales de Terre Sainte', p. 440.

52. 'Eracles', ii, p. 445; 'Gestes des Chiprois', p. 753; 'Annales de Terre Sainte', pp. 449–50; Ibn al-Furat, ii, pp. 49, 195–6; *Tab. ord. Theut.*, nos. 119–22.

53. See *Cart. gen. Hosp.*, nos. 2301, 2394, 2587, 2810, 2816–17, 2845.

54. John of Joinville, pp. 306–8, 336; Matthew Paris, *Chronica maiora*, vi, p. 206.

55. Innocent IV, *Reg.*, no. 6463.

56. See 'Eracles', ii, p. 442; 'Annales de Terre Sainte', p. 446; *Chronicon de Lanercost*, p. 61; 'Rothelin', pp. 630–1 (which refers to treaties with both Damascus and Egypt). See also Matthew Paris, v, p. 522; Ibn al-Furat, ii, pp. 40, 190.

57. 'Rothelin', pp. 631–3; 'Documents relatifs à la successibilité', p. 401. See 'Annales de Terre Sainte', p. 446. It may be that John was trying to recover Ascalon. See *Cart. gen. Hosp.*, no. 2853.

58. Alexander IV, *Reg.*, nos. 1492–3, 2174–5.

59. Ibn al-Furat, ii, pp. 43–4, 53–4; al-'Aini, pp. 216–17; al-Maqrizi, i A, p. 194; 'Eracles', ii, p. 447; 'Gestes des Chiprois', p. 756.

60. 'Annales de Terre Sainte', p. 451. See Ibn al-Furat, ii, pp. 67, 68.

61. Ibn al-Furat, ii, p. 43.

62. Pope Urban IV, *Registre*, nos. 473, 869. See 'Emprunts de Saint Louis en Palestine et en Afrique', ed. G. Servois, *BEC*, sér. 4, iv (1858) p. 293.

63. 'Gestes des Chiprois', pp. 678–9.

64. 'Gestes des Chiprois', p. 725.

65. See *Cart. gen. Hosp.*, no. 309.

66. Francesco Amadi, p. 186. Taking into account the fact that in the 1180s Toron owed the service of 15 knights (John of Jaffa, p. 423) this must represent a capital value and not annual returns.

67. *Cart. gen. Hosp.*, nos. 2972, 2985, 3047, 3071, 3326; 'Eracles', ii, p. 446; 'Annales de Terre Sainte', p. 450; Riley-Smith, *Knights of St*

John, pp. 133–4. Some of the properties in Acre may have been held by rear-vassals; James Vidal, for instance, does not appear in the list of vassals at Arsur in 1261, but both before and after that date he held a fief of Balian of Arsur.

68. For example see *Cart. gen. Hosp.*, no. 2174; 'Documents et mémoires de Chypre', iii, pp. 647–8; Pope Gregory IX, *Registre*, no. 4551; 'Eracles', ii, pp. 339–40; 'Gestes des Chiprois', pp. 666, 676, 679, 712.

69. See *Cart. gen. Hosp.*, no. 2853; 'Inventaire de l'Hôpital', no. 321.

70. *Cart. gen. Hosp.*, no. 2985. See above, and p. 6. One occasionally finds the use of the word 'client' for rear-vassal. *Chartes de Josaphat*, ed. Delaborde, nos. 18 (p. 46), 29 (p. 69) (cf. nos. 6, 8); *Cart. gen. Hosp.*, no. 783 (p. 495).

71. See below, pp. 43–4 for *gastinae*.

72. *Urkunden Venedig*, no. 299 (pp. 368, 373, 374, 375–9, 387). See *Cart. gen. Hosp.*, no. 2852, in which reference was made to villages of rear-vassals in an area that was domain of the lords of Sidon.

73. See Riley-Smith, 'Some lesser officials', pp. 17–18.

74. *Tab. ord. Theut.*, nos. 108, 110–11, 114–15, 117–18. For the *Iklim* of Jazzin, see *Palestine under the Moslems*, comp. G. Le Strange, p. 346.

75. *Cart. gen. Hosp.*, no. 495.

76. *Tab. ord. Theut.*, nos. 115, 118. Their father had also been called Andrew. For other examples of vassals of rear-vassals, see *Cart. gen. Hosp.*, nos. 139, 173, 192, 202 (p. 156), 2915.

77. John of Jaffa, p. 332.

78. John of Jaffa, pp. 302–3. See *Cart. gen. Hosp.*, nos. 480, 603, 1146; *Les Archives*, no. 50.

79. John of Jaffa, pp. 27, 28. See *Cart. gen. Hosp.*, no. 2985; *Recherches géographiques*, p. 39.

80. John of Jaffa, p. 254; and see p. 261; Philip of Novara, 'Livre', p. 494, in which they were to take charge of the body and fortresses of a lord in a minority.

81. 'Livre au roi', p. 608.

82. For example, see *Tab. ord. Theut.*, no. 115.

83. John of Jaffa, pp. 332–5, 389–90; Philip of Novara, 'Livre', pp. 531–2. A seigneurial court did not necessarily meet in the fief: for the court of Toron meeting in Acre, see *Tab. ord. Theut.*, no. 84.

84. Richard ('Pairie', pp. 76–7) has suggested that it was Baldwin III who took action against Gerard; the jurists mentioned only King Amalric.

85. John of Jaffa, pp. 214–15, 317–20; Philip of Novara 'Livre', pp. 517, 518, 525–7; James of Ibelin, pp. 454, 455. Liege-homage had to be performed within a year and a day of the acquisition of a fief;

otherwise the fief was lost for the lifetime of the king. Geoffrey Le Tor, p. 438.

86. John of Jaffa, p. 254; and see p. 303.

87. For the general principle, see Philip of Novara, 'Livre', p. 537.

88. John of Jaffa, pp. 321-2.

89. John of Jaffa, pp. 317-20; Philip of Novara, 'Livre', pp. 526-7.

90. 'Livre au roi', p. 634; and see p. 608.

91. 'Liber iurium', no. 718.

92. *Cart. gen. Hosp.*, no. 2748 (pp. 788-9).

93. 'Inventaire de l'Hôpital', no. 288; *Tab. ord. Theut.*, no. 111.

94. *Chartes de Josaphat*, ed. Delaborde, no. 55 (p. 115).

95. 'Inventaire de l'Hôpital', no. 321; *Urkunden Venedig*, no. 369 (p. 152). See also *Cart. gen. Hosp.*, nos. 2902 (p. 862), 3317 § 2; 'Documents et mémoires de Chypre' iii, p. 663.

96. *Cart. gen. Hosp.*, nos. 2985, 3213, 3326.

97. 'La fondation d'une église latine en Orient par Saint Louis: Damiette', ed. J. Richard, *BEC*, cxx (1962), p. 53.

98. John of Jaffa (pp. 313-14) envisaged the possibility that a vassal might already have made liege-homage elsewhere, but he also stated that this ought to be made to the chief lord. Geoffrey Le Tor (p. 440) wrote that every fief-holder should make *ligece* to the crown, unless he could prove that he owed it to another or was exempted from it. Of the great lords, Philip of Montfort's liege lord seems to have been the King of France. 'Quatre titres des Génois', no. 4 (p. 229).

99. See below, p. 37.

100. *Cart. gen. Hosp.*, nos. 2274, 2661 (note), 2688, 2725, 2738, 2748, 2753, 2845, 2852-3, 2985, 3326, 3346, 3408; *Tab. ord. Theut.*, nos. 100, 103, 108, 110-11, 114-15, 117-20, 122, 125; 'Chartes du Mont-Thabor', ed. J. Delaville Le Roulx, no. 26; *Recherches géographiques*, p. 40.

101. For example, see *Cart. gen. Hosp.*, nos. 2661 (note), 2688, 2845, 2852-3; *Tab. ord. Theut.*, nos. 100, 108, 111, 114, 117-18.

102. *Maugustel* in Arsur: *Cart. gen. Hosp.*, no. 2274. *Antiaume* in Haifa and Scandelion: 'Chartes du Mont-Thabor,' no. 26; *Tab. ord. Theut.*, no. 125. *Villiers* in Sidon and Tyre: *Tab. ord. Theut.*, nos. 103, 108, 110-11, 114-15, 117-18; *Cart. gen. Hosp.*, nos. 2688, 2852, 3346. *Meinebeuf* in Sidon and Beirut: *Cart. gen. Hosp.*, no. 2688; *Tab. ord. Theut.*, nos. 114, 119-20, 122; *Recherches géographiques*, p. 40. *Pinckeney* in Caesarea and Jaffa: *Cart. gen. Hosp.*, nos. 2661 (note), 2725, 2738; 'Annales de Terre Sainte', p. 451. *of Troies* in Caesarea and Jaffa; *Cart. gen. Hosp.*, nos. 2661, 2725, 2738, 2853. *Mimars* in Beirut and Sidon: *Recherches géographiques*, p. 40; *Tab. ord. Theut.*, nos. 115, 119-20, 122. *Babyn* in Beirut: *Recherches géographiques*, p. 40. *Aleman* in Jaffa: *Cart. gen. Hosp.*, nos. 2845, 2853. *of Fenion* in Sidon and Tyre: *Tab. ord.*

Theut., no. 114; *Cart. gen. Hosp.*, nos. 3346, 3408. In one charter (*Tab. ord. Theut.*, no. 84) a Lord of Haifa witnessed as a vassal of the Lady of Toron.

103. *Tab. ord. Theut.*, no. 103; *Cart. gen. Hosp.*, nos. 2688, 2810. He was the nephew of Odo of Montbéliard and he married Ralph of Tiberias's second daughter. 'Eracles', ii, p. 404; 'Les lignages', p. 455.

104. *Cart. gen. Hosp.*, nos. 2748, 2852; *Tab. ord. Theut.*, nos. 108, 111, 117–18.

105. *Cart. gen. Hosp.*, nos. 2661 (note), 2725, 2738, 3346, 3408. See Philip of Novara, 'Livre', p. 539.

106. *Tab. ord. Theut.*, no. 98; *Cart. gen. Hosp.*, nos. 2353, 2845, 2852–3, 2902, 3045; *Recherches géographiques*, p. 36; *Cod. dipl. geros.*, i, pp. 157, 161.

107. *Tab. ord. Theut.*, no. 100.

108. *Cart. gen. Hosp.*, nos. 2612, 2693, 2714, 2732, 3045, 3213, 3323, 3414; *Recherches géographiques*, p. 36; *Urkunden Venedig*, no. 343; 'Abrégé du Livre des Assises de la Cour des Bourgeois', p. 246. For his part in the military campaign of 1260, see 'Eracles', ii, p. 445.

109. *Reg. Hier.*, no. 1297a; 'Documents relatifs à la successibilité', pp. 416, 418.

110. 'Eracles', ii, pp. 464, 479; 'Gestes des Chiprois', p. 789. But see Florio Bustron, p. 115.

111. *Cart. gen. Hosp.*, no. 3213.

112. *Tab. ord. Theut.*, nos. 100, 125; *Cart. gen. Hosp.*, nos. 2753, 2934–5, 3326. The fief held of Arsur in 1269 must have been a *fief-rente* on revenues from Acre.

113. Philip of Novara, 'Livre', p. 541.

114. Philip of Novara, 'Livre', p. 538.

115. John of Jaffa, pp. 336–7; see editorial note.

116. A possible payment of relief is to be found in *Cart. gen. Hosp.*, no. 480; but it is an isolated example. It may be that exemption from relief was another privilege to encourage settlement granted early in the twelfth century. I am informed by Mr Peter Edbury that there is no sign of the payments of relief in Cyprus.

117. Assises d'Antioche, p. 16.

118. John of Jaffa, pp. 261–4, 280–1; Philip of Novara, 'Livre', pp. 494–5, 537; Geoffrey Le Tor, p. 440; James of Ibelin, p. 461; 'Livre au roi, pp. 630–1. See John of Jaffa, pp. 267, 370; *Tab. ord. Theut.*, no. 12; *Urkunden Venedig*, no. 299 (p. 379); *Cart. gen. Hosp.*, no. 2280 (esp. p. 595). But see also *Tab. ord. Theut.*, no. 22 and the peculiar and early *Cart. du St-Sépulcre*, no. 77.

119. James of Ibelin, p. 461; 'Livre au roi', p. 628. If the parent or friends of a girl aged over twelve wanted her to marry someone other

than the man proposed by the lord, they could offer the lord a sum of money to accept their candidate. John of Jaffa, pp. 264–5.

120. See John of Jaffa, pp. 260, 264.

121. Riley-Smith, *Knights of St John*, p. 438.

CHAPTER 3 THE DOMAIN IN THE COUNTRYSIDE

1. *Cart. gen. Hosp.*, no. 941.

2. *Tab. ord. Theut.*, no. 100 (p. 78); *Cart. gen. Hosp.*, no. 3323. See also *Cart. gen. Hosp.*, nos. 309, 402, 409, 2936.

3. *Tab. ord. Theut.*, no. 108; *Cod. dipl. geros.*, i, p. 288.

4. These were apparently called *curtiles*. See *Cart. gen. Hosp.*, nos. 350, 2688; *Tab. ord. Theut.*, nos. 114, 117, 118 (p. 105), 119 (p. 107), 120. But they were also to be found in or near towns: for example, *Cart. gen. Hosp.*, nos. 94, 3408.

5. See *Cart. gen. Hosp.*, no. 2693; *Urkunden Venedig*, no. 299 (pp. 372, 374, 376, 378).

6. John of Jaffa, pp. 403–6 (which may be an interpolation); Philip of Novara, 'Livre', p. 519. See *Cart. gen. Hosp.*, nos. 783 (p. 495 where, in Antioch, a differentiation was made between Christian and Muslim serfs), 2902 (p. 862), 3039 § 12; 'Quatre titres des Génois', no. 4 (p. 228).

7. *Cart. du St-Sépulcre*, nos. 33–4; 'Sankt Samuel', p. 69; *Cart. gen. Hosp.*, no. 191; and see no. 457.

8. *Cart. du St-Sépulcre*, nos 48, 52, 54–5, 144; *Tab. ord. Theut.*, no. 7; 'Chartes de l'abbaye cistercienne de St-Serge de Giblet en Syrie', ed. E. Petit, *Mémoires de la société nationale des Antiquaires de France*, sér. 5, viii (1887), p. 27; *Urkunden Venedig*, no. 299 (pp. 372, 374, 375, 376, 378, 383–4). See William of Tyre, p. 1111; *Tab. ord. Theut.*, no. 3 (p. 3).

9. *Cart. du St-Sépulcre*, no. 75; *Cart. gen. Hosp.*, no. 1372 (p. 135).

10. 'Un diplôme', p. 314.

11. *Cart. du St-Sépulcre*, nos. 43–4; *Les Archives*, no. 45.

12. *Cart. gen. Hosp.*, no. 7; *Cart. du St-Sépulcre*, no. 97; 'Chartes du Mont-Thabor', no. 4. See also *Cart. du St-Sépulcre*, nos. 26 (p. 49), 29, 53 (p. 98), 54 (p. 102), 144 (p. 263); *Cart. gen. Hosp.*, nos. 20, 45, 71, 79, 82, 128, 207, 225, 470, 521, 2915; P. Riant, 'Une dépendance italienne de l'église de Bethléem. Varazze en Ligurie (1139–1424)', *Atti della società ligure di storia patria*, xvii (1885), p. 658; *Chartes de Josaphat*, ed. Delaborde, nos. 6 (p. 30), 8 (p. 34).

13. *Cart. gen. Hosp.*, no. 2853; and see also no. 180. It might be worth mentioning here two incomprehensible phrases – 'cum raitabilis

villanis' and 'cum . . . rusticis et raitabilis' in *Cart. gen. Hosp.*, nos. 623, 782. See C. Cahen, 'Notes sur l'histoire des croisades et de l'Orient latin. 2. Le régime rural syrien au temps de la domination franque', *Bulletin de la Faculté des Lettres de l'Université de Strasbourg*, xxix (1950–51) p. 299.

14. Prawer, 'Étude de quelques problèmes agraires et sociaux d'une seigneurie croisée au XIIIe siecle' (suite), *Byzantion*, xxiii (1953), pp. 152–9. See Cahen, op. cit., p. 295. It is clear that villeins could hold very equal proportions of arable land. *Urkunden Venedig*, no. 299 (pp. 381, 384).

15. *Urkunden Venedig*, no. 299 (pp. 370–84). Note the fantastic claims made of the size of villages near Ascalon in *Urkunden Venedig*, no. 300 (p. 398).

16. *Tab. ord. Theut.*, nos. 31, 43, 119 (p. 107), 120 (p. 110), 121 (p. 111), 122; *Recherches géographiques*, pp. 41, 42; *Cod. dipl. geros.*, i, p. 288; *Cart. gen. Hosp.*, nos. 1250, 3029.

17. *Urkunden Venedig*, no. 299 (pp. 369, 380–1). See Prawer, 'Étude de quelques problèmes agraires', pp. 26–9; and Cahen, 'Le régime rural', p. 295, who have both drawn attention to alternative names for this sort of carrucate. But see also *Cart. du St-Sépulcre*, no. 64.

18. *Urkunden Venedig*, no. 299 (pp. 368–84); *Cart. gen. Hosp.*, no. 2845. See Cahen, op. cit., p. 295; Prawer, op. cit., pp. 27–8; also *Urkunden Venedig*, no. 299 (pp. 377–9). The trouble is compounded by the fact that the *modius* and another measure, the *ghirara*, varied from place to place. Prawer, op. cit., pp. 58–61. This kind of carrucate may also have been known as a *modiata*. See *Cart. gen. Hosp.*, no. 7.

19. John of Jaffa (p. 62) also used the Byzantine words *prastia* and *abbaye*, which were sometimes used of villages in Cyprus and in the north. See also *Cart. gen. Hosp.*, no. 783 (pp. 494–5); *Tab. ord. Theut.*, no. 105. I am at a loss to explain the term 'in casalibus ct casatis' to be found in *Cart. gen. Hosp.*, nos. 519, 596, 676.

20. 'Chartes de St-Serge', pp. 26–8; *Cart. du St-Sépulcre*, nos. 71, 127, 155; 'Le chartier de Sainte-Marie-Latine et l'établissement de Raymond de Saint-Gilles à Mont-Pèlerin', ed. J. Richard, *Mélanges Louis Halphen*, p. 612; *Urkunden Venedig*, no. 299 (pp. 370–84); *Tab. ord. Theut.*, no. 46.

21. See *Chartes de Josaphat*, ed. Delaborde, no. 10; *Cart. gen. Hosp.*, nos. 350, 573; and also *Cart. gen. Hosp.*, no. 2688.

22. 'Gestes des Chiprois', p. 768; *Urkunden Venedig*, no. 299 (p. 383). For the house of the *rays*, see below, pp. 48–9.

23. See *Cart. gen. Hosp.*, nos. 168, 470.

24. See *Cart. du St-Sépulcre*, nos. 64–5; *Chartes de Josaphat*, ed. Delaborde, no. 57 (p. 118); *Recherches géographiques*, pp. 41–5; *Urkunden Venedig*, no. 299 (p. 377); R. Röhricht, *Beiträge zur Geschichte der*

Kreuzzüge, ii, p. 288; Benvenisti, op. cit., p. 221; Riley-Smith, *Knights of St John*, pp. 427–8. See also *Tab. ord. Theut.*, nos. 15, 112 (p. 93).

25. *Recherches géographiques*, p. 37; 'Frag. cart. St-Lazare', no. 3; *Tab. ord. Theut.*, no. 128 (p. 120); *Urkunden Venedig*, no. 299 (pp. 370, 381–3); *Cart. gen. Hosp.*, nos. 207, 340, 1718; 'Livre des Assises des Bourgeois', p. 243.

26. For example, see *Urkunden Venedig*, no. 299 (esp. pp. 379–83); *Cart. gen. Hosp.*, no. 250.

27. See below, pp. 44–5.

28. See *Tab. ord. Theut.*, no. 128 (p. 126); 'Frag. cart. St-Lazare', nos. 7–8; 'Chartes de l'abbaye de Notre-Dame de la vallée de Josaphat en Terre Sainte', ed. C. Kohler, *ROL*, vii (1899) no. 30.

29. See A. Granott, *The Land System in Palestine*, p. 198.

30. *Urkunden Venedig*, no. 299 (pp. 379–84). Cf. Granott, op. cit., p. 166.

31. See, for example, 'Frag. cart. St-Lazare', no. 6.

32. For example, *Tab. ord. Theut.*, nos. 49, 61; *Urkunden Venedig*, no. 299 (p. 380); *Cart. gen. Hosp.*, no. 244; 'Quatre titres des Génois', no. 3 (pp. 222–3). In parts of the County of Tripoli it seems that very hard pruning could lead to two or three crops of grapes. Burchard of Mt Sion, p. 88; James of Vitry, *Lettres*, p. 93. See *Cart. gen. Hosp.*, no. 82; also 'Livre des Assises des Bourgeois', p. 243; *Urkunden Venedig*, no. 299 (p. 383).

33. *Cart. gen. Hosp.*, no. 311; *Cod. dipl. geros.*, i, p. 235. For the way the mills worked, see Benvenisti, op. cit., pp. 257–8

34. For woods, see for instance *Tab. ord. Theut.*, no. 84; *Cart. du St-Sépulcre*, nos. 55 (witnessed by a forestarius), 71; *Cart. gen. Hosp.*, nos. 309, 1002; *Recherches géographiques*, p. 37. For individual types of tree, *Tab. ord. Theut.*, no. 40; *Urkunden Venedig*, no. 299 (pp. 370, 377, 381); 'Le chartrier de Sainte-Marie-Latine', p. 612; *Cart. du St-Sépulcre*, no. 127; *Cart. gen. Hosp.*, no. 309; Burchard of Mt Sion, p. 87.

35. *Urkunden Venedig*, no. 299 (pp. 373, 374–5, 381); Ibn al-Furat, ii, p. 66.

36. *Urkunden Venedig*, no. 299 (pp. 371–4, 379–84); *Cart. gen. Hosp.* nos. 94, 97, 2845, 2853; *Cart. du St-Sépulcre*, no. 125; *Recherches géographiques*, pp. 38–9. See Prawer, 'Étude de quelques problèmes agraires', pp. 43–9.

37. *Urkunden Venedig*, no. 299 (p. 373); *Cod. dipl. geros.*, i, p. 288; *Cart. gen. Hosp.*, nos. 168, 223, 311, 480, 754. For corn on the threshing floors, see also William of Tyre, pp. 487, 1021, 1064, 1104.

38. For instance, *Recherches géographiques*, p. 42; *Itinéraires à Jérusalem*, pp. 255–6. It will be seen that I take rather a different view to Prawer, 'Étude de quelques problèmes agraires', pp. 31–40.

39. 'Livre des Assises des Bourgeois', pp. 170–1; *Tab. ord. Theut.*,

nos. 32, 73–4; *Chartes de Josaphat*, ed. Delaborde, no. 47; *Les Archives*, nos. 5, 34; 'Quatre titres des Génois', no. 3 (pp. 222, 223); *Reg. Hier.*, no. 642a; 'Chartes de Josaphat', ed. Kohler, nos. 64, 69; *Cart. gen. Hosp.*, nos. 954, 966.

40. *Cart. gen. Hosp.*, nos. 1215, 1473. I have counted 46 of these independent *gastinae*.

41. Prawer, op. cit., pp. 33–6.

42. *Urkunden Venedig*, no. 299 (p. 377).

43. *Cod. dipl. geros.*, i, p. 206; *Cart. gen. Hosp.*, no. 133.

44. *Urkunden Venedig*, no. 299 (p. 377); *Chartes de Josaphat*, ed. Delaborde, no. 43. And possibly 'Chartes de Josaphat', ed. Kohler, nos. 39, 48; *Cart. gen. Hosp.*, nos. 198, 390.

45. *Cart. gen. Hosp.*, no. 763. See also *Tab. ord. Theut.*, no. 38.

46. Naria and Cellorie in the Principality of Antioch. *Cart. gen. Hosp.*, nos. 231, 522, 1593, 2003, 3120, 3197, 3203; Pope Innocent III, 'Opera Omnia'. ccxvi, cols. 697–8; *Les Archives*, no. 19.

47. *Cod. dipl. geros.*, i, p. 206. See also *Tab. ord. Theut.*, no. 115 (p. 97); 'Un diplôme', pp. 313, 315; *Cod. dipl. geros.*, i, p. 250; 'Chartes de Josaphat', ed. Kohler, nos. 1, 9; *Cart. du St-Sépulcre*, nos. 97, 140, 144; *Cart. gen. Hosp.*, nos. 103, 107, 183, 311, 457, 754, 2296, 3346; *Chartes de Josaphat*, ed. Delaborde, no. 39; 'Frag. cart. St-Lazare', no. 16.

48. *Tab. ord. Theut.*, nos. 7, 73–4, 77–8, 81, 100 (p. 78), 108, 111, 117–18, 119 (p. 107), 120 (p. 110), 121 (p. 111), 122; *Hist. dipl. Fred. secundi*, iii, p. 118, iv, p. 793; *Chartes de Josaphat*, ed. Delaborde, nos. 15, 32, 41, 47; 'Sankt Samuel', pp. 68–9; *Documenti delle città toscane*, nos. 23 (p. 27), 31 (p. 36); *Cod. dipl. geros.*, i, p. 248; 'Chartes de St-Serge', p. 27; 'Elf deutschordensurkunden aus Venedig und Malta', ed. H. Prutz, *Altpreussische Monatsschrift*, xx (1883) nos. 8–9; *Urkunden Venedig*, no. 299 (pp. 370–71, 376); 'Chartes de Josaphat', ed. Kohler, no. 21; *Cart. du St-Sépulcre*, no. 144; *Cart. gen. Hosp.*, nos. 311, 350, 521, 621, 783 (p. 494), 1426, 1993, 2482, 2688, 2852, 2936; *Recherches géographiques*, p. 38; *Itinéraires à Jérusalem*, pp. 255–6.

49. *Tab. ord. Theut.*, nos. 90, 114; *Cart. gen. Hosp.*, nos. 115, 209, 457–8, 1250, 2688, 2748, 2915. See James of Vitry, 'Historia', p. 1068; 'Inventaire de l'Hôpital', no. 183.

50. *Tab. ord. Theut.*, nos. 77–8, 100 (p. 78), 117 (p. 104), 118 (p. 105), 119 (p. 107), 120 (p. 110); *Hist. dipl. Fred. secundi*, iv, pp. 793–4; *Cart. gen. Hosp.*, nos. 1426, 1442, 2482, 3029. See also *Cart. gen. Hosp.*, nos. 621, 2852; *Recherches géographiques*, p. 38.

51. *Cart. gen. Hosp.*, no. 621. See *Cod. dipl. geros.*, i, p. 248, and Naria mentioned above.

52. *Chartes de Josphat*, ed. Delaborde, no. 43; *Cart. du St-Sépulcre*, no. 140. But see *Recherches géographiques*, p. 38. Some of the *gastinae* in *Tab. ord. Theut.*, no. 117 appear to have belonged to families.

53. 'Chartes de Josaphat', ed. Kohler, no. 7; *Chartes de Josaphat*, ed. Delaborde, no. 20; *Cart. du St-Sépulcre*, nos. 73, 127; 'Chartes du Mont-Thabor', no. 1.

54. Granott, op. cit., pp. 169 ff.

55. John of Jaffa, p. 395; Philip of Novara, 'Livre', p. 533. See also Geoffrey Le Tor, p. 437. It must be admitted that after an exhaustive study one is bound to reach the same conclusions as did Cahen ('Le régime rural', p. 294) and Benvenisti (op. cit., pp. 216–17), who drew attention to one direct translation of *khirbat* into *gastina*.

56. *Urkunden Venedig*, no. 299 (p. 373); *Tab. ord. Theut.*, no. 12. See 'La fondation d'une église', ed. Richard, p. 53. For references to jurisdiction and *justicia*, see *Cart. gen. Hosp.*, nos. 621, 2693, 3029; *Tab. ord. Theut.*, nos. 77–8, 84, 108, 117, 118 (p. 105), 119 (p. 107), 120 (p. 110), 121 (p. 111); *Hist. dipl. Fred. secundi*, iv, pp. 793, 794.

57. See Ibn Jubair, pp. 316–17.

58. Above all, see *Urkunden Venedig*, no. 299 (pp. 371, 372, 373, 374); but for the word *kharaj*, see *Cart. gen. Hosp.*, nos. 129, 941, 2199; 'Frag. cart. St-Lazare', no. 9; *Tab. ord. Theut.*, no. 112 (p. 93); and also Ibn Jubair, p. 316. For *kharaj* in Egypt at this time, see H. Rabie, *The Financial System of Egypt*, pp. 73–9.

59. *Urkunden Venedig*, no. 299 (pp. 371, 373); *Cod. dipl. geros.*, i, p. 288; *Cart. gen. Hosp.*, nos. 457, 480; *Tab. ord. Theut.*, nos. 6, 34 (both forgeries), 112 (pp. 92–3); 'Gestes des Chiprois', p. 749; Ibn al-Furat, ii, p. 128. See *Cart. gen. Hosp.*, no. 2388; Ibn Jubair, p. 315; Matthew Paris, *Chron. maiora*, iv, p. 343; H. Wangelin, *Das arabische Volksbuch vom König AzZāhir Baibars*, p. 12.

60. *Urkunden Venedig*, no. 299 (pp. 380–3); *Tab. ord. Theut.*, no. 112 (p. 93); *Cart. du St-Sépulcre*, no. 81; 'Frag. cart. St-Lazare', no. 10; 'Chartes de Josaphat', ed. Kohler, no. 30.

61. *Tab. ord. Theut.*, nos. 15, 112 (p. 93); *Urkunden Venedig*, no. 299 (pp. 371, 372, 373, 374, 381); *Cart. gen. Hosp.*, nos. 941, 1414, 2199 (p. 529); Gregory IX, *Reg.*, no. 4474. See Cahen (op. cit., p. 300) for the suggestion that *monet* is a transliteration of the Arabic *mu'na*, meaning provisioning.

62. *Urkunden Venedig*, no. 299 (p. 383).

63. *Tab. ord. Theut.*, no. 3.

64. Ibn Jubair, p. 316. See Gregory IX, *Reg.*, nos. 4013 (col. 841), 4551. For the links between this and the old *dhimmi* payments, see below, pp. 83–4.

65. *Cart. gen. Hosp.*, no. 7; *Cart. du St-Sépulcre*, nos. 33–4.

66. *Tab. ord. Theut.*, nos. 34 (a forgery), 112 (p. 93). In the County of Tripoli a rent was paid on the oxen used for ploughing. *Cart. gen. Hosp.*, nos. 79, 82. Cf. Rabie, op. cit., pp. 79–80.

67. *Tab. ord Theut.*, no. 112 (p. 92); *Cod. dipl. geros.*, i, p. 241. See *Cart. gen. Hosp.*, no. 510; *Cod. dipl. geros.*, i, p. 288.

68. *Tab. ord. Theut.*, no. 112 (p. 92).

69. *Urkunden Venedig*, no. 299 (pp. 369, 371, 374–5).

70. Rabie, op. cit., pp. 74 ff., 77 ff.

71. 'Chartes de Josaphat', ed. Kohler, no. 10; also *Cart. gen. Hosp.*, nos. 140, 941; *Cart. du St-Sépulcre*, no. 76; *Tab. ord. Theut.*, no. 12. See *Cart. gen. Hosp.*, nos. 79, 82.

72. 'Frag. cart. St-Lazare', no. 9. And perhaps near Acre; see *Tab. ord. Theut.*, no. 34 (a forgery).

73. *Urkunden Venedig*, no. 299 (pp. 380–1); *Cart. gen. Hosp.*, no. 941.

74. *Urkunden Venedig*, no. 299 (pp. 371, 372, 373, 374, 381–3).

75. *Tab. ord. Theut.*, no. 112 (p. 93). See also *Chartes de Josaphat*, ed. Delaborde, no. 42; *Cart. gen. Hosp.*, no. 2693.

76. *Chartes de Josaphat*, ed. Delaborde, nos. 28 (p. 64), 42, 49 (p. 101); *Cart. gen. Hosp.*, nos. 397, 579, 941, 1414, 1829, 2482 (p. 674); *Tab. ord. Theut.*, no. 112; Gregory IX, *Reg.*, nos. 4013, 4474; *Urkunden Venedig*, no. 299 (p. 383).

77. *Chartes de Josaphat*, ed. Delaborde, no. 42; *Tab. ord. Theut.*, no. 112 (p. 93); *Cart. gen Hosp.*, no. 941; *Urkunden Venedig*, no. 299 (p. 383); *Recherches géographiques*, p. 38.

78. *Cart. gen. Hosp.*, nos. 397, 941, 1414. See also 'Chartes de Josaphat', ed. Kohler, no. 10.

79. *Recherches géographiques*, pp. 38–9. Boon work may also be mentioned in *Cart. gen. Hosp.*, no. 932.

80. *Urkunden Venedig*, no. 299 (p. 375). *Cart du St-Sépulcre*, no. 74 (confirmation in nos. 53 (p. 99), 54 (p. 104), 124, 144 (p. 264), 156 (p. 280)). Cf. Prawer, 'Étude de quelques problèmes agraires' (suite), pp. 165–6. Cypriot peasants did two days boon work a week. 'Doc. rel. au service militaire', p. 430.

81. *Tab. ord. Theut.*, nos. 15, 112 (p. 93); *Cart. gen. Hosp.*, no. 941; 'Chartes de Terre Sainte', ed. Delaville Le Roulx, no. 1. See 'Frag. Cart. St-Lazare', no. 21; also Prawer, op. cit., p. 166.

82. *Cart. gen. Hosp.*, nos. 494, 1718, 1911; *Tab. ord. Theut.*, no. 112 (p. 93); Riley-Smith, *Knights of St John*, pp. 433–4.

83. *Recherches géographiques*, p. 39; *Cart. gen. Hosp.*, no. 2853.

84. John of Jaffa, p. 354; Geoffrey Le Tor, p. 438; *Tab. ord. Theut.*, no. 12; Benvenisti, op. cit., pp. 233–45. Cypriot knights did stay at times on their estates. 'Gestes des Chiprois', p. 692.

85. Riley-Smith, 'Some lesser officials', pp. 1–2, 9–15.

86. See William of Tyre, p. 395; N. Elisséeff, *Nūr ad-Dīn*, iii, pp. 881–2.

87. See *Cart. gen. Hosp.*, no. 2747; Ibn Jubair, p. 317.

88. *Cart. gen. Hosp.*, nos. 2693, 2747.

89. *Cart. gen. Hosp.*, no. 2915.

90. *Urkunden Venedig*, no. 299 (p. 371).

91. *Cart. gen. Hosp.*, nos. 2693, 2747.

92. *Cart. gen. Hosp.*, no. 2747; Ibn Jubair, p. 317. See *Urkunden Venedig*, no. 299 (pp. 374–5).

93. *Urkunden Venedig*, no. 299 (p. 373).

94. See perhaps *Cart. gen. Hosp.*, no. 2693.

95. Riley-Smith, op. cit., pp. 10–11.

96. *Urkunden Venedig*, no. 299 (pp. 379–84). He was called here a *prepositus*.

97. *Urkunden Venedig*, no. 299 (pp. 371, 372, 373). See also *Chartes de Josaphat*, ed. Delaborde, no. 10.

98. *Urkunden Venedig*, no. 299 (p. 383); Ibn Jubair, p. 317; *Cart. gen. Hosp.*, nos. 2693, 2747.

99. See Benvenisti, op. cit., pp. 218–27.

100. J. Prawer, 'Colonisation Activities in the Latin Kingdom of Jerusalem', *Revue belge de philologie et d'histoire*, xxix (1951) *passim*. To his sources one could add for the twelfth century: 'Frag. cart. St-Lazare', no. 31; *Cart. gen. Hosp.*, nos. 140 and perhaps 491; 'Un diplôme', p. 314.

101. *Tab. ord. Theut.*, no. 128 (p. 121).

102. *Recherches géographiques*, p. 39. For its foundation, see Prawer, 'Colonisation Activities', p. 1116. For possible thirteenth-century settlements in the northern Christian states, see *Cart. gen. Hosp.*, nos. 2148, 3197.

103. *Tab. ord. Theut.*, no. 112 (p. 93); *Chartes de Josaphat*, ed. Delaborde, no. 4; 'Chartes de Josaphat', ed. Kohler, nos. 4, 44; *Cart. gen. Hosp.*, no. 350.

104. See 'Quatre titres des Génois', no. 4 (p. 226); *Cod. dipl. geros.*, i, p. 50; *Cart. du St-Sépulcre*, no. 155; *Cart. gen. Hosp.*, nos. 3045, 3408; *Urkunden Venedig*, no. 299 (pp. 368–9); Burchard of Mt Sion, pp. 24, 26. For cultivation, see Burchard of Mt Sion, p. 87.

105. *Recherches géographiques*, pp. 38–9; *Urkunden Venedig*, no. 299 (p. 369).

106. See the reference to *sucre Nabeth* in 'Livre des Assises des Bourgeois', p. 279.

107. *Tab. ord. Theut.*, nos. 8 (a forgery), 18, 34 (a forgery); *Urkunden Venedig*, no. 299 (p. 368); 'Quatre titres des Génois', nos. 3 (pp. 222–4), 4 (p. 226); *Cart. du St-Sépulcre*, no. 155. For the way the presses worked, see Benvenisti, op. cit., pp. 253–6; and for the production process, Burchard of Mt Sion, p. 87. Rents in sugar were paid at Easter. 'Chartes du Mont-Thabor', no. 14; *Cart. gen. Hosp.*, nos. 625, 2224; *Les Archives*, no. 73.

108. For instance *Documenti delle città toscane*, nos. 23 (p. 26), 31 (p. 36); 'Chartes de Josaphat', ed. Kohler, no. 57.

109. 'Chartes de Josaphat', ed. Kohler, no. 17; *Chartes de Josaphat*, ed. Delaborde, nos. 12, 18 (p. 45), 28 (p. 64), 29 (p. 68), 49 (p. 101).

110. *Urkunden Venedig*, no. 299 (pp. 369–70); *Documenti delle città toscane*, nos. 23 (pp. 26–7), 31 (p. 36); 'Quatre titres des Génois', nos. 2 (p. 219), 3 (p. 223), 4 (pp. 226, 228); Burchard of Mt Sion, p. 24.

111. *Documenti delle città toscane*, nos. 25 (p. 30), 27, 32 (p. 38); *Cod. dipl. geros.*, i, pp. 50–51; *Tab. ord. Theut.*, no. 91; and see below, pp. 50–2.

112. *Cart. gen. Hosp.*, nos. 97, 2274.

113. *Cart. du St-Sépulcre*, no. 90; *Cart. gen. Hosp.*, nos. 222, 665; *Tab. ord. Theut.*, no. 61; *Les Archives*, no. 15. For the way the mills worked, see Benvenisti, op. cit., pp. 247–52. Some millstones came from Transjordan. *Cart. gen. Hosp.*, no. 207.

114. *Urkunden Venedig*, no. 299 (pp. 369–70); *Cart. du St-Sépulcre*, no. 90; *Cart. gen. Hosp.*, nos. 665, 3045; *Tab. ord. Theut.*, no. 61. See *Cart. gen. Hosp.*, no. 2298. One four-wheel mill, Recordane, still stands. See Benvenisti, op. cit., pp. 249–51.

115. See *Cart. gen. Hosp.*, no. 622; *Urkunden Venedig*, no. 299 (pp. 369–70). For the mills near Acre, see below, pp. 50–2.

116. *Cart. du St-Sépulcre*, no. 90; *Cart. gen. Hosp.*, no. 665. See also perhaps *Recherches géographiques*, p. 22; *Cart. gen. Hosp.*, no. 2298.

117. *Cod. dipl. geros.*, i, pp. 50–1. See also *Cart. gen. Hosp.*, no. 454.

118. *Cart. gen. Hosp.*, nos. 2117, 3045; and also nos. 2107, 2120–21, 3032; Riley-Smith, *Knights of St John*, p. 446.

119. *Cart. du St-Sépulcre*, no. 119. For Tripoli, see *Cart. gen. Hosp.*, no. 596.

120. *Cart. du St-Sépulcre*, no. 155.

121. *Cart. gen. Hosp*, no. 2801.

122. *Urkunden Venedig*, no. 299 (p. 368); 'Quatre titres des Génois', nos. 3 (p. 223), 4 (p. 226); and also *Cart. gen. Hosp.*, nos. 3346, 3408; 'Inventaire de l'Hopital', no. 195.

123. Riley-Smith, 'Some lesser officials', pp. 15–16.

124. E. Tyan, *Histoire de l'organisation judiciaire en pays d'Islam*, i, p. 258.

125. *Cart. gen. Hosp.*, nos. 480, 2693. See 'Gestes des Chiprois', p. 764; *La Règle du Temple*, pp. 108, 134. The dragoman of a religious house was perhaps in charge of *casalia* scattered over a wide area. See Riley-Smith, 'Some lesser officials, p. 16.

126. *Cart. gen. Hosp.*, no. 28; 'Chartes de Josaphat', ed. Kohler, no. 5; *Cod. dipl. geros.*, i, p. 40.

127. 'Frag. cart. St-Lazare', no. 9.

128. *Cart. gen. Hosp.*, no. 2985.

129. *Cart. gen. Hosp.*, nos. 115, 168.

130. *Tab. ord. Theut.*, no. 2.

131. *Tab. ord. Theut.*, no. 17.

132. *Tab. ord. Theut.*, no. 16. The removal of the dragoman and scribe from their offices apparently gave Joscelin full control of the territory. Geoffrey also owned lands further to the west, on the other side of the castellany of Chastiau-dou-rei. 'Chartes du Mont-Thabor', no. 14.

133. *Cart. gen. Hosp.*, no. 480.

134. Peter is to be found in a list of witnesses with precedence over the Viscount of Cacho. *Cart. gen. Hosp.*, no. 115.

135. Riley-Smith, 'Some lesser officials', p. 16.

136. *Cart. gen. Hosp.*, no. 480.

137. *Cart. gen. Hosp.*, no. 2985.

138. To these the words of the 'Livre des Assises des Bourgeois' (pp. 343–4) on the writing of false charters presumably applied.

139. See Rabie, op. cit., p. 158, for the duties of a *kātib*.

140. Here the variant reading seems to be the better one.

141. 'Livre des Assises des Bourgeois', pp. 344–5.

142. John of Jaffa, p. 394.

143. *Cart. gen. Hosp.*, no. 2902 (p. 862).

144. See Rabie, op. cit., pp. 154, 160; H. L. Gottschalk, 'Dīwān, ii, Egypt', *The Encyclopaedia of Islam*, ii, p. 329.

145. *Cart. gen. Hosp.*, nos. 398, 495, 516–18, 941, 1146, 2747–8, 2925, 2985; *Les Archives*, nos. 39, 61; 'Deux chartes des croisés', pp. 10–11; *Cod. dipl. geros.*, i, pp. 288–9; *Tab. ord. Theut.*, nos. 2, 16–17, 112; 'Elf deutschordensurkunden', nos. 8, 10; 'Liber iurium', no. 256; John of Jaffa, p. 424; *Recherches géographiques*, p. 38; 'Eracles', ii, p. 111.

146. For town-*rayses*, see below, pp. 90–1.

147. See Rabie, op. cit., pp. 136–7; Elisséeff, *Nūr ad-Dīn*, iii, p. 807.

148. That of George in Nablus. John of Jaffa, p. 424.

149. *Cod. dipl. geros.*, i, p. 288. In one village the *scribanus* had authority only in that part owned by his lord: evidence that here he acted only for him.

150. *Tab. ord. Theut.*, no. 16; *Cart. gen. Hosp.*, no. 1996.

151. *Cart. gen. Hosp.*, no. 2985. Its holder had to provide the service of a *scribe*.

152. *Tab. ord. Theut.*, nos. 2, 17.

153. *Tab. ord. Theut.*, no. 16.

154. John of Jaffa, p. 424.

155. *Cart. Gen. Hosp.*, nos. 495, 516–18, 551; *Les Archives*, no. 39. Before granting the village to the Hospitallers Constance issued privileges for its Christian inhabitants. *Cart. gen. Hosp.*, no. 491.

156. *Cart. gen. Hosp.*, no. 2985.

157. *Cod. dipl. geros.*, i, pp. 288–9. If he had to surrender the *scribanage*, Soquerius would be recompensed with 40 besants.

158. For its name, see John of Jaffa, p. 412.

159. *Cart. du St-Sépulcre*, no. 55. For *secretarii* in Antioch, see *Cart. du St-Sépulcre*, no. 86; *Documenti delle città toscane*, no. 58 (p. 90). The *secrete* in the kingdom itself was mentioned in 'Livre au roi', pp. 613–14, 642–3. A document of 1195 contains a reference to it; but this was written in the margin at an indeterminate date. *Tab. ord. Theut.*, no. 31.

160. John of Jaffa, pp. 407–9.

161. John of Jaffa, p. 227. Assignments on fiefs would therefore be registered. 'Livre au roi', pp. 642–3; Philip of Novara, 'Livre', p. 550. For proof of territorial fiefs, see 'La Clef des Assises de la Haute Cour', p. 595. The list of services and rights of justice in John of Jaffa (pp. 419–27) is assumed to have come from the *secrete* registers.

162. 'Livre au roi', pp. 613, 614; John of Jaffa, pp. 257, 409, 412; 'Clef des Assises', p. 595; Philip of Novara, 'Livre', p. 511; 'Bans et ordonnances des rois de Chypre', p. 369. The marshal had his own scribe in the *secrete*.

163. John of Jaffa (pp. 407–8) mentioned *baillis* and scribes, but it is clear that viscounts were also involved. For Cypriot evidence, see 'Abrégé des Assises des Bourgeois', pp. 241, 243; 'Bans et ordonnances', p. 372.

164. *Tab. ord. Theut.*, no. 31. For the *modius*, see *Urkunden Venedig*, no. 299 (p. 369); Francesco Balducci Pegolotti, p. 64; 'Eracles', ii, p. 152.

165. See Rabie, op. cit., pp. 144–9; Gottschalk, 'Dīwān', pp. 327–31. Two Muslims, clearly referring to the *secrete*, called it the *amwal*. Ibn Jubair (ed. in *RHC. Or.*, iii) p. 455; Ibn al-Athir, i, p. 675.

166. Philip of Novara, 'Livre', p. 511. See 'Bans et ordonnances', p. 365.

167. *Cart. du St-Sépulcre*, nos. 86, 88–9.

168. *Tab. ord. Theut.*, no. 2; *Urkunden Venedig*, no. 299 (p. 370); *Cart. gen. Hosp.*, nos. 2693, 2949, 3213. It seems likely that the curious name of Homo Dei was a Latin version of the Arabic 'Abd-Allah. For another example, see *Reg. Hier.*, no. 500; but against this should be placed the Venetian Johannes Homodei of *Reg. Hier.*, no. 1293b.

169. John of Jaffa, p. 407.

170. *Cart. gen. Hosp.*, no. 244. If it was a *bailli* of Nazareth who appeared in a document of 1255 then he was an agent of the archbishop. *Cart. gen. Hosp.*, no. 2748.

171. *Recherches géographiques*, pp. 30–2; *Cart. gen. Hosp.*, no. 2245. See also 'Chartes de Josaphat', ed. Kohler, no. 30.

172. See Richard, *Le royaume latin*, pp. 89–90.

173. William of Tyre, p. 1111. For lists of inhabitants, most of them in the royal domain, see above, pp. 40–1.

174. 'Chartes de Josaphat', ed. Kohler, no. 71.

CHAPTER 4   THE DOMAIN IN THE TOWNS

1. See William of Tyre, p. 975; 'Chartes du Mont-Thabor', no. 15; *Chartes de Josaphat*, ed. Delaborde, no. 35; 'L'ordre de Montjoye', ed. J. Delaville Le Roulx, *ROL*, i (1893) no. 1 (p. 52); 'Gestes des Chiprois', p. 805.

2. As late as the middle of the twelfth century the sea route from the Red Sea to India, opened by the Fatimids, was still believed to be the main way to the Far East. William of Tyre, p. 931. It was, however, already in decline.

3. The following description of the goods passing through Acre is based upon 'Livre des Assises des Bourgeois', pp. 274–87; Francesco Balducci Pegolotti, pp. 63–9; *Urkunden Venedig*, no. 300; *Documents inédits sur le commerce de Marseille au moyen âge*, ed. L. Blancard, *passim*. When making use of other material, I have referred to it in a note.

4. See editor's note, Francesco Balducci Pegolotti, p. 419.

5. See also *Documenti del commercio veneziano nei secoli XI-XIII*, ed R. Morozzo della Rocca and A. Lombardi, nos. 62, 513.

6. 'Livre des Assises des Bourgeois', pp. 220–33; John of Jaffa, pp. 129, 207.

7. For the enslavement of prisoners-of-war, see 'Frag. cart. St-Lazare', no. 22; 'De constructione castri Saphet', pp. 382, 384; 'Gestes des Chiprois', p. 756; 'Eracles' ii, pp. 363, 447.

8. *Urkunden Vendig*, no. 300 (p. 398); Innocent IV, *Reg.*, no. 2122. See also *Documenti del commercio veneziano*, nos. 411–12, 425. It is clear that there were also eastern slave-dealers. John of Jaffa, p. 207.

9. See below, pp. 87–8.

10. James of Vitry, *Lettres*, p. 88; *Cart. gen. Hosp.*, nos. 2168, 3039 § 9 (see § 48); Gregory IX, *Reg.*, no. 4147. Cf. *Cart. gen. Hosp.*, no. 3105. A slave who fled from paynim into Palestine and became a Christian gained his freedom, but one who fled from his owner within the kingdom and then converted was not released from servitude. 'Livre des Assises des Bourgeois', pp. 299–300. This passage contains the following splendid, but rather empty phrase: 'this is the land of the Franks and for this reason ought all to be free'. It may, however, be a later addition. For the legal position of slaves, see also 'Livre des Assises des Bourgeois', pp. 55–6, 219, 225–6, 251–3; John of Jaffa, pp. 114, 187; and note the curious views of Philip of Novara ('Livre', p. 502) on the marriage of a slave to a freewoman.

11. Innocent IV, *Reg.*, no. 2122; 'Livre des Assises des Bourgeois', pp. 228–9.

12. Mentioned by Francesco Balducci Pegolotti (p. 69) as being exported in the fourteenth century. But it must have been sold in Acre earlier.

13. Note the reference to a Pisan vessel charged with nuts in the port of Acre. 'Gestes des Chiprois', p. 797.

14. Mentioned by Francesco Balducci Pegolotti (p. 69) as being exported in the fourteenth century.

15. See Riley-Smith, *Knights of St John*, pp. 439–43.

16. For Acre, see J. Prawer, 'L'établissement des coutumes du marché à Saint-Jean d'Acre', *RHDFE*, sér. 4, xxix (1951), pp. 335–7. For Tyre, 'Liber iurium', nos. 374 (col. 358), 405 (col. 406); 'Quatre titres des Génois', no. 4 (p. 226). For Jaffa, Gregory IX, *Reg.*, no. 4013.

17. *Chartes de Josaphat*, ed. Delaborde, appendice, pp. 123–5; *Sacrae antiquitatis monumenta historica*, ed. C. L. Hugo, i, p. 36 (see also pp. 37–8); R. Röhricht, *Studien zur Geschichte des Fünften Kreuzzüges*, pp. 69–70, no. 45. The Lords of Caesarea were very much in debt, 1212–13 (*Cart. gen. Hosp.*, nos. 1400, 1414), but after this there is no sign of financial troubles until the 1250s (see the references to the Lords of Sidon and Beirut and the Count of Jaffa, above, p. 30). In the 1270s the Lords of Scandelion were deeply in debt. 'Elf deutschordensurkunden', nos. 8–9.

18. Ibn al-Furat, ii, pp. 43–4. See also H. A. R. Gibb, 'The Aiyūbids', *A History of the Crusades*, ed.-in-chief K. M. Setton, ii, p. 694.

19. Matthew Paris, 'Itinéraire de Londres à Jérusalem', ed. H. Michelant and G. Raynaud, *Itinéraires à Jérusalem*, p. 137. It should be noted that Matthew Paris (p. 127) gave the sum of 500 pounds of silver – in one redaction sterling – a *day* for Damascus.

20. 'Livre au roi', p. 617.

21. *Tab. ord. Theut.*, no. 3 (p. 4).

22. Ibn Jubair, p. 316. See also *Cart. gen. Hosp.*, no. 3029. Ibn Jubair's merchants were taking the shorter, but rougher, route through Toron which was suitable for mule trains: caravans of camels went the easier but longer way from Damascus through Tiberias. Ibn Jubair, p. 324. Others in the caravan were subjected to a poll-tax.

23. Philip of Novara 'Livre', p. 533; John of Jaffa, p. 395. John but not Philip, referred to it as wasteland.

24. Prawer, 'Étude de quelques problèmes agraires', pp. 36–40.

25. *Cart. gen. Hosp.*, nos. 531, 2688, 2748, 3029; *Chartes de Josaphat*, ed. Delaborde, no. 49 (p. 102); *Tab. ord. Theut.*, nos. 117 (p. 104), 118 (p. 105), 119 (p. 107), 120 (p. 110); *Recherches géographiques*, p. 38. For *chemin reau* and *chemin* meaning definitely a road, see 'Livre des Assises

des Bourgeois', p. 309; 'Livre au roi', p. 617; *Cart. gen. Hosp.*, no. 2753; 'Chartes du Mont-Thabor', no. 26.

26. *Cart. gen. Hosp.*, no. 2853.

27. 'Quatre titres des Génois', no. 4; *Urkunden Venedig*, no. 369; *Cart. gen. Hosp.*, nos. 3346, 3408.

28. *Cart. gen. Hosp.*, no. 77 (see also *Documenti delle città toscane*, nos. 6, 24); *Urkunden Venedig*, no. 271 (p. 261). For Jaffa under John, see above, pp. 27–8, 30–1.

29. *Cart. du St-Sépulcre*, nos. 127, 155; and for Oultrejourdain and the Dead Sea, *Cart. gen. Hosp.*, nos. 207, 521.

30. 'Liber iurium', no. 718.

31. 'nerçi/verzi'.

32. 'Liber iurium', nos. 569, 585; *Urkunden Venedig*, nos. 261–2; Mayer, *Marseilles Levantehandel*, no. 8 (pp. 191–2).

33. *Chartes de Josaphat*, ed. Delaborde, app., p. 125; 'Annales mon. Burtonensis', p. 494.

34. A. Germain, *Histoire de la commune de Montpellier*, ii, pp. 513–15.

35. *Cod. dipl. geros.*, i, p. 157.

36. *Recherches géographiques*, pp. 49–50. And see also Pope Honorius III, *Regesta*, no. 6130.

37. 'Liber iurium', no. 11; *Urkunden Venedig*, nos. 40–1, 300 (p. 397); *Documenti delle città toscane*, no. 5.

38. *Urkunden Venedig*, nos. 40–1. But cf. the interpretation of Richard (*Le royaume latin*, p. 221).

39. See Richard, *Le royaume latin*, p. 220.

40. *Documenti delle città toscane*, no. 5.

41. *Documenti delle città toscane*, no. 11.

42. Richard, *Le royaume latin*, pp. 220–2.

43. *Documenti delle città toscane*, nos. 23–5, 32–3, 35–6; 'Liber iurium', nos. 363, 374 (col. 358), 401 (col. 401). The Provençals' courts in Tyre and Acre were allowed to judge all upon whom the commune imposed taxes, although there was a reservation of High Justice. Mayer, *Marseilles Levantehandel*, nos. 4 (p. 182), 5 (pp. 185–6).

44. 'Liber iurium', nos. 405 (col. 406), 410.

45. 'Eracles', ii, pp. 202–3; *Documenti delle città toscane*, nos. 37, 40; see also no. 45. Particularly striking is the return to the old situation on the matter of *tallea*. See below, p. 83.

46. *Urkunden Venedig*, no. 299 (pp. 358–60, 369, 375, 384–5, 387–9).

47. *Urkunden Venedig*, no. 299 (pp. 357–8, 384–9).

48. *Urkunden Venedig*, no. 369 (p. 152).

49. 'Livre des Assises des Bourgeois', pp. 161–3. See John of Jaffa, p. 309. For the date of the burgess laws, see below, p. 268 note 186.

50. 'Quatre titres des Génois', no. 4 (pp. 225–6). See *Reg. Hier.*, no. 659.

51. *Urkunden Venedig*, no. 300; 'Quatre titres des Génois', no. 2 (pp. 215–21). See also the interesting *Documenti delle città toscane*, no. 37. For the population of Acre, see Benvenisti, *Crusaders in the Holy Land*, pp. 26–7.

52. 'Liber iurium', nos. 8, 11, 20, 256, 276, 363, 374–5, 379, 392, 401, 410, 477, 569, 585, 718; *Documenti delle città toscane*, nos. 1, 5, 22–5, 31–2, 37; *Urkunden Venedig*, nos. 40–1, 68, 261–2, 369; Mayer, *Marseilles Levantehandel*, nos. 4 (p. 182), 5 (p. 185), 8 (p. 192); *Memorie di Amalfi*, i, p. 201; *Recherches géographiques*, p. 47; 'Quatre titres des Génois', no. 4 (pp. 225–6); 'Chartae', *HPM*, i, no. 544.

53. *Urkunden Venedig*, nos. 46, 61; 'Liber iurium', nos. 405, 516 (although the second of these may contain a reference to the gate tolls); *Documenti delle città toscane*, nos. 4, 6, 13, 50, 53, 58, 70; *Memorie di Amalfi*, i, p. 202; *Acta imperii inedita saeculi XIII*, ed. E. Winkelmann, i, no. 302; *Cod. dipl. geros.*, i, p. 158; *Cart. gen. Hosp.*, no. 2801; Germain, *Histoire de Montpellier*, ii, p. 513; *Epistolae saeculi XIII e regestis pontificum Romanorum selectae*, ii, no. 125; Röhricht, 'Amalrich I', p. 489.

54. *Documenti delle città toscane*, nos. 23–5, 31–2, 65 (and see no. 66); *Breve* from the 'Statuti pisani', in *Documenti delle città toscane*, pp. 380–1.

55. The only general exemptions were for the Genoese in Antioch, Laodicea, Gibel, Tripoli, Gibelet, Tyre, Acre, Haifa, Jerusalem, Jaffa and Ascalon: 'Liber iurium', nos. 256, 374, 379, 401, 410, 477, 516, 718; 'Quatre titres des Génois', no. 4 (p. 225); and for the Amalfitans in Acre: *Memorie di Amalfi*, i, p. 201 – it is of interest that a contemporary charter to merchants from Marseilles did not give them full exemption. Mayer, *Marseilles Levantehandel*, no. 5 (p. 185).

56. 'Liber iurium', nos. 405, 585; *Recherches géographiques*, pp. 47–8. See *Urkunden Venedig*, no. 300 (pp. 397–8).

57. *Documenti delle città toscane*, nos. 4, 6, 13, 50; *Urkunden Venedig*, nos. 61, 250; *Memorie di Amalfi*, i, p. 202; Germain, *Histoire de Montpellier*, ii, p. 513; Röhricht, 'Amalrich I', p. 489; Mayer, *Marseilles Levantehandel*, no. 5 (p. 185).

58. Freedom from charges on selling only: Mayer, *Marseilles Levantehandel*, no. 8 (p. 192). Freedom from tax on buying only: 'Liber iurium', no. 569; *Urkunden Venedig*, nos. 68, 261.

59. See *Cart. gen. Hosp.*, no. 77; 'Sankt Samuel', p. 68; and 'La fondation d'une église', p. 54.

60. *Urkunden Venedig*, no. 40.

61. *Urkunden Venedig*, no. 41.

62. *Documenti delle città toscane*, nos. 23–5, 31–2; Mayer, *Marseilles Levantehandel*, no. 4 (p. 183).

63. *Recherches géographiques*, pp. 47–50.

64. 'Liber iurium', no. 374: confirmed by Henry of Champagne, no. 405.

65. *Urkunden Venedig*, no. 63; but see no. 299 (p. 385).

66. Francesco Balducci Pegolotti, p. 64. For the *platea* in the Genoese quarter, see 'Gestes des Chiprois', p. 816.

67. 'Quatre titres des Génois', no. 4 (pp. 227–8). The Genoese had to pay for measurement in Beirut and Cyprus, but they were absolved from it in Haifa; 'Liber iurium', nos. 585, 693, 718. The Venetians had to pay for measurement of certain commodities in Tripoli. *Recherches géographiques*, p. 48. For *mensuragium*, see also William of Tyre, p. 534.

68. See the emphasis on the payment of tolls by visiting Muslim merchants in 'Livre des Assises des Bourgeois', p. 276.

69. 'Liber iurium', no. 405.

70. *Urkunden Venedig*, no. 300 (pp. 397–8).

71. 'Quatre titres des Génois', no. 4 (p. 226).

72. *Urkunden Venedig*, no. 300 (p. 398).

73. Germain, *Histoire de Montpellier*, ii, p. 513. See also the terms of a charter for Provençals from Henry of Cyprus in 1236. Mayer, *Marseilles Levantehandel*, no. 10 (p. 194).

74. *Urkunden Venedig*, no. 300 (p. 398).

75. 'Quatre titres des Génois', no. 4 (p. 225).

76. 'Liber iurium', no. 405. If there was no sale the Genoese need pay no customs. In 1243, however, Bohemond V of Tripoli reduced by two-thirds the 'passage usé' paid by those Provençals who brought goods from paynim into Tripoli by sea and loaded their boats with them. Germain, *Histoire de Montpellier*, ii, p. 513.

77. *Cod. dipl. geros.*, i, p. 158 – although it seems that the charge on entry would be subtracted from it.

78. *Recherches géographiques*, pp. 47–8.

79. *Recherches géographiques*, pp. 47–8.

80. 'Livre des Assises des Bourgeois', pp. 282–3; and for shop-keepers, see p. 277; *Urkunden Venedig*, no. 299 (p. 359). See also J. Richard, 'Colonies marchandes privilégiées et marché seigneurial. La Fonde d'Acre et ses "droitures"', *Le moyen âge*, lix (1953) pp. 333–40. The date of this statute has been much debated. See Richard, loc. cit.; Prawer, 'L'établissement des coutumes', pp. 338–44; C. Cahen, 'À propos des coutumes du marché d'Acre', *RHDFE*, sér. 4, xli (1963) pp. 287–90.

81. *Urkunden Venedig*, no. 299 (pp. 384–5). For John and the *chaine* dues of Acre, see Honorius III, *Reg.*, no. 3826.

82. Except in the fields we have discussed above. In 1231 there does however seem to have been a strong attempt to make the Genoese pay customs duties in the port of Acre. *Annales Januenses*, iii, pp. 55–6.

83. *Documenti delle città toscane*, nos. 4, 6, 13, 50, 53, 58, 70; Röhricht, 'Amalrich I', p. 489; *Urkunden Venedig*, nos. 46, 55, 61, 68, 250; *Acta imperii inedita*, i, no. 302; Germain, *Histoire de Montpellier*, ii, pp. 513–

15; 'Liber iurium', no. 718; *Cod. dipl. geros.*, i, pp. 157–61; *Epistolae saeculi XIII*, ii, no. 125; *Recherches géographiques*, pp. 47–50. And see below, pp. 76–8.

84. *Urkunden Venedig*, no. 68.

85. Mayer, *Marseilles Levantehandel*, no. 5 (p. 185).

86. *Documenti delle città toscane*, no. 53.

87. *Cart. gen. Hosp.*, no. 2801; *Recherches géographiques*, pp. 47–50.

88. Mayer, *Marseilles Levantehandel*, no. 5 (p. 185).

89. *Urkunden Venedig*, no. 300 (p. 398); *Documenti delle città toscane*, no. 66.

90. *Urkunden Venedig*, nos. 94 (p. 382), 307, 361; Röhricht, 'Amalrich I', p. 489.

91. Mayer, *Marseilles Levantehandel*, no. 23 (pp. 207–9); and see pp. 123 ff.

92. 'Liber iurium', nos. 569, 585. On shipwreck, see also the charter from the Lord of Haifa; 'Liber iurium', no. 718.

93. This is the reading suggested by the editors.

94. *Urkunden Venedig*, nos. 261–2.

95. Mayer, *Marseilles Levantehandel*, no. 8 (pp. 191–2).

96. 'Liber iurium', no. 718.

97. See Matthew Paris, 'Itinéraire', p. 137; Ibn Jubair, p. 323; James of Vitry, *Lettres*, p. 149.

98. 'Documents et mémoires de Chypre', ii, pp. 74 ff.

99. See *Calendar of the Patent Rolls*. 4 Edward I, p. 132; and also *Documents inédits sur le commerce de Marseille, passim*.

100. 'Livre des Assises des Bourgeois', pp. 75–8, 80–1, 129–32. See also *Assises d'Antioche*, p. 82.

101. 'Livre des Assises des Bourgeois', p. 276–7. See also *Documenti del commercio veneziano*, nos. 90, 155, 167, 181, 301, 306, 312, 454. There was a ban on the export of armour to Egypt that reflected the crusading laws. 'Livre des Assises des Bourgeois', pp. 79–80. But see Urban IV, *Reg.* no. 866.

102. 'Actes passés en 1271, 1274 et 1279 à Aïas (Petite Armenie) et à Beyrouth par devant des notaires génois', ed. C. Desimoni, *AOL*, i (1881) pp. 443–4, 451–2, 456–7, 462, 475, 479, 486, 491–2, 498, 503, 506–8, 526–30, 532–3; and see pp. 455, 499. See also Mayer, *Marseilles Levantehandel*, nos. 5 (p. 185), 8 (p. 192); *Memorie di Amalfi*, i, p. 201.

103. D. H. von Soden, 'Bericht über die in der Kubbet in Damaskus gefundenen Handschriftenfragmente', *Sitzungsberichte der Königlich Preussischen Akademie der Wissenschaften* (1903) p. 827; Benjamin of Tudela, p. 18.

104. *Urkenden Venedig*, no. 299 (pp. 384–5).

105. This perhaps equalled 5,699 saracen besants. We know that it equalled 22,797 saracen besants and 7 caroubles in Armenian money –

and that in 1252 there were four Armenian besants to one of Acre. *Cart. gen. Hosp.*, no. 2581.

106. 'Documents et mémoires de Chypre', ii, pp. 74–9; 'Actes passés par devant des notaires génois', pp. 441–2. The names in the documents do not always correspond and the figures given may not be accurate.

107. *Cart. gen. Hosp.*, nos. 3105, 3263.

108. 'Livre des Assises des Bourgeois', pp. 110–14. For native servants, see 'Livre des Assises des Bourgeois', p. 112; 'Gestes des Chiprois', pp. 775–6.

109. 'Livre des Assises des Bourgeois', pp. 235–6, 238.

110. 'Livre des Assises des Bourgeois', pp. 78–9.

111. 'Livre des Assises des Bourgeois', pp. 171–2; 'Eracles', ii, p. 152.

112. See 'Livre des Assises des Bourgeois', pp. 73, 118–21; *Cart. gen. Hosp.*, nos. 399, 2732; *Tab. ord. Theut.*, no. 41.

113. *Urkunden Venedig*, no. 299 (p. 359); *Les Archives*, no. 27. See 'Livre des Assises des Bourgeois', p. 283; *Cart. gen. Hosp.* no. 2888; *Recherches géographiques*, p. 47.

114. *Urkunden Venedig*, no. 299 (p. 359; and see p. 385).

115. 'Livre des Assises des Bourgeois', pp. 73–4; 'Chartes du Mont-Thabor', no. 20; *Recherches géographiques*, p. 48.

116. *Cart. gen. Hosp.*, no. 2732; *Recherches géographiques*, p. 48. And perhaps also milk: *Urkunden Venedig*, no. 299 (p. 385).

117. 'Livre des Assises des Bourgeois', p. 70; *Urkunden Venedig*, no. 299 (pp. 359–60, 385). See also *Cart. gen. Hosp.*, nos. 250, 469, 508, 648.

118. *Tab. ord. Theut.*, no. 92; *Cart. gen. Hosp.*, no. 3105; 'Quatre titres des Génois', no. 2 (pp. 219, 221).

119. 'Livre des Assises des Bourgeois', pp. 345–6; 'Quatre titres des Génois', no. 3 (p. 223); 'Liber iurium', nos. 363 (col. 347), 374 (col. 358), 405 (col. 406); 'Bans et ordonnances', p. 357. See *Cart. gen. Hosp.*, nos. 249, 376; *Cart. du St-Sépulcre*, nos. 80, 105.

120. *Urkunden Venedig*, no. 299 (p. 385). See *Cart. gen. Hosp.*, nos. 399, 648; *Les Archives*, no. 27.

121. C. Enlart, *Les monuments des croisés dans le royaume de Jérusalem*, ii, p. 236.

122. *Urkunden Venedig*, no. 299 (p. 386); 'L'ordre de Montjoye', no. 1 (p. 52).

123. *Urkunden Venedig*, no. 299 (p. 385); Usamah ibn Munqidh, pp. 164–5; *Cart. gen. Hosp.*, no. 469. See 'Chartes de Josaphat,' ed. Kohler, no. 44; Ibn al-Furat, ii, p. 108; S. D. Goitein, *A Mediterranean Society*, i, pp. 126–7.

124. See *Cart. gen. Hosp.*, nos. 249, 376, 422, 483, 508.

125. *Tab. ord. Theut.*, no. 128 (p. 126). See *Cart. gen. Hosp.*, nos. 207, 532, 554; 'Chartes de Josaphat', ed. Kohler, no. 49.

126. *Documenti delle città toscane*, no. 71 F; 'Actes passés par devant des notaires génois', p. 454; 'Quatre titres des Génois', no. 2 (p. 220).

127. 'Livre des Assises des Bourgeois', pp. 114–15. See *Cart. gen. Hosp.*, no. 648.

128. 'Titres de l'hôpital des Bretons d'Acre', ed. J. Delaville Le Roulx, *AOL*, i (1881) pp. 426, 427; *Cart. gen. Hosp.*, no. 2127. See 'Chartes de Terre Sainte', ed. Delaville Le Roulx, no. 3.

129. See for instance *Itinéraires a Jérusalem*, pp. 149–50.

130. 'Quatre titres des Génois', no. 3 (p. 223); *Documenti delle città toscane*, nos. 23 (p. 26), 31 (p. 36).

131. *Tab. ord. Theut.*, nos. 92, 128 (p. 126). For Jerusalem, see 'Chartes de Terre Sainte', ed. Delaville Le Roulx, no. 3; *Cart. gen. Hosp.*, nos. 249, 376, 2127; *Cod. dipl. geros.*, i, pp. 235–6. See also *Itinéraires à Jérusalem*, pp. 43, 150, 155.

132. 'Livre des Assises des Bourgeois', pp. 345–6; 'Bans et ordonnances', pp. 357–8.

133. Goitein, *A Mediterranean Society*, i, pp. 197 ff. See *Assises d'Antioche*, p. 82.

134. For examples, see *Documents inédits sur le commerce de Marseille*, i, pp. 273, 288–90, 297, 310, 323–5, 328–9, 335, 341–2, 348–9, 352, 363, 365, 368.

135. For La Change in Acre, see 'Eracles', ii, p. 221; 'Gestes des Chiprois', p. 740; and see also *Cart. du St-Sépulcre*, nos. 32, 48, 52–4, 144; William of Tyre, p. 392; *Cart. gen. Hosp.*, nos. 84, 225; *Assises d'Antioche*, pp. 80–2; 'Frag. cart. St-Lazare', no. 24. For the control by the customs house, see *Documents inédits sur le commerce de Marseille*, i, pp. 153, 156–8, 162–3, 315, 324, 348–9, 363, 365. In 'Quatres titres des Génois' (no. 4 (p. 228)) the word printed as 'bocharie' ought surely to read 'bancerie'.

136. See *Cart. gen. Hosp.*, nos. 84, 225, 250, 312, 375, 554, 2033, 2330; 'Chartes de Terre Sainte', ed. Delaville Le Roulx, no. 3; *Recherches géographiques*, p. 22; *Cart. du St-Sépulcre*, no. 80; *Les Archives*, no. 27; 'Quatre titres des Génois', no. 2 (pp. 215, 217, 220, 221).

137. *Cart. gen. Hosp.*, nos. 573 (doubtful), 3653 bis; Pope Honorius IV, *Registre*, nos. 183, 617. Note the 'change de Sarazins' in Acre. 'Gestes des Chiprois', p. 805.

138. Prawer, *Histoire*, i, p. 531; 'Elf deutschordensurkunden', nos. 8–9. And see also 'Eracles', ii, p. 187.

139. See Nicholas IV, *Reg.*, no. 5080.

140. 'Gestes des Chiprois' pp. 797–8. See James of Vitry, 'Historia', p. 1071; 'Liber iurium', nos. 374 (col. 358), 405 (col. 406); 'Chartes de Josaphat', ed. Kohler, no. 69.

141. *Palestine under the Moslems*, p. 410. See *Documenti del commercio veneziano*, no. 158.

142. *Urkunden Venedig*, no. 299 (p. 367); Mayer, *Marseilles Levantehandel*, no. 5 (p. 185).

143. *Cart. gen. Hosp.*, nos. 2002, 2280; *Urkunden Venedig*, no. 299 (p. 367); 'Documents et mémoires de Chypre', iii, p. 666. In Acre the Genoese may have had their own. 'Quatre titres des Génois', no. 2 (pp. 217, 220).

144. *Tab. ord. Theut.*, nos. 56–7, 104; *Cart. gen. Hosp.*, nos. 311, 2001–2, 2280, 3514–15; *Documenti delle città toscane*, nos. 4, 13.

145. Benjamin of Tudela, pp. 20–8; according to him they had a monopoly of dye-working in Jerusalem.

146. *Urkunden Venedig*, no. 299 (pp. 359, 367).

147. Benjamin of Tudela, p. 18; he also referred (p. 16) to Jews engaged in glassmaking in Antioch. For Tyre, see also James of Vitry, 'Historia', p. 1098 (who also made mention of glass manufacturing in Acre); *Urkunden Venedig* nos. 63 (p. 168), 299 (p. 385). A specimen of glass produced in Tyre at this time is on display in the King Edward VII Gallery of the British Museum. One might here add the references to houses which had belonged to the king in Tyre 'ubi fiebant cartule' (*Documenti delle città toscane*, nos. 23 (p. 26), 31 (p. 36)) and one in Antioch 'ubi fiunt calamite' (Riant, 'Une dépendance', p. 659).

148. *Recherches géographiques*, p. 36; 'Livre au roi' p. 619. See also *Cart. gen. Hosp.*, no. 144 and perhaps no. 754; *Tab. ord. Theut.*, no. 15 (p. 15).

149. 'Eracles', ii, p. 474; and, although it has never been identified, for its position, see p. 330; *Cart. gen. Hosp.*, no. 3045.

150. See 'Liber iurium', nos. 8 (col. 16), 345 (col. 332), 346 (col. 333), 349 (col. 335); *Tab. ord. Theut.*, nos. 76, 80, 86, 91; *Cart. gen. Hosp.*, nos. 312, 2714; Riant, 'Une dépendance', p. 657; *Hist. dipl. Fred. secundi*, iii, p. 127. See 'Chartes de Josaphat,' ed. Kohler, no. 71; *Urkunden Venedig*, no. 299 (pp. 368–70); James of Vitry, *Lettres*, p. 93; and also *Chartes de Josaphat*, ed. Delaborde App. p. 124; *Cart. gen. Hosp.*, nos. 1718, 3408; Urban IV, *Reg.*, no. 344 (p. 162).

151. *Cart. gen. Hosp.*, nos. 84, 225, 391; *Cart. du St-Sépulcre*, nos. 127, 155; 'Chartes de St-Serge', p. 27; *Urkunden Venedig*, no. 299 (p. 370).

152. *Cart. gen. Hosp.*, no. 521; *Cart. du St-Sépulcre*, no. 145; 'Chartes de Josaphat', ed. Kohler, no. 64; and see no. 12 for a gardener.

153. I hope to make this the subject of a future article.

154. John of Jaffa, pp. 63–4; Philip of Novara, 'Livre', pp. 484–5; 'Livre des Assises des Bourgeois', pp. 65–6; 'Abrégé des Assises des Bourgeois', p. 251. See Prawer, 'Assise de Teneure', p. 83, 85. Also

Cart. gen. Hosp., no. 2732; *Tab. ord. Theut.*, no. 41; *Urkunden Venedig,* no. 299. (pp. 358–61).

155. John of Jaffa, p. 26. This is not entirely clear in 'Livre des Assises des Bourgeois', pp. 270–4.

156. *Cart. gen. Hosp.*, nos. 472, 648, 891, 966; and see no. 941.

157. See for example *Cart. gen. Hosp.*, no. 2902 (p. 861).

158. See 'Livre des Assises des Bourgeois', pp. 115–17, 122–4.

159. 'Livre des Assises des Bourgeois', p. 66.

160. 'Livre au roi', pp. 619, 633; 'Eracles', ii, p. 474. See 'Abrégé des Assises des Bourgeois', p. 251.

161. For example see *Tab. ord. Theut.*, nos. 73–4; *Chartes de Josaphat,* ed. Delaborde, nos. 36, 47.

162. 'Livre des Assises des Bourgeois', pp. 65–6, 117, 123; Philip of Novara, 'Livre', p. 550. See for instance *Documenti delle città toscane,* no. 37 and 'Illustrazioni', pp. 439–40. The Genoese called the city of Acre outside their own quarter the 'borgesia'. 'Quatre titres des Génois', no. 2 (pp. 219, 221). See also the reference to a 'visconte dou Bort' (sic) in Acre. 'Gestes des Chiprois', p. 810. Some cases, however, obviously involved both the seigneurial and burgess courts. See *Tab. ord. Theut.*, no. 36; *Cart. gen. Hosp.*, no. 2714.

163. 'Livre des Assises des Bourgeois', pp. 65–6, 117, 122–4; *Recherches géographiques*, p. 37. For burgess services, see 'Frag. cart. St-Lazare', no. 18; *Memorie di Amalfi*, i, pp. 202, 203–4; *Documenti delle città toscane*, no. 19; *Cart. du St-Sépulcre*, no. 54 (p. 104); *Cod. dipl. geros.*, i, p. 287. Note the 65 young men from the burgess colony of Mahumeria near Jerusalem serving at Gaza in 1170. William of Tyre, p. 977.

164. *Cart. du St-Sépulcre*, nos. 80, 136–9; *Cart. gen. Hosp.*, nos. 508, 663, 803; and see no. 783 (p. 495).

165. For inventories of normal rents, see *Cod. dipl. geros.*, i, pp. 235–6; *Cart. du St-Sépulcre*, no. 185; 'Quatre titres des Génois', no. 2; *Urkunden Venedig*, no. 300.

166. William of Tyre, p. 1112; Pope Innocent III, *Register*, no. 512.

167. *Cart. gen. Hosp.* nos. 437, 648; Innocent III, *Reg.*, no. 512. See Cahen, *Syrie du Nord*, p. 558.

168. See William of Tyre, p. 1112.

169. *Documenti delle città toscane*, nos. 23 (p. 27), 24 (p. 28), 25 (p. 30), 31 (p. 37), 32. A problem concerns the phrase 'pro communi', which I have translated as 'for all'; there are other possible interpretations. For other other references to *tallea*, see *Documenti delle città toscane*, nos. 27 (p. 33), 28 (p. 34); *Tab. ord. Theut.*, no. 74; *Chartes de Josaphat*, ed. Delaborde, no. 47 (p. 98). See 'Inventaire de l'Hôpital', no. 182.

170. See above, p. 68.

171. *Urkunden Venedig*, no. 299 (pp. 358–9); and see above, p. 45, for the poll-tax on Muslims. For the *jawali* tax, see Rabie, *Financial System*, pp. 108–13.

172. *Urkunden Venedig*, no. 299 (pp. 360, 385).

173. *Urkunden Venedig*, no. 299 (pp. 359–60); *Assises d'Antioche*, p. 78. See also 'La fondation d'une église', p. 54.

174. *Urkunden Venedig*, no. 299 (p. 359). For *hilali*, see Rabie, op. cit., pp. 105–6.

175. *Urkunden Venedig*, no. 300 (pp. 390, 391, 397). See also 'Quatre titres des Génois', nos. 2 (pp. 218, 219), 4 (p. 227); Röhricht, 'Amalrich I', p. 489.

176. James of Vitry, 'Historia', p. 1088.

177. Usamah ibn Munqidh, pp. 165–6; 'Liber iurium', nos. 374, 405. It was in Tyre that Usamah (p. 166) saw a woman in a public bath.

178. *Urkunden Venedig*, no. 299 (p. 365).

179. *Cart. gen. Hosp.*, no. 941; *Urkunden Venedig*, nos. 299 (pp. 365–6), 300; 'Quatre titres des Génois', no. 2 (p. 219). See 'Chartes du Mont-Thabor', no. 19 (p. 908); *Cart. gen. Hosp.*, no. 3029 (p. 32); also 'Documents et mémoires de Chypre', ii, p. 55.

180. Usamah ibn Munquidh, p. 165; and see *Urkunden Venedig*, no. 299 (p. 379).

181. *Cart. du St-Sépulcre*, no. 80.

182. John of Jaffa, pp. 24, 419–21; but his list is far from complete: there is in it, for instance, no reference to the burgess courts at Cacho and Legio. See *Cart. gen. Hosp.*, no. 94, 115; *Documenti delle città toscane*, no. 25 (p. 31).

183. John of Jaffa, pp. 23, 47; Philip of Novara, 'Livre', pp. 560–2. See 'Livre des Assises des Bourgeois', pp. 314–15, 318–19.

184. 'Abrégé des Assises des Bourgeois', pp. 241, 243.

185. This is what seems to have happened in at least one rural colonial settlement, although the rents could be sent to wherever the *dispensator* ordered. *Cart. du St-Sépulcre*, no. 135. See also *Cart. gen. Hosp.*, no. 2126.

186. See J. Prawer, 'Étude préliminaire sur les sources et la composition du "Livre des Assises des Bourgeois"', *RHDFE*, sér. 4, xxxii (1954). For problems, see M. Grandclaude, *Étude critique sur les livres des Assises de Jérusalme*, pp. 123–7. The date I have given for the redaction is different from those proposed by Grandclaude (op. cit., pp. 66–70) and Prawer ('L'établissement des coutumes', pp. 346–8). Since it is a compilation, references to internal evidence do not of course prove anything; but John of Jaffa (p. 23) seems to have referred to it; and the work itself ('Livre des Assises des Bourgeois', p. 160) mentioned a scribe of the court, who was only established in the 1260s. See below, p. 87.

187. *Urkunden Venedig*, nos. 299 (p. 360), 369 (p. 154); *Les Archives*, no. 34; *Tab. ord. Theut.*, nos. 86, 91; *Cart. gen. Hosp.*, nos. 2015, 3514; 'Chartes de Josaphat', ed. Kohler, no. 71. And see Prawer, 'Colonisation Activities', pp. 1090–3, 1112–13.

188. See John of Jaffa, pp. 22, 24–5; 'Livre des Assises des Bourgeois', pp. 244–8, 295–7; 'Livre des Assises des Bourgeois', ed. Beugnot, p. 155; *Recherches géographiques*, p. 39 (although this refers to Casal Imbert in the royal domain). The courts of the merchants from Provence and perhaps Ancona had to follow the custom of the kingdom. Mayer, *Marseilles Levantehandel*, no. 5 (p. 186); *Cod. dipl. geros.*, i, p. 158.

189. *Tab. ord. Theut.*, no. 92.

190. 'Livre des Assises des Bourgeois', pp. 45–8, 121, 159–60; John of Jaffa, p. 23.

191. *Les Archives*, no. 34; *Cart. gen. Hosp.*, nos. 312, 538, 554; but see also no. 2127.

192. 'Quatre titres des Génois', no. 4 (p. 227). See 'Abrégé des Assises des Bourgeois', pp. 240–1.

193. 'Livre des Assises des Bourgeois', pp. 51–2, 333–4; although fourteen jurors were listed in 1251, 'Abrégé des Assises des Bourgeois' pp. 246–7. Six from Haifa witnessed a charter in 1201. *Cart. gen. Hosp.*, no. 1146.

194. See *Cart. gen. Hosp.*, nos. 663, 2015, 2033, 2949, 3334; 'Abrégé des Assises des Bourgeois', pp. 246–7, and below, pp. 123–4.

195. 'Livre des Assises des Bourgeois', pp. 51–2. It was perhaps from their ranks that were drawn the investigators into taxable properties in the towns before the great general tax of 1183. William of Tyre, pp. 1110–12.

196. John of Jaffa, p. 23; *Urkunden Venedig*, no. 299 (p. 360). See 'Livre des Assises des Bourgeois', pp. 49–50.

197. 'Livre des Assises des Bourgeois', pp. 51–2, 333–4.

198. 'Livre des Assises des Bourgeois', pp. 49, 58, 152–3; 'Abrégé des Assises des Bourgeois', p. 245. See Philip of Novara, 'Livre', pp. 561–2.

199. John of Jaffa, p. 112; Philip of Novara, 'Livre', pp. 482–3. For differences, see 'Livre des Assises des Bourgeois', pp. 157–8, 317–18; 'Abrégé des Assises des Bourgeois', pp. 336–7; Philip of Novara, 'Livre', pp. 481, 561–2.

200. 'Livre des Assises des Bourgeois', pp. 46–7; *Cart. gen. Hosp.*, no. 3334. See John of Jaffa, pp. 23–4; 'Abrégé des Assises des Bourgeois', p. 249. For punishments, see 'Quatre titres des Génois', no. 4 (pp. 225–6); *Urkunden Venedig*, no. 369 (p. 152). For *esgarts, conoissances* and *recorts*, see below, p. 132.

201. *Cart. gen. Hosp.*, nos. 2662, 2949, 3334; and see nos. 444, 663,

2015, 2126, 2212, 2714. In Jerusalem in 1163 there was a ceremony which involved placing hands upon an altar. *Cart. gen. Hosp.*, no. 312.

202. 'Livre des Assises des Bourgeois', p. 66; *Urkunden Venedig* no. 299 (p. 361); *Cart. gen. Hosp.*, no. 3334. See also *Cart. gen. Hosp.*, no. 554; *Les Archives*, no. 34; *Cart. du St-Sépulcre*, no. 103.

203. 'Abrégé des Assises des Bourgeois', pp. 237, 238, 243–4.

204. *Urkunden Venedig*, no. 299 (p. 359). See Tyan, *Histoire de l'organisation judiciaire*, pp. 617–50. For the Mamluk *Muhtasib*, see Goitein, *A Mediterranean Society*, i, p. 270.

205. John of Jaffa, pp. 198–9, 212, 289–91, 293, 295; Geoffrey Le Tor, p. 449; James of Ibelin, p. 464; Philip of Novara, 'Livre', pp. 501, 552, 553.

206. See 'Livre au roi' p. 643; John of Jaffa, pp. 342–3; 'Eracles', ii, p. 53.

207. 'Livre des Assises des Bourgeois', p. 312.

208. 'Livre des Assises des Bourgeois', p. 158; *Urkunden Venedig*, nos. 299 (p. 361), 300 (pp. 392, 395); 'Quatre titres des Génois', no. 3 (p. 224); *Cod. dipl. geros.*, i, p. 159; 'Actes passés par devant des notaires génois', p. 527 (for the Genoese in Beirut).

209. 'Quatre titres des Génois', no. 4 (p. 227). Cf. 'Abrégé des Assises des Bourgeois', pp. 240–1. For other references to *placiers*, see *Cart. du St-Sépulcre*, nos. 88, 92, 103; *Chartes de Josaphat*, ed. Delaborde, no. 7. In 1155–6 the Viscount of Jaffa was assisted by a *privignus* whose office might have been similar to that of a *placier*. 'Frag. cart. St-Lazare', nos. 14–15.

210. 'Abrégé des Assises des Bourgeois', pp. 246–9; *Cart. gen. Hosp.*, no. 2949; and see nos. 2662, 2714.

211. *Cart. gen. Hosp.* no. 3334; 'Livre des Assises des Bourgeois', p. 160, in which a differentiation was made between the scribe of the court and the scribe of the town. As early as 1187 the Viscount of Nablus had his own seal, but this may have been a personal one. 'Chartes de Josaphat', ed. Kohler, no. 49.

212. See for instance John of Jaffa, p. 114.

213. John of Jaffa, pp. 98–9, 395; James of Ibelin, p. 466; Philip of Novara 'Livre', p. 533.

214. 'Livre des Assises des Bourgeois', pp. 220–2, 229. Also *Cart. gen. Hosp.*, nos. 409, 783 (p. 495) and above pp. 62–3. Early in the twelfth century Muslims were not permitted to wear Frankish clothing. *Sacrorum concilium*, xxi, col. 264. It is interesting to compare this with the clothing requirements laid on *dhimmis* in Muslim states, especially remembering what has been said above (pp. 83–4) about poll-tax.

215. John of Jaffa, p. 395; 'Livre des Assises des Bourgeois,' pp. 88–91, 156–7, 270–4; Ernoul, p. 209; Philip of Novara, 'Livre', pp.

533, 546. But cf. Burchard of Mt Sion, p. 89; James of Vitry, 'Historia', pp. 1089 ff.; James of Vitry *Lettres*, pp. 84–5.

216. John of Jaffa, pp. 114, 395; Philip of Novara, 'Livre', pp. 501–2, 533; Geoffrey Le Tor, p. 443; James of Ibelin, p. 466; 'Livre des Assises des Bourgeois', pp. 88–92, 156–7. See also John of Jaffa, p. 187; 'Livre des Assises des Bourgeois' pp. 347–8; *Analecta novissima*, ed. J. B. Pitra, i, p. 581; Honorius III, *Reg.*, no. 3494; *Assises d'Antioche*, p. 38.

217. Tyan, *Histoire de l'organisation judiciaire, passim.*

218. See above, p. 87. For references to criminal jurisdiction, see 'Quatre titres des Génois', no. 4 (pp. 225–6); *Urkunden Venedig*, no. 369 (p. 152).

219. *Cart. gen. Hosp.*, no. 3180 § 6.

220. For rabbinical courts, see Prawer, *Histoire*, i, p. 533, ii, pp. 412–18. For the *Qadi* of Gibel, see Ibn-al-Athir, i, pp. 717, 719; Abu-Shamah, iv, pp. 352–3; Baha' ad-Din, p. 130.

221. See Riley-Smith, 'Some lesser officials', pp. 2–9.

222. John of Jaffa, p. 26. For a reference to a Syrian custom, see 'Livre des Assises des Bourgeois', p. 112.

223. John of Jaffa, p. 26.

224. *Cart. gen. Hosp.*, no. 532; John of Jaffa, p. 424. It was, on the other hand, quite common for the indigenous to take Latin names; and Sade (Sa'di?) of Tyre was described as 'rays des Sarrazins', but his brother had the good Latin name of William. 'Inventaire de l'Hôpital', no. 140.

225. John of Jaffa, p. 26, note 28.

226. 'Chartes de Josaphat', ed. Kohler, no. 10; *Cart. du St-Sépulcre*, nos. 103, 116. For court see *Cart. du St-Sépulcre*, no. 80.

227. *Cart. gen. Hosp.*, nos. 530–32; *Chartes de Josaphat*, ed. Delaborde, no. 43; 'Chartes de Josaphat,' ed. Kohler, nos. 39, 46, 48; John of Jaffa, p. 424.

228. 'Inventaire de l'Hôpital', no. 140.

229. 'Frag. cart. St-Lazare', nos. 7–8.

230. *Cart. gen. Hosp.*, nos. 160, 467, 932; 'Chartes du Mont-Thabor', no. 13.

231. Usamah ibn Munqidh, p. 169; *Cart. gen. Hosp.*, nos. 367, 522.

232. *Cart. gen. Hosp.*, no. 457.

233. 'Livre des Assises des Bourgeois', pp. 270–87; John of Jaffa, p. 26.

234. See Riley-Smith, 'Some lesser officials', pp. 6–7.

235. *Cart. gen. Hosp.*, no. 2748, in which he was entitled 'bais', which is more likely to be *bail* than *rays*.

236. A Venetian report of 1243 (*Urkunden Venedig*, no. 299 (esp. pp. 358–60, 384–5), seems to suggest a separation of the functions

recognisably belonging to the *Cour de la Fonde* and the *Cour des Syriens*.

237. *Lacrimae Nicossienses*, comp. T. J. Chamberlayne, i, pp. 31, 64; 'Bans et ordonnances', p. 377.

238. John of Jaffa, pp. 284–5; Philip of Novara, 'Livre', p. 539; 'Quatre pièces teut.,' no. 3; *Tab. ord. Theut.*, no. 14.

239. 'Frag. cart. St-Lazare', nos. 27–9; 'Sankt Samuel,' p. 70; *Tab. ord. Theut.*, no. 64; *Cart. gen. Hosp.* no. 2280 (pp. 594–5); 'Un diplôme', p. 312.

240. *Tab. ord. Theut.*, nos. 5, 19, 63–4; 'Frag. cart. St-Lazare', nos. 28–9; *Cart. gen. Hosp.*, nos. 1032, 2002, 2280; *Hist. dipl. Fred. secundi*, iii, pp. 117–18, 122–3, 125, 130; *Recherches géographiques*, p. 51; 'Quatre pièces teut.', no. 3; Röhricht, 'Amalrich I', p. 493; *Urkunden Venedig*, no. 299 (p. 367). See 'Contributi alle relazioni tra Genova e l'Oriente. Una lettera del Pontifice Innocenzo III e un privilegio di Guido Re di Gerusalemme e Signore di Cipro', ed. A. Ferreto, *Giornale ligustico*, xxi (1896), p. 44; *Cart. gen. Hosp.*, no. 311. For references to the customary terms of Acre and Tyre, see *Tab. ord. Theut.*, nos. 14, 17.

241. John of Jaffa, pp. 274, 373; 'Chartes de Terre Sainte', ed. Delaville Le Roulx, no. 4; 'Frag. cart. St-Lazare', nos. 26, 30, 33. See also *Assises d'Antioche*, pp. 40–2. For two rather peculiar examples, see 'Frag. cart. St Lazare', no. 40; 'Papst-Kaiser-und Normannenurkenden aus Unteritalien', ed. W. Holtzmann, *QFIAB*, xxxv (1955), p. 57.

242. *Urkunden Venedig*, no. 299 (p. 367); *Cart. gen. Hosp.*, no. 1031; *Cod. dipl. geros.*, i, p. 63; 'Frag. cart. St-Lazare, no. 27.

243. The present Khan al-'Umdan in Acre, almost certainly on the site of the *Cour de la Chaine*, is built on Frankish foundations.

244. 'Livre des Assises des Bourgeois', pp. 75–82 (see 'Livre des Assises des Bourgeois', ed. Beugnot, p. 47). R. B. Patterson ('The Early Existence of the *Funda* and *Catena* in the Twelfth-Century Latin Kingdom of Jerusalem', *Speculum* xxxix (1964) pp. 474–7) has argued that the *Cours de la Chaine* and *de la Fonde* existed before the reign of Amalric. But maritime jurisdiction was only one – and in a sense the least important – of the functions of the *chaine*. It is clear that some office existed from the first and was probably inherited from the Muslims. By creating a court the Latins were characteristically turning a financial office into a tribunal.

245. See 'Quatre titres des Génois', no. 4 (p. 226); Benjamin of Tudela, p. 18; and also 'Liber iurium', nos. 374, 405.

246. *Tab. ord. Theut.*, nos. 5, 17, 63–4; 'Frag. cart. St-Lazare, no. 28; *Documenti delle città toscane*, no. 27. 'Quatre pièces teut.', no. 3; *Cart. gen. Hosp.*, nos. 1031–2, 2280; *Hist. dipl. Fred. secundi*, ii, pp. 533–4, 537, iii, pp. 117–18, 122–3, 125, 130; John of Jaffa, p. 274.

247. *Documenti delle città toscane*, no. 65; *Cod. dipl. geros.*, i, p. 158;

'Eracles', ii, p. 475; *Cart. du St-Sépulcre*, no. 46. The following may have been officers of the *chaine*: Menardus in the twelfth century, and Bernard, Thomas and Simon (the last two father and son), in the thirteenth. *Cart. gen. Hosp.*, nos. 180, 1276, 2166, 2483.

248. 'Livre des Assises des Bourgeois', p. 344.

249. Prawer, 'Étude de quelques problèmes agraires', pp. 58–61. For Egypt I have relied on C. Cahen, 'Douanes et commerce dans les ports méditerranéens de l'Égypte médiévale d'après le *Minhādj* d'al-Makhzūmī', *Journal of the Economic and Social History of the Orient*, vii (1964) *passim*; Goitein, *A Mediterranean Society*, i, *passim*; Rabie, *Financial System*, pp. 89 ff.

250. See 'Eracles', ii, pp. 75, 76; and also Abu-Shamah, iv, p. 310. For pilots at Tyre, see William of Tyre, p. 562.

251. See the description of the ports of Acre and Tyre by Theoderic, (pp. 90–1, 110–11) and also the narrative in 'Eracles' (ii, p. 395).

252. In 1181 the charge on a ship entering a port was one silver mark. F. Wilken, *Geschichte der Kreuzzüge*, vii, 'Beylagen', 5, pp. 33–4. See also *Documenti delle città toscane*, nos. 50, 58; 'Liber iurium', nos. 569, 585; *Urkunden Venedig*, nos. 261–2; Mayer, *Marseilles Levantehandel*, no. 5 (p. 185); *Memorie di Amalfi*, i, p. 201 (note difference between 'anchoragii' and 'ancorandi'); *Recherches géographiques*, p. 47. Also *Documenti delle città toscane*, nos. 1 B, 5; *Chartes de Josaphat*, ed. Delaborde, nos. 18 (p. 46), 28 (p. 65), 29 (p. 69), 49 (p. 102); *Analecta novissima*, i, p. 556; *Cart. gen. Hosp.*, no. 1372. The list of duties given in *Hist. dipl. Fred. secundi* (ii, p. 535) are to be found in a charter issued in Sicily and so may not accurately reflect conditions in the port of Acre.

253. For Latin Jerusalem, see 'Livre des Assises des Bourgeois', ed. Beugnot, pp. 48–9.

254. See H. Antoniadis-Bibicou, *Recherches sur les Douanes à Byzance*, pp. 107–22.

255. *Cart. du St-Sépulcre*, no. 46.

256. See Ibn al-Athir, i, p. 689.

257. 'Livre des Assises des Bourgeois', pp. 274 (rubric), 275–6; *Cart. du St-Sépulcre*, no. 46; Mayer, *Marseilles Levantehandel*, no. 5 (p. 185). But on the other hand, *Cod. dipl. geros.*, i, p. 158; *Documenti delle città toscane*, no. 70; *Acta imperii inedita*, i, no. 302; 'Livre des Assises des Bourgeois', p. 276 (on sugar).

258. *Annales Januenses*, iii, p. 56; 'Livre des Assises des Bourgeois', p. 275 (perhaps only on re-exports); Francesco Balducci Pegolotti, p. 69.

259. See 'Liber iurium', nos. 401, 410.

260. 'Livre des Assises des Bourgeois', pp. 275–6, 344–5; *Recherches géographiques*, p. 47; *Cod. dipl. geros.*, i, p. 158; *Epistolae saeculi XIII*, ii,

no. 125; 'Quatre titres des Génois', no. 4 (p. 226); Germain, *Histoire de Montpellier*, ii, p. 513. See 'Liber iurium', no. 569; *Urkunden Venedig*, no. 262. But cf. the charter of King Guy in which he promised that the merchants from Marseilles would not be forced against their will to sell what they had brought in. Mayer, *Marseilles Levantehandel*, no. 5 (p. 185).

261. See Francesco Balducci Pegolotti, pp. 63–4; *Documents inédits sur le commerce de Marseille, passim*; *Cart. gen. Hosp.*, nos. 77, 2298; also 'Sankt Samuel', p. 68.

262. 'Livre des Assises des Bourgeois', pp. 274–87. One reference in the 'Livre des Assises des Bourgeois' (p. 345) suggests that some dues were paid in kind. For date, see Prawer, 'L'établissement des coutumes', pp. 329–51; Richard, 'Colonies marchandes', pp. 325–40. But cf. the arguments of Cahen, 'À propos des coutumes', pp. 287–90.

263. *Cod. dipl. geros.*, i, p. 158.

264. For pilgrims and passengers: *Urkunden Venedig*, nos. 40–1, 300 (p. 397). For sailors: *Recherches géographiques*, p. 47. See 'Liber iurium', nos. 569, 585; *Urkunden Venedig*, nos. 261–2; Germain, *Histoire de Montpellier*, ii, p. 513; and also *Documenti delle città toscane*, nos. 23–5, 31–2, 50, 58; Mayer, *Marseilles Levantehandel*, nos. 4 (p. 182), 5 (p. 185); *Memorie di Amalfi*, i, p. 201.

265. *Cart. gen. Hosp.*, no. 990.

266. *Urkunden Venedig*, nos. 63, 299 (p. 385); *Cart. gen. Hosp.*, nos. 79, 82; *Cod. dipl. geros.*, i, p. 63; 'Frag. cart. St-Lazare', nos. 27, 33; 'Un diplôme', p. 312; 'L'ordre de Montjoye', no. 1 (p. 52).

267. Gate tolls seems to have been included in the surviving list of charges imposed in Acre, but so were *chaine* dues. 'Livre des Assises des Bourgeois', pp. 274–87. In 1191, before Acre was retaken, the Hospitallers and Templars had promised to take into custody 'redditus fori, et rerum venalium, et redditus portus Acrae': there was here no reference to the gates. *Gesta regis Henrici secundi*, ii, p. 170.

268. Ibn Jubair, p. 317.

269. *Tab. ord. Theut.*, no. 19; and see nos. 5, 7, 13–14; *Documenti delle città toscane*, no. 27; 'Quatre pièces teut.' no. 3: 'Frag. cart. St-Lazare', no. 29.

270. 'Livre des Assises des Bourgeois', pp. 270–4; 'Eracles', ii, p. 475.

271. See also the farming of the *Chaine* of Limassol in Cyprus by King Aimery in 1199 for two years for 28,500 white besants. 'Inventaire de l'Hôpital', no. 187. On the other hand a description of the tolls imposed on Venetians in Acre in 1244 (*Urkunden Venedig*, no. 300 (p. 398)) suggests that the gates were not being farmed then.

272. 'Livre des Assises des Bourgeois', pp. 277, 284; *Urkunden Venedig*, no. 63 (p. 168); 'Quatre titres des Génois', no. 4 (pp. 225–6); *Cart. du St-Sépulcre*, nos. 45, 184; William of Tyre, p. 534.

273. See 'Livre des Assises des Bourgeois', pp. 280, 283, 285; *Urkunden Venedig*, no. 300 (p. 398); and perhaps *Tab. ord. Theut.*, nos. 18, 22. But see *Cart. du St-Sépulcre*, no. 184.

274. 'Livre des Assises des Bourgeois', pp. 283, 285, 286.

275. *Urkunden Venedig*, no. 300 (p. 398); 'Livre des Assises des Bourgeois', pp. 279, 280, 285, 286.

276. See S. Y. Labib, *Handelsgeschichte Ägyptens im Spätmittelalter*, pp. 211 ff.

277. See *Documenti delle città toscane*, no. 6; also *Documenti del commercio veneziano*, no. 513; Philip of Novara, 'Livre', p. 549. A *funduq* could itself be endowed with rights. See Urban IV, *Reg.*, no. 1019.

278. For instance in Acre a *platea* in which onions were sold: interesting because onions are included in the surviving list of charges (*Cart. gen. Hosp.*, no. 2919); in Antioch a *funde del vin* (*Cart. gen. Hosp.*, no. 2001); in Laodicea a *fundum fructus* (*Cart. gen. Hosp.*, no. 437); in Gibel a *platea telarum* (*Les Archives*, no. 52; *Cart. gen. Hosp.*, nos. 1684, 2143); in the lordship of Margat a *platea tincturia* (*Cart. gen. Hosp.*, no. 941); in Tyre a 'vastina que fuit fontica de çucaro' (*Documenti del commercio veneziano*, no. 513) and 'cum uno fontico . . . in quo vendentur mercimonia' . . . 'item ex alio fontico . . . cum tubis et zallamellis, vocinis et tanburis et aliis instrumentis ad ludendum' (*Urkunden Venedig*, no. 299 (p. 385).

279. 'Livre des Assises des Bourgeois', pp. 274–87. See also Francesco Balducci Pegolotti, pp. 63–9.

280. 'Livre des Assises des Bourgeois', pp. 282–3, but cf. Prawer, 'L'établissement des coutumes', pp. 331–44; Richard, 'Colonies marchandes', pp. 336–40; Cahen, 'À propos des coutumes', pp. 288–9.

281. See *Tab. ord. Theut.*, nos. 73–4; 'Rothelin', p. 635.

282. 'Livre des Assises des Bourgeois', p. 282.

283. *Documenti delle città toscane*, no. 27; *Hist. dipl. Fred. secundi*, iii, p. 128.

284. 'Livre des Assises des Bourgeois', pp. 270–4. See above, pp. 90–1.

285. 'Livre des Assises des Bourgeois', pp. 271, 300–1, 344–5. The *mensurator* of Beirut was mentioned in a charter of 1223. 'Liber iurium', no. 585.

286. John of Jaffa, p. 213.

287. *Tab. ord. Theut.*, nos. 5, 14, 19, 63–4; *Urkunden Venedig*, no. 299 (p. 367); *Cart. gen. Hosp.*, nos. 1215, 2001–2, 2280; *Hist. dipl. Fred. secundi*, iii, pp. 117–18, 122–3, 125, 130; 'Frag. cart. St-Lazare', nos. 29–30; 'Sankt Samuel', pp. 69–70; 'L'ordre de Montjoye', no. 1 (p. 52).

288. Richard, 'Colonies marchandes', p. 330.

289. *Cart. gen. Hosp.*, no. 2001. The *fonde* was known here as the *commerc*.

290. *Cart. gen. Hosp.*, nos. 311, 437.

291. *Les Archives*, p. 52; *Cart. gen. Hosp.*, nos. 1684, 2143.

292. *Cart. gen. Hosp.*, no. 941.

293. *Cart. gen. Hosp.*, nos. 620, 2002, 2280; *Recherches géographiques*, pp. 47–8, 51. In the last of those documents two sources of revenue in Tripoli, which were printed as 'drina' and 'paudico', must in fact have been 'duana' and 'fundico': i.e. the *chaine* and the *fonde*.

294. *Tab. ord. Theut.*, nos. 4–5. See 'Gestes des Chiprois', pp. 683–4, 813.

295. *Cart. gen. Hosp.*, nos. 3514–15.

296. *Urkunden Venedig*, no. 299 (pp. 359–60, 385); and see no. 63 (p. 168). For the *muhtasib*, see also above, pp. 86–7. For Damascus, see Elisséeff, *Nūr-ad-Dīn*, iii, *passim*. But for what seem to have been references to a *fonde* in Tyre more like that in Acre, see *Cart. gen. Hosp.*, nos. 3346, 3408; *Tab. ord. Theut.*, no. 14. A possible explanation of this may lie in the fact that for a few years before its capture by the Franks Tyre had been divided between Damascus and Egypt in the proportions one-third to two-thirds. It is possible that the Venetian third had belonged to and been administered by Damascus.

297. John of Joinville, p. 90.

298. Francesco Balducci Pegolotti, p. 64; *Urkunden Venedig*, no. 299 (p. 385); 'Liber iurium', no. 585; *Recherches géographiques*, p. 48; and also 'Sankt Samuel', p. 68.

299. An obviously corrupt variant gave the charge on wax ($11\frac{5}{24}$%) at $2\frac{5}{24}$%.

300. Of the various commodities taxed at this rate, cinnamon was listed twice, once obviously as a transit good, while $4\frac{1}{6}$% was charged on Venetian goods passing through Acre from Islamic countries. It was an easy duty to take, being one carouble in the besant. See also Ibn Jubair, p. 316.

301. 'Livre des Assises des Bourgeois', pp. 274–87; although it is perhaps better to look at Beugnot's edition (pp. 173–81); *Urkunden Venedig*, no. 300. For Egypt and Greece, see Cahen 'Douanes et commerce', pp. 243 ff.; Antoniadis-Bibicou, *Recherches sur les douanes, passim*.

302. Cahen, 'Douanes et commerce', pp. 240–1, 251–2; Goitein, *A Mediterranean Society*, i, pp. 192–3, 218–19.

303. Cahen, op. cit., pp. 240–3, 254; Goitein, op. cit., p. 193; Rabie, op. cit., pp. 89–90.

304. 'Livre des Assises des Bourgeois', pp. 63–4, 300–1. In the Principality of Antioch merchants registered their transactions in the prince's offices. *Assises d'Antioche*, pp. 82–4.

305. 'nichil plus accipiemus ab illis gentibus, que vobiscum negociantur, nisi quantum soliti sunt dare, et quanta accipimus ab illis, qui

cum aliis negociantur gentibus', *Urkunden Venedig*, no. 40 (this does not appear in the confirmation, no. 41). It was to the payment by both parties that Bohemond VII of Tripoli seems to have been referring in 1277 when his charter mentioned goods owing 'II. dreitures'. *Recherches géographiques*, pp. 47–8. See also Germain, *Histoire de Montpellier*, ii, p. 513. For Egypt and Greece, see Cahen, op. cit., p. 254; Antoniadis-Bibicou, op. cit., p. 112.

PART II: CONSTITUTIONAL CONFLICT

CHAPTER 5   THE FATHERS OF THE BARONIAL MOVEMENT

1. William of Tyre, pp. 1004–5.

2. *Annales Januenses*, i, p. 135. For Miles, see William of Tyre, pp. 1008–9.

3. William of Tyre, p. 1009. Earlier references to Rohard (*Reg. Hier.*, nos. 303, 356, 400, 413, 450, 451a, 487, 512, 513a, 514, 517–18, 525, 531, 536–8; William of Tyre, p. 842) seem to disprove William's statement that he was a mediocre man. He must have been made castellan in 1174: his predecessor was still in office in 1173 (*Reg. Hier.*, no. 503) and the first reference to him in that position was in the following year (*Reg. Hier.*, no. 512).

4. William of Tyre, pp. 1007–10. The writer of *Annales Januenses* (i, p. 135) reported that Miles had been assassinated by the lords of Beirut – presumably by a member of the family which had had to sell its fief because of the payment of heavy ransoms and was later to be granted Blanchegarde. See 'Les lignages', p. 458, though it is confused and probably erroneous. For a mission to the West from Jerusalem at this time, see *Chronica regia Coloniensis*, p. 125.

5. William of Tyre, p. 1008.

6. A good example of this view can be found in Runciman, *Crusades*, ii, p. 405.

7. William of Tyre, pp. 1007, 1009.

8. Especially in M. W. Baldwin, *Raymond III of Tripolis and the Fall of Jerusalem*, passim.

9. See Baldwin, op. cit., pp. 156–60.

10. See Ibn al-Athir, i, p. 674; Ibn Jubair, p. 324.

11. *Annales Januenses*, i, pp. 136–7.

12. William of Tyre, p. 1062.

13. William of Tyre, pp. 1077–9; H. E. Mayer, 'Kaiserrecht und Heiliges Land', *Aus Reichsgeschichte und Nordischer Geschichte*, p. 202.

14. See William of Tyre, pp. 1027–9; *Gesta regis Henrici secundi*, i, p. 116; also Ernoul, p. 33.

15. *Tab. ord. Theut.*, nos. 10–14, 16–17; *Cart. gen. Hosp.*, no. 625.

16. Ernoul, pp. 82–7; 'Eracles', ii, pp. 57–62.

17. See Ernoul, pp. 114, 131, 178; 'Eracles', ii, pp. 26, 29, 50–52.

18. William of Tyre, p. 1028.

19. William of Tyre, pp. 1068–9; Ibn Jubair, p. 316. The references in *Tab. ord. Theut.* (nos. 14, 17) probably refer to Chastiau-dou-rei and so it seems that Joscelin did not acquire Chastel Neuf at this time.

20. William of Tyre, pp. 1049, 1062–3, 1069–70; Ernoul, pp. 48, 56–60. The account by Ernoul (p. 48) suggests that the affair with Baldwin had begun even before Sibylla married William Longsword. Her feelings may have changed on seeing Baldwin after his imprisonment: to encourage him to pay the ransom Saladin had two of his teeth drawn.

21. William of Tyre, p. 1062; *Gesta regis Henrici secundi*, i, pp. 343, 359.

22. Ernoul, pp. 60, 135; 'Eracles', i, p. 1117; ii, p. 30; William of Tyre, pp. 1116–17, 1122–3, 1127.

23. William of Tyre, pp. 1116–17.

24. This may be what was behind the many later reports that the baronage were only willing to accept Sibylla if she divorced Guy. *Gesta regis Henrici secundi*, i, p. 358; Robert of Clari, p. 35; *Récits d'un ménestrel de Rheims*, pp. 14–15.

25. There are chronological difficulties here. William of Tyre (p. 1128) merely reported that it was thought at this time that Raymond should govern the land. It was his continuators who gave details of the arrangements made and their accounts suggest that the promise of the regency was made a few months later.

26. William of Tyre, pp. 1122–3, 1127–8, 1133–4; 'Eracles', ii, pp. 1–3, 8; 'Gestes des Chiprois', p. 658; Mayer, 'Kaiserrecht', pp. 203–6.

27. Ernoul, pp. 115–19; 'Eracles', ii, pp. 6–8. See Arnold of Lübeck, p. 164. The writer of 'Eracles' (ii, p. 4) reported a very improbable scene in which the dying Baldwin IV made his liegemen promise to consider Raymond for the throne in the event of his nephew's death: improbable because this would seem to have granted elective rights to the High Court; and see in this regard Arnold of Lübeck, p. 165. On the other hand Sicard of Cremona (col. 603) believed that baronial assent was necessary before Guy could be crowned.

28. 'Eracles', ii, pp. 5–6, 7.

29. Ernoul, p. 117; 'Eracles', ii, p. 7.

30. Maria was to live on until after 1207 and it would be interesting to know whether she had any influence over her son, John of Beirut. See *Thesaurus nov. anecdot.*, i, col. 807.

31. William of Tyre, p. 889.

32. Ernoul, pp. 129–34; 'Eracles', ii, pp. 25–9; Arnold of Lübeck, pp. 164–5. See Mayer, 'Das Pontifikale', pp. 157–8, 161–2. The fact

that the coronation took place on a Friday caused comment. 'Eracles', ii, p. 29.

33. That it caused a great stir is clear from the accounts in *Gesta regis Henrici secundi*, i, pp. 358–9; Roger of Wendover, ii, pp. 420–21; Robert of Clari, p. 35; *Récits d'un ménestrel de Rheims*, pp. 15–17.

34. See for example William of Tyre, pp. 1116–17, 1134.

35. Agnes died in 1185 and presumably Toron passed to Joscelin although there is no evidence that he was granted it until October 1186. *Tab. ord. Theut.*, no. 21.

36. See *Tab. ord. Theut.*, nos. 17, 21.

37. John of Jaffa (p. 422) gave the knightage of Galilee as 100 knights, but the author of the *Annales Januenses* (i, p. 136) rated it at 80.

38. See above, p. 9.

39. One rather inaccurate account placed him among Sibylla's opponents. *Récits d'un ménestrel de Rheims*, p. 14.

40. These calculations are based on the admittedly incomplete list given by John of Jaffa (pp. 422–6) which has been dated to this period. See Smail, *Crusading Warfare*, pp. 89–90.

41. Ernoul, pp. 135–9; 'Eracles', ii, pp. 30–4. Raymond's close relations with the Muslims and Saladin's exploitation of his ambitions were well known to the Christians. See Röhricht, *Geschichte*, p. 420 note 3. See *Tab. ord. Theut.*, no. 21, in which Joscelin of Courtenay was confirmed in his possession of Toron, although it is clear that there was to be a meeting of the High Court to decide Humphrey of Toron's rights. See also *Tab. ord. Theut.*, no. 23.

42. Ernoul, pp. 141–53; 'Eracles', ii, pp. 34–45. See 'Imad ad-Din in Abu-Shamah, iv, pp. 257–8.

43. Ernoul, pp. 130, 137, 142; 'Eracles', ii, pp. 32, 35–6. See Arnold of Lübeck, p. 166.

44. Ibn al-Athir (i, p. 675) reported that a reckoning was demanded of what had been collected from the *amwal*.

45. Mayer, 'The Commune of Tyre', *passim*.

46. See Baldwin, *Raymond III*, pp. 125, 129.

47. Ernoul, pp. 179–83; 'Eracles', ii, pp. 74–8.

48. *Annales Januenses*, i, p. 145. See Mayer, 'The Commune of Tyre', p. 449, and also *Itinerarium peregrinorum et gesta regis Ricardi*, ed. H. E. Mayer, p. 305.

49. Ambroise, col. 11; *Itinerarium peregrinorum et gesta regis Ricardi*, ed. W. Stubbs, p. 150. Cf. Mayer, 'Kaiserrecht', pp. 196–8; H. Fichtenau, 'Akkon, Zypern und das Lösegeld für Richard Löwenherz', *Archiv für österreichische Geschichte*, cxxv (1966), pp. 11–25 *passim*.

50. See Mayer, 'The Commune of Tyre', pp. 452–3.

51. *Cart. gen. Hosp.*, no. 858; Mayer, 'The Commune of Tyre', pp. 454–6. In 1189 Sibylla referred to herself in a letter as 'once queen'. *Scriptores rerum Germanicarum*, ed. M. Freher, i, p. 410.

52. Ambroise, cols. 72–3.

53. Ernoul, pp. 256–7; 'Eracles', ii, p. 124.

54. 'Eracles', ii, p. 125.

55. Ernoul, p. 257; 'Eracles', ii, p. 124.

56. Robert of Clari, pp. 36–7, who added that Conrad argued that there was a shortage of corn in the city and he could not feed Guy and Sibylla and their followers.

57. *Itinerarium peregrinorum*, ed. Mayer, p. 305. See *Annales Januenses*, i, p. 145; Baha' ad-Din, p. 144.

58. Robert of Clari, p. 36; *Annales Januenses*, i, p. 145; Ralph of Diceto, ii, p. 70; *Gesta regis Henrici secundi*, ii, p. 93; 'Eracles', ii, pp. 125, 128; *Itinerarium peregrinorum*, ed. Mayer, p. 306; Haymarus Monachus, p. 76; *Documenti delle città toscane*, nos. 31–2 (see also nos. 23–5, 27–8); *Cart. gen. Hosp.*, no. 858.

59. *Itinerarium peregrinorum*, ed. Mayer, p. 312; Arnold of Lübeck, p. 177.

60. *Itinerarium peregrinorum*, ed. Mayer, p. 321; 'Liber iurium', nos. 374–5.

61. 'Eracles', ii, p. 151; Ernoul, p. 267. See Runciman, *Crusades*, iii, p. 30 note 2.

62. Ernoul, p. 267; 'Eracles', ii, p. 152.

63. 'Eracles', ii, p. 151; *Itinerarium peregrinorum*, ed. Mayer, pp. 352–4 – and see pp. 322, 335.

64. Innocent III, 'Opera Omnia', ccxvi, col. 981. See 'Eracles', ii, p. 154.

65. 'Eracles', ii, pp. 151–2. Isabella had been betrothed at 8 and married at 11.

66. Innocent III, 'Opera Omnia', ccxvi, cols. 908–1; 'Eracles', ii, pp. 151–6; *Itinerarium peregrinorum*, ed. Mayer, pp. 352–5; Ernoul, pp. 267–8 (in which it was stated that Humphrey was bribed to abandon the case); 'De excidio regni et regibus Jerusalem', p. 166.

67. Innocent III, 'Opera Omnia', ccxvi, cols. 978, 980–1; 'Gesta Innocentii PP. III', col. civ; *Corpus iuris canonici*, ed. E. Friedberg, ii, cols. 726–7. On Conrad's earlier wives, see Runciman, *Crusades*, iii, p. 32 note 1.

68. 'Eracles', ii, p. 154. See *Tab. ord. Theut.*, no. 21.

69. See the witness lists to *Documenti delle città toscane*, no. 33; 'Liber iurium,' no. 401.

70. 'De excidio regni', pp. 166–7. This source also mentions Louis of Thuringia who had gone home. See also *Gesta regis Henrici secundi*, ii, pp. 170, 171. Henry of Champagne, who had arrived earlier than Richard, seems to have agreed to Isabella's marriage to Conrad. Innocent III, 'Opera Omnia', ccxvi, col. 980.

71. *Gesta regis Henrici secundi*, ii, pp. 170–1; *The Crusade and Death of*

Richard I, p. 28. For the exercise of the rights of a crusader, see *Documenti delle città toscane*, no. 35.

72. *Gesta regis Henrici secundi*, ii, pp. 183–4; *Itinerarium peregrinorum*, ed. Stubbs, pp. 235–6 (in which Conrad's lands were called a *comitatus*); Ambroise, col. 135 (dated before the fall of Acre); Sicard of Cremona, cols. 614–15 (in which Conrad was also given the inheritance of half of the County of Jaffa and Ascalon); *The Crusade and Death of Richard*, p. 34.

73. *Gesta regis Henrici secundi*, ii, pp. 173–4; Ambroise, cols. 144–5, 218, 232–3; *Itinerarium peregrinorum*, ed. Stubbs, pp. 336–7; Baha' ad-Din, pp. 304, 317–18, 329–30, 332–3; 'Eracles', ii, pp. 198–9; Ernoul, p. 293. For French intransigence, see also Runciman, *Crusades*, iii, pp. 52–74 *passim*. Saladin was later to return to Reynald half of Sidon and to give Balian Caymont. 'Eracles', ii, pp. 198–9.

74. Ambroise, cols. 218–21; *Itinerarium peregrinorum*, ed. Stubbs, pp. 321–24.

75. Ambroise, cols. 229–34; *Itinerarium peregrinorum*, ed. Stubbs, pp. 334–8. See Sicard of Cremona, col. 616.

76. The sources blame variously Richard, Humphrey of Toron, Guy of Lusignan and Muslims for his death. After the assassination the French made an abortive attempt to gain control of Tyre. Ambroise, cols. 238–9; *Itinerarium peregrinorum*, ed. Stubbs, p. 342.

77. The writer of 'Eracles' (ii, p. 193) reported that he was reluctant because Isabella was pregnant. It is likely that Maria of Montferrat had already been born, but see also Abu-Shamah, v, p. 53.

78. It is possible that the story of the disinheritance of Conrad's heirs belongs to the period when there was a growing fear of Hohenstaufen claims. Ernoul, pp. 290–1; 'Eracles', ii, pp. 193–5. Richard's initiative was also reported in *Annales Januenses*, i, p. 147, and Abu-Shamah, v, p. 52. A variation seems to appear in the narrative of Alberic of Trois Fontaines (p. 869) in which the initiative belonged to Philip Augustus.

79. Ambroise, cols, 239–43; *Itinerarium peregrinorum*, ed. Stubbs, pp. 342–3, 346–50. The Church later considered this marriage to be invalid. Innocent III, 'Opera Omnia', ccxvi, cols. 978, 980–1. It might be added that Balian of Nablus was now prepared to negotiate with Saladin for Richard. See 'Eracles', ii, p. 199; Baha' ad-Din, p. 385; Abu-Shamah, v, pp. 77–8.

CHAPTER 6   A SCHOOL OF FEUDAL JURISTS

1. *Reg. Hier.*, nos. 373, 690, 698, 701, 810; 'Eracles', ii, p. 209; Philip of Novara, 'Livre', pp. 545–6, 570.

2. Philip of Novara, 'Livre', pp. 545–6, 570; 'Eracles', ii, p. 399;

'Gestes des Chiprois', p. 724. See Philip of Novara, 'Livre', pp. 515, 525; John of Jaffa, p. 384; also *Reg. Hier.*, nos. 1049, 1054–5, 1071, 1092.

3. Philip of Novara, 'Livre', pp. 515, 525, 570; John of Jaffa, p. 384; 'Eracles', ii, p. 387; 'Gestes des Chiprois', p. 706; 'Les lignages', p. 465; *Reg. Hier.*, nos. 942, 1037, 1054–5.

4. Philip of Novara, 'Livre', p. 525; 'Gestes des Chiprois', pp. 672, 676, 685, 688, 694; 'Eracles', ii, pp. 368, 375 ff.; *Reg. Hier.*, nos. 929, 938, 1017. See Richard, *Le royaume latin*, p. 160; and also Honorius III, *Reg.*, nos. 5108, 6272; Gregory IX, *Reg.*, no. 1084.

5. Philip of Novara, 'Livre', p. 570.

6. Philip of Novara, 'Livre', p. 515; John of Jaffa, p. 384. See the Arnaldus Forzon of *Reg. Hier.*, no. 1049.

7. Philip of Novara, 'Livre', p. 515; John of Jaffa, p. 384; 'Les lignages', p. 464; *Reg. Hier.*, nos. 1037, 1049, 1156.

8. Philip of Novara, 'Livre', p. 515; John of Jaffa, p. 384; *Reg. Hier.*, nos. 1037, 1049.

9. Philip of Novara, 'Livre', p. 515; John of Jaffa, p. 384; *Reg. Hier.*, nos. 929, 1078.

10. Philip of Novara, 'Livre', p. 559.

11. Philip of Novara, 'Livre', p. 570; see also pp. 522–3, 525, 544, 559–60; John of Jaffa, p. 430.

12. Philip of Novara, 'Livre', p. 525.

13. Philip of Novara, 'Livre', loc. cit.

14. Philip of Novara, 'Livre', pp. 515–16; John of Jaffa, pp. 383–4.

15. Philip of Novara, 'Livre', pp. 525, 539, 544, 559–60, 570; John of Jaffa, pp. 103, 327.

16. Philip of Novara, 'Livre', pp. 525, 539–40, 544, 559–60, 570.

17. Geoffrey Le Tor, pp. 435–6. See Du Cange, *Les familles*, pp. 600–1; and above, p. 17. For proof that this was the Geoffrey Le Tor who wrote the law-book I would refer the reader to the work at present being prepared by one of my pupils, Mr Peter Edbury.

18. Philip of Novara, 'Livre', p. 525; 'Gestes des Chiprois', p. 731; *Reg. Hier.*, nos. 1110b, 1120.

19. Philip of Novara, 'Livre', p. 515; John of Jaffa, p. 384; *Reg. Hier.*, nos. 1036, 1038. Perhaps he was able to plead in Nicosia because he was not a subject of Cyprus. His political leanings are not known, but it is worth remembering that one of his descendants supported an attempted *coup d'état* in 1242 in Acre in favour of Richard Filangieri. 'Gestes des Chiprois', p. 728.

20. See *Reg. Hier.*, nos. 710, 716, 1036, 1038.

21. Philip of Novara, 'Livre', p. 523. See also 'Abrégé des Assises des Bourgeois', p. 339.

22. Philip of Novara, 'Livre', p. 525; John of Jaffa, p. 220; 'Abrégé des Assises des Bourgeois', p. 339; 'Documents relatifs à la successibilité', p. 401. *Reg. Hier.*, nos. 974–5, 1027, 1063, 1073, 1181.

23. Ernoul, p. 149; and see pp. 491 ff.

24. See Philip of Novara, 'Livre', p. 570.

25. 'Gestes des Chiprois', p. 705; also 'Abrégé des Assises des Bourgeois', pp. 246–8, 326–39. See below, pp. 133 ff.

26. 'Gestes des Chiprois', pp. 708–9, 711–12, 719. See Philip of Novara, 'Livre', p. 544.

27. See John of Jaffa, p. 220; Philip of Novara, 'Livre', p. 540; 'Abrégé des Assises des Bourgeois', p. 339.

28. John of Jaffa, p. 325; Philip of Novara, 'Livre', pp. 517, 528; 'Gestes des Chiprois', pp. 711–12.

29. See above, p. 241 note 118.

30. 'Documents et mémoires de Chypre', iii, pp. 647–8; see also pp. 648–9, and Odo of Châteauroux, 'Letter', ed. L. d'Achéry, *Spicilegium*, iii, pp. 626, 628; Innocent IV, *Reg.*, no. 6465.

31. John of Joinville, pp. 86–8, 282–4; and see p. 232.

32. Grandclaude, *Etude critique*, p. 88. For his death, see 'Gestes des Chiprois', p. 766.

33. Grandclaude, op. cit., pp. 143–8. Grandclaude ('Classement sommaire', pp. 444–5) has noted a number of interpolations, mostly taken from the work of Philip of Novara and associated with one group of manuscripts, for which he has postulated a common fourteenth-century source. But some of these interpolations were obviously inserted by John himself, which suggests that the question is complicated. Mr Peter Edbury is at present examining this.

34. For his life, see J. L. La Monte, intr. to translation of Philip of Novara, *The Wars of Frederick II against the Ibelins in Syria and Cyprus*, pp. 7–17.

35. He was able to speak before the High Court in 1243, which probably means that he already had a fief in Palestine; soon afterwards he was given a money-fief in Acre. 'Gestes des Chiprois', pp. 731–2. See also *Recherches géographiques*, p. 44.

36. 'Documents relatifs à la successibilité', pp. 404, 406; 'Abrégé des Assises des Bourgeois', pp. 318, 337, 341. See also Philip of Novara, 'Livre', p. 540.

37. La Monte, op. cit., pp. 16–17; C. Kohler, intr. to Philippe de Novare, *Mémoires*, pp. v–xiv.

38. Grandclaude, ('Classement sommaire', pp. 426–31) suggested that the third redaction was never completed. See Grandclaude, *Étude critique*, pp. 80–1 (although his dates are in error because of his lack of knowledge of the regnal dates of Henry I and the acquisition of the County of Jaffa by John); and also Philip of Novara, 'Livre', pp. 475–

6; Philip of Novara, *Les Quatre Ages de l'Homme*, p. 123. The 'Livre', as it comes down to us, also contains later interpolations. See especially Philip of Novara, 'Livre', pp. 530–1.

39. Grandclaude, *Étude critique*, pp. 130–5.

40. See 'Abrégé des Assises des Bourgeois', pp. 248, 339.

41. See W. H. Rüdt de Collenberg, *The Rupenides, Hethumides and Lusignans*, Table IIIa (H 3). He was referred to as Count of Jaffa and Lord of Ramle in 'Annales de Terre Sainte' (p. 456), but against this should be set 'Les lignages' (p. 452) in which there is reference only to a Guiotin as John's son. Guiotin of course may have been a younger son who inherited the titular rights on James's death.

42. 'Doc. rel. au service militaire', pp. 430–4; James of Ibelin, p. 453 note 1; 'Annales de Terre Sainte', p. 456; Grandclaude, *Étude critique*, pp. 148–9. See *Reg. Hier.*, nos. 1250, 1368, and below, p. 225.

43. Philip of Novara, 'Livre', pp. 515, 544; John of Jaffa, pp. 383–4.

44. Philip of Novara, 'Livre', p. 525.

45. John of Jaffa, pp. 103, 112–13, 220, 383. See above, p. 283 note 33.

46. William of Tyre, pp. 705–6.

47. 'Eracles', ii, pp. 231, 463.

48. Philip of Novara, 'Livre', pp. 559–60.

49. 'Abrégé des Assises des Bourgeois', pp. 339–40.

50. Philip of Novara, 'Livre', pp. 539–40.

51. Philip of Novara, 'Livre', pp. 563–7; and see also p. 570.

52. John, the 'Old Lord' of Beirut entered the Templars on his deathbed and Julian of Sidon died a brother of St Trinity after being a Templar for a time, but I can only think of one high churchman in the thirteenth century – Simon of Maugustel, Archbishop of Tyre – who was related to a Palestinian feudal family.

53. *Cart. du St-Sépulcre*, no. 36.

54. *Cart. gen. Hosp.*, nos. 665, 1336; Honorius III, *Reg.*, no. 6272; Innocent IV, *Reg.*, no. 7397; Alexander IV, *Reg.*, no. 316; Urban IV, *Reg.*, nos. 1183, 2429, 2431; Pope Nicholas III, *Registre*, nos. 19, 54.

55. *Cart. gen. Hosp.*, no. 100.

56. James of Vitry, *Lettres*, p. 110.

57. Innocent IV, *Reg.*, no. 7116; 'Documents et mémoires de Chypre', iii, p. 667; *Cart. gen. Hosp.*, no. 2280. And this in spite of the famous prohibition of Pope Honorius III. *Analecta novissima*, i, pp. 570–3.

58. Matthew Paris, *Chron. maiora*, iii, pp. 396–9.

59. 'Guillaume de Tyr étudiant', ed. R. B. C. Huygens, *Latomus*, xxi (1962), pp. 822–4; Innocent III, 'Opera Omnia', ccxvi, col. 697; *Analecta novissima*, i, pp. 570–3; 'Documents et mémoires de Chypre', iii, p. 623; Innocent IV, *Reg.*, nos. 509, 5101, 8059. But cf. the exiled

chapter of Nazareth in 1252: it had no school and one member was illiterate. Innocent IV, *Reg.*, no. 5538.

60. *Cart. gen. Hosp.*, no. 1193 (p. 39).

61. Philip of Novara, 'Livre', p. 565; Philip of Novara, *Les Quatre Ages*, pp. 12–13. See James of Vitry ('Historia', p. 1088) on the employment by the lords of chaplains. There is some evidence for royal libraries. King Amalric's was used by William of Tyre. Mayer, 'Das Pontifikale', p. 145.

62. Philip of Novara, 'Livre', p. 570.

63. See Philip of Novara, 'Livre', p. 492; John of Jaffa, p. 103.

64. John of Jaffa, pp. 71–3; Philip of Novara, 'Livre', pp. 481, 512.

65. See *Cart. gen. Hosp.*, no. 1032; John of Jaffa, p. 419; also *Tab. ord. Theut.*, nos. 78, 85.

66. John of Jaffa, pp. 405–6: although these pages may be a four-teenth-century interpolation. See Grandclaude, 'Classement sommaire', p. 445.

67. *Tab. ord. Theut.*, no. 16.

68. *Cart. gen. Hosp.*, no. 480; John of Jaffa, p. 303. See also *Cart. gen. Hosp.*, no. 2353.

69. *Tab. ord. Theut.*, nos. 27, 36, 53 (p. 44); *Cart. gen. Hosp.*, no. 1526. See *Documenti delle città toscane*, no. 37; *Hist. dipl. Fred. secundi*, iii, pp. 123–5.

70. *Cart. gen. Hosp.*, nos. 468, 1032, 1996, 3213, 3323, 3326; 'Chartes de Josaphat; ed. Kohler, nos. 2–3; *Hist. dipl. Fred. secundi*, iii, pp. 117–21; *Chartes de Josaphat*, ed. Delaborde, no. 43; *Tab. ord. Theut.*, nos. 41, 53, 56; *Reg. Hier.*, no. 865.

71. *Cart. gen. Hosp.*, no. 2693.

72. *Tab. ord. Theut.*, no. 37. See 'Chartes du Mont-Thabor', no. 4.

73. John of Jaffa, p. 27; and see pp. 31–3.

74. See especially John of Jaffa, pp. 46, 53–4: he advised pleaders to speak briefly.

75. John of Jaffa, pp. 143 ff. – and see p. 298; Philip of Novara, 'Livre', p. 540.

76. See John of Jaffa, pp. 113–14.

77. See John of Jaffa, pp. 115 ff.

78. For instance, see John of Jaffa, pp. 56–63.

79. John of Jaffa, pp. 73, 226, 252, 256, 408; Philip of Novara, 'Livre', p. 529. Dealt with at some length was the situation in which a president failed to attend a meeting that had been arranged beforehand: so long as a plaintiff presented himself before two liegemen, these could have it legally recorded at a future sitting of the court that he had met his obligations and so would not lose his case by default. John of Jaffa, pp. 89–93, 253, 255–7.

80. John of Jaffa, pp. 23, 32–3, 255–7; James of Ibelin, p. 453. See below, pp. 196–7.
81. See below, pp. 142 ff.
82. John of Jaffa, pp. 69, 112–13, 303 note *a*; Philip of Novara, 'Livre', pp. 492, 529; 'Abrégé des Assises des Bourgeois', pp. 238 note *a*, 246–8. For an example, see *Cart. gen. Hosp.*, no. 1526.
83. John of Jaffa, pp. 46–7.
84. John of Jaffa, pp. 34–5.
85. See Philip of Novara, 'Livre', p. 537 and note *b*.
86. John of Jaffa, p. 124; 'Livre au roi', pp. 622–3.
87. John of Jaffa, pp. 33–45; Beugnot, intr. to *RHC Lois*, i, p. xliii.
88. See John of Jaffa, pp. 33–5, 53; Philip of Novara, 'Livre', pp. 564–7.
89. See John of Jaffa, p. 53; Philip of Novara, 'Livre', pp. 482–3.
90. John of Jaffa, pp. 36, 44–5.
91. John of Jaffa, pp. 33, 112, 124–5, 147; Philip of Novara, 'Livre', pp. 482–3; 'Abrégé des Assises des Bourgeois', p. 247.
92. Philip of Novara, 'Livre', p. 569; and see pp. 565–6.
93. John of Jaffa, pp. 25–6, 429; Philip of Novara, 'Livre', pp. 521–2. Philip had known some of those who had guard of the *Letres*.
94. 'Abrégé des Assises des Bourgeois', pp. 246–50. For the scribe of the *Cours des Bourgeois*, see above, p. 87.
95. Philip of Novara, 'Livre', p. 536.
96. Philip of Novara, 'Livre', p. 521; John of Jaffa, p. 429. See also Philip of Novara, 'Livre', p. 523.
97. Alexander IV, *Reg.*, no. 1936.
98. Philip of Novara, 'Livre', p. 536; and see pp. 566, 570, the last of which appears to be a reference to John of Jaffa.
99. Philip of Novara, 'Livre', pp. 491, 525; John of Jaffa, p. 27. There are many references to past pleaders: for instance see John of Jaffa, p. 285.
100. Philip of Novara, 'Livre', p. 523; and pp. 523–4, where apparently the court of Jerusalem had precedence over that of Cyprus. See also John of Jaffa, p. 362.
101. Philip of Novara, 'Livre', p. 544.
102. And Kings Baldwin III, Amalric and Baldwin IV had been interested in history. William of Tyre, pp. 705–6, 884–5, 1005.
103. See 'Gestes des Chiprois', pp. 672, 793.
104. See John of Jaffa, pp. 107–9; also *Tab. ord. Theut.*, no. 53 (p. 44).
105. 'Eracles', ii, pp. 172–3, 175–6; Ernoul, pp. 274–6.
106. 'Eracles', ii, pp. 329, 343–4, 348–9, 366; Ernoul, p. 449; 'La fondation d'une église', *passim*; Ibn al-Furat, ii, pp. 13, 179.
107. John of Jaffa, pp. 29, 216; 'Eracles', ii, p. 475. That this was not only a thirteenth-century idea can be demonstrated from the word-

ing of a confirmation made by Baldwin I in 1115 'by reason of the royal power given me by God'. *Chartes des Josaphat*, ed. Delaborde, no. 5. But cf. Mayer, 'Kaiserrecht', *passim*. For Antioch, see Innocent III, 'Opera Omnia', ccxvi, col. 793.

108. 'Eracles', i, p. 45; although (pp. 367, 376–7) he followed William in making Godfrey's election as ruler a matter for the barons.

109. 'Eracles', ii, p. 389; John of Jaffa, p. 21.

110. 'Eracles', ii, p. 389; 'Les lignages', p. 441; John of Jaffa, p. 22.

111. Richard, 'Pairie', p. 71.

112. William of Tyre, p. 472.

113. See J. W. Gough, *The social contract*, pp. 3, 8–48.

114. Philip of Novara, 'Livre', p. 541.

115. See John of Jaffa, p. 31.

116. John of Jaffa, p. 22.

117. 'Eracles', ii, p. 389.

118. 'Livre des Assises des Bourgeois', pp. 350–1; John of Jaffa, p. 157; and see Philip of Novara, 'Livre', p. 542.

119. John of Jaffa, p. 23.

120. John of Jaffa, pp. 24–5. See Philip of Novara, 'Livre', p. 522; 'Documents relatifs à la successibilité', p. 410.

121. 'Documents relatifs à la successibilité', pp. 404, 406, 408, 409, 411, 413, 414; 'Doc. rel. au service militaire', p. 431.

122. 'Eracles', ii, p. 389.

123. John of Jaffa, pp. 310–12; James of Ibelin, pp. 453–4; 'Documents relatifs à la successibilité', p. 397. There is an interesting variant in the 'Livre des Assises des Bourgeois' (p. 62) in which the king swore to maintain the gifts of other kings, good usages and customs, to give right to all and to maintain the liegemen against all persons by the usage of the court and specifically by means of the judgements of the liegemen themselves. Homage seems always to have been received *before* the coronation. See 'Eracles', ii, pp. 154, 311; 'Documents relatifs à la successibilité', p. 419.

124. 'Documents relatifs à la successibilité', pp. 418–19.

125. Albert of Aix, p. 532. See Mayer, 'Das Pontifikale', p. 197. There was no reference to this oath in a description of the acceptance of Isabella as rightful heiress in 1191 ('Eracles', ii, p. 154), but the 'Livre au roi' (p. 608) may reflect it.

126. See Mayer, 'Das Pontifikale', *passim*; and especially pp. 196–9 for coronations in the thirteenth century.

127. *Cart. du St-Sépulcre*, no. 154; Mayer, 'Das Pontifikale', p. 194; 'Un rituel et un bréviaire du Saint-Sépulcre de Jérusalem (XIIe–XIIIe siècle),' ed. C. Kohler, *ROL*, viii (1900/1901) p. 443; John of Jaffa, pp. 29–30.

128. Mayer, 'Das Pontifikale', p. 197 note 250.

129. But see the description of the royal oath in the anonymous 'Tractatus de locis' (p. 157) of *c.* 1190.

130. John of Jaffa, pp. 27, 41, 87–8, 322, 389.

131. John of Jaffa, pp. 23, 43, 76, 240, 322, 330–1, 389–92; 'Livre des Assises des Bourgeois', pp. 61–2. See *Tab. ord. Theut.*, nos. 21, 41; *Hist. dipl. Fred. secundi*, iii, pp. 123–5.

132. John of Jaffa, p. 315; and see pp. 137, 250–1, 315, 321, 323–30, 332–5, 385–6; Philip of Novara, 'Livre', pp. 517–18, 527–8; 'Livre au roi', pp. 623–4; 'Eracles', ii, p. 390.

133. Grandclaude, *Étude critique*, pp. 120–3. One cannot accept the suggestion of M. Grandclaude ('Caractère du "Livre au roi",' *RHDFE*, sér. 4, v (1926) pp. 308–14) that it is a collection of judgements.

134. 'Livre au roi', pp. 607–8.

135. 'Livre au roi', p. 624.

136. 'Livre au roi', pp. 616–17. See below, pp. 146–7.

137. 'Livre au roi', pp. 609, 634.

138. 'Livre au roi', p. 623; and see p. 624.

139. See below, pp. 190–1, 193.

140. John of Jaffa, pp. 103, 315; and see pp. 23, 400–1; 'Livre au roi', p. 625; Geoffrey Le Tor, p. 445; Philip of Novara 'Livre', pp. 543–5.

CHAPTER 7   THE ASSISE SUR LA LIGECE

1. See John of Jaffa, pp. 397, 421–7; Philip of Novara, 'Livre', p. 553; also Smail, *Crusading Warfare*, pp. 92–3. For bans of another kind in the royal domain, see 'Bans et ordonnances', p. 357; 'Documents et mémoires de Chypre', iii, pp. 671–3. For the royal *banier*, see above, p. 87. It is not known whether lords could issue *levées en masse* in their lordships. Philip of Montfort may have done so on one occasion ('Gestes des Chyprois', p. 757), but his lordship, Tyre, was technically royal domain.

2. 'Livre au roi', pp. 616–17. See also the references to royal majesty and rights in *Cart. gen. Hosp.*, no. 84; *Cart. du St-Sépulcre*, nos. 53–4; *Cod. dipl. geros.*, i, p. 248.

3. 'Livre des Assises des Bourgeois', p. 82 (see 'Livre des Assises des Bourgeois', ed. Beugnot, p. 47). The same source (pp. 335–7) made reference to rights of treasure trove, but it may be that this was enjoyed only in the royal domain.

4. Richard, *Le royaume latin*, pp. 100–1; Mayer, 'Das Pontifikale', pp. 184–7.

5. Mayer, 'Das Pontifikale', pp. 173–80, 184.

6. The *assise* was attributed to Baldwin II, but there seems to be a good deal of sense in the views of Prawer ('Étude sur le droit', suite, pp. 38–42).

7. See John of Jaffa, pp. 158–62, 303–5, 307–10; also Prawer, 'Étude sur le droit', suite, p. 36.

8. 'Livre au roi', pp. 616–17.

9. Prawer, 'Étude sur le droit', *passim*.

10. Prawer, 'Étude sur le droit', p. 523 note 16. See 'Livre au roi', p. 616 note *c*.

11. William of Tyre, pp. 629–30.

12. Philip of Novara, 'Livre', pp. 490, 560.

13. See especially J. E. A. Jolliffe, *Angevin Kingship*, pp. 50–86.

14. See 'Livre des Assises des Bourgeois', p. 197.

15. John of Jaffa, pp. 158–62, 303–5, 307–10.

16. *Corpus iuris canonici*, ii, col. 54; 'Eracles', ii, pp. 203–5; *Cart. du St-Sépulcre*, no. 128 (p. 236). But see *Cart. gen. Hosp.*, no. 1432.

17. 'Les lignages', p. 454; *Reg. Hier.*, nos. 828, 933, 978. See nos. 829, 892.

18. 'Les lignages', p. 458.

19. Cahen, *La Syrie du Nord*, pp. 608–9.

20. Riley-Smith, *Knights of St John*, pp. 141–4.

21. 'Chartes du Mont-Thabor', nos. 13, 22; *Cart. gen. Hosp.*, nos. 3197–8; *Chartes de Josaphat*, ed. Delaborde, no. 44; 'Documents inédits concernant l'Orient latin et les croisades (XIIe–XIVe siècle)', ed. C. Kohler, *ROL*, vii (1899) nos. 7–8.

22. *Recherches géographiques*, pp. 31, 39; *Tab. ord. Theut.*, nos. 89, 99–100; 'Frag. cart. St-Lazare', no. 38; 'Chartes des Josaphat', ed. Kohler, no. 78; *Cart. gen. Hosp.*, nos. 2245, 2748, 2934, 3051 (p. 64). See Innocent IV, *Reg.*, no. 5538; James of Vitry, *Lettres*, p. 84; 'Eracles', ii, p. 455; 'Gestes des Chiprois', p. 766. For a twelfth-century parallel see William of Tyre, p. 486.

23. *Cart. gen. Hosp.*, no. 2482; *Urkunden Venedig*, no. 343 (p. 34); *Tab. ord. Theut.*, nos. 119, 121.

24. 'Eracles', ii, p. 390.

25. John of Jaffa, pp. 214–15.

26. Prawer, 'La noblesse', pp. 65–6.

27. John of Jaffa, pp. 369–92 (esp. pp. 389–90); Philip of Novara, 'Livre', pp. 508–17; James of Ibelin, pp. 456–7.

28. John of Jaffa, pp. 215, 320, 323; Philip of Novara, 'Livre', p. 527.

29. See especially John of Jaffa, pp. 333–4.

30. These seem to have been refusal of *esgart* on escheat or *esgart* of court, or failure to hold to the decision of a court by *esgart*, *conoissance* or *recort*, of failure to pay what was due on a money-fief, or to support

by holding a court a vassal deprived of his fief by another, or banishment.

31. John of Jaffa, pp. 323–9, 332–5, 387–8; Philip of Novara, 'Livre', pp. 517–18, 527–9. Although at one point John of Jaffa wrote that a lord should be formally summoned 'several times' in court before the withdrawal of service was justified, it seems that appeals were generally made three times; or six times for the payment of money-fiefs. John of Jaffa, pp. 326, 371, 377, 389–90; Philip of Novara, 'Livre', pp. 508, 510, 528. It has been rightly pointed out that in all cases known in which the *Assise* was raised the crown was involved. Prawer, 'La noblesse', p. 71.

32. Aimery was in Tyre in August 1198 and Ralph of Tiberias was with him. *Cart. gen. Hosp.*, no. 1032.

33. Of the versions of this incident, the most circumstantial gave the number of Germans as four. 'Eracles', ii, pp. 224, 228–9; Ernoul, pp. 310–11.

34. 'Eracles', ii, p. 216.

35. 'Eracles', ii, pp. 219–20; Ernoul, pp. 306–7.

36. 'Eracles', ii, pp. 222–3; Ernoul, pp. 309–10; Innocent III, *Reg.*, nos. 437–8, 487; Innocent III, 'Opera Omnia', ccxiv, cols. 475–8. Aimery's coronation oath appears to contain some concession to the Church. *Cart. du St-Sépulcre*, no. 154. It is not clear where the coronation took place. Mayer, 'Das Pontifikale', p. 193.

37. Philip of Novara, 'Livre', p. 569; John of Jaffa, pp. 429–30.

38. Ernoul, p. 59. See *Reg. Hier.*, nos. 518, 525.

39. Philip of Novara, 'Livre', p. 569; John of Jaffa, p. 430. For the office, see below, p. 291 note 48.

40. 'Les lignages', p. 443; Ernoul, p. 59. They must have been married before the end of 1175. *Reg. Hier.*, no. 530b.

41. The writer of Ernoul (p. 59) reported that he owed the constableship to Agnes. See also John of Jaffa, p. 430; Philip of Novara, 'Livre', p. 569; *Reg. Hier.*, nos. 601, 613–14, 617–19, 624–5.

42. See *Reg. Hier.*, nos. 653–5.

43. Runciman, *Crusades*, iii, p. 19.

44. See *Reg. Hier.*, nos. 683–4, 693, 696–8, 701–2.

45. The writer of 'Eracles' (ii, p. 208) reported that Aimery claimed that he had never had seizin of the fief, but he also wrote in error that Aimery had been given the county by Guy and Sibylla.

46. See especially J. Richard, 'L'abbaye cistercienne de Jubin et le prieuré Saint-Blaise de Nicosie', *Epeteris*, iii (1969–70) pp. 69–70.

47. 'Eracles', ii, pp. 194, 202–3, 208–9: the latter of these references dates the dispute inaccurately after Guy's death; Aimery is to be found in Cyprus by August 1194. Richard, 'L'abbaye cistercienne de Jubin', pp. 69–70. The author of 'Eracles' (ii, pp. 212–13) suggested that the

two men also quarrelled over the appointment of a new patriarch, but the election of Haymarus did not take place until the following year. For the Pisans, see *Documenti delle città toscane*, nos. 37, 40. For John of Ibelin's constableship, see La Monte, *Feudal Monarchy*, p. 253.

48. For the importance of the chamberlain and constable in court, see 'Livre des Assises des Bourgeois', pp. 335–6; John of Jaffa, pp. 400, 410, 414; 'Livre au roi', pp. 615–16.

49. He was still alive in August 1194. Richard, loc. cit.

50. G. F. Hill, *A History of Cyprus*, ii, pp. 44–66; E. C. Furber, 'The Kingdom of Cyprus 1191–1291', *A History of the Crusades*, ed.-in-chief, K. M. Setton, ii, pp. 604–5.

51. Henry may have promised to grant what was owed for Cyprus as the dowry of his eldest daughter. 'Eracles', ii, pp. 199, 208–9, 212–13, 219; Ernoul, pp. 293–4; 'Doc. rel. au service militaire', p. 428. See Innocent III, 'Opera Omnia', ccxv, col. 830; *Thesaurus nov. anecdot.*, i, cols. 806–7.

52. Philip of Novara, 'Livre', pp. 523, 544, 569–70; John of Jaffa, pp. 429–30.

53. John of Jaffa, p. 430. Philip of Novara ('Livre', pp. 522–3) wrote of a commission of ten; but a normal *inquisitio* of the king and two vassals, together with Ralph, sounds more likely.

54. See Grandclaude, *Étude critique*, pp. 44–50; Richard, *Le royaume latin*, p. 203.

55. The royal charter witnessed by Ralph in October 1198 (*Reg. Hier.*, no. 747) is a forgery. See Mayer, *Marseilles Levantehandel*, pp. 43 ff.

56. 'Eracles', ii, p. 230; and see p. 224; Ernoul, p. 311.

57. This is clear from the accounts of Philip of Novara ('Livre', p. 518) and John of Jaffa (pp. 327–8). The writer of the account in 'Eracles' (ii, p. 224) and Ernoul (p. 311) reported that Aimery had no proof of guilt.

58. *Reg. Hier.*, nos. 740; 'Les lignages', p. 455.

59. Ernoul, p. 170; 'Eracles', ii, p. 65.

60. *Reg. Hier.*, nos. 665–8.

61. Ralph of Diceto, ii, p. 80.

62. Innocent III, 'Opera Omnia', ccxvi, col. 980.

63. *Reg. Hier.*, nos. 717, 720–2, 722a, 724, 727, 735, 740, 740b, 743–4, 821, 853, 892, 898, 930, 933–4. For the duties of a seneschal, see John of Jaffa, pp. 30, 31, 407–9.

64. Prawer, 'Estates', pp. 4 ff.

65. Philip of Novara, 'Livre', pp. 518, 528–9; John of Jaffa, pp. 327–8. From October 1198 to August 1200 there survives no charter from Aimery witnessed by his vassals; but see *Reg. Hier.*, no. 761a which has survived only in an abstract – and one of my pupils has

shrewdly pointed out that the same conditions prevailed in the years *after* 1200! We may only be faced by the accidental loss of documents. The reason given for the perseverance of the knights – that Ralph had suffered on account of the stand he had made – is not clear to me; for surely Ralph would have been banished anyway.

66. 'Eracles', ii, pp. 230–1; Philip of Novara, 'Livre', p. 570.

67. 'Eracles', ii, pp. 231, 314–15; Philip of Novara, 'Livre', pp. 543–4, 570; John of Jaffa, p. 401. See Cahen, *La Syrie du Nord*, p. 609.

68. Geoffrey of Villehardouin, ii, p. 125.

69. *Reg. Hier.*, no. 821.

70. Philip of Novara, 'Livre', p. 525; *Reg. Hier.*, nos. 933–4.

71. It is, however, curious that the writers of 'Eracles' (ii, pp. 224, 230) and Ernoul (p. 311) did not refer to Ralph's resistance.

72. See John of Jaffa, p. 328.

73. 'Eracles', ii, pp. 357–60; Ernoul, pp. 451–2. See *Hist. dipl. Fred. secundi*, ii, pp. 708–10. Frederick may already had had relations with the Holy Land. See the curious letter, dated to 1224, to the people of Acre, addressed as 'universitas', asking them to treat the Genoese with favour. *Acta imperii inedita*, i, no. 263

74. E. Kantorowicz, *Frederick II*, p. 140; 'Eracles', ii, pp. 358–9.

75. T. C. Van Cleve, 'The Crusade of Frederick II', *A History of the Crusades*, ed.-in-chief, K. M. Setton, ii, pp. 440–2, 446–7.

76. See *Hist. dipl. Fred. secundi*, iii, pp. 32–4; also Van Cleve, 'The Crusade of Frederick II', p. 447 note 64.

77. See letter of the patriarch in Matthew Paris, *Chron. maiora*, iii, p. 179; also 'Eracles', ii, p. 366. But the writer of 'Breve chronicon de rebus siculis' (p. 898), who was present, reported that Frederick sailed in a fleet of 40 galleys. Cf. 'Gestes des Chiprois', p. 676.

78. 'Gestes des Chiprois', pp. 670, 679; 'Eracles', ii, pp. 360–1. The island was under papal protection. Honorius III, *Reg.*, nos. 1522, 1524; also no. 679, and below, note 80. For Philip's *bailliage*, see below, pp. 192–3.

79. 'Gestes des Chiprois', p. 672. For the interpretation of a corrupt sentence, see Hill, *History of Cyprus*, ii, p. 90 note 2. The text of this source gives the coming-of-age as twenty-five years, but this has rightly been corrected to fifteen. For the dates of attaining majority in Germany, see La Monte, *The Wars of Frederick II*, p. 64 note 1.

80. *Epistolae saeculi XIII*, i, no. 292. See also Honorius III, *Reg.*, nos. 5813, 5822, 5824–5, 5839.

81. 'Gestes des Chiprois', p. 672.

82. Alberic of Trois Fontaines, p. 933; 'Breve chron. de rebus siculis', p. 900. For the citadel of Beirut, see Willbrand of Oldenburg, pp. 166–7. A biography of John, which amounts to no more than a narrative of the main incidents in his life, was compiled by J. L. La

Monte, 'John d'Ibelin. The Old Lord of Beirut, 1177–1236', *Byzantion*, xii (1937) pp. 417–48.

83. Richard, *Le royaume latin*, pp. 240–41, esp. p. 241 note 2.

84. See below, pp. 213–14.

85. 'Gestes des Chiprois', p. 672.

86. 'Gestes des Chiprois', p. 676.

87. 'Eracles', ii, p. 366.

88. 'Eracles', ii, p. 367; 'Gestes des Chiprois', pp. 677, 679.

89. See 'Breve chron. de rebus siculis', p. 900.

90. 'Gestes des Chiprois', pp. 677–80. The writer of 'Eracles' (ii, p. 367) made Frederick demand an account of the *bailliage* of Jerusalem, not that of Cyprus.

91. 'Gestes des Chiprois', pp. 680–1; 'Eracles', ii, pp. 368–9; 'Breve chron. de rebus siculis', p. 900.

92. See the words of John of Beirut in 'Gestes des Chiprois', p. 679.

93. Philip of Novara ('Gestes des Chiprois', p. 681) wrongly believed that Frederick already knew of war in southern Italy before coming to an agreement in Cyprus.

94. 'Gestes des Chiprois', pp. 681–2. The revenues of Cyprus were to be sent to Frederick on the mainland. The author of 'Eracles' (ii, p. 369) reported that the emperor received the *bailliage* of Cyprus.

95. 'Gestes des Chiprois', p. 682.

96. He left the Cypriots in Jaffa when he went up to the Holy City. 'Eracles', ii, p. 374.

97. 'Gestes des Chiprois', pp. 682–4; letter from the patriarch in Matthew Paris, *Chron. maiora*, iii, pp. 179–80, 183–4. See Hill, *History of Cyprus*, ii, pp. 100–1.

98. *Hist. dipl. Fred. secundi*, ii, pp. 531–8, 671–2; 'Eracles', ii, pp. 359, 364; 'Gestes des Chiprois', p. 674; 'Annales de Terre Sainte', p. 438; 'Documents relatifs à la successibilité,' p. 399.

99. *Documenti delle città toscane*, no. 65 (see nos. 64, 66); *Annales Januenses*, iii, p. 56. For his policies in Sicily, see Kantorowicz, *Frederick II*, pp. 121–4.

100. Riley-Smith, *Knights of St John*, pp. 166–9.

101. 'Gestes des Chiprois', p. 679.

102. Kantorowicz, *Frederick II*, pp. 114–19; Richard, *Le royaume latin*, p. 237.

103. 'Eracles', ii, p. 364. It is worth asking whether the actions taken against the Italians, the Templars and John of Beirut were really *quo warranto* proceedings, stemming from the same motives as the Law of Privileges.

104. 'Documents relatifs a la successibilité', p. 399. The author of 'Eracles' (ii, p. 367) was clearly in error in reporting that Thomas of Acerra was *bailli* later in 1228.

105. 'Gestes des Chiprois', p. 682.

106. See *Reg. Hier.*, nos. 994–5, 1003–14, 1016.

107. See Riley-Smith, *Knights of St John*, pp. 141–3.

108. See Runciman, *Crusades*, iii, p. 187. Balian of Sidon was among those who took the oath on the emperor's behalf and he also went to Damascus to try to get the agreement of the Damascenes. *Hist. dipl. Fred. secundi*, iii, p. 106.

109. Mayer, 'Das Pontifikale', pp. 200–10. See the letter of Frederick in *Constitutiones et acta publica imperatorum et regum*, ii, p. 166; and 'Breve chron. de rebus siculis', p. 901. One wonders whether Frederick treated Jerusalem as his own possession by right of conquest. This seems to be suggested in a commentary on his treaty by the patriarch. *Hist. dipl. Fred. secundi*, iii, pp. 87, 108. It was later under the authority of the imperial *bailli* in Tyre. See *Reg. Hier.*, no. 1107. See also 'Eracles', ii, pp. 374, 384; Ernoul, p. 466. On the other hand Jerusalem followed the laws of the kingdom (Röhricht, 'Amalrich I', p. 493) and Frederick's attitude to Toron in 1229 (see below, pp. 171–2), which was also acquired by the treaty, does not suggest that he regarded it as his by right of conquest.

110. For other objections, see Riley-Smith, *Knights of St John*, pp. 166–7.

111. Letter from the patriarch in Matthew Paris, *Chron. maiora*, iii, pp. 181–3; 'Gestes des Chiprois', p. 683.

112. Philip of Novara, 'Livre', pp. 517, 528; John of Jaffa, p. 325.

113. For the estates of the Teutonic Knights, see W. Hubatsch, 'Montfort und die Bildung des Deutschordensstaates im Heiligen Lande', *Nachrichten der Akademie der Wissenschaften in Göttingen. Phil.-Hist. Klasse* (1966) pp. 182–6; K. Forstreuter, *Der Deutsche Orden am Mittelmeer*, pp. 35–49.

114. John of Jaffa, pp. 112–13, 325–6.

115. John of Jaffa, p. 112. See below, p. 172.

116. This may be confirmed in the patriarch's letter, in which a condition of peace between the emperor and his opponents was that 'ablatis ... bonis nostris restitutis, ita quod essent omnia in eo statu et libertate, qua erant die qua ingressus est civitatem', although this could be a reference to the looting by the imperial forces in late March. Matthew Paris, *Chron. maiora*, iii, p. 183.

117. John of Jaffa, p. 326.

118. *Hist. dipl. Fred. secundi*, iii, pp. 123–5.

119. Letter from the patriarch in Matthew Paris, *Chron. maiora*, iii, p. 182; *Hist. dipl. Fred. secundi*, iii, p. 120; *Acta imperii inedita*, i, no. 302.

120. 'Gestes des Chiprois', pp. 683–4; *Acta imperii inedita*, i, no. 303; 'Documents relatifs à la successibilité', p. 399.

121. Hill, *History of Cyprus*, ii, pp. 101–9. The force, according to Philip of Novara ('Gestes des Chiprois', p. 700) consisted of 600 knights, 100 mounted sergeants, 700 foot and 3,000 armed sailors; and according to the author of 'Eracles' (ii, pp. 385–6) of 300 knights and 200 crossbowmen and mounted sergeants.

122. 'Gestes des Chiprois', p. 695.

123. *Hist. dipl. Fred. secundi*, iii, p. 267.

124. John of Jaffa, p. 267. See above, p. 239 note 82.

125. 'Eracles', ii, p. 380; and see p. 386.

126. 'Gestes des Chiprois', pp. 700–1; 'Eracles', ii, pp. 385–8.

127. See 'Eracles', ii, p. 391.

128. 'Eracles', ii, p. 385. See Gregory IX, *Reg.*, no. 529.

129. 'Eracles', ii, p. 388; 'Gestes des Chiprois', p. 704.

130. 'Eracles', ii, pp. 388–9, 395; 'Gestes des Chiprois', p. 711. The speech of Balian of Sidon, quoted below, and the papal letters of the 1230s (see *Epistolae saeculi XIII*, i, nos. 656, 674, and below, pp. 203 ff.) make it clear that he was accepted. The account in 'Eracles' is ambiguous, probably deliberately.

131. 'Eracles', ii, pp. 389–90.

132. 'Eracles', ii, pp. 390–1.

133. They may have been in Ravenna in December. *Tab. ord. Theut.*, no. 76. But it is possible that they never went. See Hill, *History of Cyprus*, p. 110 note 4.

134. 'Gestes des Chiprois', pp. 701–2. In another version ('Eracles', ii, p. 392) he dwelt on the obligations of a king to help a vassal. But the king had no duty to aid a vassal recover a fief outside his kingdom. See 'Doc. rel. au service militaire', p. 431.

135. 'Gestes des Chiprois', pp. 702 ff; 'Eracles', ii, pp. 392 ff.

136. 'Eracles', ii, pp. 391–2. See Prawer, 'Estates', pp. 20–2.

137. For John of Beirut, see 'Gestes des Chiprois', pp. 707, 722, 724. For the structure of the commune, see Prawer, 'Estates', pp. 23–5; J. S. C. Riley-Smith, 'The Assise sur la ligece and the Commune of Acre', *Traditio*, xxvii (1971), p. 196 note 84.

138. Mayer, 'The Commune of Tyre', *passim*; La Monte, 'Communal Movement', pp. 122–4; Prawer, 'Estates', pp. 27–36. I do not find the arguments of Mayer ('Zwei Kommunen', *passim*) that there was an earlier commune in Acre convincing.

139. See Prawer, 'Estates', p. 23.

140. See particularly the statement of Philip of Novara that the imperial ban ran in Tyre. 'Gestes des Chiprois', p. 731. See also *Reg. Hier.*, nos. 1086, 1107; also below, pp. 213–14.

141. 'Acte de soumission des barons du royaume de Jérusalem à Frédéric II', ed. R. Röhricht, *AOL*, i (1881) pp. 402–3; *Urkunden Venedig*, no. 299 (p. 355).

142. La Monte, 'Communal Movement', pp. 124–30. See Mayer, 'The Commune of Tyre', p. 445.

143. *Cart. gen. Hosp.*, nos. 2015, 2033.

144. Prawer, 'Estates', pp. 14–27.

145. Riley-Smith, 'Assise sur la ligece', pp. 198–9.

146. 'Documents relatifs à la successibilité', p. 399, although John did refer to the attempt to appoint Philip of Maugustel in 1233. Balian of Sidon was entitled *bailli* in a document of 28 September 1231. *Cart. gen. Hosp.*, no. 1996. After that date and before October 1233 neither he nor Odo seem to have used the title. *Cart. gen. Hosp.*, nos. 2001–3, 2033; 'Documents et mémoires de Chypre', iii, p. 636. It has been suggested that the vassals would have felt that the emperor in appointing Richard Filangieri could not undo by letters what he had done in person in the High Court. Prawer, 'Estates', p. 19. But we will see (below, pp. 202–3) that this argument, presented by John of Caesarea when he resisted the appointment of Philip of Maugustel in 1233, was of doubtful legality.

147. 'Eracles', ii, p. 394.

148. 'Documents relatifs à la successibilité', p. 399. Cf. 'Gestes des Chiprois', p. 722.

149. 'Documents relatifs à la successibilité, p. 399.

150. See below, pp. 190–1, 193.

151. 'Eracles', ii, p. 395; 'Gestes des Chiprois', p. 711. The second source put the capture of the ships after the Battle of Casal Imbert, but this is unlikely.

152. 'Gestes des Chiprois', p. 722; 'Documents relatifs à la successibilité', p. 399.

153. *Epistolae saeculi XIII*, i, nos. 649–50.

154. *Epistolae saeculi XIII*, i, nos. 578, 593–4, 656–7, 673–5; 'Eracles', ii, pp. 406–7; and see also 'Acte de soumission', *passim*.

155. *Urkunden Venedig*, no. 299 (p. 355).

156. 'Eracles', ii, p. 390.

157. 'Eracles', ii, pp. 393–4. There are many examples of the narrower meaning of *homes*, but perhaps the best is in the description of how Hugh of Antioch-Lusignan required the regency 'as *homes* et à la *gent* de Acre'. 'Documents relatifs à la successibilité', p. 415. Cf. the description of the commune by the writer of 'Eracles' (ii, p. 406) as 'la communauté des *gens* do roiaume de Jerusalem'.

158. 'Eracles', ii, pp. 394–5; 'Gestes des Chiprois', pp. 704, 705–6, 707–8. See Richard of San Germano, p. 181. The commune may have received its formal structure at this time, but that it had been originally founded late in 1231 is clear from a statement by the writer of 'Eracles' (ii, p. 392) that the news of its establishment was sent to John of Beirut while he was still in Cyprus.

159. 'Eracles', ii, pp. 392, 393.

160. 'Eracles', ii, p. 391.

161. See Prawer, 'Estates', pp. 36–9; La Monte, 'Communal Movement', pp. 128–9.

162. There may be an indirect reference to these events in Philip of Novara, 'Livre', pp. 531–2.

CHAPTER 8   THE BAILLIAGE

1. William of Tyre, pp. 1007–10.

2. 'Livre au roi', p. 610; John of Jaffa in 'Documents relatifs à la successibilité' pp. 397–8.

3. 'Eracles', ii, p. 320.

4. See above, p. 167.

5. 'Livre au roi', p. 610; 'Documents relatifs à la successibilité', p. 398. See John of Jaffa, p. 267.

6. 'Documents relatifs à la successibilité', p. 398.

7. 'Eracles', ii, p. 305. See Ernoul, p. 407. An abstract of a letter from the Archbishop of Caesarea in 'Anon. cont. app. Roberti de Monte' (p. 342) contained the statement that John had been chosen by the Templars and Hospitallers. This is obviously corrupt, although it may reflect their influence.

8. 'Documents relatifs à la successibilité', p. 399.

9. John of Jaffa, p. 312.

10. William of Tyre, p. 1010.

11. 'Documents relatifs à la successibilité', p. 398; John of Jaffa, p. 305. See Geoffrey Le Tor, pp. 437–8, 439.

12. But this was not automatically the case with the relative of a minor regent. See below, p. 190.

13. Although he seems to have taken custody of Baldwin IV in 1174.

14. John of Jaffa, p. 312. See 'Eracles', ii, p. 6.

15. 'Livre au roi', p. 610. See 'Documents relatifs à la successibilité', pp. 397–8. In 1243 Alice repealed all Frederick II's gifts. This may have been an act of politics, but it may have applied only to those charters issued since Conrad came of age. 'Documents relatifs à la successibilité', p. 400.

16. 'Documents relatifs à la successibilité', p. 398; *Tab. ord. Theut.*, nos. 100 (pp. 79, 80), 119 (p. 108), 121 (p. 113); *Cart. gen. Hosp.*, no. 2753; *Recherches géographiques*, pp. 39, 42–3. See *Tab. ord. Theut.*, no. 105. A similar phrase, perhaps because it was during a time of lieutenancy, is to be found in a charter of 20 April 1228, when Queen Yolande was still alive, although in Italy. *Tab. ord. Theut.* no. 63 (p. 52) (confirmed by Frederick II in 1229. *Hist. dipl. Fred. secundi*, iii, p. 118).

17. *Chronica de Mailros*, p. 156; 'Documents relatifs à la successibilité', pp. 400, 401; 'Gestes des Chiprois', pp. 731–2; 'Annales de Terre Sainte', p. 441. But Alice seems to have sworn an oath more similar to those of the kings. *Urkunden Venedig*, no. 299 (p. 355).

18. See *Tab. ord. Theut.*, no. 105.

19. 'Annales de Terre Sainte', p. 442; 'Documents relatifs à la successibilité', p. 401; *Tab. ord. Theut.*, nos. 105, 106 (p. 86); *Recherches géographiques*, p. 34; *Cart. gen. Hosp.*, nos. 2612, 3047; 'Abrégé des Assises des Bourgeois' p. 246. At this time Melisende's claims to 'dominium et baiulatum' were referred to by the pope. *Epistolae saeculi XIII*, ii, no. 675.

20. 'Documents relatifs à la successibilité', p. 416.

21. *Tab. ord. Theut.*, nos. 7, 77–9, 81. See *Reg. Hier.*, no. 1097.

22. *Tab. ord. Theut.*, nos. 106–7; *Recherches géographiques*, pp. 29–36. See *Reg. Hier.*, nos. 1342c, 1367.

23. John of Jaffa, p. 263.

24. 'Livre au roi', p. 610.

25. 'Eracles', ii, p. 447; 'Gestes des Chiprois', p. 756.

26. 'Documents relatifs à la successibilité', p. 398.

27. 'Documents relatifs à la successibilité', pp. 400, 401; *Cart. gen. Hosp.*, no. 2693. The phrase was also used of the lieutenancies of Balian of Sidon and Odo of Montbéliard. 'Documents relatifs à la successibilité', p. 399. On the other hand John of Jaffa was referred to as *bailli*. 'Eracles', ii, p. 441; 'Annales mon. Burtonensis', p. 368.

28. 'Documents relatifs a la successibilité', p. 398; Alexander IV, *Reg.*, no. 1936.

29. *Tab. ord. Theut.*, no. 41; *Cart. gen. Hosp.*, nos. 1346, 2693. See *Cart. gen. Hosp.*, no. 2753; *Cod. dipl. geros.*, i, pp. 157–61; *Recherches géographiques*, ed. Rey, p. 40. The first two of these charters were issued with the consent of the minor.

30. William of Tyre, pp. 1027–8.

31. William of Tyre, p. 1116.

32. 'Documents relatifs à la successibilité', pp. 399–400. If a king was taken by the Muslims, then election of a lieutenant was made by the vassals. For an early example, see Fulcher of Chartres, pp. 450, 454; William of Tyre, pp. 538, 545.

33. 'Eracles', ii, pp. 305.

34. 'Annales de Terre Sainte', p. 442.

35. See Appendix E; and cf. La Monte, *Feudal Monarchy*, pp. 252–6.

36. 'Eracles', ii, pp. 360–2; 'Gestes des Chiprois', pp. 669, 670, 673. But see also Honorius III, *Reg.* no. 5824, from which it appears that the pope thought that Philip had been chosen by the vassals.

37. 'Acte de soumission', p. 403; *Epistolae saeculi XIII*, i, no. 674.

38. 'Eracles', ii, p. 224; Ernoul, p. 311; *Epistolae saeculi XIII*, i, nos. 656, 674.

39. See for instance William of Tyre, p. 1028; 'Eracles', ii, pp. 334, 437.

40. *Epistolae saeculi XIII*, i, nos. 656, 674. We will see that there was inserted a saving clause – and it should be remembered that the papal proposals were rejected in Acre. But they had been drawn up after negotiations with representatives of the kingdom.

41. 'Eracles', ii, pp. 388, 479; 'Gestes des Chiprois', p. 704.

42. 'Eracles', ii, pp. 474–5. By 1287 the lieutenants had their own seals. 'Gestes des Chiprois', p. 799.

43. *Cart. gen. Hosp.*, nos. 2067, 2612, 2902.

44. *Cod. dipl. geros.*, i, pp. 157–61.

45. L. de Mas Latrie, *Histoire de l'île de Chypre*, i, p. 406; Prawer, 'Estates', pp. 39–42; Mayer, 'The Commune of Tyre', pp. 443–5.

46. See above, p. 180. For meetings of this kind in the thirteenth century, see 'Abrégé des Assises des Bourgeois', pp. 246–9, and perhaps *Cart. gen. Hosp.*, no. 2033.

47. William of Tyre, pp. 758–9; Ernoul, p. 311; 'Eracles', ii, pp. 224, 322–3; Letter from St Louis, ed. F. Duchesne, *Historiae Francorum Scriptores*, v, p. 431.

48. See above, p. 15.

49. 'Doc. rel. au service militaire', *passim*.

50. William of Tyre, pp. 1027, 1133, 1137; 'Eracles', ii, pp. 2, 222–3, 305–6; Ernoul, pp. 309–10, 407–8; Innocent III, *Reg.*, no. 438. See Mayer, 'Kaiserrecht', pp. 203–6; Riley-Smith, *Knights of St John*, pp. 148–50.

51. Riley-Smith, *Knights of St John*, pp. 128–9.

52. See *Thesaurus nov. anecdot.*, i, cols. 1012–13; *Chron. de Mailros*, pp. 156–62; 'Annales mon. Burtonensis', pp. 368–9; 'Lettre des chrétiens de Terre-Sainte à Charles d'Anjou (22 avril 1260)', ed. H. F. Delaborde, *ROL*, ii, (1894), pp. 211–15; *Foedera, conventiones, litterae et acta publica inter reges Angliae et alios*, ed. T. Rymer *et al.*, i, p. 395. See also *Cart. gen. Hosp.*, no. 3098, obviously an answer by Pope Urban IV to another letter of this type and addressed to individual leaders and the barons and 'communities' of the Holy Land.

53. William of Tyre, pp. 903, 1110–12. There was also an annual subvention for the repair of the walls of Jerusalem paid in the 1170s by the temporal and spiritual lords. William of Tyre, pp. 1048–9.

54. 'Gestes des Chiprois', p. 731 (referred also to the Pisans); 'Documents relatifs à la successibilité', p. 400; *Urkunden Venedig*, no. 299 (p. 355).

55. 'Rothelin', p. 634.

56. 'Documents relatifs à la successibilité', pp. 414–15.

57. 'Documents relatifs à la successibilité', p. 415. The Hospitallers do not seem to have been present; and the Genoese were now based in Tyre.

58. 'Eracles', ii, p. 474. The Templars and Venetians deliberately absented themselves.

59. 'Gestes des Chiprois', p. 784.

60. Innocent IV, *Reg.*, no. 53.

61. 'Documents relatifs à la successibilité', p. 415.

62. 'Gestes des Chiprois', pp. 731–2.

63. 'Documents relatifs à la successibilité', pp. 401–15.

64. 'Documents relatifs à la successibilité', pp. 400, 414–15, 416; 'Gestes des Chiprois', p. 732; *Urkunden Venedig*, no. 299 (p. 355); 'Eracles', ii, p. 420. See 'Rothelin', p. 634; also 'Documents relatifs à la successibilité', p. 399; 'Eracles', ii, p. 447; 'Gestes des Chiprois', p. 756.

65. *Urkunden Venedig*, no. 299 (p. 355).

66. See 'Rothelin', p. 634. On the other hand the Templars and Hospitallers do appear to have spoken in the debate in 1197 on the choosing of a consort for Isabella of Jerusalem.

67. J. S. C. Riley-Smith, 'A note on confraternities in the Latin kingdom of Jerusalem', *Bulletin of the Institute of Historical Research*, xliv (1971) *passim.*

68. He administered justice firmly. 'Gestes des Chiprois', p. 750; 'Eracles', ii, p. 444; 'Annales de Terre Sainte', p. 448.

69. For Baibars's view, see Ibn al-Furat, ii, p. 55.

70. 'Eracles', ii, pp. 395–8; 'Gestes des Chiprois', pp. 707–10, 737.

71. Hill, *History of Cyprus*, ii, pp. 113–14, 116–26.

72. *Epistolae saeculi XIII*, i, no. 450. See 'Eracles', ii, p. 389; Francesco Amadi, p. 147; *Tab. ord. Theut.*, nos. 78, 85; Röhricht, 'Amalrich I', p. 493; *Hist. dipl. Fred. secundi*, iv, p. 793.

73. 'Gestes des Chiprois', p. 708.

74. *Epistolae saeculi XIII*, i, nos. 467–9. The matter was made delicate by Frederick's treatment of the Military Orders in Sicily. Riley-Smith, *Knights of St John*, pp. 171–2.

75. *Epistolae saeculi XIII*, i, nos. 474–5.

76. *Epistolae saeculi XIII*, i, nos. 476–8. See *Cart. gen. Hosp.*, no. 2026.

77. Gregory IX, *Reg.*, no. 1037.

78. *Epistolae Saeculi XIII*, i, no. 534.

79. Richard Filangieri may have visited Italy at this time ('Gestes des Chiprois', p. 719), although this has been doubted. See Hill, *History of Cyprus*, ii, p. 123 note 2; La Monte, *The Wars of Frederick II*, p. 156 note 4.

80. 'Documents relatifs à la successibilité', p. 399; 'Gestes des Chiprois', pp. 721–2.

81. 'Annales de Terre Sainte', p. 449. At least six months had elapsed since the death of the previous lieutenant.

82. 'Acte de soumission', pp. 402–3.

83. 'Gestes des Chiprois', p. 722; 'Documents relatifs à la successibilité', p. 399. For another episode in John's violent life, see 'Les lignages', p. 457. For Philip of Maugustel and Richard Filangieri, see also *Tab. ord. Theut.*, nos. 78, 84–5.

84. 'Gestes des Chiprois', pp. 722–4.

85. *Cart. gen. Hosp.*, no. 2067. See 'Documents relatifs à la successibilité', p. 399, and the reference to Odo in 'Gestes des Chiprois', p. 729. But no other document witnessed by Odo contained a reference to his *bailliage*. See 'Catalogue d'actes des comtes de Brienne, 950–1356', comp. H. d'Arbois de Jubainville, *BEC*, xxxiii (1872) p. 174; *Thesaurus nov. anecdot.*, i, cols. 1012–13.

86. The best description of this plan is to be found in *Epistolae saeculi XIII*, i, no. 656 i.

87. *Epistolae saeculi XIII*, i, no. 593.

88. *Epistolae saeculi XIII*, i, no. 578, (addressed to Odo of Montbéliard, the barons and knights of Jerusalem).

89. *Epistolae saeculi XIII*, i, no. 594.

90. *Epistolae saeculi XIII*, i, no. 656 i.

91. *Epistolae saeculi XIII*, i, nos. 649–50.

92. *Epistolae saeculi XIII*, i, no. 656 i. For Frederick's complaints, in which he also referred to the favour shown to the Patriarch of Jerusalem, see the *gravamina* of 1236. Gregory IX, *Reg.*, no. 2483.

93. *Epistolae saeculi XIII*, i, nos. 656 i and ii, 657; 'Eracles', ii, pp. 406–7.

94. *Epistolae saeculi XIII*, i, nos. 673–5; 'Eracles', ii, p. 406. See also Gregory IX, *Reg.*, no. 3082.

95. 'Eracles', ii, pp. 406–7. For Genoa and Cyprus, see 'Documents et mémoires de Chypre', ii, pp. 51–8. But for a group in Acre which at this time may have supported the emperor, see *Tab. ord. Theut.*, no. 84.

96. Gregory IX, *Reg.*, no. 2483. See also 'Documents et mémoires de Chypre', ii, pp. 61–3 (see iii, pp. 629–30); Gregory IX, *Reg.*, no. 3181.

97. 'Gestes des Chiprois', pp. 724–5.

98. See 'Documents relatifs à la successibilité', p. 399; 'Gestes des Chiprois', p. 729; also a letter of 1239 written by the leaders of the kingdom, including Walter of Brienne, Odo of Montbéliard, Balian of Sidon and John of Caesarea (*Thesaurus nov. anecdot.*, i, cols. 1012–13). In 1237 the pope had written on the freeing of crusaders from Muslim prisons to the leaders in the East, among them an unnamed *bailli*. Gregory IX, *Reg.*, no. 3993.

99. See the letter written by Frederick to Henry III of England in

1240, in which the claimed that he or his son had originally intended to join the crusade. *Hist. dipl. Fred. secundi*, v, pp. 921–3.

100. See his letter. Matthew Paris, *Chron. maiora*, iv, p. 139.

101. 'Gestes des Chiprois', p. 728; 'Eracles', ii, p. 421; Riley-Smith, *Knights of St John*, pp. 132–3, 173.

102. 'Acte de soumission', pp. 402–3. Attention has been drawn to the last of these proposals by Prawer ('Estates', p. 26); and to Mayer ('Zwei Kommunen', pp. 444–5) this is perhaps evidence for the existence of a commune before 1231. But there is every reason for believing that this clause, which had recurred in the various papal proposals for peace (see above, pp. 203 ff.), referred merely to the confraternity, the constitution of which, *pace* Prawer, would have been important both to the members of the commune and to the regent, since it was in possession of royal charters.

103. 'Gestes des Chiprois', pp. 728–30; 'Annales de Terre Sainte', p. 441; Richard of San Germano, p. 212. See Riley-Smith, *Knights of St John*, pp. 179–80 for the date. The fear of *conjurationes* was later reflected in a clause in an agreement between Philip of Montfort and the Genoese in 1264. See 'Quatre titres des Génois', no. 4 (p. 228).

104. See Ibn al-Furat, ii, pp. 1 ff., 170–5; Riley-Smith, *Knights of St John*, pp. 175–82.

105. See *Cart. gen. Hosp.*, no. 2301; although this was confirmed by Conrad.

106. For instance, see *Hist. dipl. Fred. secundi*, v, pp. 313, 324; vi, pp. 76, 197, 227, 444, 474, 567. According to the edition of Frederick's will in *Constitutiones et acta publica imperatorum* (ii, p. 386), he left, depending on the wishes of Conrad, either the Kingdom of Arles or that of Jerusalem to his son Henry, who could have had no possible right to the latter. But a recently discovered variant gives the far more likely reading of either the Kingdom of Arles or the Kingdom of Sicily. 'Ein unveröffentliches Testament Kaiser Friedrichs II', ed. G. Wolf, *Zeitschrift für die Geschichte des Oberrheins*, civ (1956) p. 7; and see pp. 33–4.

107. See *Regesta imperii V*, no. 4534. There are a few exceptions in which Conrad was entitled 'Rex' before 1251. See *Regesta imperii V*, no. 4384 of 1236; and *Hist. dipl. Fred. secundi*, vi, pp. 886–7, of 1249, which were certainly forgeries. In one document of 1244 Conrad entitled himself 'heres et dominus regni Ierusalem'. 'Zwei unbekannte Diplome der lateinischen Könige von Jerusalem aus Lucca', ed. R. Hiestand, *QFIAB*, l (1971) p. 55.

108. 'Livre au roi', p. 610.

109. 'Documents relatifs à la successibilité', p. 399. Thomas left for the East in June 1242, according to Richard of San Germano (p. 215),

but that author's chronology is sometimes rather suspect. Perhaps Thomas was intended to replace Richard Filangieri in Tyre.

110. 'Zwei unbekannte Diplome', pp. 55–6; *Cart. gen. Hosp.*, no. 2301 (although here Frederick referred to 'our court in the kingdom'); *Epistolae saeculi XIII*, ii, no. 564. In two charters, which unfortunately survive only in abstracts. Thomas seems to have claimed to act for both father and son. *Cart. gen. Hosp.*, nos. 2320, 2331.

111. 'Gestes des Chiprois', pp. 730–2; 'Documents relatifs à la successibilité', pp. 399–400; *Urkunden Venedig*, no. 299 (pp. 354–5); 'Eracles', ii, p. 420. Recently M. L. Bulst-Thiele ('Zur Geschichte der Ritterorden und des Königreiches Jerusalem im 13. Jahrhundert bis zur Schlacht bei la Forbie am 17. Okt. 1244', *Deustsches Archiv*, xxii (1966) p. 215 note 56) has revived the suggestion that the appointment of Alice of Cyprus as *bailli* and the capture of Tyre should be dated to 1242. This rests on a statement in 'Gestes des Chiprois' (p. 736) that Raymond of Toulouse was in Italy and interceded with the emperor for Richard Filangieri. But every source agrees that the events took place *after* Conrad came of age – that is in 1243 – and in fact the moves made by the baronial leaders and the legal expedients invented by them would have been senseless had not Conrad attained his majority.

112. The writer of 'Eracles' (ii, p. 420) reported that Ralph of Soissons spoke for Alice.

113. See Ibn al-Furat, ii, p. 170 note 6. The Templars planned to build a castle to defend Jerusalem. Matthew Paris, *Chron. maiora*, iv, p. 290; *Acta imperii inedita*, i, no. 434.

114. *Urkunden Venedig*, no. 299 (p. 355)

115. 'Documents relatifs à la successibilité', p. 400; *Urkunden Venedig*, no. 299 (p. 355); 'Gestes des Chiprois', p. 732; 'Eracles', ii, p. 420.

116. 'Gestes des Chiprois', pp. 731, 735; 'Documents relatifs à la successibilité', pp. 400–1; 'Eracles', ii, p. 423; *Urkunden Venedig*, no. 299 (p. 358). Philip of Novara wrote ('Gestes des Chiprois', p. 735) that it was said that Alice might have received the city of Tyre if she had requested it before its citadel was taken from the imperialists. I do not understand this.

117. *Urkunden Venedig*, no. 299 (p. 357).

118. 'Gestes des Chiprois', p. 735; 'Eracles', ii, p. 420.

119. 'Annales de Terre Sainte', pp. 441–2; 'Gestes des Chiprois', p. 741. See 'Documents relatifs à la successibilité', p. 401.

120. *Epistolae saeculi XIII*, ii, no. 675.

121. *Epistolae saeculi XIII*, ii, no. 124 (especially pp. 93–4).

122. *Epistolae Saeculi XIII*, ii, no. 291. In 1244 Henry had sent to Frederick for news, obviously concerned at the way matters were developing. *Hist. dipl. Fred. secundi*, vi, pp. 914–15.

123. *Epistolae saeculi XIII*, ii, nos. 125, 336; Mayer, *Marseilles Levante-handel*, nos. 13–4, 17–21 (pp. 197–9, 201–6).

124. See *Epistolae saeculi XIII*, ii, no. 675. He never seems formally to have referred to Conrad as such in his letters, but he recognised Conradin as king after Conrad's death. See below, p. 215.

125. See Riley-Smith, *Knights of St John*, p. 182.

126. Innocent IV, *Reg.*, no. 2801; *Epistolae saeculi XIII*, ii, no. 565.

127. *Epistolae saeculi XIII*, ii, nos. 412, 564, 568. See the letter of November to the Bishop of Tripoli, permitting him to use Church money to aid his relatives who had been despoiled by Frederick's supporters. *Epistolae saeculi XIII*, ii, no. 607; and also Innocent IV, *Reg.*, no. 4364.

128. *Epistolae saeculi XIII*, ii, no. 582. The permission was renewed for Odo on 12 February 1253. Innocent IV, *Reg.*, no. 6337.

129. *Epistolae saeculi XIII*, ii, no. 324. In 1247 the King of Cyprus was granted for five years the privilege that he could not be excommunicated or an interdict laid on his lands without the express command of the Holy See. This was repeated in 1252 with special reference to the royal chapel in Nicosia. Innocent IV, *Reg.*, nos. 3067, 5893.

130. *Epistolae saeculi XIII*, ii, no. 411. See also a letter to the patriarch in 1248 ordering him to take counsel with Henry and the barons on the defence of the kingdom against Islam. *Epistolae saeculi XIII*, ii, no. 566.

131. Innocent IV, *Reg.*, nos. 2524, 2884. The pope also intervened on behalf of Balian's bailiff in Cyprus, who in the course of a dispute over lands had been excommunicated by the Archbishop of Nicosia, and he issued a dispensation for Balian's nephew for marriage within the prohibited degrees. Innocent IV, *Reg.*, nos. 3149–51.

132. Innocent IV, *Reg.*, nos. 6455–8.

133. Although of course they could be enjoyed by crusaders. Cf. the rights granted to Geoffrey of Sargines in 1262. Urban IV, *Reg.*, nos. 53–6.

134. 'Documents relatifs à la successibilité', p. 401; *Urkunden Vene-dig*, no. 299 (p. 358).

135. 'Gestes des Chiprois', p. 741. See below, pp. 224–5. It seems that the lord of Beirut had custody of the castle of Acre in the early 1250's. 'Abrégé des Assises des Bourgeois', p. 246.

136. *Tab. ord. Theut.*, nos. 105, 119, 121; *Recherches géographiques*, pp. 38–40, 41–5.

137. See above, p. 125.

138. *Tab. ord. Theut.*, no. 105.

139. 'Documents relatifs à la successibilité', p. 401; *Cart. gen. Hosp.*, no. 2693.

140. Innocent IV, *Reg.*, i, pp. xliv–v. The papacy may have retained some kind of authority. See the confirmations of privileges, some

forged, claimed by Marseilles. Alexander IV, *Reg.*, no. 752; Mayer, *Marseilles Levantehandel*, nos. 23–6 (pp. 207–12).

141. 'Documents relatifs à la successibilité', p. 401; 'Eracles', ii, p. 441; 'Annales de Terre Sainte', p. 446. John was already regent in September ('Annales mon. Burtonensis', pp. 368–9; for date, see *Reg. Hier.*, no. 1221), but he cannot have been before the 22nd of that month. (See *Cart. gen. Hosp.*, no. 2693.)

142. 'Documents relatifs à la successibilité', p. 401; 'Eracles', ii, p. 442; 'Annales de Terre Sainte', p. 446; *Recherches géographiques*, p. 40 (dated 15 September 1256); *Cod. dipl. geros.*, i, p. 157.

143. For date, see Richard, *Le royaume latin*, p. 287 note 3.

144. For a general history of the war, see Prawer, *Histoire*, ii, pp. 365 ff.

145. *Annales Januenses*, iv, p. 33; 'Annales de Terre Sainte', p. 447; 'Gestes des Chiprois', p. 743; Martino da Canale, p. 460.

146. *Cod. dipl. geros.*, i, pp. 157–61. For Ancona's support of Genoa, see also *Annales Januenses*, iv, p. 36.

147. But he was involved in one violent dispute with Philip of Montfort. 'Gestes des Chiprois', p. 752.

148. Andrew Dandolo (p. 308), and 'Annales de Terre Sainte', (p. 448) add to John of Jaffa and the Templars another John of Ibelin. For John of Jaffa's attitude from the start, see 'Gestes des Chiprois', pp. 743, 746; Francesco Amadi, p. 204 (who dated from his *bailliage* his personal dislike of the Genoese).

149. See Alexander IV, *Reg.*, nos. 741, 2510 'Eracles', ii, p. 441 'Annales de Terre Sainte', p. 448; Hill, *History of Cyprus*, ii, p. 149. It may be that John of Jaffa was involved in an adulterous relationship with Plaisance: this view has been convincingly revived by my pupil Mr Peter Edbury.

150. 'Rothelin', p. 634; 'Eracles', ii, p. 443; 'Annales de Terre Sainte', pp. 447–8; 'Gestes des Chiprois', pp. 742, 743–4; 'Documents relatifs à la successibilité', pp. 401–2; Martino da Canale, p. 460; Andrew Dandolo, p. 308. The writer of 'Rothelin' (loc. cit) confused him with Hugh of Brienne in an otherwise detailed account.

151. 'Documents relatifs à la successibilité', pp. 401–2. See John of Jaffa, p. 263; Geoffrey Le Tor, p. 440; James of Ibelin, p. 461. The author of 'Rothelin' (p. 634) was here mistaken.

152. 'Gestes des Chiprois', pp. 744–5; *Annales Januenses*, iv, pp. 35–6. See 'Rothelin', pp. 634–5.

153. 'Rothelin', p. 634; 'Eracles', ii, p. 443; 'Annales de Terre Sainte', p. 448. See 'Gestes des Chiprois', p. 747; *Cart. gen. Hosp.*, no. 2902.

154. 'Annales de Terre Sainte', p. 448; 'Gestes des Chiprois', p. 750; 'Eracles', ii, p. 444; 'Lettre des chrétiens', pp. 211–15.

155. See Prawer, *Histoire*, ii, pp. 368–9.

156. 'Gestes des Chiprois', p. 756; 'Eracles', ii, p. 447; *Cart. gen. Hosp.*, no. 3029; *Foedera*, i, p. 395; Urban IV, *Reg.*, nos. 183, 344. Geoffrey had returned to the West, but he was leaving for the East in February and was in Palestine by April 1262. Urban IV, *Reg.*, nos. 53–6 (and see no. 2177); 'Gestes des Chiprois', loc. cit.

157. 'Gestes des Chiprois', p. 756; 'Eracles', ii, p. 447; 'Documents relatifs à la successibilité', p. 402. See above, p. 190.

158. Geoffrey was the first man to make homage to Hugh of Antioch-Lusignan in 1264. 'Documents relatifs à la successibilité', pp. 414–15. For Isabella's death, see 'Eracles', ii, p. 448. In July Henry of Antioch was still her lieutenant. *Cart. gen. Hosp.*, no. 3098.

159. Urban IV, *Reg.*, no. 867.

160. 'Documents relatifs à la successibilité', pp. 401–15.

161. 'Documents relatifs à la successibilité', pp. 403–4, 407, 410–11, 413.

162. She had died even before the marriage of Henry to Plaisance. 'Documents relatifs à la successibilité', pp. 405, 409, 412.

163. 'Documents relatifs à la successibilité', pp. 407, 411, 414.

164. 'Documents relatifs à la successibilité', pp. 406, 408.

165. 'Documents relatifs à la successibilité', pp. 402, 405–6, 412.

166. 'Documents relatifs à la successibilité', pp. 402, 405–7, 409–10, 412–13. See John of Jaffa, pp. 224–5; Geoffrey Le Tor, pp. 435–6.

167. 'Documents relatifs à la successibilité', pp. 404, 408; 'Livre au roi', p. 630.

168. 'Documents relatifs à la successibilité', p. 402. See p. 412.

169. 'Documents relatifs à la successibilité', pp. 403, 411. This argument was also echoed in John of Jaffa (p. 227) and Geoffrey Le Tor (p. 436).

170. 'Documents relatifs à la successibilité', pp. 414–15.

171. *Thesaurus. nov. anecdot.*, i, cols. 1013–14; 'Gestes des Chiprois', p. 769; Ibn al-Furat, ii, p. 129; E. Lourie, 'An offer of the suzerainty and escheat of Cyprus to Alphonso III of Aragon by Hugh de Brienne in 1289', *English Historical Review*, lxxxiv (1969).

172. Clement IV, *Reg.*, nos. 602, 690, 699, 705; and see nos. 427, 601. For a charter issued by Conradin himself in 1268, *Documenti delle città toscane*, no. 70.

173. 'Documents relatifs à la successibilité', pp. 415–16, where it is revealed that the High Court was twice convoked. For date, see 'Annales de Terre Sainte', p. 453.

174. 'Eracles', ii, p. 457; 'Gestes des Chiprois', p. 772.

175. 'Gestes des Chiprois', p. 771.

176. 'Gestes des Chiprois', p. 773.

177. 'Documents relatifs à la successibilité', pp. 416–17; 'Gestes des Chiprois', p. 773. It was wrongly thought in 1324 that the meeting of the court had been held in Acre. 'Documents relatifs à la successibilité', p. 421.

178. 'Documents relatifs à la successibilité', pp. 417–18.

179. 'Documents relatifs à la successibilité', p. 421.

180. Ibn al-Furat, ii, p. 129.

181. 'Documents relatifs à la successibilité', pp. 418–19. Geoffrey of Sargines was mentioned as being among those who made homage, although it is possible that he was already dead.

182. Pope Gregory X, *Registre*, no. 103.

183. 'Gestes des Chiprois', p. 773.

184. Gregory X, *Reg.*, nos. 3, 103; 'Gestes des Chiprois', p. 773. See 'Eracles', ii, p. 475.

185. See 'Documents relatifs à la successibilité', p. 419.

186. 'Eracles', ii, p. 464. The text gave as a member the Bishop of Jaffa: there was no such prelate and the word 'Jaffe' ought perhaps to read 'Baffe'.

187. 'Commerce et expéditions militaires de la France et de Venise au moyen âge', ed. L. de Mas Latrie, '*Mélanges historiques*, iii, p. 13. See also 'Lettre des chrétiens', *passim*.

188. Ibn al-Furat, ii, pp. 131, 156–7; 'Eracles', ii, p. 461; 'Emprunts de Saint Louis', p. 293.

189. Ibn al-Furat, ii, p. 130. The author of 'Eracles' (ii, p. 475) reported that negotiations went on for a long time.

190. 'Eracles', ii, pp. 475–6; 'Gestes des Chiprois', p. 777.

191. See 'Gestes des Chiprois', pp. 777, 783; 'Eracles', ii, p. 476; C. Minieri Riccio, *Genealogia di Carlo I. di Angio*, pp. 142–3; *Syllabus membranarum ad regiae Siclae archivum pertinentium*, ii, pp. 151, 225–9. Charles II continued to make the payments to Maria. When he made homage for Sicily to Pope Nicholas III on 24 May 1278 Charles I stated that he was in the second year of his reign in Jerusalem. Nicholas III, *Reg.*, no. 302. But when he had made homage to Pope John XXI on 7 October 1276 he had called himself only King of Sicily. Pope John XXI, *Registre*, no. 163.

192. 'Eracles', ii, p. 474; 'Gestes des Chiprois', p. 783.

193. Ibn al-Furat, ii, p. 164. A reference to a dispute with feudatories in the early 1270's (Gregory X, *Reg.*, 'App.', no. 810) probably concerned the military services of the Cypriot vassals. See also 'Doc. rel. au service militaire', *passim*; 'Eracles', ii, pp. 463–4.

194. See 'Quattro documenti genovesi sulle contese d'Oltramare nel secolo XIII', ed. G. Bigoni, *Archivio storico italiano*, ser. 5, xxiv (1899) pp. 63, 64. If the 'Livre des Assises des Bourgeois' dates from this period then the very strong statement (pp. 161–3) according to

which the communal courts had no jurisdiction over property has obvious significance.

195. Philip of Novara, 'Livre', pp. 530–1; *Cart. gen. Hosp.*, nos. 3047, 3323, 3326.

196. See 'Gestes des Chiprois', p. 773; and also *Cart. gen. Hosp.*, no. 3346; above, p. 215. This may account for Philip of Montfort's apparent delay in recognising Hugh's *bailliage* in 1268. 'Documents relatifs à la successibilité', p. 416.

197. 'Gestes des Chiprois', pp. 773, 790, 804.

198. *Urkunden Venedig*, no. 369 (pp. 155, 157–8).

199. James of Ibelin, pp. 459, 463.

200. 'Eracles', ii, p. 474.

201. 'Gestes des Chiprois', p. 783, although Hugh's departure was wrongly dated.

202. Although Hugh claimed the Templars had accepted him. 'Documents relatifs à la successibilité', p. 419.

203. 'Eracles', ii, pp. 474–5; 'Gestes des Chiprois', p. 783; 'Annales de Terre Sainte', p. 456. In 1275 Balian of Arsur had been 'vicar' of the kingdoms of Jerusalem and Cyprus for Hugh. *Codex ep. Rudolphi*, p. 66.

204. 'Gestes des Chiprois', pp. 783–4; 'Eracles', ii, pp. 478, 479.

205. For the Venetians, see Andrew Dandolo, p. 324.

206. 'Eracles', ii, pp. 478–9; 'Gestes des Chiprois', p. 784; 'Annales de Terre Sainte', p. 456. According to Florio Bustron (p. 115) the leading knights took a neutral stance but he named among them James Vidal and Balian of Arsur. The date of the submission was presumably before September 1278, by which time the Hospitallers and Bohemond of Tripoli had recognised Roger. *Cart. gen. Hosp.*, nos. 3672–3; in the second of these documents Roger was called 'vicair et bail'. In February, March and April 1278 Charles was referring to him as his vicar-general in the kingdom and in the first of these months a Hospitaller ship in Italy was being prepared to carry him supplies. *Cart. gen. Hosp.*, no. 3650 (and see no. 3701); 'Documents et mémoires de Chypre', ii, pp. 80–1.

207. For the close relations between Isabella's father and the House of Cyprus, see 'Documents et mémoires de Chypre', iii, pp. 660–2.

208. For the support of the Angevins by the French troops, see 'Documents et mémoires de Chypre', iii, pp. 671–3; 'Bans et ordonnances', p. 357. Both documents date from 1286. The role of the French troops deserves further study. For them, see Richard, *Le royaume latin*, pp. 297–300; J. Richard, 'Saint Louis dans l'histoire des croisades', *Bulletin de la Société d'Emulation du Bourbonnais* (1970) pp. 243–4; J. R. Strayer, 'The Crusades of Louis IX', *A History of the Crusades*, ed. K. M. Setton, ii, p. 508. For the actions of earlier French

kings, see R. C. Smail, 'Latin Syria and the West, 1149–1187', *Transactions of the Royal Historical Society*, 5th series, xix (1969) *passim*.

CONCLUSION

1. Certain historians, among them F. M. Powicke (*The Thirteenth Century*, p. 134) and Prawer ('Estates', pp. 26–7) have drawn attention to the possibility that England, through Simon of Montfort, felt the influence of the constitutional ideas of the Palestinian jurists. For all their learning this is impossible of proof. None of Simon's ideas that are known to us, except perhaps his belief that Parliament could meet without the presence of the king, have any convincing links with those of the feudatories of Jerusalem.

APPENDIXES

A CHRONOLOGICAL TABLE
(Monarchs in capital letters; regents in italics)

1099	15 July	Taking of Jerusalem by the First Crusade.
	22 July	Election of GODFREY OF BOUILLON as Advocate of the Holy Sepulchre.
1100	18 July	Death of GODFREY.
	25 December	Coronation of BALDWIN I.
1104	May	Taking of Acre.
1118	2 April	Death of BALDWIN I.
	14 April	Coronation of BALDWIN II.
1120	January	Council of Nablus.
1124	7 July	Taking of Tyre.
1131	21 August	Death of BALDWIN II.
	14 September	Coronation of FULK OF ANJOU.
1143	10 November	Death of FULK.
	25 December	Coronation of MELISENDE and BALDWIN III.
1148		Second Crusade in Palestine.
1163	10 February	Death of BALDWIN III.
	18 February	Coronation of AMALRIC.
c. 1166		Issuing of the *Assise sur la ligece*.
1174	11 July	Death of AMALRIC.

	15 July	Coronation of BALDWIN IV.
		Regency of *Miles of Plancy* or *Rohard of Jaffa*.
	Autumn	Assassination of *Miles of Plancy*.
		Regency of *Raymond of Tripoli*.
1177		BALDWIN's majority.
		Philip of Flanders in Palestine.
		Lieutenancy of Reynald of Châtillon.
1180	March/April	Marriage of Sibylla of Jerusalem and Guy of Lusignan.
1183	early in year	Lieutenancy of Guy of Lusignan.
	20 November	Dismissal of Guy from the lieutenancy.
		Coronation of BALDWIN V.

1184	December/ January	Lieutenancy of Raymond of Tripoli.
1185	March	Death of BALDWIN IV.
		Regency of *Raymond of Tripoli*.
1186	late Summer	Death of BALDWIN V.
		Coronation of SIBYLLA and GUY OF LUSIGNAN.
1187	4 July	Battle of Hattin.
	14 July	Arrival in Tyre of Conrad of Montferrat.
	2 October	Surrender of the city of Jerusalem to Saladin.
1187–9		Saladin's conquest of nearly all of Palestine.
1189	27 August	Siege of Acre by GUY OF LUSIGNAN.
1190–2		Third Crusade in Palestine.
1190	Autumn	Death of SIBYLLA.
	24 November	Marriage of Conrad of Montferrat and Isabella of Jerusalem.
1191	12 July	Recapture of Acre.
1192	April	Conrad of Montferrat recognised as king-elect.
	28 April	Conrad of Montferrat assassinated.
	5 May	Marriage of Isabella of Jerusalem and Henry of Champagne.
	May	Sale of Cyprus by Richard of England to GUY OF LUSIGNAN.
1194	Autumn	Death of GUY OF LUSIGNAN.
		Accession of Aimery of Lusignan to Lordship of Cyprus.
1197	September	Aimery of Lusignan crowned King of Cyprus.
	10 September	Death of Henry of Champagne.
	Autumn	Marriage of ISABELLA OF JERUSALEM and AIMERY OF LUSIGNAN.
1198	January	Coronation of ISABELLA and AIMERY.
	Autumn	Dispute between KING AIMERY and Ralph of Tiberias; application of the *Assise sur la ligece*.
1202–4		Fourth Crusade.
1205	1 April	Death of AIMERY OF LUSIGNAN.
		Lieutenancy of John of Beirut.
	Summer	Death of ISABELLA OF JERUSALEM.

		Regency of *John of Beirut* for MARIA OF JERUSALEM.
1210	14 September	Marriage of MARIA OF JERUSALEM and JOHN OF BRIENNE.
	3 October	Coronation of MARIA and JOHN.
1212		Death of MARIA OF JERUSALEM.
		Regency of *JOHN OF BRIENNE* for YOLANDE (ISABELLA).
1217–21		Fifth Crusade in Palestine and Egypt.
1225	August	Coronation of YOLANDE (ISABELLA).
	9 November	Marriage of YOLANDE (ISABELLA) and the Emperor FREDERICK II.
1228	1 May	Death of YOLANDE (ISABELLA).
		Regency for CONRAD of *Balian of Sidon* and *Odo of Montbéliard*.
	September	Arrival of *FREDERICK* in Palestine and his assumption of the regency.
1229	18 February	Treaty with Egypt by which city of Jerusalem regained.
	April	Successful application against *FREDERICK* of the *Assise sur la ligece*.
	May	Departure from Palestine of *FREDERICK*.
		Appointment of Balian of Sidon and Garnier l'Aleman as lieutenants.
	Autumn	Debate on claim to the throne of Alice of Cyprus.
1231	October	Siege of Beirut by imperial forces; arrival of *FREDERICK*'s lieutenant, Richard Filangieri.
1231–43		The Commune of Acre.
1232	early in year	Failure of the vassals in Acre to raise the siege of Beirut.
	3 May	Battle of Casal Imbert.
	15 June	Battle of Agridi.
1233	early in year	Rejection by the commune of the lieutenancy of Philip of Maugustel.
1236		Agreement with *FREDERICK* negotiated at the papal curia rejected by the commune.
		Death of John of Beirut.
1239–41		Crusades of Thibaut of Champagne and Richard of Cornwall.

1243	25 April	CONRAD's majority.
		Regency of *Odo of Montbéliard*.
	5 June	Acceptance of *Alice of Cyprus* as regent.
1244	23 August	Fall of the city of Jerusalem to the Khwarizmians.
	17 October	Battle of Gaza.
1245	17 July	Deposition of *FREDERICK* from the empire.
1246		Death of *Alice of Cyprus*.
		Regency of *Henry of Cyprus*.
1247	17 June	Loss of Tiberias.
	15 October	Loss of Ascalon.
1249–54		Crusade of St Louis IX of France in Egypt and Palestine.
1250	13 December	Death of the Emperor *FREDERICK II*.
1253	18 January	Death of *Henry of Cyprus*.
		Regency of *John of Arsur*.
1254		Regency of *Philip Chamberlain*.
	21 May	Death of CONRAD.
	22–30 September	Election of *John of Jaffa* as regent for CONRADIN.
1256		Regency of *John of Arsur*.
1256–61		War of St Sabas.
1258	February	Acceptance of *Hugh of Cyprus* as regent; regency of his mother *Plaisance* on his behalf.
1261	September	Death of *Plaisance*.
		Regency of *Geoffrey of Sargines*.
1263	Spring	Acceptance of *Isabella of Cyprus* as regent for *Hugh of Cyprus*.
1264	after June	Death of *Isabella of Cyprus*.
		Regency of *Geoffrey of Sargines*.
		Acceptance of *Hugh of Antioch-Lusignan* as regent for *Hugh of Cyprus*.
1265	5 March	Loss of Caesarea.
	29 April	Loss of Arsur.
1266	July	Loss of Saphet.
1267		CONRADIN's majority.
	5 December	Death of *Hugh of Cyprus*; succession of *Hugh of Antioch-Lusignan* to the throne of Cyprus.
1268	7 March	Loss of Jaffa.
	April	Acceptance of *Hugh of Antioch-Lusignan* as regent for CONRADIN.

	15 April	Loss of Beaufort.
	18 May	Loss of Antioch.
	29 October	Execution in Naples of CONRADIN.
1269	24 September	Coronation as King of Jerusalem of HUGH OF ANTIOCH-LUSIGNAN; his right to throne challenged by Maria of Antioch.
1269–72		Aragonese and English crusades in Palestine.
1271	12 June	Loss of Montfort.
1276	October	Departure of HUGH from Palestine.
1277	18 March	Sale by Maria of Antioch to CHARLES OF ANJOU of the crown of Jerusalem.
	September	Arrival in Acre of CHARLES's vicar, Roger of San Severino.

1284	4 March	Death of HUGH OF ANTIOCH-LUSIGNAN.
		Succession of JOHN to the thrones of Cyprus and Jerusalem.
1285	7 January	Death of CHARLES OF ANJOU.
		Succession of CHARLES II to the thrones of Naples and Jerusalem.
	20 May	Death of JOHN.
		Succession of HENRY to the thrones of Cyprus and Jerusalem.
1286	29 June	Surrender to HENRY of the citadel of Acre by the Angevin garrison.
	15 August	Coronation of HENRY.
1289	26 April	Loss of Tripoli.
1291	18 May	Fall of Acre and loss of all Palestine.

B THE ROYAL HOUSE OF JERUSALEM
Kings in capital letters; regents in italics)

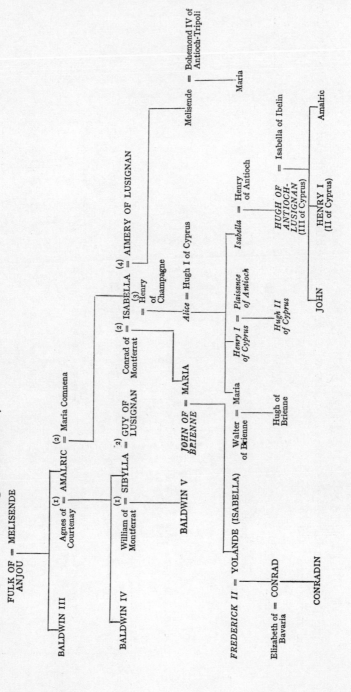

C THE IBELINS AND THE LORDS OF THE KINGDOM OF JERUSALEM

(This Table contains only the names of nobles who played a significant part in the history of the Kingdom and are referred to in the text.)

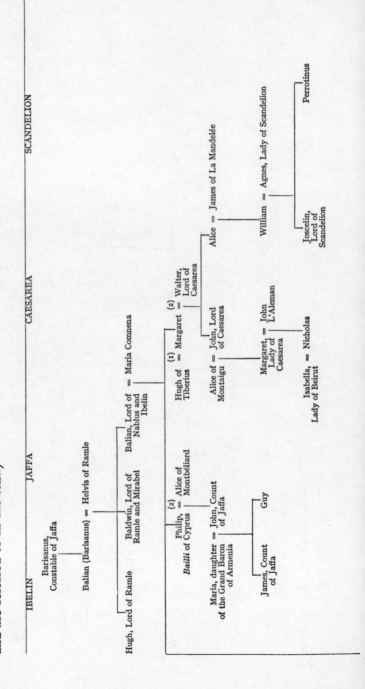

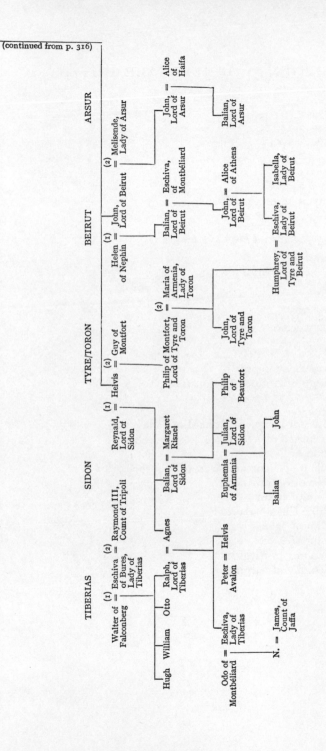

(continued from p. 316)

D THE REGENTS OF JERUSALEM, 1174–1277

Parents of a minor

1212–25   John of Brienne
1228–43   Frederick II

Nearest relatives of a minor

1174–7   Raymond of Tripoli
1258–67   Hugh of Cyprus

Nearest relatives of uncrowned kings who were of age

1243–6   Alice of Cyprus
1246–53   Henry of Cyprus
1268   Hugh of Antioch-Lusignan (of Cyprus)

Parent of a minor regent

1258–61   Plaisance of Cyprus

Nearest relatives of a minor regent

1263–4   Isabella of Cyprus
1264–7   Hugh of Antioch-Lusignan

Vassal regents

1174   Miles of Plancy or Rohard of Jaffa
1185–6   Raymond of Tripoli
1205–10   John of Beirut
1228   Balian of Sidon and Odo of Montbéliard
1243   Odo of Montbéliard
1253–4   John of Arsur
1254   Philip Chamberlain
1254–6   John of Jaffa
1256–8   John of Arsur
1261–3   Geoffrey of Sargines
1264   Geoffrey of Sargines

Date	Names	Nominator	Reference
1177	Reynald of Châtillon	Baldwin IV	William of Tyre, p. 1028
1183	Guy of Lusignan	Baldwin IV	William of Tyre, p. 1116
1184–5	Raymond of Tripoli	Baldwin IV	William of Tyre, p. 1134; 'Eracles', ii, p. 3
1205	John of Beirut	Isabella	'Eracles', ii, p. 305
1218	Garnier L'Aleman (Acre)	John of Brienne	'Eracles', ii, p. 334
1222–5	Odo of Montbéliard (Acre)	John of Brienne	'Eracles', ii, p. 355; Ernoul, p. 448
1225–6	Odo of Montbéliard	Yolande	'Eracles', ii, p. 359
1226–8	Thomas of Acerra	Yolande[1]	'Eracles', ii, p. 364; 'Gestes des Chiprois' p. 674; 'Annales de Terre Sainte', p. 438; 'Documents relatifs à la successibilité', p. 399
1229	Balian of Sidon (Acre)	Frederick II	See above, p. 171
1229–31	Balian of Sidon Garnier L'Aleman } (Acre) Reynald of Haifa (Jerusalem)	Frederick II	'Documents relatifs à la successibilité', p. 399; 'Eracles', ii, p. 384; 'Gestes des Chiprois', p. 684; Reg. Hier., no. 1027
1231–43	Richard Filangieri[2] (Tyre and Jerusalem)	Frederick II	See above, pp. 175 ff. also Reg. Hier., nos. 1058–9, 1086, 1107
1231–9	Balian of Sidon } (Acre) Odo of Montbéliard	Frederick II	See above, pp. 180 ff. also 'Documents relatifs à la successibilité', p. 399; Reg. Hier., no. 1046
1239–43	Odo of Montbéliard (Acre)	Frederick II	'Documents relatifs à la successibilité', p. 399; 'Gestes des Chiprois', p. 729
1246–7	Balian of Beirut (Acre) } Philip of Montfort (Tyre)[3]	Henry of Cyprus	'Gestes des Chiprois' p. 741; 'Annales de Terre Sainte', p. 442; Innocent IV, Reg., no. 2884; Epistolae saeculi XIII, ii, no. 411
1247–8	John of Arsur	Henry of Cyprus	'Gestes des Chiprois', p. 741; 'Eracles', ii, p. 436; 'Annales de Terre Sainte', p. 442; Francesco Amadi, p. 198

1248–9	John Fuinon	Henry of Cyprus	'Eracles', ii, p. 436; 'Annales de Terre Sainte', p. 442
1249–52	John of Arsur	Henry of Cyprus	'Eracles', ii, p. 437; 'Annales de Terre Sainte', p. 443; 'Abrégé des Assises des Bourgeois', p. 246; *Reg. Hier.*, no. 1200
1253	John of Jaffa[4]	Henry of Cyprus	Innocent IV, *Reg.*, nos. 6455–8
1258	John of Arsur	Plaisance of Cyprus	'Rothelin', p. 634; 'Eracles', ii, p. 443; 'Gestes des Chiprois', p. 747; 'Annales de Terre Sainte', p. 448; *Reg. Hier.*, no. 1269
1259–61	Geoffrey of Sargines	Plaisance of Cyprus	'Annales de Terre Sainte', p. 448; 'Gestes des Chiprois', p. 750; 'Eracles', ii, p. 444; *Reg. Hier.*, no. 1291a
1263–4	Henry of Antioch	Isabella of Cyprus	'Eracles', ii, p. 447; 'Annales de Terre Sainte', pp. 450–1; *Reg. Hier.*, no. 1332a
1264–7	Geoffrey of Sargines	Hugh of Antioch-Lusignan	*Cart. gen. Hosp.*, no. 3213; Clement IV, *Reg.*, nos. 824–5, 838, 918, 1110, 1130, 1200; *Thesaurus nov. anecdot.*, ed. Martène and Durand, i, cols. 1013–14
1268	Balian of Arsur	Hugh of Antioch-Lusignan	'Eracles', ii, p. 457; 'Gestes des Chiprois', p. 772
1275	Balian of Arsur (entitled Vicar)	Hugh of Antioch-Lusignan	*Codex ep. Rudolphi*, pp. 66–7
1276–7	Balian of Arsur	Hugh of Antioch-Lusignan	'Eracles', ii, pp. 474–5; 'Gestes des Chiprois', pp. 783–4; 'Annales de Terre Sainte', p. 456
1277–	Roger of San Severino	Charles of Anjou	'Eracles', ii, p. 478; 'Gestes des Chiprois', pp. 783–4; 'Annales de Terre Sainte', p. 456; *Reg. Hier.*, nos. 1424b, 1425. See above, pp. 226 ff.

NOTES TO APPENDIX E

1. According to the sources Thomas was appointed by the Emperor Frederick II, but of course it was the fact that Yolande had been crowned queen in Palestine that enabled this to be done.

2. In 1243 Richard briefly appointed his brother Lothair to rule until the emperor should send a replacement. After 1243 Thomas of Acerra claimed to represent Frederick and Conrad, although he had to reside outside the kingdom in the County of Tripoli.

3. Tyre was to remain in the hands of members of the family of Montfort until 1289.

4. This may be inferred, although it was nowhere specifically stated.

BIBLIOGRAPHY

OF ORIGINAL SOURCES AND SECONDARY WORKS QUOTED OR REFERRED TO IN THE TEXT OR NOTES

DOCUMENTS AND COLLECTIONS OF MATERIALS

Acta imperii inedita saeculi XIII, ed. E. Winkelmann, 2 vols (Innsbruck, 1880–5).

'Acte de soumission des barons du royaume de Jérusalem à Frédéric II', ed. R. Röhricht, *AOL*, i (1881).

'Actes passés en 1271, 1274 et 1279 à l'Aïas (Petite Arménie) et à Beyrouth par devant des notaires génois', ed. C. Desimoni, *AOL*, i (1881).

Pope Alexander IV, *Registre*, ed. C. Bourel de la Roncière *et al.*, 2 vols (Paris, 1902–31).

Analecta novissima. Spicilegii Solesmensis altera continuatio, ed. J. B. Pitra, 2 vols (Paris, 1885–8).

Les Archives, la Bibliothèque et le trésor de l'ordre de Saint-Jean de Jérusalem à Malte, ed. J. Delaville Le Roulx (Bibliothèque des Écoles d'Athènes et de Rome. Série I, 32) (Paris, 1883).

'Bans et ordonnances des rois de Chypre, 1286–1362', *RHC Lois* ii.

Calendar of the Patent Rolls preserved in the Public Record Office. Edward I. A.D. 1272–1281, prep. under the superintendence of The Deputy Keeper of the Records (London, 1901).

Cartulaire de l'église du Saint-Sépulcre de Jérusalem, ed. E. de Rozière. (Collection des documents inédits sur l'histoire de France, sér. I, 5) (Paris, 1849).

Cartulaire général de l'ordre des Hospitaliers de St.-Jean de Jérusalem (1100–1310), ed. J. Delaville Le Roulx, 4 vols (Paris, 1894–1906).

'Catalogue d'actes des comtes de Brienne, 950–1356', comp. H. d'Arbois de Jubainville, *BEC*, xxxiii (1872).

'Chartae', *HPM* i.

'Chartes de l'abbaye cistercienne de St.-Serge de Giblet en Syrie', ed. E. Petit, *Mémoires de la Société nationale des Antiquaires de France*, sér. 5, viii (1887).

'Chartes de l'abbaye de Notre-Dame de la vallée de Josaphat en Terre Sainte (1108–1291). Analyse et extraits', ed. C. Kohler, *ROL*, vii (1899).

Chartes de la Terre Sainte provenant de l'abbaye de Notre Dame de Josaphat, ed. H. F. Delaborde (Bibliothèque des Écoles françaises d'Athènes at de Rome. Série I, 19) (Paris, 1880).

'Chartes de Terre Sainte', ed. J. Delaville Le Roulx, *ROL*, xi (1905/8).

'Chartes du Mont-Thabor', ed. J. Delaville Le Roulx, *Cart. gen. Hosp.*, ii.

'Le chartrier de Ste-Marie Latine et l'établissement de Raymond de St-Gilles à Mont Pèlerin', ed. J. Richard, *Mélanges Louis Halphen* (Paris, 1951).

Pope Clement IV, *Registre*, ed. E. Jordan (Paris, 1893–1945).

Codex epistolaris Rudolphi I, ed. M. Gerbert (St Blasien, 1772).

Codice diplomatico del sacro militare ordine gerosolimitano oggi di Malta, ed. S. Pauli, 2 vols (Lucca, 1733–7).

'Commerce et expéditions militaires de la France et de Venise au moyen âge', ed. L. de Mas Latrie, *Collection des documents inédits sur l'histoire de France. Mélanges historiques. Choix de documents*, iii (Paris, 1880).

Constitutiones et acta publica imperatorum et regum, ed. L. Weiland *et al.* (*M.G.H. Legum sectio IV*), 7 vols (Hanover/Leipzig, 1893–1927).

'Contributi alle relazioni tra Genova e l'Oriente. Una lettera del Pontifice Innocenzo III e un privilegio di Guido, Rè di Gerusalemme e Signore di Cipro', ed. A. Ferreto, *Giornale ligustico*, xxi (1896).

Corpus iuris canonici, ed. E. Friedberg, 2 vols (Leipzig, 1879–81).

'Deux chartes des croisés dans les archives arabes', ed. C. Clermont-Ganneau, *Recueil d'archéologie orientale*, vi (1903/5).

'Un diplôme inédit d'Amaury I, roi de Jérusalem, en faveur de l'abbaye du Temple-Notre-Seigneur (1166)', ed. F. Chalandon, *ROL*, viii (1900–1).

Documenti del commercio veneziano nei secoli XI–XIII, ed. R. Morozzo della Rocca and A. Lombardi (Regesta chartarum Italiae, 28–9), 2 vols (Rome, 1940).

Documenti sulle relazioni delle città toscane coll' Oriente cristiano e coi Turchi fino all'anno 1531, ed. G. Müller (Documenti degli archivi toscani, 3) (Florence, 1879).

'Documents et mémoires servant de preuves à l'histoire de l'île de Chypre sous les Lusignans', ed. L. de Mas-Latrie, *Histoire de l'île de Chypre*, ii, iii.

'Documents inédits concernant l'Orient latin et les croisades (XIIe–XIVe siècle)', ed. C. Kohler, *ROL*, vii (1899).

Documents inédits sur le commerce de Marseille au moyen âge, ed. L. Blancard, 2 vols (Marseilles, 1884–5).

'Elf deutschordensurkunden aus Venedig und Malta', ed. H. Prutz, *Altpreussische Monatsschrift*, xx (1883).

'Emprunts de Saint Louis en Palestine et en Afrique', ed. G. Servois, *BEC*, sér. 4, iv (1858).

Epistolae saeculi XIII e regestis pontificum Romanorum selectae per G. H. Pertz, ed. C. Rodenberg (*MGH*), 3 vols (Berlin, 1883–94).

'Étude sur un texte latin énumérant les possessions musulmanes dans le royaume de Jérusalem vers l'année 1239', ed. P. Deschamps, *Syria*, xxiii (1942–3).

Foedera, conventiones, litterae et acta publica inter reges Angliae et alios, ed. T. Rymer *et al.* and Record Commission, 4 vols in 7 pts (London, 1816–69).

'La fondation d'une église latine en Orient par Saint Louis: Damiette', ed. J. Richard, *BEC*, cxx (1962).

'Fragment d'un cartulaire de l'ordre de Saint-Lazare, en Terre Sainte', ed. A. de Marsy, *AOL*, ii (1884).

Pope Gregory IX, *Registre*, ed. L. Auvray, 3 vols and tables (Paris, 1896–1955).

Pope Gregory X, *Registre*, ed. J. Guiraud and L. Cadier (Paris, 1892–1906).

Historia diplomatica Frederici secundi, ed. J. L. de Huillard-Bréholles, 6 pts in 12 vols (Paris, 1852–61).

Pope Honorius III, *Regesta*, ed. P. Pressutti, 2 vols (Rome, 1888–95).

Pope Honorius IV, *Registre*, ed. M. Prou (Paris, 1888).

Pope Innocent III, 'Opera Omnia', *PL*, ccxiv–ccxvi.

—— *Register*, ed. O. Hageneder and A. Haidacher, i (Graz, 1964).

Pope Innocent IV, *Registre*, ed. E. Berger, 4 vols (Paris, 1884–1921).

'Inventaire de pièces de Terre Sainte de l'ordre de l'Hôpital', ed. J. Delaville Le Roulx, *ROL*, iii (1895).

Itinéraires à Jérusalem et descriptions de la Terre Sainte rédigés en français aux XIe, XIIe et XIIIe siècles, ed. H. Michelant and G. Raynaud (Société de l'Orient latin. Série géographique, 3) (Geneva, 1882).

James of Vitry, *Lettres*, ed. R. B. C. Huygens (Leyden, 1960).

Pope John XXI, *Registre*, ed. J. Guiraud and L. Cadier (Paris, 1892–1906).

Lacrimae Nicossienses. Recueil d'inscriptions funéraires, la plupart françaises, existant encore dans l'île de Chypre, comp. T. J. Chamberlayne (Paris, 1894).

'Lettre des chrétiens de Terre-Sainte à Charles d'Anjou (22 Avril 1260)', ed. H. F. Delaborde, *ROL*, ii (1894).

'Lettres inédites concernant les croisades (1275–1307)', ed. C. Kohler and C. V. Langlois, *BEC*, lii (1891).

'Liber iurium reipublicae Ianuensis', *HPM* vii/ix.

King Louis IX of France 'Epistola de captione et liberatione sua', ed. F. Duchesne, *Historiae Francorum Scriptores*, v (Paris, 1649), pp. 428–32.

Memorie storico-diplomatiche dell' antica città e ducato di Amalfi, ed. M. Camera, 2 vols (Naples, 1876–81).

Pope Nicholas III, *Registre*, ed. J. Gay and S. Vitte (Paris, 1898–1938).

Pope Nicholas IV, *Registre*, ed. E. Langlois, 2 vols (Paris, 1886–93).

Odo of Châteauroux, 'Letter', ed. L. d'Achéry, *Spicilegium*, iii (Paris, 1723), pp. 624–8.

'L'ordre de Montjoye', ed. J. Delaville Le Roulx, *ROL*, i (1893).

Palestine under the Moslems. Description of Syria and the Holy Land from 650–1500. Translated from Medieval Arabic Geographers, comp. G. Le Strange (London, 1890).

'Papst-Kaiser- und Normannenurkunden aus Unteritalien', ed. W. Holtzmann, *QFIAB*, xxxv (1955).

'Les Porcellets de Syrie', ed. F. Benoit, *Congrès de Marseille* (Institut historique de Provence), 1929.

'Quatre pièces relatives à l'ordre teutonique en Orient', *AOL*, ii (1884).

'Quatre titres des propriétés des Génois à Acre et à Tyr', ed. C. Desimoni, *AOL*, ii (1884).

'Quattro documenti genovesi sulle contese d'Oltramare nel secolo XIII', ed. G. Bigoni, *Archivio storico italiano*, ser. 5, xxiv (1899).

Recherches géographiques et historiques sur la domination des Latins en Orient, ed. E. G. Rey (Paris, 1877).

Regesta imperii V. Die Regesten des Kaiserreichs unter Philipp, Otto IV., Friedrich II., Heinrich (VII.), Conrad IV., Heinrich Raspe, Wilhelm und Richard. 1198–1272, comp. J. F. Böhmer, J. Ficker and E. Winkelmann (Innsbruck, 1881–1901).

Regesta regni Hierosolymitani 1097–1291, comp. R. Röhricht (Innsbruck, 1893). *Additamentum*, 1904.

Rerum Germanicarum Scriptores, ed. M. Freher, 3 vols. 3rd ed. B. G. Struve (Strasbourg, 1717).

'Un rituel et un bréviaire du Saint-Sépulcre de Jérusalem (XIIe–XIIIe siècle)', ed. C. Kohler, *ROL*, vii (1900/1901).

Sacrae antiquitatis monumenta historica, dogmatica, diplomatica, ed. C. L. Hugo, 2 vols (Estival, 1725–31).

Sacrorum conciliorum nova et amplissima collectio, ed. G. D. Mansi, 31 vols (Florence/Venice, 1759–98).

'Sankt Samuel auf dem Freudenberge und sein Besitz nach einem unbekannten Diplom König Balduins V', ed. H. E. Mayer, *QFIAB*, xliv (1964).

Syllabus membranarum ad regiae Siclae archivum pertinentium, comp. A. A. Scotti (Naples, 1824–45).

Tabulae ordinis Theutonici, ed. E. Strehlke (Berlin, 1869).

Thesaurus novus anecdotorum, ed. E. Martène and U. Durand, 5 vols (Paris, 1717).

'Titres de l'hôpital des Bretons d'Acre', ed. J. Delaville Le Roulx, *AOL*, i (1881).

'Ein unveröffentliches Testament Kaiser Friedrichs II', ed. G. Wolf, *Zeitschrift für die Geschichte des Oberrheins*, civ (1956).

Pope Urban IV, *Registre*, ed. J. Guiraud, 4 vols (Paris, 1901–58).
Urkunden zur älteren Handels- und Staatsgeschichte der Republik Venedig mit besonderer Beziehung auf Byzanz und die Levante, ed. G. L. F. Tafel and G. M. Thomas (Fontes rerum Austriacarum. Sectio 2, 12–14), 3 vols (Vienna, 1856–7).
'Zwei unbekannte Diplome der lateinischen Könige von Jerusalem aus Lucca', ed. R. Hiestand, *QFIAB*, l (1971).
(See also the books and articles marked with asterisks and listed under Secondary Works.)

LEGAL TEXTS AND NARRATIVE SOURCES

'Abrégé du Livre des Assises de la cour des Bourgeois', *RHC Lois*, ii.
Abu-Shamah, 'Kitab al-raudatain fi akhbar al-daulatain'. extr. ed. and tr., *RHC Or.*, iv–v.
al-'Aini, ''Iqd al-juman fi tarikh ahl al-zaman', extr. ed. and tr., *RHC Or.*, ii.
Alberic of Trois Fontaines, 'Chronicon', *MGHS*, xxiii.
Albert of Aix, 'Historia Hierosolymitana', *RHC Or.*, iv.
Ambroise, *L'Estoire de la guerre sainte*, ed. G. Paris (Collection des documents inédits sur l'histoire de France, sér. I, 24) (Paris, 1897).
Andrew Dandolo, 'Chronica Venetiarum', *RISNS*, xii, 1.
'Annales de Terre Sainte', ed. R. Röhricht and G. Raynaud, *AOL*, ii (1884).
Annales Januenses, ed. L. T. Belgrano and C. Imperiale di St Angelo (Fonti per la storia d'Italia. Scrittori, 10–15), 6 vols (Rome, 1890–1929).
'Annales monasterii Burtonensis', ed. H. R. Luard, *Annales monastici*, i (Rolls Series, 36) (London, 1864).
Arnold of Lübeck, 'Chronica Slavorum', *MGHS*, xxi.
Assises d'Antioche, ed. and tr. L. M. Alishan (Venice, 1876).
Baha' ad-Din, *Kitab al-nawadir al-sultaniya wa'l-mahasin al-yusufiya*, tr. C. W. Wilson (London, 1897).
Benjamin of Tudela, *Itinerary*, ed. and tr. M. N. Adler (London, 1907).
'Breve chronicon de rebus siculis', ed. J. L. A. de Huillard-Bréholles, *Hist. dipl. Fred. secundi*, i.
Burchard of Mt. Sion, 'Descriptio Terrae Sanctae', *PMAQ*.
Chronica de Mailros, ed. J. Stevenson (Bannatyne Club, 49) (Edinburgh, 1835).
Chronica regia Coloniensis, ed. G. Waitz, *MGHS rer. Germ.*, xviii.
Chronicon de Lanercost, ed. J. Stevenson (Edinburgh, 1839).
'La Clef des Assises de la Haute Cour du royaume de Jérusalem et de Chypre', *RHC Lois*, i.

The Crusade and Death of Richard I, ed. R. C. Johnston (Anglo-Norman texts, 17) (Oxford, 1961).

'De constructione castri Saphet', ed. R. B. C. Huygens, *Studi medievali*, ser. 3, vi (1965).

'De excidio regni et regibus Jerusalem' and 'Tractatus de locis et statu sancte terre ierosolimitane', ed. G. M. Thomas, 'Ein Tractat über das heilige Land und den dritten Kreuzzug', *Sitzungsberichte der philosophisch-historischen Klasse der Bayrischen Akademie der Wissenschaften*, part 2 (Munich, 1865).

'Document relatif au service militaire', *RHC Lois*, ii.

'Documents relatifs à la successibilité au trône et à la régence', *RHC Lois*, ii.

Ernoul, *Chronique d'Ernoul et de Bernard le Trésorier*, ed. L. de Mas-Latrie (Paris, 1871).

'L'Estoire de Eracles empereur et la conqueste de la Terre d'Outremer', *RHC Oc.*, i–ii.

Florio Bustron, *Chronique de l'île de Chypre*, ed. R. de Mas-Latrie (Collection des documents inédits sur l'histoire de France. Mélanges historiques, 5) (Paris, 1886).

Francesco Amadi, *Chroniques de Chypre d'Amadi et de Strambaldi*, ed. R. de Mas-Latrie, 2 vols (Paris, 1891–3).

Francesco Balducci Pegolotti, *La pratica della mercatura*, ed. A. Evans (Monographs of the Mediaeval Academy of America, 24) (Cambridge, Mass., 1936).

Fulcher of Chartres, 'Historia Hierosolymitana. Gesta Francorum Iherusalem peregrinantium', *RHC Oc.*, iii.

Geoffrey Le Tor, 'Livre', *RHC Lois*, i.

Geoffrey of Villehardouin, *La conquête de Constantinople*, ed. E. Faral (Les classiques de l'histoire de France an moyen âge, 19), 2 vols (Paris, 1961).

'Gesta Innocentii PP. III', *PL*, ccxiv.

Gesta regis Henrici secundi et Ricardi primi, ed. W. Stubbs (Rolls Series 49), 2 vols (London, 1867).

'Les Gestes des Chiprois', *RHC arm.*, ii.

Haymarus Monachus, 'De expugnata Accone liber tetrastichus', ed. P. Riant, *De Haymaro Monacho* (Paris, 1865).

Ibn al-Athir, 'Kamil al-tawarikh', extr. ed. and tr., *RHC Or.*, i–ii.

Ibn al-Furat, *Tarikh al-Duwal wa'l Muluk*, extr. ed. and tr. U. and M. C. Lyons, *Ayyubids, Mamlukes and Crusaders*. Historical Introduction and Notes by J. S. C. Riley-Smith, 2 vols (Cambridge, 1971).

Ibn al-Qalanisi, *Dhail tarikh Dimashq*, extr. tr. H. A. R. Gibb (University of London Historical Series, 5) (London, 1932).

Ibn Jubair, *Rihla*, tr. R. J. C. Broadhurst (London, 1952).
    Use has also been made of the edition in *RHC Or.*, iii.

Itinerarium peregrinorum et gesta regis Ricardi, 1st part ed. H. E. Mayer,
    Schriften der Monumenta Germaniae historica, 18) (Stuttgart,
    1962). 2nd part ed. W. Stubbs, *Chronicles and Memorials of the Reign
    of Richard I* (Rolls series, 38), i (London, 1864).
James of Ibelin, 'Livre', *RHC Lois*, i.
James of Vitry, 'Historia orientalis seu Hierosolymitana', ed. J.
    Bongars, *Gesta Dei per Francos*, i (Hannau, 1611).
John of Jaffa, 'Livre des Assises de la Haute Cour', *RHC Lois*, i.
John of Joinville, *Histoire de Saint Louis*, ed. N. de Wailly (Paris,
    1874).
'Les lignages d'Outremer', *RHC Lois*, ii.
'Livre au roi', *RHC Lois*, i.
'Livre des Assises de la Cour des Bourgeois', ed. E. H. Kausler, *Les
    Livres des Assises et des Usages dou reaume de Jérusalem*, i (Stuttgart,
    1839).
    Use has also been made of the edition by A. A. Beugnot, *RHC
    Lois*, ii.
al-Maqrizi, *Kitab al-suluk li-ma'rifat duwal al-muluk*, extr. tr. M. E.
    Quatremère, 4 pts in 2 vols (Paris, 1837–45).
Martino da Canale, 'La Cronaca dei Veneziani', ed. G. Galvani *et al.*,
    Archivio storico italiano, viii (1845).
Matthew Paris, *Chronica maiora*, ed. H. R. Luard (Rolls Series, 57), 7
    vols (London, 1872–83).
—— 'Itinéraire de Londres à Jérusalem', ed. H. Michelant and G.
    Raynaud, *Itinéraires à Jérusalem*.
Menko, 'Chronicon Werumensium', *MGHS*, xxiii.
Philip of Novara, 'Memoirs': see 'Les Gestes des Chiprois'.
—— 'Livre de forme de plait', *RHC Lois*, i.
—— *Les Quatre Âges de l'Homme*, ed. M. de Fréville (Paris, 1888).
Ralph of Diceto, *Opera historica*, ed. W. Stubbs (Rolls Series, 68), 2 vols
    (London, 1876).
Récits d'un ménestrel de Rheims au treizième siècle, ed. N. de Wailly (Paris,
    1876).
La Règle du Temple, ed. H. de Curzon (Paris, 1886).
Richard of San Germano, 'Chronica', *RISNS*, vii, 2.
Robert of Clari, *La conquête de Constantinople*, ed. P. Lauer (Paris, 1956).
Roger of Howden, *Chronica*, ed. W. Stubbs (Rolls Series, 51), 4 vols
    (London, 1868–71).
Roger of Wendover, *Chronica sive flores historiarum*, ed. H. O. Coxe, 4
    vols (London, 1841–2).
'Rothelin', 'Continuation de Guillaume de Tyr de 1229 à 1261, dite du
    manuscrit de Rothelin', *RHC Oc.*, ii.
Sicard of Cremona, 'Cronica', *RIS*, vii.
Theoderic, *Libellus de locis sanctis*, ed. T. Tobler (St Gallen, 1865).

'Tractatus de locis et statu sancte terre ierosolimitane', *see* 'De excidio regni et regibus Jerusalem'.

Usamah ibn Munqidh, *Kitab al-i'tibar*, tr. P. K. Hitti (Columbia University Records of Civilisation. Sources and Studies, 10) (New York, 1929).

Willbrand of Oldenburg, 'Itinerarium Terrae Sanctae', *PMAQ*.

William of Tyre, 'Historia rerum in partibus transmarinis gestarum', *RHC Oc.*, i.

—— 'Lost chapter', ed. R. B. C. Huygens, 'Guillaume de Tyr étudiant. Un chapitre (xix, 12) de son "Histoire" retrouvé', *Latomus*, xxi (1962).

SECONDARY WORKS

(Books and articles marked with asterisks contain printed documents to which reference has been made.)

Antoniadis-Bibicou, H. *Recherches sur les Douanes à Byzance* (Cahiers des Annales, 20) (Paris, 1963).

Baldwin, M. W. *Raymond III of Tripolis and the Fall of Jerusalem (1140–1187)* (Princeton, 1936).

Benvenisti, M. *The Crusaders in the Holy Land* (Jerusalem, 1970).

Beugnot, A. A. 'Introduction aux Assises de la Haute Cour', *RHC Lois*, i.

Bloch, M. *Feudal Society*, tr. L. A. Manyon (London, 1961).

Boutruche, R. *Seigneurie et Féodalité*. 2nd ed. (Paris, 1968).

Bulst-Thiele, M. L. 'Zur Geschichte der Ritterorden und des Königreichs Jerusalem im 13. Jahrhundert, bis zur Schlacht bei la Forbie am 17 Okt. 1244', *Deutsches Archiv*, xxii (1966).

Cahen, C. *La Syrie du Nord à l'époque des croisades et la principauté franque d'Antioche* (Institut français de Damas. Bibliothèque orientale, 1) (Paris, 1940).

—— 'Notes sur l'histoire des croisades et de l'Orient latin. 2. Le régime rural syrien au temps de la domination franque', *Bulletin de la Faculté des Lettres de l'Université de Strasbourg*, xxix (1950/51).

—— 'La féodalité et les institutions politiques de l'Orient latin', *Oriente e Occidente nel Medioevo* (Accademia nazionale dei Lincei. Fondazione 'Alessandro Volta'. XII Convegno 'Volta') (Rome, 1957).

—— 'A propos des coutumes du marché d'Acre', *RHDFE*, sér. 4, xli (1963).

—— 'Douanes et commerce dans les ports méditerranéens de l'Égypte médiévale d'après le *Minhadj* d'al-Makhzūmī', *Journal of the Economic and Social History of the Orient*, vii (1964).

Chandon de Brailles, F. 'Le droit des "coins" dans le royaume de Jérusalem', *Syria*, xxiii (1942/3).
—— 'Bulles de l'Orient latin', *Syria*, xxvii (1950).
Colson, J. 'Aux origines des assemblées d'État. L'exemple de l'Orient latin', *Revue des études byzantines*, xii (1954).
Deschamps, P. *Les châteaux des croisés en Terre Sainte, ii. La défense du royaume de Jérusalem* (Haut Commissariat de la République française en Syrie et au Liban. Service des Antiquités et Beaux-Arts. Bibliothèque archéologique et historique, 34) (Paris, 1939).
Du Cange, C. du Fresne, *Les familles d'Outremer*, ed. E. G. Rey (Collection des documents inédits sur l'histoire de France, 18) (Paris, 1869).
Elisséeff, N. *Nūr-ad-Dīn*, 3 vols (Damascus, 1967).
Enlart, C. *Les monuments des croisés dans le royaume de Jérusalem. Architecture religieuse et civile.* (Haut Commissariat de la République française en Syrie et au Liban. Service des Antiquités et Beaux-Arts. Bibliothèque archéologique et historique, 7–8), 2 vols and 2 folders of Plates (Paris, 1925–8).
Fichtenau, H. 'Akkon, Zypern und das Lösegeld für Richard Löwenherz', *Archiv für österreichische Geschichte*, cxxv (1966).
Forstreuter, K. *Der Deutsche Orden am Mittelmeer* (Quellen and Studien zur Geschichte des Deutschen Ordens, 2) (Bonn, 1967).
Furber, E. C. 'The Kingdom of Cyprus, 1191–1291', *A History of the Crusades*, ed.-in-chief K. M. Setton, ii.
*Germain, A. C. *Histoire de la commune de Montpellier*, 3 vols (Montpellier, 1851).
Gibb, H. A. R. 'The Aiyūbids', *A History of the Crusades*, ed.-in-chief K. M. Setton, ii.
Goitein, S. D. *A Mediterranean Society*, i (Berkeley and Los Angeles, 1967).
Gottschalk, H. L. 'Dīwān. ii. Egypt', *The Encyclopaedia of Islam*, ii (Leyden, 1965).
Gough, J. W. *The social contract; a critical study of its development*, 2nd ed. (Oxford, 1957).
Grandclaude, M. *Étude critique sur les livres des Assises de Jérusalem* (Paris, 1923).
—— 'Caractère du "Livre au roi"', *RHDFE*, sér. 4, v (1926).
—— 'Classement sommaire des manuscrits des principaux livres des Assises de Jérusalem', *RHDFE*, sér. 4, v (1926).
—— 'Liste d'Assises remontant au premier royaume de Jérusalem (1099–1187)', *Mélanges Paul Fournier* (Paris, 1929).
Grousset, R. *Histoire des croisades et du royaume franc de Jérusalem*, 3 vols (Paris, 1934–6).
Hill, G. F. *A History of Cyprus*, 4 vols (Cambridge, 1940–52).
Hubatsch, W. 'Montfort und die Bildung des Deutschordensstaates im

Heiligen Lande'. *Nachrichten der Akademie der Wissenschaften in Göttingen. Phil.-Hist. Klasse* (1966).

Jolliffe, J. E. A. *Angevin Kingship.* 2nd ed. (London, 1963).

Kantorowicz, E. H. *Frederick II, 1194–1250,* tr. E. O. Lorimer (London, 1931).

Kohler, C. Introduction to *Mémoires de Philippe de Novare.* (Les classiques de l'histoire de France au moyen âge, 10) (Paris, 1913).

Labib, S. Y. *Handelsgeschichte Ägyptens im Spätmittelalter (1171–1517).* (Vierteljahrschrift für Sozial- und Wirtschaftsgeschichte. Beihefte, 46) (Wiesbaden, 1965).

La Monte, J. L. 'The Communal Movement in Syria in the Thirteenth Century', *Haskins Anniversary Essays in Mediaeval History* (Boston/New York, 1929).

—— *Feudal Monarchy in the Latin Kingdom of Jerusalem, 1100–1291.* (Monographs of the Mediaeval Academy of America, 4) (Cambridge, Mass., 1932).

—— Introduction to translation of Philip of Novara, *The Wars of Frederick II against the Ibelins in Syria and Cyprus* (Columbia University Records of Civilisation. Sources and Studies, 25) (New York, 1936).

—— 'John d'Ibelin. The Old Lord of Beirut, 1177–1236', *Byzantion,* xii (1937).

—— 'The Lords of Sidon in the Twelfth and Thirteenth Centuries', *Byzantion,* xvii (1944/5).

—— 'The Lords of Caesarea in the Period of the Crusades', *Speculum,* xxii (1947).

*Lourie, E. 'An offer of the suzerainty and escheat of Cyprus to Alphonso III of Aragon by Hugh de Brienne in 1289', *English Historical Review,* lxxxiv (1969).

Lyon, B. D. *From Fief to Indenture* (Harvard Historical Studies, 68) (Cambridge, Mass., 1957).

*Mas-Latrie, L. de, *Histoire de l'île de Chypre sous le règne des princes de la maison de Lusignan,* 3 vols (Paris, 1852–61).

Mayer, H. E. *Bibliographie zur Geschichte der Kreuzzüge.* Hanover, 1960. Supplement to 1967 in *Historische Zeitschrift. Sonderheft,* 3 (1969).

—— *The Crusades,* tr. J. Gillingham (Oxford, 1972).

*—— 'Das Pontifikale von Tyrus und die Krönung der lateinischen Könige von Jerusalem', *Dumbarton Oaks Papers,* xxi (1967).

—— 'On the beginnings of the Communal Movement in the Holy Land: The Commune of Tyre', *Traditio,* xxiv (1968).

—— 'Zwei Kommunen in Akkon?', *Deutsches Archiv,* xxvi (1970).

*—— *Marseilles Levantehandel und ein akkonensisches Fälscheratelier des 13. Jahrhunderts* (Bibliothek des Deutschen Historischen Instituts in Rom, 38) (Tübingen, 1972).

Mayer, H. E. 'Kaiserrecht und Heiliges Land', *Aus Reichgeschichte und Nordischer Geschichte* (Kieler Historische Studien, 1972).

Meynial, E. 'De quelques particularités des successions féodales dans les Assises de Jérusalem', *RHDFE*, xvi (1892).

*Minieri Riccio C. *Genealogia di Carlo I. di Angio, prima generazione* (Naples, 1857).

Patterson, R. B. 'The Early Existence of the *Funda* and *Catena* in the Twelfth-Century Latin Kingdom of Jerusalem', *Speculum*, xxxix (1964).

Petit-Dutaillis, C. *L'essor des États d'occident, France, Angleterre, Péninsule Ibérique* (Paris, 1937).

Poole, A. L. *Obligations of Society in the XII and XIII Centuries* (Oxford, 1946).

Prawer, J. 'The Assise de Teneure and the Assise de Vente. A Study of Landed Property in the Latin Kingdom', *Economic History Review*, ser. 2, iv (1951).

—— 'Colonisation Activities in the Latin Kingdom of Jerusalem', *Revue belge de philologie et d'histoire*, xxix (1951).

—— 'L'établissement des coutumes du marché à Saint-Jean d'Acre et la date de composition du Livre des Assises des Bourgeois', *RHDFE*, sér. 4, xxix (1951).

—— 'Étude de quelques problèmes agraires et sociaux d'une seigneurie croisée au XIIIe siècle', *Byzantion*, xxii–xxiii (1952–3).

—— 'Étude préliminaire sur les sources et la composition du "Livre des Assises des Bourgeois"', *RHDFE*, sér. 4, xxxii (1954).

—— 'Les premiers temps de la féodalité du royaume latin de Jérusalem', *Tijdschrift voor rechtsgeschiedenis*, xxii (1954).

—— 'La noblesse et le régime féodal du royaume latin de Jérusalem', *Le moyen âge*, lxv (1959).

—— 'Étude sur le droit des Assises de Jérusalem', *RHDFE*, sér. 4, xxxix–xl (1961–2).

—— 'Estates, Communities and the Constitution of the Latin Kingdom', *Proceedings of the Israel Academy of Sciences and Humanities*, ii (1966).

—— *Histoire du royaume latin de Jérusalem*, 2 vols (Paris, 1969–70).

—— and Benvenisti, M. 'Crusader Palestine'. Sheet 12/IX of the *Atlas of Israel* (Jerusalem, 1960).

Rabie, H. *The Financial System of Egypt A.H. 564–741/A.D. 1169–1341.* (London Oriental Series, 25) (London, 1972).

Reid, R. R. 'Barony and Thanage', *English Historical Review*, xxxv (1920).

*Riant, P. 'Une dépendance italienne de l'église de Bethléem. Varazze en Ligurie (1139–1424)', *Atti della società ligure di storia patria*, xvii (1885).

Richard, J. 'Pairie d'Orient latin. Les quatre baronnies des royaumes de Jérusalem et de Chypre', *RHDFE*, sér. 4, xxviii (1950).
—— 'Colonies marchandes privilégiées et marché seigneurial. La Fonde d'Acre et ses "droitures"', *Le moyen âge*, lix (1953).
—— *Le royaume latin de Jérusalem* (Paris, 1953).
—— 'Les listes des seigneuries dans "Le Livre de Jean d'Ibelin". Recherches sur l'Assebebe et Mimars', *RHDFE*, sér. 4, xxxii (1954).
—— 'Le statut de la femme dans l'Orient latin', *Recueils de la société Jean Bodin, xii. La femme*, 2e partie (Brussels, 1962).
*—— 'L'abbaye cistercienne de Jubin et le prieuré Saint-Blaise de Nicosie', *Epeteris*, iii (1969/70).
—— 'Saint Louis dans l'histoire des croisades', *Bulletin de la Société d'Emulation du Bourbonnais* (1970).
Richter, P. 'Beiträge zur Historiographie in den Kreuzfahrerstaaten', *Mitteilungen des Instituts für österreichische Geschichtsforschung*, xiii–xv (1892–4).
Riley-Smith, J. S. C. *The Knights of St John in Jerusalem and Cyprus, c. 1050–1310* (London, 1967).
—— 'The Assise sur la ligece and the Commune of Acre', *Traditio*, xxvii (1971).
—— 'A note on confraternities in the Latin Kingdom of Jerusalem', *Bulletin of the Institute of Historical Research*, xliv (1971).
—— 'Some lesser officials in Latin Syria', *English Historical Review*, lxxxvii (1972).
*Röhricht, R. *Beiträge sur Geschichte der Kreuzzüge*, 2 vols (Berlin, 1874–8).
*—— 'Amalrich I., König von Jerusalem', *Mitteilungen des Instituts für österreichische Geschichtsforschung*, xii (1891).
*—— *Studien zur Geschichte des Fünften Kreuzzuges* (Innsbruck, 1891).
—— *Geschichte des Königreichs Jerusalem 1100–1291* (Innsbruck, 1898).
Rüdt de Collenberg, W. H. *The Rupenides, Hethumides and Lusignans. The Structure of the Armeno-Cilician Dynasties* (Paris, 1963).
—— 'Les premiers Ibelins', *Le moyen âge*, lxxi (1965).
Runciman, S. *A History of the Crusades*, 3 vols (Cambridge, 1951–5).
Schlumberger, G. *Numismatique de l'Orient latin* (Paris, 1878). *Supplément*, 1882.
——, Chalandon, F. and Blanchet, A. *Sigillographie de l'Orient latin* (Haut Commissariat de la République française en Syrie et au Liban. Service des Antiquités et Beaux-Arts. Bibliothèque archéologique et historique, 37) (Paris, 1943).
Setton, K. M. (ed.-in-chief). *A History of the Crusades*, 2 vols so far (Philadelphia, 1955 ff.).
Smail, R. C. *Crusading Warfare (1097–1193). A Contribution to Medieval*

Military History (Cambridge Studies in Medieval Life and Thought. New Series, 3) (Cambridge, 1956).

—— 'Latin Syria and the West, 1149–1187', *Transactions of The Royal Historical Society*, 5th series, xix (1969).

*Soden, D. H. von, 'Bericht über die in der Kubbet in Damaskus gefundenen Handschriftenfragmente', *Sitzungsberichte der königlich Preussischen Akademie der Wissenschaften* (1903).

Strayer, J. R. 'The Crusades of Louis IX', *A History of the Crusades*, ed.-in-chief K. M. Setton, ii.

Tyan, E. *Histoire de l'organisation judiciaire en pays d'Islam*. 2nd ed. (Leyden, 1960).

Van Cleve, T. C. 'The Crusade of Frederick II', *A History of the Crusades*, ed.-in-chief K. M. Setton, ii.

Wangelin, H. *Das arabische Volksbuch vom König Aẓ Ẓāhir Baibars* (Bonner orientalistische Studien, 17) (Stuttgart, 1936).

*Wilken, F. *Geschichte der Kreuzzüge*, 7 vols in 8 parts (Leipzig, 1807–32).

INDEX

INDEX

The following abbreviations are used:

Archb.	Archbishop (of)	L	Lord (of)
B	Bishop (of)	P	Patriarch (of)
C	Count (of)	Pr.	Prince (of)
K	King (of)	S	Sultan (of)